Adobe®
DREAMWEAVER® CS6
COMPLETE

Corinne L. Hoisington

Jessica L. Minnick

COURSE TECHNOLOGY
CENGAGE Learning

SHELLY
CASHMAN
SERIES®

Australia • Brazil • Japan • Korea • Mexico • Singapore • Spain • United Kingdom • United States

COURSE TECHNOLOGY
CENGAGE Learning™

Adobe® Dreamweaver® CS6 Complete
Corinne L. Hoisington, Jessica L. Minnick

Editor-in-Chief: Marie Lee

Executive Editor: Kathleen McMahon

Senior Product Manager: Emma F. Newsom

Associate Product Manager:
    Crystal Parenteau

Editorial Assistant: Sarah Ryan

Director of Marketing: Cheryl Costantini

Marketing Manager: Mark Linton

Marketing Coordinator: Benjamin Genise

Print Buyer: Julio Esperas

Director of Production: Patty Stephan

Content Project Manager: Matthew Hutchinson

Development Editor: Lisa Ruffolo

Copyeditor: Suzanne Huizenga

Proofreader: Kathy Orrino

Indexer: Rich Carlson

QA Manuscript Reviewers: Jeffrey Schwartz,
    Serge Palladino, Danielle Shaw,
    Susan Whalen

Art Director: GEX Publishing Services

Cover Designer: Lisa Kuhn, Curio Press, LLC

Cover Photo: Tom Kates Photography

Text Design: Joel Sadagursky

Compositor: PreMediaGlobal

For product information and technology assistance, contact us at
Cengage Learning Customer & Sales Support, 1-800-354-9706

For permission to use material from this text or product,
submit all requests online at **cengage.com/permissions**
Further permissions questions can be emailed to
permissionrequest@cengage.com

Library of Congress Control Number: 2012945760
ISBN-13: 978-1-133-52594-3
ISBN-10: 1-133-52594-6

Course Technology
20 Channel Center Street
Boston, Massachusetts 02210
USA

Cengage Learning is a leading provider of customized learning solutions with office locations around the globe, including Singapore, the United Kingdom, Australia, Mexico, Brazil, and Japan. Locate your local office at:
international.cengage.com/region

Cengage Learning products are represented in Canada by Nelson Education, Ltd.

For your course and learning solutions, visit **www.cengage.com**

To learn more about Course Technology,
visit **www.cengage.com/coursetechnology**

Purchase any of our products at your local college bookstore or at our preferred online store **www.cengagebrain.com**

Printed in the United States of America
1 2 3 4 5 6 7 17 16 15 14 13 12

Adobe DREAMWEAVER CS6 COMPLETE

Contents

Preface   vii

Adobe **Dreamweaver CS6**

INTRODUCTION

Web Site Development and Adobe Dreamweaver CS6

Objectives	**DW 1**
Web Site Planning and Design Basics	**DW 2**
Types of Web Sites	DW 2
Browser Considerations	DW 4
Web Site Navigation	DW 7
Mobile Site Access	DW 8
Planning a Web Site	**DW 8**
Planning Basics	DW 9
Design	DW 10
Accessibility Guidelines	DW 12
Role of Social Networking	DW 13
Web Site Hosting	**DW 14**
Project Management	**DW 16**
Testing the Site	DW 16
Maintaining the Site	DW 16
Web Programming Languages	**DW 17**
HTML and XHTML	DW 17
HTML5	DW 18
DHTML	DW 18
XML	DW 18
PHP	DW 18
ASP	DW 18
jQuery	DW 18
Web Page Authoring Programs	**DW 19**
About Adobe Dreamweaver CS6	DW 19
Chapter Summary	**DW 21**
Apply Your Knowledge	**DW 21**
Extend Your Knowledge	**DW 22**
Make It Right	**DW 22**
In the Lab	**DW 22**
Cases and Places	**DW 24**

CHAPTER ONE

Creating a New Web Site with Dreamweaver

Objectives	**DW 25**
What Is Dreamweaver CS6?	**DW 26**
Project — Small Business Incubator	
Web Site Plan	**DW 26**
Overview	DW 27
Starting Dreamweaver	**DW 28**
To Start Dreamweaver	DW 28
Touring the Dreamweaver Window	**DW 30**
Dreamweaver Workspace	DW 30
Displaying Document Views	DW 35
Opening and Closing Panels	DW 37
To Show, Hide, and Move Panels	DW 37
To Reset the Classic Workspace	DW 39
To Display the Standard Toolbar	DW 40
To Access Preferences	DW 41
Understanding HTML5	**DW 42**
Understanding CSS3	**DW 43**
Creating a New Site	**DW 43**
Defining a Local Site	DW 43
Creating the Local Root Folder and Subfolders	DW 44
Using Site Setup to Create a Local Site	DW 45
To Quit and Restart Dreamweaver	DW 45
To Use Site Setup to Create a Local Site	DW 46
Selecting a Predefined Template	DW 49
To Select a Template Layout	DW 50
To Name and Save the Home Page	DW 51
To Edit Navigation Link Text	DW 53
To Format Text Using Heading Styles	DW 54
To Create a Link	DW 56
To Save the Home Page	DW 57
To Add a Second Page	DW 58
To Create an Unordered List	DW 59
To Add the Links to the Second Page	DW 61
To Change the Web Page Title	DW 62

To Check Spelling .... DW 63
Previewing a Web Page in a Browser ...... DW 63
To Choose a Browser and Preview the Web Site ... DW 64
Dreamweaver Help .... **DW 65**
To Access Dreamweaver Help .... DW 65
To Quit Dreamweaver .... DW 65
Chapter Summary .... **DW 66**
Apply Your Knowledge .... **DW 66**
Extend Your Knowledge .... **DW 67**
Make It Right .... **DW 69**
In the Lab .... **DW 70**
Cases and Places .... **DW 75**

CHAPTER TWO
Designing a Web Site
Using a Template and CSS
Objectives .... **DW 77**
Designing Web Pages with CSS .... **DW 78**
Project — Custom Template and Style Sheet ... **DW 78**
Overview .... DW 79
Anatomy of a Style Sheet .... **DW 80**
Understanding the Structure of a Style ... DW 81
Identifying Types of Style Sheets .... DW 82
Creating a Dreamweaver Web Template ... **DW 84**
Organizing the Site Structure .... DW 84
To Create a New Site .... DW 86
To Create Folders for the Image and CSS Files ... DW 87
To Create a Blank HTML Template .... DW 88
To Save the HTML Page as a Template ...... DW 90
Adding CSS Styles .... **DW 92**
To Add a Div Tag .... DW 93
Setting CSS Rule Definitions .... **DW 97**
To Select CSS Rule Definitions .... DW 97
To Add the Logo Div Tag and Define
  Its CSS Rules .... DW 100
To Add the Navigation Div Tag and
  Define Its CSS Rules .... DW 104
To Add the Image Div Tag and Define
  Its CSS Rules .... DW 107
To Add the Content Div Tag and Define
  Its CSS Rules .... DW 109
To Add the Footer Div Tag and Define
  Its CSS Rules .... DW 111
Creating an Editable Region of a Template ... **DW 113**
To Create an Editable Region .... DW 113
To Close the Template .... DW 115
Creating a New Page from a Template ...... **DW 115**
To Create a Page from a Template .... DW 115
To View the Site in Live View .... DW 118
Chapter Summary .... **DW 119**
Apply Your Knowledge .... **DW 119**
Extend Your Knowledge .... **DW 122**
Make It Right .... **DW 123**
In the Lab .... **DW 125**
Cases and Places .... **DW 136**

CHAPTER THREE
Adding Graphics
and Links
Objectives .... **DW 139**
Introduction .... **DW 140**
Project — Promotional Images .... **DW 140**
Overview .... DW 142
Modifying a Template .... **DW 143**
To Modify a Dreamweaver Template by
  Editing a CSS Rule .... DW 144
To Modify a Dreamweaver Template by
  Adding an Editable Region .... DW 146
Adding Graphics To the Web Site .... **DW 148**
Understanding Image File Formats .... DW 149
Adding Alt Text to Provide Accessibility ... DW 150
To Copy Files into the Images Folder ...... DW 150
To Insert a Logo Image in the Template ... DW 152
Marketing a Site with Facebook and Twitter ... **DW 153**
To Insert Social Networking Icons in the
  Template .... DW 155
To Insert an Image on the Home Page ..... DW 157
Creating Additional Pages for the Site ..... **DW 159**
To Create the Services Web Page .... DW 159
To Create the Portfolio Web Page .... DW 161
To Create the Pricing Web Page .... DW 164
To Create the Session Web Page .... DW 165
To Create the Contact Web Page .... DW 166
Adding Links to the Gallery Site .... **DW 168**
To Add Relative Links to the
  Gallery Template .... DW 170
To Add Absolute Links to the
  Gallery Template .... DW 172
To Add an E-mail Link to the
  Gallery Template .... DW 174
Formatting Links .... **DW 175**
To Format a Link as Rollover Text .... DW 176
Modifying the CSS Style Sheet .... **DW 178**
Creating Compound Styles .... DW 178
To Add New CSS Rules with a
  Compound Selector .... DW 178
Adding an Image Placeholder .... **DW 180**
To Define an Image Placeholder .... DW 181
To Replace an Image Placeholder .... DW 183
To Add Image Placeholders .... DW 184
Chapter Summary .... **DW 186**
Apply Your Knowledge .... **DW 186**
Extend Your Knowledge .... **DW 187**
Make It Right .... **DW 189**
In the Lab .... **DW 190**
Cases and Places .... **DW 199**

CHAPTER FOUR
Exploring Tables and Forms

Objectives	DW 201
Introduction	DW 202
Project — Formatted Tables and Forms	DW 202
Overview	DW 203
Understanding Tables	**DW 204**
Designing Table Layouts	DW 205
Adding a Summary to Provide Accessibility	DW 206
To Insert a Table into the Services Page	DW 207
To Add Text to the Table	DW 209
Formatting Tables	**DW 210**
Setting Cell, Row, and Column Properties	DW 211
Selecting Table Elements	DW 213
To Format Table Text	DW 214
To Format the Table Caption	DW 215
Understanding the HTML Structure of a Table	DW 216
To Insert a Table into the Pricing Page	DW 217
Merging and Splitting Cells in a Table	DW 219
To Merge Cells in a Table	DW 220
To Add Text to the Pricing Table	DW 221
To Align the Table	DW 223
To Adjust the Table Width	DW 224
To Adjust the Column Width	DW 225
Changing the Default Cell Alignment	DW 227
To Align Text within a Table Cell	DW 228
To Set the Background Color of Cells in a Table	DW 229
Understanding How Forms Work	**DW 231**
Creating a Form	DW 231
Form Processing	DW 231
To Insert a Form into a Web Page	DW 232
Using the Form Property Inspector	DW 234
To Insert a Table to Design the Form	DW 235
To Add Labels to the Table	DW 236
Adding Form Objects	**DW 237**
Adding Text Fields	DW 238
To Add Text Fields to a Form	DW 239
Adding a Menu	DW 243
To Add a Menu to a Form	DW 243
Text Field Properties	DW 246
To Add an Initial Value to a Text Field	DW 247
Adding Radio Buttons in a Radio Group	DW 248
To Add a Radio Group	DW 248
To Add Submit and Reset Buttons to a Form	DW 250
Chapter Summary	**DW 253**
Apply Your Knowledge	**DW 254**
Extend Your Knowledge	**DW 255**
Make It Right	**DW 256**
In the Lab	**DW 258**
Cases and Places	**DW 267**

CHAPTER FIVE
Creating Interactive Web Pages with Spry and Adobe Widgets

Objectives	DW 269
Introduction	DW 270
Project — Interactive Web Pages	DW 270
Overview	DW 271
Understanding the Spry Framework	**DW 272**
Spry Widget Options	DW 273
Adding Spry to a Web Page	**DW 274**
Using Spry Validation Widgets	DW 275
To Open the Contact Web Page and Select the Spry Category on the Insert Bar	DW 275
To Add Spry Validation to a Required Text Field	DW 276
To Add Spry Validation to Another Required Text Field	DW 279
To Add Spry Validation to an E-mail Text Field	DW 281
To Add Spry Validation to a Phone Number Text Field	DW 283
To Add Spry Validation to Another Required Text Field	DW 284
To Add Spry Validation to a Radio Group	DW 287
To Test the Spry Validation Form in a Browser	DW 290
Using Spry Collapsible Panels	DW 292
To Add Spry Collapsible Panels to a Web Page	DW 292
To Add Panel Headings	DW 296
Using the Adobe Widget Browser	**DW 297**
To Check Your Computer for the Adobe AIR Application	DW 298
To Download and Install Adobe AIR	DW 299
To Create an Adobe Account	DW 300
To View and Add Widgets from Adobe Exchange to My Widgets	DW 303
Editing and Formatting Widgets	DW 306
To Create a Widget Preset for the LightBox Gallery Widget	DW 306
Adding an Adobe Widget to a Web Page	**DW 309**
To Add the LightBox Gallery Widget to a Web Page	DW 311
To Add Images to the Portrait Photography LightBox Gallery Widget	DW 314
To Add Images to the Family Photography LightBox Gallery Widget	DW 317
To Add Images to the Baby Photography LightBox Gallery Widget	DW 319
Chapter Summary	**DW 322**
Apply Your Knowledge	**DW 322**
Extend Your Knowledge	**DW 323**
Make It Right	**DW 324**
In the Lab	**DW 325**
Cases and Places	**DW 329**

CHAPTER SIX
Enhancing Web Pages with
Audio and Video
Objectives   **DW 331**
Introduction   **DW 332**
Project — Web Pages with Multimedia   **DW 332**
  Overview   DW 333
Adding Multimedia with Plug-ins or HTML5   **DW 334**
Adding Sound   **DW 335**
  Understanding Audio Codecs   DW 336
  Embedding a Sound File Using a Plug-In   DW 338
  To Embed a Background Sound
      Using a Plug-In   DW 338
  Setting the Parameters of a Sound File   DW 340
  To Set the Parameters of a Sound File   DW 341
Adding an Audio File with HTML5 Code   **DW 343**
  Coding HTML5 Audio   DW 344
  To Add an Audio File Using HTML5 Code   DW 345
  To Display an HTML5 Audio Control in
      Different Browsers   DW 348
  To Remove an HTML5 Audio Control and Loop   DW 350
Adding Video   **DW 351**
  Understanding Video Formats   DW 351
  Embedding a Video File Using a Plug-In   DW 351
  To Embed a Video Using a Plug-In   DW 352
  To Set the Parameters of a Video File   DW 354
Adding a Video File with HTML5 Code   **DW 357**
  Coding HTML5 Video   DW 357
  To Add a Video File Using HTML5 Code   DW 358
Chapter Summary   **DW 362**
Apply Your Knowledge   **DW 362**
Extend Your Knowledge   **DW 363**
Make It Right   **DW 363**
In the Lab   **DW 365**
Cases and Places   **DW 368**

Appendices

APPENDIX A
Adobe Dreamweaver CS6 Help
Getting Help with Dreamweaver CS6   **APP 1**
  The Dreamweaver Help Menu   APP 1
Exploring the Dreamweaver CS6 Help System   **APP 3**
  Using the Help and Tutorials List   APP 4
  To Find Help Using the Help and Tutorials List APP 4
  Using the Search Feature   APP 5
  To Use the Adobe Community Help
      Search Feature   APP 5
Context-Sensitive Help   **APP 6**
  To Display Context-Sensitive Help on Text
      Using the Options Menu   APP 6
Using the Reference Panel   **APP 7**
  To Use the Reference Panel   APP 7
  Apply Your Knowledge   APP 9

APPENDIX B
Changing Screen Resolution
Changing Screen Resolution   **APP 11**
  To Change the Screen Resolution   APP 12

APPENDIX C
For Mac Users
For the Mac User of this Book   **APP 15**
  Keyboard Differences   APP 15
  To Start Adobe Dreamweaver CS6   APP 16
  To Create a New HTML File   APP 17
  Save a File in Dreamweaver   APP 19
  Print a File in Dreamweaver   APP 19
  Close a File in Dreamweaver   APP 20
  Quit Dreamweaver   APP 20

APPENDIX D
Project Planning Guidelines
Using Project Planning Guidelines   **APP 21**
  Determine the Project's Purpose   APP 22
  Analyze Your Audience   APP 22
  Gather Possible Content   APP 22
  Determine What Content to Present to
      Your Audience   APP 22
Summary   **APP 23**

Index   **IND 1**

Quick Reference Summary   **QR 1**

Preface

The Shelly Cashman Series® offers the finest textbooks in computer education. We are proud of the fact that our previous Dreamweaver® books have been so well received. With each new edition of our Dreamweaver® books, we make significant improvements based on the software and comments made by instructors and students. For this Adobe® Dreamweaver® CS6 text, the Shelly Cashman Series® development team carefully reviewed our pedagogy and analyzed its effectiveness in teaching today's Dreamweaver® student. Students today read less, but need to retain more. They need not only to be able to perform skills, but to retain those skills and know how to apply them to different settings. Today's students need to be continually engaged and challenged to retain what they're learning.

With this Adobe® Dreamweaver® CS6 text, we continue our commitment to focusing on the user and how they learn best.

Objectives of This Textbook

Adobe® Dreamweaver® CS6: Complete is intended for a first course that offers an introduction to Dreamweaver® CS6 and creation of Web sites. No experience with a computer is assumed, and no mathematics beyond the high school freshman level is required. The objectives of this book are:

- To teach the fundamentals of Dreamweaver® CS6

- To expose students to proper Web site design and management techniques

- To acquaint students with the proper procedures to create Web sites suitable for coursework, professional purposes, and personal use

- To develop an exercise-oriented approach that allows learning by doing

- To introduce students to new input technologies

- To encourage independent study and provide help for those who are working independently

New to This Edition

HTM5 and CSS3
Engaging coverage of the latest HTML5 and CSS3 standards including style sheets which provide students with a solid understanding of professional Web design.

Professional Web Design
Explore creative designed centered solutions for creating a business and personal site that captures the attention of your targeted audience.

Mobile Web Site
Design a mobile Web site using a Web standards approach for delivering content beyond the desktop.

Web Accessibility
Integration of guidelines and standards for Web accessibility and disability access to the Web.

Social Networking
Coverage of social networking within a Web site to market business products and connect social trends.

The Shelly Cashman Approach

A Proven Pedagogy with an Emphasis on Project Planning
Each chapter presents a practical problem to be solved, within a project planning framework. The project orientation is strengthened by the use of Plan Ahead boxes, which encourage critical thinking about how to proceed at various points in the project. Step-by-step instructions with supporting screens guide students through the steps. Instructional steps are supported by the Q&A, Experimental Step, and BTW features.

A Visually Engaging Book that Maintains Student Interest
The step-by-step tasks, with supporting figures, provide a rich visual experience for the student. Call-outs on the screens that present both explanatory and navigational information provide students with information they need when they need to know it.

Supporting Reference Materials (Appendices and Quick Reference)
The appendices provide additional information about the Application at hand and include such topics as the Help Feature and customizing the application. With the Quick Reference, students can quickly look up information about a single task, such as creating a site, and find page references of where in the book the task is illustrated.

Integration of the World Wide Web
The World Wide Web is integrated into the Dreamweaver CS6 learning experience by (1) BTW annotations; and (2) BTW, Q&A, and Quick Reference Summary Web pages.

End-of-Chapter Student Activities
Extensive end-of-chapter activities provide a variety of reinforcement opportunities for students where they can apply and expand their skills. To complete some of these assignments, you will be required to use the Data Files for Students. Visit http://www.cengage.com/ct/studentdownload for detailed access instructions or contact your instructor for information about accessing the required files.

Instructor Resources
The Instructor Resources include both teaching and testing aids and can be accessed via CD-ROM or at **www.cengage.com/login**.

INSTRUCTOR'S MANUAL Includes lecture notes summarizing the chapter sections, figures and boxed elements found in every chapter, teacher tips, classroom activities, lab activities, and quick quizzes in Microsoft Word files.

SYLLABUS Easily customizable sample syllabi that cover policies, assignments, exams, and other course information.

FIGURE FILES Illustrations for every figure in the textbook in electronic form.

POWERPOINT PRESENTATIONS A multimedia lecture presentation system that provides slides for each chapter. Presentations are based on chapter objectives.

SOLUTIONS TO EXERCISES Includes solutions for all end-of-chapter and chapter reinforcement exercises.

TEST BANK & TEST ENGINE Test Banks include 112 questions for every chapter, featuring objective-based and critical thinking question types, and including page number references and figure references, when appropriate. Also included is the test engine, ExamView, the ultimate tool for your objective-based testing needs.

DATA FILES FOR STUDENTS Includes all the files that are required by students to complete the exercises. Visit www.cengage.com/ct/studentdownload for detailed instructions.

Learn Online

CengageBrain.com is the premier destination for purchasing or renting Cengage Learning textbooks, ebooks, eChapters and study tools, at a significant discount (eBooks up to 50% off Print). In addition, CengageBrain.com provides direct access to all digital products including eBooks, eChapters and digital solutions (i.e. CourseMate, SAM) regardless of where purchased. The following are some examples of what is available for this product on www.cengagebrain.com.

STUDENT COMPANION SITE Online practice opportunities and learning tools are available for no additional cost at www.cengagebrain.com can help reinforce chapter terms and concepts.

ADOBE DREAMWEAVER CS6 COURSEMATE CourseMate with ebook for Adobe Dreamweaver CS6 keeps today's students engaged and involved in the learning experience. Adobe Dreamweaver CS6 CourseMate includes an integrated, multi-media rich eBook, and a variety of interactive learning tools, including quizzes, activities, videos, and other resources that specifically reinforce and build on the concepts presented in the chapter. These interactive activities are tracked within CourseMate's Engagement Tracker, making it easy to assess students' retention of concepts. All of these resources enable students to get more comfortable using technology and help prepare students to use the Internet as a tool to enrich their lives. Available at the Comprehensive level in Spring 2013.

CourseNotes

Course Technology's CourseNotes are six-panel quick reference cards that reinforce the most important and widely used features of a software application in a visual and user-friendly format. CourseNotes serve as a great reference tool during and after the student completes the course. CourseNotes are available for software applications such as Adobe Photoshop CS6, Microsoft Office 2010, and Windows 7. Topic-based CourseNotes are available for Best Practices in Social Networking, Hot Topics in Technology, and Web 2.0. Visit www.cengage.com/ct/coursenotes to learn more!

course|notes™
quick reference guide

About Our Covers

The Shelly Cashman Series is continually updating our approach and content to reflect the way today's students learn and experience new technology. This focus on student success is reflected on our covers, which feature real students from Naugatuck Valley Community College using the Shelly Cashman Series in their courses, and reflect the varied ages and backgrounds of the students learning with our books. When you use the Shelly Cashman Series, you can be assured that you are learning computer skills using the most effective courseware available.

Textbook Walk-Through

The Shelly Cashman Series Pedagogy: Project-Based — Step-by-Step — Variety of Assessments

Plan Ahead boxes prepare students to create successful projects by encouraging them to think strategically about what they are trying to accomplish before they begin working.

Step-by-step instructions now provide a context beyond the point-and-click. Each step provides information on why students are performing each task, or what will occur as a result.

Plan
Ahead

General Project Guidelines

When creating a Dreamweaver Web site, the actions you perform and the decisions you make will affect the appearance and characteristics of the entire Web site. When creating Web pages, such as the ones shown in Figure 1–1 on the previous page, you should follow these general guidelines:

1. **Review the Dreamweaver workspace window.** Become familiar with the various layouts and available panels.

2. **Define the local site.** Create the local site using Dreamweaver's Site Setup dialog box.

3. **Determine the location for the local site.** Select the location and storage media where you will save the site. Keep in mind that in Chapter 2, you will begin a site and then modify those pages, and add new pages as you progress through this book. Storage media can include a hard disk, USB flash drive, network drive, or cloud computing drive.

4. **Select the words and heading sizes for the text.** Text accounts for the bulk of the content on most Web pages, but Web site visitors often avoid long blocks of text. It is best to be brief. Include headings to organize the text into sections. Use lists whenever possible. Use common words and simple language.

5. **Identify how to format various elements of the text.** Determine which text will be headings and subheadings, paragraphs, and bulleted and numbered lists on the Web page.

6. **Review final tasks.** Prepare to display a Web page to others by adding professional finishing touches such as a Web page title and by checking the spelling of the text.

When necessary, more specific details concerning the above guidelines are presented at appropriate points in the chapter. The chapter also identifies the actions performed and decisions made regarding these guidelines during the creation of the Web site pages shown in Figure 1–1 on the previous page.

Starting Dreamweaver

Screen Resolution
BTW
If you use a screen resolution higher than 1024 x 768, the location of on-screen tools might vary slightly from the book.

If you are using a computer to step through the project in this chapter and you want your screen to match the figures in this book, you should change your screen's resolution to 1024 × 768. For information about how to change a screen's resolution, read the "Changing Screen Resolution" appendix. The browser used to display the Web page figures is Internet Explorer 9. The browser text size is set to Medium.

To Start Dreamweaver

The following steps, which assume Windows 7 is running, start Dreamweaver, based on a typical installation. You may need to ask your instructor how to start Dreamweaver for your computer.

Creating a New Web Site with Drea

1
- Click the Start button on the Windows 7 taskbar to display the Start menu.

- Type Dreamweaver CS6 in the 'Search programs and files' text box, and watch the search results appear on the Start menu (Figure 1–2).

Q&A
Why do I have documents and files in my list of results?

Any documents containing the words, Dreamweaver CS6, and any files that have been opened with Dreamweaver CS6 may appear in your list.

Figure 1–2

2
- Click Adobe Dreamweaver CS6 in the search results on the Start menu to start Dreamweaver and display the Welcome screen.

- If necessary, click the Workspace Switcher button on the Application bar, and then click Classic to switch to the Classic workspace (Figure 1–3).

Q&A
What is the Classic workspace?

Eleven predefined workspace layouts designed for application developers, coders, and Web designers allow you to customize your workspace according to your role or target device. The Classic workspace provides all the tools necessary for a beginning Web designer's needs and omits features for advanced designers and programmers.

Q&A
Why does the Application bar appear on two rows in Figure 1–3?

If your screen resolution is set to 1024 × 768, the Application bar appears on two rows. If you are using a higher screen resolution, the Application bar appears on one row at the top of the Dreamweaver window.

Figure 1–3

Navigational callouts in red show students where to click.

Explanatory callouts summarize what is happening on screen.

Textbook Walk-Through

❸

- Click HTML in the Create New list to create a blank HTML document.

- If the Dreamweaver window is not maximized, click the Maximize button next to the Close button on the Application bar to maximize the window.

Figure 1–4

- If the Design button is not selected, click the Design button on the Document toolbar to view the page design.

- If the Insert bar is not displayed, click Window on the Application bar and then click Insert to display the Insert panel (Figure 1–4).

Q&A What if a message is displayed regarding default file types?
If a message is displayed, click the Close button.

Q&A What is a maximized window?
A maximized window fills the entire screen. When you maximize a window, the Maximize button changes to a Restore Down button.

Other Ways		
1. Double-click Dreamweaver icon on desktop, if one is present	2. Click Adobe Dreamweaver CS6 on Start menu	3. Click Adobe Dreamweaver icon on taskbar, if present

MAC For a detailed example of starting Dreamweaver using the Mac operating system, refer to the "To Start Adobe Dreamweaver CS6" steps in the For Mac Users appendix at the end of this book.

reamweaver Window

indow open, take time to tour your new Web design weaver workspace lets you view documents and object olbar buttons for the most common operations so that you to your documents. In Dreamweaver, a document is an ed in a browser as a Web page. Figure 1–4 shows how the looks the first time you start Dreamweaver after installation ork efficiently, you should learn the basic terms and concepts space, and understand how to choose options, use inspectors ences that best fit your work style.

Workspace

workspace is an integrated environment in which the anels are incorporated into one large application window. tomized workspace, Dreamweaver provides the Web site workspace layouts as shown in the Workspace Switcher

---

To View the Site in Live View

Live view provides a realistic rendering of what your page will look like in a browser, but lets you make any necessary changes without leaving Dreamweaver. The following steps display the page in Live view.

❶

- Click the Live button on the Document toolbar to display a Live view of the site (Figure 2–67).

Experiment

- Click the Code, Split, and Design buttons to view the page in different views. When you are finished, click the Live button to return to Live view.

❷

- Click the Live button again to return to Design view.

Figure 2–67

Other Ways
1. Press ALT+F11

To View the Site in the Browser

The following steps preview the Gallery Web site home page using Internet Explorer.

❶ Click the 'Preview/Debug in browser' button on the Document toolbar.

❷ Click Preview in IExplore in the Preview/Debug in browser list to display the Gallery Web site in the Internet Explorer browser.

❸ Click the Internet Explorer Close button to close the browser.

To Quit Dreamweaver

The following steps quit Dreamweaver and return control to the operating system.

❶ Click the Close button on the right side of the Application bar to close the window.

❷ If Dreamweaver displays a dialog box asking you to save changes, click the No button.

Chapter Summary

In this chapter, you have learned how to create a Web site template using the design building blocks of CSS style sheets. You defined a new Web site, created a Dreamweaver Web Template, and defined regions of the page using a style sheet. You defined each region with CSS rules that provided consistent site formatting. You also learned how to create an editable region within a template. You added a page to the site based on the template and placed text in the editable region. You displayed the completed Web page in Live view and in a browser. The following tasks are all the new Dreamweaver skills you learned in this chapter:

1. Create a New Site (DW 86)
2. Create Folders for the Image and CSS Files (DW 87)
3. Create a Blank HTML Template (DW 88)
4. Save the HTML Page as a Template (DW 90)
5. Add a Div Tag (DW 93)
6. Select CSS Rule Definitions (DW 97)
7. Add the Logo Div Tag and Define Its CSS Rules (DW 100)
8. Add the Navigation Div Tag and Define Its CSS Rules (DW 104)
9. Add the Image Div Tag and Define Its CSS Rules (DW 107)
10. Add the Content Div Tag and Define Its CSS Rules (DW 109)
11. Add the Footer Div Tag and Define Its CSS Rules (DW 111)
12. Create an Editable Region (DW 113)
13. Close the Template (DW 115)
14. Create a Page from a Template (DW 115)
15. View the Site in Live View (DW 118)

Apply Your Knowledge

Reinforce the skills and apply the concepts you learned in this chapter.

Creating a New Web Page Template

Instructions: First, create a new HTML5 Web page template and save it. Next, insert div tags in the template and create a new external style sheet file. Finally, add new CSS rules so that the completed template in Live view looks like Figure 2–68. The CSS rule definitions for the template are provided in Table 2–2.

Figure 2–68

Continued >

Chapter Summary includes a concluding paragraph, followed by a listing of the tasks completed within a chapter together with the pages on which the step-by-step, screen-by-screen explanations appear.

Apply Your Knowledge usually requires students to open and manipulate a file from the Data Files that parallels the activities learned in the chapter.

Textbook Walk-Through

Extend Your Knowledge

Extend the skills you learned in this chapter and experiment with new skills. You may need to use Help to complete the assignment.

Attaching an External Style Sheet to a Web Page

Note: To complete this assignment, you will be required to use the Data Files for Students. Visit www.cengage.com/ct/studentdownload for detailed instructions or contact your instructor for information about accessing the required files.

Instructions: A volunteer service organization wants to create a Web site using style sheets. You are creating a Web page for the organization that explains the difference between internal and external style sheets. Apply styles to a page by attaching an external style sheet to an existing Web page. The completed Web page is shown in Figure 2–69.

Figure 2–69

Perform the following tasks:

1. Use Windows Explorer to copy the CSS folder and the extend2.html file from the Chapter 02\ Extend folder into the *your last name and first initial*\Extend folder (the folder named perezm\ Extend, for example, which you created in Chapter 1).

2. Start Dreamweaver and open extend2.html.

3. On the CSS Styles panel, click the Attach External Style Sheet button to display the Attach External Style Sheet dialog box. (*Hint*: Point to the buttons in the lower-right part of the CSS Styles panel to find the Attach Style Sheet button.) Click the Browse button in the Attach External Style Sheet dialog box, and then navigate to find and then select the extend2.css file located in the CSS folder in the Extend root folder. Add the CSS file as a link, and then accept your changes.

4. Replace the text Your name here with your name.

   eets.

   your document in your browser. Compare your document to changes and then save your changes.

   nat specified by your instructor.

Extend Your Knowledge projects at the end of each chapter allow students to extend and expand on the skills learned within the chapter. Students use critical thinking to experiment with new skills to complete each project.

Make It Right

Analyze a Web page and correct all errors and/or improve the design.

Formatting and Checking the Spelling of a Web Page

Note: To complete this assignment, you will be required to use the Data Files for Students. Visit www.cengage.com/ct/studentdownload for detailed instructions, or contact your instructor for information about accessing the required files.

Instructions: Start Dreamweaver. You are working with a neighborhood association that wants to learn about Dreamweaver. An association member created a Web page and asks you to improve it. First, you will enhance the look of the Web page by applying styles, aligning text, and adding bullets. Next, you will make the Web page more useful by adding links to text and inserting a document title. Finally, you will check the spelling. The modified Web page is shown in Figure 1–65.

Figure 1–65

Perform the following tasks:

1. Use the Site Setup dialog box to define a new local site in the *your last name and first initial* folder (the F:\perezm folder, for example). Enter `Right` as the new site name and save it.

2. Click the 'Browse for folder' icon to navigate to your USB flash drive. Create a new subfolder within the *your last name and first initial* folder and name it `Right`. Open the folder and then select it as the local site folder. Save the Right site.

3. Using Windows Explorer, copy the right1.html file from the Chapter 01\Right folder into the

---

Make It Right projects call on students to analyze a file, discover errors in it, and fix them using the skills they learned in the chapter.

16. Replace the text, Your name here., with your name.

17. Title the document CSS Rules.

18. Save your changes and then view the Web page in your browser. Compare your page to Figure 2–70. Make any necessary changes and then save your changes.

19. Submit the document in the format specified by your instructor.

In the Lab

Design and/or create a Web document using the guidelines, concepts, and skills presented in this chapter. Labs are listed in order of increasing difficulty.

Lab 1: Designing a New Template for the Healthy Lifestyle Web Site

Note: To complete this assignment, you will be required to use the Data Files for Students. Visit www.cengage.com/ct/studentdownload for detailed instructions or contact your instructor for information about accessing the required files.

Problem: In an effort to reduce health insurance costs, your company wants to provide resources for living a healthy lifestyle. You have been asked to create an internal Web site for your company with information about how to live a healthy lifestyle. This Web site will be used as a resource by employees at your company. You thoughtfully have planned the design of the Web site and now are ready to create a template for the site.

Define a new Web site and create a new HTML5 template. Use div tags and CSS rules in your template design. The template in Live view is shown in Figure 2–71, and the final Web page is shown in Figure 2–72. The CSS rule definitions for the template are provided in Table 2–4.

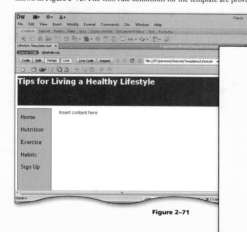

Figure 2–71

In the Lab assignments require students to utilize the chapter concepts and techniques to solve problems on a computer.

Table 1–3 Business Plan Tips	
Section	**Text**
Heading	Business Plan Tips
Paragraph 1	Understand your target audience. Identify demographics of your target audience.
Paragraph 2	Identify your industry and describe your products and services. Identify the benefits of your products and services.
Paragraph 3	Define your business model. How many employees do you need?
Paragraph 4	Describe how you will market your products and services. What is the best way to reach your target audience?
Paragraph 5	How much money do you need to get started? How will you obtain capital?

1. Start Dreamweaver. Use the Site Setup dialog box to define a new local site using BusinessPlan as the site name.

2. Click the 'Browse for folder' icon and then create a new subfolder in the *your last name and first initial* folder named BusinessPlan. Open and select the BusinessPlan folder, and then save the site.

3. On the Dreamweaver Welcome screen, click More in the Create New list. Create a blank HTML page using the 1 column liquid, centered layout, and HTML5 as the DocType. Save the new Web page using index.html as the file name.

4. Enter Business Plan as the Web page title.

5. Delete all the text on the page, replacing it with the text shown in Table 1–3. Press the ENTER key after typing each line or paragraph.

6. Press the ENTER key two times after typing the last sentence. Type your first and last names.

7. Select all of the text below the heading and use the Ordered List button in the Property inspector to create a numbered list for the text.

8. Save your changes and then view your document in your browser. Compare your document to Figure 1–68. Make any necessary changes and then save your work.

9. Submit the document in the format specified by your instructor.

Cases and Places

Apply your creative thinking and problem solving skills to design and implement a solution.

1: Protecting Yourself from Identity Theft

Personal

You recently read an article about the growing trend of identity theft. The article has prompted you to create an educational Web site on how people can protect themselves from identity theft. Define a new local site in the *your last name and first initial* folder and name it Protect Yourself from Identity Theft. Name the new subfolder Theft. Create and save a new HTML Web page. Name the file protect. Use your browser to conduct some research on ways to protect yourself from identity theft. Create a heading for your Web page. Apply the Heading 1 format to the title and center-align the title on the page. Below the heading, create an unordered list of 10 different ways to protect yourself from identity theft. Title the document ID Theft. Check the spelling in the document. Include your name at the bottom of the page. Submit the document in the format specified by your instructor.

Cases & Places exercises call on students to create open-ended projects that reflect academic, personal, and business settings.

Continued >

Web Site Development and Adobe Dreamweaver CS6

mozcann/iStockphoto.com

Objectives

You will have mastered the material in this chapter when you can:

- Identify the 10 types of Web sites
- Define Web browsers and identify their main features
- Discuss how to connect to the Internet using an ISP or a data plan
- Discuss how to plan a Web site for your targeted audience
- Design a Web page with a focal point and appropriate colors, text, and images
- Design a site using accessibility guidelines

- Discuss the role of social networking within Web sites
- Identify the steps in hosting a Web site
- Understand how a Web project is managed
- Discuss how to test, publish, and maintain a Web site
- Recognize the HTML versions and the programming languages of the Web
- Discuss the advantages of using Web page authoring programs such as Dreamweaver

Web Site Development and Adobe Dreamweaver CS6

Web Site Planning and Design Basics

You make judgments about a Web site's visual appeal within seconds of opening a page on the site. This first impression influences subsequent judgments about the site's credibility and your willingness to make purchases. A Web site provides prospective customers with distinct impressions of a business through its online presence. A clean, professional design with intuitive navigation keeps you on a Web page instead of pressing the Back button in the browser. When you walk into a local physical store, you are more apt to make a purchase if the store is well organized, sells quality products, and establishes a positive shopping experience. Similarly, a good Web site is an online storefront providing a friendly environment with the same high level of attention to design and detail as a physical store.

To make that quality first impression, carefully plan your Web site before actually building it by defining its purpose and intended target audience. For example, the goal of a Web site for a local bed and breakfast inn is to encourage travelers to book a reservation at the inn. The site should provide the necessary information to book a stay: contact information, location, photos of the inn, rates, a neighborhood description, proximity to attractions, and a list of amenities, while also conveying a visual image representative of the inn's style. A well-planned site clearly communicates pertinent information to your target audience. Depending on the purpose, the site's goals may also include posting opinions, sharing personal interests, creating a social community, or generating revenue.

Types of Web Sites

Web sites can be classified into 10 categories according to their purpose: search engine/portal, social network, business, informational/educational, news, personal, blog, Web 2.0, e-commerce, and entertainment, as shown in Figure I–1. A search engine or a **portal** Web site (Figure I–1a) provides a variety of Internet services from a single, convenient location. Most portals offer free services such as search engines; e-mail; images; local, national, and worldwide news; sports; weather; reference tools; maps; stock quotes; newsgroups; and calendars. Popular search engines include Google, Bing, Yahoo!, and WolframAlpha. A **social network** (Figure I–1b) is an online community such as Facebook, LinkedIn, or Twitter that encourages members to share their interests, stories, photos, music, and videos with other members. A **business** Web site (Figure I–1c) displays content that markets or sells products or services. An **informational/educational** Web site (Figure I–1d) contains factual information, such as research and statistics. Web pages for governmental agencies, schools, and nonprofit organizations are examples of informational Web pages. A **news** Web site (Figure I–1e) features news articles and information about current events. By contrast, a **personal** Web site (Figure I–1f) is published by an individual or a family and is not associated with any organization. A **blog** (Figure I–1g), short for Weblog, uses a regularly updated journal format to reflect the interests, opinions, and personality of the author and sometimes of site visitors. Blogs can be created using free services such as Blogger.com. A **Web 2.0** site (Figure I–1h) shares user-created content with site visitors. Popular Web 2.0 sites include Erly, Flickr, Pinterest, and Animoto.

(a) search engine/portal

(b) social network

(c) business

(d) informational/educational

(e) news

(f) personal

(g) blog

(h) Web 2.0

(i) e-commerce

(j) entertainment

Figure I–1

E-commerce Web sites (Figure I–1i) such as Amazon, eBay, and Expedia specialize in generating revenue through sales and auctions of products and services. An **entertainment** Web site (Figure I–1j) offers an interactive and engaging environment and may contain music, video, sports, games, and other similar features. As you progress through this book, you will learn more about different types of Web pages.

Browser Considerations

The medium through which you access Web pages is quickly changing. Web pages are opened in a **browser**, a software application that displays content from the **World Wide Web (WWW)**. Browsers are the interface through which you view sites on your own Internet-connected device. You can access your favorite browser on a tablet (a slate device such as an iPad or a Windows or Android tablet), laptop or desktop computer (PC or Mac), or smartphone. The more popular Web browser programs, shown in Figure I–2, are Microsoft Internet Explorer, Mozilla Firefox, Apple Safari, Google Chrome, and Opera.

(a) Internet Explorer

(b) Mozilla Firefox

(c) Apple Safari

(d) Google Chrome

(e) Opera

Figure I–2

This book uses Internet Explorer (Figure I–3) as the primary browser. Using the browser's Tools menu, you can designate any page on the Web as the home page. Important features of Internet Explorer are summarized in Table I–1.

Entering a unique address or **Uniform Resource Locator (URL)** into a browser retrieves a Web page from a Web server, interprets the code within the page, and then displays the page within the browser. **Hypertext Transfer Protocol (HTTP)** is the protocol, or standard, that enables the host computer to transfer data to the client computer. The Web consists of a system of global network servers, also known as **Web servers**, that support specially formatted documents and provide a means for sharing these resources with many people at the same time. As you design a Web page, be aware that different browsers do not display pages identically. During the design and testing phases, ensure that your Web site looks and functions in the ways you intended. What you see when you surf the Web is your browser's interpretation of the underlying code, so testing your page in various browsers helps you create a consistent, positive experience.

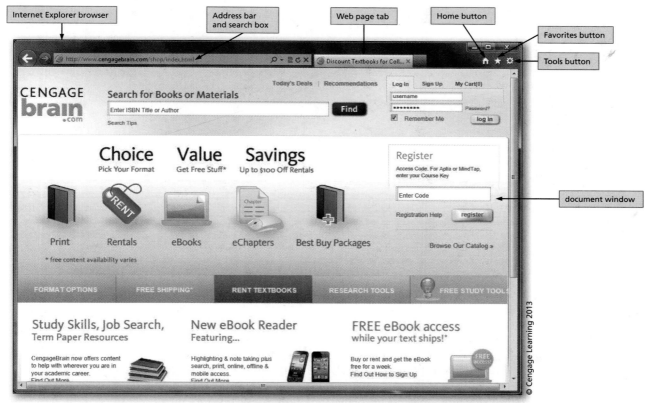

Figure I–3

Table I–1 Internet Explorer Features

Feature	Description
Address bar and search box	Displays the Web site address, or URL, of the Web page you are viewing or searches for the term entered on a search provider site such as Bing.
Web page tab	Provides the option to use tabs to switch from one site to another in a single browser window. The Web page tab also displays the title of the Web page.
Home button	Opens the default home page.
Favorites button	Lets you view favorites, feeds, and history.
Tools button	Provides access to print, zoom, and safety features and lets you view downloads and manage add-ons.
Document window	Displays the Web page content.

Although nearly all Web pages have unique characteristics, most share the same basic design elements. On most Web pages, you find headings or titles, text, pictures or images, background enhancements, and hyperlinks. A **hyperlink**, or link, can connect to another place in the same Web page or site — or a page on an entirely different Web site or document on a server in another city or country. A Web page can contain a variety of link types such as hyperlinks, image links, and social network links to Facebook and Twitter as shown in Figure I–4. Clicking a link displays the Web page associated with the link in a browser window. Linked pages can appear in the same browser window, in a new tab, or in a separate browser window, depending on the code associated with the link.

Figure I–4

Most Web pages are part of a **Web site**, which is a group of related Web pages that are linked together. Most Web sites contain a home page, which is generally the first Web page visitors see when they enter the site. A **home page** (also called an **index page**) typically provides information about the Web site's purpose and content. Most Web sites also contain additional content and pages. An individual, a company, or an organization owns and manages each Web site.

To access the Web, you must connect through a regional or national **Internet service provider (ISP)** using a wireless or wired connection, or a mobile data plan for your phone, tablet, or laptop. Figure I–5 illustrates ways to access the Internet using a service provider or data plan. An ISP provides temporary connections to individuals or businesses through its permanent Internet connection.

(a)　　　　(b)

High-speed connectivity through DSL, cable modem, or satellite (wireless or wired)

Wireless connectivity through ISP or data plan

Smartphone data plan

Figure I–5

Web Site Navigation

　　If visitors to your Web site do not find what they are looking for quickly and easily, they will simply go elsewhere. Predicting how a visitor will access a Web site or at what point the visitor will enter the Web site structure is not possible. Visitors can arrive at any page within your site by a variety of ways, including clicking a hyperlink from another page or Facebook posting, using a search engine, typing a Web address directly, and so on. Therefore, every page of your Web site must provide clear answers to the three questions your visitors will ask: Where am I? Where do I go from here? How do I get to the home page? Once a visitor arrives at a Web site, navigation, the pathway through your site, must be clear and intuitive. Good site navigation uses a consistent and uniform layout for each page. For example, if one page provides a link at the bottom of the window to return to the home page, then all pages should provide navigation to the home page in the same location. Using intuitive navigation greatly enhances the usability of your Web site, which leads to higher user satisfaction and return rates. Every page within your site must provide the visitor with a sense of location, or context within the site.

BTW

Web Page Navigation Charts
To create a visual representation of your site navigation for planning purposes, consider using an organizational chart included in Microsoft Word or PowerPoint. For larger, more complex Web sites, you can chart and organize your content using Microsoft Visio or SmartDraw.

BTW

BTWs
For a complete list of the BTWs found in the margins of this book, visit the Dreamweaver BTW chapter resource on the student companion site located at www. cengagebrain.com.

Mobile Site Access

Using a mobile device with a monthly **data plan** subscription, you can connect to a wireless data network to access the Web, check e-mail, stream music, and download applications (apps). Terms of the data plan are set by the service provider, such as AT&T and Verizon, and typically limit the user to a certain amount of bandwidth per month based on a tiered rate plan (Figure I–5).

An **AirCard**, a type of wireless broadband modem, enables users to connect their laptop to the Internet with their data plan when not connected to a local Wi-Fi (Wireless Fidelity) network. Mobile devices come equipped with default browsers such as Safari for the iOS platform, a built-in Android browser for Android tablets and phones, and Internet Explorer for the Windows tablet or phone. In addition, a wide variety of free browsers are available for download.

Savvy businesses are investing in a mobile presence by creating mobile optimized Web pages based on each mobile device's capabilities and screen size. Using a mobile device with a data plan, you can browse the Internet while commuting on trains, racing through airports, or standing in line. Their small size gives users instant access, from anywhere at any time, as an alternative to sitting at a desk, tethered to a traditional desktop computer. Mobile Web browsers can display the content of most Web sites, but pages that are coded specifically to display on a mobile device provide a more personal, mobile-friendly experience, as shown in Figure I–6. By customizing a Web site for a phone or tablet, navigation is optimized for the mobile world, including an automatic touch interaction to directly call a company or instantly display a map and directions to your meeting.

Figure I–6

Planning a Web Site

The first step in building your first Web site is to design a detailed plan to ensure success. Defining your site's purpose, its target audience, the intended Web platform, and the proposed design is a crucial aspect of Web development. You need to make sure that visitors are immediately drawn into your site through captivating content, a compelling call to action, ease of use, and a sense of community.

Planning Basics

Those who rush into publishing their Web site without proper planning usually design sites that are unorganized and difficult to navigate. Visitors to this type of Web site often lose interest quickly and do not return. As you begin planning your Web site, consider the following guidelines to ensure that you set and attain realistic goals.

Purpose and Goal   Determine the purpose and goal of your Web site. Create a focus by developing a mission statement, which conveys the intention of the Web site. Consider the 10 basic types of Web sites mentioned previously. Will your Web site consist of one basic type or a combination of two or more types? For example, a business Web site's purpose may be to market new products and services or provide customer support. By focusing on the goals that you hope to achieve, you can effectively plan a site that fits your organization's business model.

Target Audience   Knowing your target audience is essential to good design because the needs of your intended visitors help shape the content of a site as well as its look and feel. Figure I–7 shows the Web site for a popular outdoor company named REI that is customized to its target audience. The intended audience at the REI site is anyone who enjoys nature and outdoor adventures. Notice the image on the REI home page during the month of January is customized to the time of the year. Visitors in the winter are most likely focused on snow activities including sledding and skiing, and interested in clothing that provides warmth during the winter season. Easy navigation using a wide variety of links is provided for the major categories of products sold at REI. A search tool at the top of the site enables quick and easy navigation to the desired products. Knowing the information that your target audience is searching for simplifies their purchasing experience at this site. Creating a welcoming, easy-to-navigate experience is vital to any site, so consider the characteristics of your target audience such as interest, gender, education, age range, income, profession/job field, and computer proficiency.

Multiplatform Display   Where will your target audience view your Web site? Will it be displayed on a Mac laptop using Safari, a Windows tablet using Internet Explorer, an Android phone on a built-in browser, or a desktop PC using Mozilla Firefox? Planning for Web presentation involves verifying that your site will function in a variety

Figure I–7

of browsers based on the intended layout and in different screen resolutions. **Screen resolution** refers to the number of pixels in a display, such as 1280 × 800. The layout of a Web site can change depending on the user's screen resolution. Creating a multi-platform Web page, also called a **cross-platform site,** that provides a similar display experience across various screen sizes, resolutions, browsers, and devices is supported by a new code environment called HTML5 and CSS3, which are explained later in the chapter. Web developers must plan their sites to deploy on any device without worrying that the device itself will not support a particular graphic or effect used in the page.

Design

A Web site consists of more than information and links. A well-designed Web site creates a positive interaction with the user by focusing on a visual, aesthetically pleasing way to present information. Web users prefer a simple, clean, and functional design. Avoid a cluttered design that uses multiple fonts, inconsistent icons, flashing ads, and ubiquitous links. Consider the following Web design principles when creating a memorable site.

Focal Point   A mixture of elements including text, colors, and images all compete for your attention when you open a Web page. A design element called a **focal point** provides a dominating element that captures your attention. In Figure I–8, the United States Department of Agriculture nutrition site uses a dominant image as a focal point to immediately draw your attention to and illustrate the purpose of this site — choosing a plate full of healthy foods. A focal point in your site may be an element such as a prominent header, company logo, or central product image. Notice the amount of white space in the site in Figure I–8. **White space** is the empty space around the focal point and other design elements that enables important aspects of the page to stand out. White space does not have to be white; it can be the background color of the page. Appropriate use of white space can lead the user's eye to important content. When a Web page lacks a clear focal point and white space, competing images, flashing text, and abundant text can confuse the user.

Color as a Design Tool   Color can effectively convey information that adds interest and vitality to your site. Color should be aesthetically pleasing to your target audience and suit the content of the page. For example, in Figure I–7 on the previous page the gray and white colors fit the page's winter theme. When designing Web pages for a

Figure I–8

business environment, consider the company's branding colors. In Figure I–9, the site for the Cengage Learning publishing company incorporates the colors in the logo shown in the upper-left corner of the page. The blue color scheme of this page reinforces the site's overall message and identity.

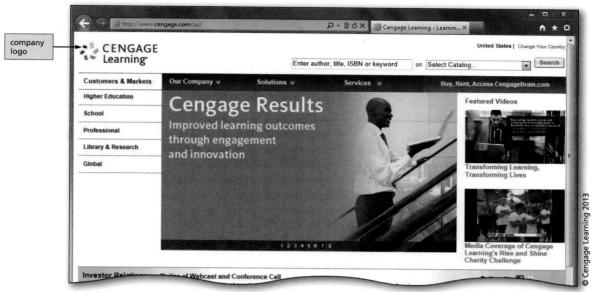

© Cengage Learning 2013

Figure I–9

The most common misuse of color is a background color that detracts from the readability of the text. How much time would you spend on a site featuring a bright yellow background and white text? A bright yellow background strains the eyes, making it impossible to read the text. Keep in mind that people use color to categorize objects in their everyday lives. Colors in the cool color group such as green and blue tend to have a calming effect. Similarly, many companies use color in their Web design to help users identify and categorize their brand with just one glance. For example, red is associated with power and energy, making it a good color for a sports car. Table I–2 describes the common colors and their related meanings.

Table I–2 Common Color Meanings	
Color	**Description**
Blue	Trust, security, conservative, technology (The most common color used on the Web)
Green	Nature, money, earth, health, good luck
White	Purity, cleanliness, innocence, precision
Red	Power, danger, passion, love, energy
Black	Sophistication, power, death, fear
Gray	Intellect, elegance, modesty
Orange	Energy, balance, warmth, brightness
Yellow	Cheer, optimism, joy, honesty
Brown	Reliability, earth, comfort
Purple	Mystery, spirituality, arrogance, royalty

Text Design Like other Web elements, good **typography**, or the appearance and arrangement of the characters that make up your text, is vital to the success of your Web page. Adding text is not just about placing letters on a site, but rather using text as a page design element to improve readability. The introductory text of a Web page should instantly convey the purpose of the site. A Web site visitor will more likely read a short and well-structured introduction while skipping longer paragraphs of text. In the Web site for the Fish restaurant shown in Figure I–10, the shading on the left provides a focal point for the text. The introductory text is short, useful, and interesting. A call to action initiated by the text requests that you view the menus. The site clearly defines what its targeted audience wants to view first — the menus.

On an opening page, shorter text can captivate your audience. But when longer paragraphs are necessary to provide more detailed information, the text should be easy to read. A font face or font family is the typeface that will be applied to the text by a Web browser. Select fonts with good readability — especially when developing pages for smaller, mobile devices.

Image Design Images provide an instant focal point to any site and give viewers an immediate cue about page content. In the Fish restaurant example in Figure I–10, the image of Asian food on the home page conveys the flavor of the cuisine and the ambiance of this restaurant. Even a cursory glance at this opening communicates a positive impression for that type of cuisine and atmosphere.

An image can stimulate visual interest, market a product, display a company logo, illustrate a process, or provide graphical information. Visitors' eyes are naturally drawn to photos of people. Creating a balance between the number of images and text elements is vital to achieving an uncluttered appearance. An image leaves a stronger impression because our brains are drawn to familiar, real-life objects rather than words alone.

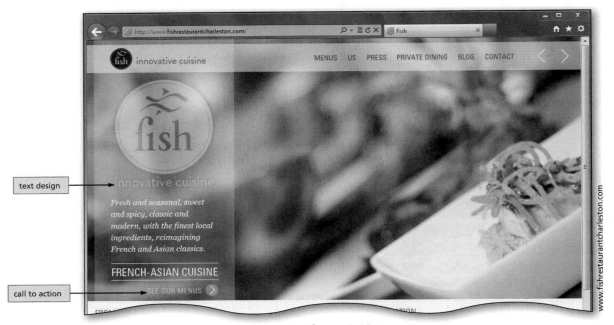

Figure I–10

Accessibility Guidelines

In your planning phase, you must ensure your site is accessible to all users. Imagine if your school's Web site was not accessible to all students regardless of physical limitations. For schools and government entities it is not only unwise, but also likely in violation of federal law. Section 508, which was added as an amendment in 1998 to the Rehabilitation Act, requires that electronic and information technology that is developed by or purchased by federal agencies be accessible to people with disabilities (www.section508.gov). Businesses seek the largest possible audience and recognize the positive return on investment (ROI) for the extra costs of building a site accessible to all customers. Table I–3 categorizes the major types of disabilities. Each requires certain kinds of adaptations in the design of the Web content, but ultimately everyone benefits from helpful illustrations and clear navigation.

Table I–3 Disability Types and Design Strategies		
Disability	**Description**	**Design Strategies**
Cognitive	Autism, learning disabilities, distractibility, inability to focus on large amounts of information	Keep text short. Break up text with headings. Use meaningful graphics.
Hearing	Deafness	Provide a transcription or summary of audio elements.
Motor	Inability to move mouse or use touch screen, slower response time	Minimize scrolling.
Visual	Blindness, poor vision, color blindness	Describe images in text (which may be read aloud by a screen reader). Use a large, easy-to-read font.

As a Web designer, removing barriers so people with disabilities have equal access to the Web is a moral and often a legal obligation under the Americans with Disabilities Act (ADA). For example, a visually impaired person often uses a screen reader, which is a software application that can vocalize screen content. A Web site image should contain information called **alternative text** describing the picture for the screen. The **World Wide Web Consortium (W3C)**, an international standards organization for the World Wide Web, provides Web standards, language specifications, and accessibility recommendations at www.w3.org to promote the growth of the Web. Forward-thinking Web developers plan their sites with accessibility in mind because it is the right thing to do. Accessibility needs to be an integral part of Web design planning rather than an afterthought. Throughout this text, accessibility is illustrated as each aspect of Web page development is covered.

Role of Social Networking

Planning a site extends beyond selecting content and following accessibility rules. Modern Web sites enable users to interact with one another and share information. These sites create a sense of community with two-way conversations between site visitors and business responses, including product reviews, targeted e-mail, a Facebook and Twitter marketing presence, YouTube links to new product video demonstrations, and blog feedback. These online interactions allow businesses to give their customers a voice and help them improve their products, services, and customer satisfaction. A Web site can provide customer reviews and ratings to help other customers. In addition, many sites incorporate Facebook pages and Twitter follower links by providing logos and inviting visitors to connect with them.

As shown in Figure I–11 on the next page, the publishing company Cengage Learning provides a Facebook and Twitter logo on its opening page to allow a user to "like" or "follow" its product line. When a visitor "likes" a business, he or she becomes a fan on Facebook, promoting that business to all of the visitor's personal contacts. Cengage Learning leverages Facebook and Twitter to provide instructors and students with the latest technology innovations, educational research, and e-book ventures. This social networking resource offers the customer a location to share learning success stories, ask questions, and post new ways to integrate classroom solutions. This presence creates an interwoven community of friends and colleagues who can quickly learn about the business from others who have liked or followed it.

Figure I–11

Web Site Hosting

Creating a good Web site begins with planning the content and structure. But selecting a Web server host, which makes a Web site visible to the world through a unique URL, is another important consideration. Each Web site requires a Web server running continuously to deliver your Web pages to visitors quickly.

Obtain a Domain Name   To allow visitors to access your Web site, you must obtain a domain name. Visitors access Web sites via an IP address or a domain name. An **IP address (Internet Protocol address)** is a number that uniquely identifies each computer or device connected to the Internet. A **domain name** is the text version of an IP address. The **Domain Name System (DNS)** is an Internet service that translates domain names into their corresponding IP addresses. The **Accredited Registrar Directory** provides a listing of domain name registrars accredited by the **Internet Corporation for Assigned Names and Numbers (ICANN)**. Your most difficult task likely will be to find a name that is not registered. Expect to pay approximately $8 to $50 per year for a domain name.

For example, a small hair salon named Shear Styles contacts a domain registrar, Network Solutions — which is shown in Figure I–12 — to create a site for its Web presence. The salon would like the URL www.shearstyles.com, but must first verify if that URL is available. As a Web domain registrar, Network Solutions determines if the site is available and the yearly cost of that domain name. The domain name ends with an extension such as .com (commercial entity), .net (network), .gov (government agency), .org (organization), or .edu (education) to represent the type of site. Domain names should be easy to recall or should reflect the organization's name so that people can easily find the site.

Obtain Server Space   Locate an ISP that will host your Web site. Recall that an ISP is a business that has a permanent Internet connection. ISPs offer connections to individuals and companies for free or for a fee. Typically, an ISP for your home Internet connection provides a small amount of server space for free to host a personal site.

enter URL to determine if domain name is available

possible domain extensions

www.networksolutions.com

Figure I–12

If you select an ISP that provides free server space, your visitors will typically be subjected to advertisements and pop-up windows. Other options to explore for free or inexpensive server space include online communities, such as Bravenet (http://bravenet .com), Biz.ly (www.biz.ly), and webs.com (www.webs.com); and your educational institution's Web server. If the purpose of your Web site is to sell a product or service or to promote a professional organization, you should consider a fee-based ISP. Shop around to determine the best fit for your site. When selecting an ISP, consider the following questions and how they apply to your particular situation and Web site:

1. What is the monthly fee? Are setup fees charged?

2. How much server space is provided for the monthly fee? Is there unlimited storage? Can you purchase additional space? If so, how much does it cost?

3. How much bandwidth is available to download multimedia files?

4. Is your site hosted on a single dedicated server or cloud-hosted servers? (Cloud hosting forms a network of connected servers that are located in different locations across the world, providing multiple backup opportunities.)

5. What is the average server uptime on a monthly basis? What is the average server downtime?

6. What are the server specifications? Can the server handle heavy usage? Does it have battery backup power?

7. Are **server logs**, which keep track of the number of accesses, available?

8. What technical support does the ISP provide, and when is it available?

9. Does the server on which the Web site will reside have CGI and PHP scripting capabilities, and provide support for Active Server Pages (ASP), SQL Database, and File Transfer Protocol (FTP)?

10. Does the server on which the Web site will reside support e-commerce with **Secure Sockets Layer (SSL)** for encrypting confidential data such as credit card numbers? Are additional fees required for these capabilities?

Publish the Web Site   You must publish, or upload, a finished Web site from your computer to a host server where your site will then be accessible to anyone on the Internet. Publishing, or uploading, is the process of transmitting all the files that constitute your Web site from your computer to the top directory, also called the root folder on the selected server or host computer. The files that make up your Web site can include Web pages, PDF documents, images, audio, video, animation, and others. You can use a variety of tools and methods to manage the upload task. Some of the more popular of these are **FTP (File Transfer Protocol)** and Web authoring programs such as Dreamweaver. These tools allow you to link to a remote server, enter a password, and then upload your files. Dreamweaver contains a built-in function similar to independent FTP programs.

Project Management

After completing the planning phase, the next step is to create, manage, and update the site. In most businesses, a **Webmaster** or Web project manager is in charge of delivering the site. Large commercial organizations employ a Web development team, shown in Figure I–13, which includes project managers, designers, programmers, a marketing group, a legal team to deal with copyright materials and permissions, editors, and strategic managers. The Webmaster works within the budget for site development, creates a schedule from start to end, and defines the quality of the work completed. The members of a Web team continue their roles throughout the development, testing, and maintenance of the site to keep the information current.

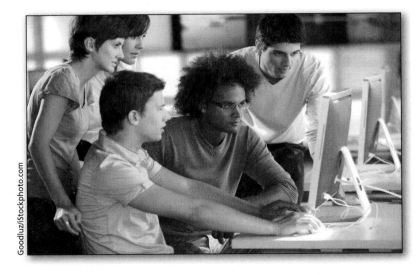

Goodluz/iStockphoto.com

Figure I–13

Test Web Pages

BTW

To test a Web page, you can use the Adobe BrowserLab at https:// browserlab.adobe.com to see how your pages are displayed in a variety of browsers and versions of browsers.

The best way to test a site is to use actual users. Each user independently reviews each page and records his or her feedback. In addition to the basic testing, safety testing with e-commerce sites is especially imperative where credit card numbers and personal information are part of the purchasing process. These security tests should report any possible vulnerabilities and recommendations to address them.

Testing the Site

A Web site's usability or ease of use is an integral part of the site's success. Due to the complexity of most Web sites with multimedia, interaction, and navigation, each page in a site must be tested on various browsers, operating systems, and platforms. Testing can take place at almost any stage of site development, but earlier is better. Among other things, the testing process verifies that the site is free of spelling and grammatical errors, all the links work correctly, and graphics appear as designed.

Maintaining the Site

An outdated Web site gives the impression that the site has been abandoned, making the visitor lose trust in the information on the site. In the long run, performing ongoing maintenance is usually less expensive than overhauling a site that is significantly out of date. Content on any site should be routinely reviewed for accuracy, currency, and alignment with the site's purpose. A Web site is a living entity, requiring the addition of updated images, topics, and videos at regular intervals. The site should be reviewed periodically for obsolete information and broken links. Use internal statistics from your ISP reports to track each visitor's behavior to determine popular pages within your site, how visitors found your site, their countries of origin, the browsers they are using, and the number of people visiting your site. Learning to use and apply the information derived from the server log will help you make your Web site successful.

Load Testing

A Web site testing **BTW** process called load testing simulates the operation of hundreds or thousands of simultaneous visitors to determine how well a site performs under a heavy load.

Web Programming Languages

When you access a Web page with your browser, the Web server reads through a coded page line by line and executes the code to display the finished page. **Hypertext Markup Language (HTML)** is the language used to develop basic Web pages. To view the HTML source code for a Web page using Internet Explorer, right-click the Web page, and then click View source. Web site programming allows you to turn a simple, static HTML page into a dynamic Web page with the use of various programming languages added within the HTML code. Web programming languages, such as PHP and ASP, provide user interaction to fill in an online application, post your Facebook status, submit a dinner review at Yelp, purchase your textbooks online, or request an online Groupon coupon, for example.

HTML and XHTML

HTML, the first language of the Web developed in 1990 to organize information in a browser, continues to evolve. HTML code, or markup, consists of **tags** shown in Figure I–14, which are a set of symbols defined in HTML. Tags start with a left angle bracket (<) followed by an HTML keyword, and end with a right angle bracket (>). For example, the tags <p>, <h1>, and <table> represent paragraph, heading size 1, and table, respectively. Many tags have a start tag, or element, such as <h1> and an end tag, or element, such as </h1> to indicate where the formatting begins and ends.

HTML is useful for creating headings, paragraphs, lists, and so on, but is limited to these general types of formatting. **XHTML (Extensible Hypertext Markup Language)** is a rewritten version of HTML using XML (Extensible Markup Language) developed in 2000 and described later in the chapter. The difference between HTML and XHTML is minor, but the primary benefit is that XHTML is more widely accepted on mobile device platforms. Some XHTML elements such as a line break <br /> do not have an end element. Instead, the right angle bracket is

Figure I–14

preceded by a space and forward slash. These are known as one-sided elements, or self-closing elements. XHMTL elements use lowercase tags in the Web page code source.

HTML5

The newest HTML standard is **HTML5**, representing the fifth major revision of the core Web language. Web developers use HTML5 to display their sites on a variety of smartphones, tablets, and computers without tailoring the code for specific hardware. HTML5 supports in-browser multimedia by adding simple tags to play audio and video elements. HTML5 enables developers to write less JavaScript code (a scripting Web language), which makes the site easier to code and update.

DHTML

HTML5 is combined with CSS3 (Cascading Style Sheets) and JavaScript to create more dynamic Web content. **CSS3** describes a template for the style and formatting of the page. The resulting combined code is called **DHTML**, which stands for Dynamic HTML, and creates movement or interactivity. DHTML is supported by modern browsers and creates a faster Web experience.

XML

The goal of HTML code is to display a Web page in a particular layout. But a different type of code, called **XML (Extensible Markup Language)**, is designed to transport data, not to display data. If a site visitor at a hotel chain Web site enters his or her home address to get directions from home to the hotel, the home address entered is supported and sent to the Web service using XML. In other words, XML code transports and stores data. Newer versions of Microsoft Office save their documents in XML, creating a direct way to carry these documents throughout the Web.

PHP

Embedded within HTML code, **PHP (Hypertext Preprocessor)** code is an open-source Web server-side scripting language that produces dynamic Web pages. A server-side scripting language means that when a visitor opens a Web page, the Web server processes the PHP code and then sends the results to the visitor's browser to be displayed within the HTML code. When you create an account to log on to a Web site, fill out a financial aid form online, search an online shopping site's database to determine if it has your size, or open a PDF form for your federal income taxes, the Web server processes the PHP code to administer each of these actions.

ASP

ASP (Active Server Pages) is very similar to PHP because both languages create dynamic Web pages. ASP leverages languages such as Visual Basic Script, JScript, and C#, among others, to create ASP code. A programmer can write code in Visual Basic using Visual Studio, and ASP code is generated automatically. ASP is a proprietary system owned by Microsoft.

jQuery

jQuery provides a full JavaScript Library that simplifies programming within an HTML document. If you have visited a site with a drag-and-drop interface, a drop-down calendar (Figure I–15), a horizontal slider, or text that could be expanded like an accordion, jQuery was most likely the code powering the effect. If your Web page requires a date picker calendar tool, jQuery provides code to paste directly in your HTML to create this widget. jQuery is a cross-browser, free open source library that contains thousands of animations, widgets, and plug-ins that cover a wide range of functionality.

Figure I–15

Web Page Authoring Programs

Web developers have several options for creating Web pages: a text editor, an HTML5 editor, software applications, or a **What You See Is What You Get (WYSIWYG)** text editor. A WYSIWYG text editor allows a user to view a document as it will appear in the final product and to edit the text, images, or other elements directly within that view. Microsoft Notepad (Figure I–16 on the next page), WordPad, and Notepad++ are each examples of a **text editor**. These simple, easy-to-use programs allow you to enter, edit, save, and print text. Software applications such as Microsoft Word and Microsoft Excel also provide a Save as Web Page command. This feature converts the application document into a file that Web browsers can display.

Web page authoring software allows you to see your design as you create it without writing code. Examples of a WYSIWYG text editor are programs such as Adobe Dreamweaver, Microsoft Expression Web, WordPress, Joomla, and Drupal. Technically, you do not need to know HTML to create Web pages in Dreamweaver; however, an understanding of HTML will help you if you need to alter Dreamweaver-generated code. If you know HTML, then you can make changes to the code in the code window (Figure I–17 on the next page) and Dreamweaver will accept the changes.

About Adobe Dreamweaver CS6

The standard in professional Web authoring, **Adobe Dreamweaver CS6** (Figure I–18 on the next page) is part of the Adobe Creative Suite, which includes Adobe Flash, Fireworks, Photoshop, Illustrator, InDesign, Acrobat, and other programs depending on the particular suite. Dreamweaver provides features that access these separate products. Dreamweaver makes it easy to get started and provides you with helpful tools to enhance your Web design and development experience. Working in a single environment, you create, build, and manage Web sites and Internet applications. Many of the new features in Dreamweaver CS6 focus on building mobile HTML5 applications for various platforms.

Dreamweaver contains coding tools and features that include references for HTML5, XML, CSS, and JavaScript, as well as code editors that allow you to edit the code directly using programming languages such as PHP, ASP, and jQuery. Using **Adobe Roundtrip technology**, Dreamweaver can import Microsoft Office or other software Web pages and delete the unused code. Downloadable extensions from the Adobe Web site make it easy to add functionality to any Web site. Examples of these extensions include shopping carts and online payment features.

HTML5 code in Notepad

```
<!DOCTYPE HTML>
<html>
<body>
<h1> Welcome to an HTML5 Page </h1>
<h2> This page displays a video </h2>|

<video width="320" height="240" controls="controls">
  <source src="movie.mp4" type="video/mp4" />
  <source src="movie.ogg" type="video/ogg" />
  <source src="movie.webm" type="video/webm" />
Your browser does not support the video tag.
</video>

</body>
</html>
```

Used with permission from Microsoft Corporation

Figure I–16

Dreamweaver HTML5 Code window

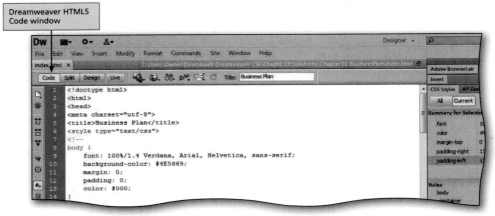

Figure I–17

Adobe Dreamweaver CS6

Figure I–18

Instead of writing individual files for every page, you can use a database to store content and then retrieve the content dynamically in response to a user's request. With this feature, you can update the information one time in one place, instead of manually editing many pages. Another key feature is **Cascading Style Sheets (CSS) styles**.

CSS3 (version 3) styles are collections of formatting definitions that affect the appearance of Web page elements. You can use CSS3 styles to format text, images, headings, tables, and so forth. Using CSS, you can make a formatting change in one place and update all the Web pages that contain that same formatting. CSS layouts are used to create a similar look and feel across Web sites. They also are used to reduce the amount of work and HTML code generated by consolidating display properties into a single file.

Dreamweaver provides the tools that help you author accessible content that complies with government guidelines. Accessibility is discussed in more detail as you progress through the book.

Dreamweaver allows you to easily publish Web sites to a local area network, which connects computers in a limited geographical area, or to the Web, so that anyone with Internet access can see them. The concepts and techniques presented in this book provide the tools you need to plan, develop, and publish professional Web sites.

Chapter Summary

In this chapter, you have learned how to plan, design, develop, test, publish, and maintain a Web site using accessibility guidelines. An overview of the basic types of Web pages also was presented. The Introduction furnished information on developing a Web site, including planning basics. The process of designing a Web site with a focal point and appropriate color, text, and images was discussed. Information about testing, publishing, and maintaining a Web site also was presented, including an overview of obtaining a domain name, acquiring server space, and uploading a Web site. Methods and tools used to create Web pages were introduced. A short overview of the languages used to create Web sites was explained. Finally, the advantages of using Dreamweaver in Web development were discussed. These advantages include a WYSIWYG text editor and a visual, customizable development environment using Cascading Style Sheets.

1. Web Site Planning and Design Basics (DW 2)
2. Planning a Web Site (DW 9)
3. Web Site Hosting (DW 15)
4. Project Management (DW 16)
5. Web Programming Languages (DW 18)
6. Web Page Authoring Programs (DW 20)

Apply Your Knowledge

Reinforce the skills and apply the concepts you learned in this chapter.

Planning a Web Site

Instructions: As discussed in this Introduction, you must plan and design your Web site thoughtfully before you create it. Use the information in Table I–4 to plan and design a Web site.

Table I–4 Planning a Web Site	
Web Site Element	**Questions to Ask**
Purpose and goal	What are the purpose and goal of your Web site? What type of Web site will you develop?
Target audience	Who is your target audience? For what purpose is the audience using your Web site?
Multiplatform display	Will your target audience view your Web site on a computer, tablet, or mobile device? Will you design a cross-platform site?
Focal point	What will you use to capture the attention of your target audience?
Color	What color(s) will you use to enhance your site? Refer to Table I–2 on page DW 12.
Text design	How will text be arranged on your pages?
Image design	What types of images will you use within your site?
Accessibility	How will your site accommodate people with disabilities?
Social networking	Will you incorporate social networking within your planning model?

Perform the following tasks:

1. Select a type of Web site to create, using Figure I–1 as a guide. Open your word processing program and answer the questions contained in Table I–4. Restate each question and use complete sentences for your answers.

2. Save the document with the file name Apply I-1_*lastname_firstname*. Submit the document in the format specified by your instructor.

Extend Your Knowledge

Extend the skills you learned in this chapter and experiment with new skills. You may need to use Help to complete the assignment.

Exploring Programming Languages

Instructions: As you learned in this Introduction, you can use many types of Web programming languages in the development of a Web site. This introduction discussed the following types of programming languages: HTML, XHTML, HTML5, DHTML, XML, PHP, ASP, and jQuery. Use the Web to identify other types of Web programming languages.

Perform the following tasks:

1. Open your Web browser and use a search engine to research three types of Web programming languages not discussed in this chapter.

2. Use your word processor to list the Web programming languages that you found and describe how each language can be used in the development of a Web site.

3. Save the document with the file name Extend I-1_*lastname_firstname*. Submit the document in the format specified by your instructor.

Make It Right

Analyze a Web site and suggest how to improve its design.

Improving Design

Instructions: Start your Web browser. Select and analyze two Web sites. Determine the focal point and typography for each Web site.

Use your word processing program to describe the focal point for each Web site and include a screen shot within your document of each site's home page. Describe the text and color design used in each Web site. Review Table I–3 on page DW 13. Discuss how the text and color design could be improved. Save your document as MIR_*lastname_firstname*. Submit the document in the format specified by your instructor.

In the Lab

Design and/or create a document using the guidelines, concepts, and skills presented in this chapter. Labs are listed in order of increasing difficulty.

Lab 1: Web Site Maintenance

Problem: Once a Web site is up and running, the Webmaster is responsible for maintaining the site. Assume you are the Webmaster for a state government agency. Develop a maintenance plan for the Web site.

Perform the following tasks:

1. Open your Web browser. Research tips on Web site maintenance.

2. Use your word processing program to describe your Web site maintenance plan.

3. Save the document with the file name Lab I-1_*lastname_firstname*. Submit the document in the format specified by your instructor.

In the Lab

Lab 2: Web Site Hosting

Problem: Determining the best ISP to host your site is vital to maintain a continuous site that attracts visitors. Assume you have developed a new Web site for a small online retail store. Conduct research on the Web to find a suitable ISP.

Perform the following tasks:

1. Start your browser. Use a search engine to find ISPs and research their services and costs.

2. Select two desirable ISPs and use your word processing program to compare their services and costs. Write a short summary explaining which ISP you would select and why.

3. Save the document with the file name Lab I-2_*lastname_firstname*. Submit the document in the format specified by your instructor.

In the Lab

Lab 3: Comparing Web Browsers

Problem: People use many different Web browsers to access the Internet. Typically, an individual will select a primary Web browser as his or her preferred browser based on its features and tools.

Perform the following tasks:

1. Open or download a Web browser that you do not normally use or have never used and examine its features and tools. Web browsers include:

    a. Microsoft Internet Explorer (http://windows.microsoft.com/en-US/internet-explorer/downloads/ie)

    b. Mozilla Firefox (www.mozilla.org/en-US/firefox/new/)

    c. Google Chrome (www.google.com/chrome/)

    d. Apple Safari (www.apple.com/safari/download/)

    e. Opera (www.opera.com/download/)

2. Open your preferred Web browser and visit a page you have visited previously. Examine the browser's features and tools and explore its ease of use.

3. Use your word processing program to identify your primary Web browser and the one you downloaded, and then compare and contrast the browsers' features and tools.

4. Describe the ease of use of the browser that you do not normally use, and explain why you would or would not use the browser as a secondary Web browser.

5. Save your document as Lab I-3_*lastname_firstname*. Submit the document in the format specified by your instructor.

Cases and Places

Apply your creative thinking and problem solving skills to design and implement a solution.

1: Determining Web Site Type

Personal

You are an expert on several video games and video game consoles. You have decided to design a Web site to share tips about certain video games and game consoles. Use a search engine to research the type of Web site you should design. Use your word processing program to write a one-page summary about the type of Web site you will design and why. Save the document as Case I-1_*lastname_firstname*. Use proper spelling and grammar. Submit the document in the format specified by your instructor.

2: Designing for Accessibility

Academic

You are the Webmaster for a small community college. As such, you must make the college's Web site accessible for students with disabilities. Start your browser and research various ways you can accomplish this task. Write a two-page summary of at least three ways you can make the Web site accessible for students with disabilities. Use proper spelling and grammar. Save the document as Case I-2_*lastname_firstname*. Submit the document in the format specified by your instructor.

3: Social Networking for a Business

Professional

Assume you are the owner of a local pest control business. You currently have a Web site and are now considering joining the world of social networking, but are unsure about the best social networking option. Start your browser and use a search engine to do some research. Use your word processing program to write a two-page summary about the information you found. Include a list of pros and cons of a business using social media. Use proper spelling and grammar. Save the document as Case I-3_*lastname_firstname*. Submit the document in the format specified by your instructor.

1 | Creating a New Web Site with Dreamweaver

Objectives

You will have mastered the material in this chapter when you can:

- Start Dreamweaver and customize the Dreamweaver workspace
- Describe the Dreamweaver workspace
- Show and hide panels
- Create a Dreamweaver Web site using a template
- Define a local site
- Add text to a Web page

- Change the format of the text headings
- Add links to a Web site
- Create an unordered list
- Save a Web site
- Check spelling
- Preview a Web site in a browser
- Use Dreamweaver Help

1 | Creating a New Web Site with Dreamweaver

What Is Dreamweaver CS6?

Adobe Dreamweaver CS6, the preferred professional Web site creation and management software, provides a rich user interface with powerful tools. Dreamweaver can be used to design a Web site that is displayed in any browser on multiple platforms, including PC and Mac computers, kiosks, tablets, and smartphones. Dreamweaver's icon-driven menus and detailed panels make it easy for users to add text, images, multimedia files, and links without typing one line of code. Dreamweaver creates code that reflects selections made in the user interface and provides content structure when rendering the page in the browser.

The Adobe Dreamweaver user interface is consistent across all Adobe authoring tools. This consistency allows for easy integration with other Adobe Web-related programs such as Adobe Flash, Photoshop, Illustrator, and Fireworks. Dreamweaver CS6 is part of the **Adobe Creative Suite 6**, a collection of graphic design, video editing, and Web development applications published by Adobe Systems. Dreamweaver CS6 runs on multiple operating systems, including Windows 8, Windows 7, Windows Vista, Windows XP, and Mac OS X. This text uses Dreamweaver CS6 on the PC platform, running the Windows 7 operating system.

Project Planning Guidelines

The process of developing a Web site that communicates specific information requires careful analysis and planning. Start by identifying the purpose and audience of the Web site and developing a Web page design. If you are working with a client, ask your client to clearly express his or her expectations, such as who will visit the site and how they will use it. The Web page design contributes to the look and feel of the Web site, which includes the amount of text displayed on each page and the format of the text. Details of these guidelines are provided in the "Project Planning Guidelines" appendix. Each chapter in this book provides practical business applications of these planning guidelines.

Project — Small Business Incubator Web Site Plan

You can use Dreamweaver CS6 to produce Web sites such as the Small Business Incubator Web site shown in Figure 1–1. A business incubator is a program that supports start-up companies by providing resources such as office space, and services such as business advice and networking opportunities. A business incubator in Condor, California plans to create the site shown in Figure 1–1 to highlight best practices for small businesses that design their own Web sites. The two-page Small Business Incubator Web site includes the index, or home, page for the Web site and introduces the design elements. The page includes a simple navigation bar in the left column and a main heading followed by a short informational paragraph in the right column. The second page displays a checklist of best practices for designing any small business Web site.

The project in this chapter uses a built-in Dreamweaver layout to create a simple HTML5 page named index as shown in Figure 1–1a. Recall that HTML5 is the most recent standard of Hypertext Markup Language (HTML), the core language for creating Web pages. After entering text into the index page, you will create a second page (Figure 1–1b) named checklist, which includes a bulleted list of best practices for small business Web site planning. Creating a two-page Web site requires a basic understanding of the Dreamweaver user interface, layouts, links, heading sizes, and bullets.

Figure 1–1

Overview

As you read this chapter, you will learn how to create the Web page project shown in Figure 1–1 by performing these general tasks:

- Customize the workspace.
- Create a new Dreamweaver HTML5 Web site with two columns.
- Enter text in the Web page.
- Change the format of the headings.
- Add links.
- Save the document.
- Add a second HTML5 page.
- Create a bulleted list.
- Check spelling.
- Preview the Web site in a browser.
- Save the Web site.

Plan Ahead

General Project Guidelines

When creating a Dreamweaver Web site, the actions you perform and the decisions you make will affect the appearance and characteristics of the entire Web site. When creating Web pages, such as the ones shown in Figure 1–1 on the previous page, you should follow these general guidelines:

1. **Review the Dreamweaver workspace window.** Become familiar with the various layouts and available panels.

2. **Define the local site.** Create the local site using Dreamweaver's Site Setup dialog box.

3. **Determine the location for the local site.** Select the location and storage media where you will save the site. Keep in mind that in Chapter 2, you will begin a site and then modify those pages, and add new pages as you progress through this book. Storage media can include a hard disk, USB flash drive, network drive, or cloud computing drive.

4. **Select the words and heading sizes for the text.** Text accounts for the bulk of the content on most Web pages, but Web site visitors often avoid long blocks of text. It is best to be brief. Include headings to organize the text into sections. Use lists whenever possible. Use common words and simple language.

5. **Identify how to format various elements of the text.** Determine which text will be headings and subheadings, paragraphs, and bulleted and numbered lists on the Web page.

6. **Review final tasks.** Prepare to display a Web page to others by adding professional finishing touches such as a Web page title and by checking the spelling of the text.

When necessary, more specific details concerning the above guidelines are presented at appropriate points in the chapter. The chapter also identifies the actions performed and decisions made regarding these guidelines during the creation of the Web site pages shown in Figure 1–1 on the previous page.

Starting Dreamweaver

BTW

Screen Resolution
If you use a screen resolution higher than 1024 x 768, the location of on-screen tools might vary slightly from the book.

If you are using a computer to step through the project in this chapter and you want your screen to match the figures in this book, you should change your screen's resolution to 1024 × 768. For information about how to change a screen's resolution, read the "Changing Screen Resolution" appendix. The browser used to display the Web page figures is Internet Explorer 9. The browser text size is set to Medium.

To Start Dreamweaver

The following steps, which assume Windows 7 is running, start Dreamweaver, based on a typical installation. You may need to ask your instructor how to start Dreamweaver for your computer.

1

- Click the Start button on the Windows 7 taskbar to display the Start menu.

- Type Dreamweaver CS6 in the 'Search programs and files' text box, and watch the search results appear on the Start menu (Figure 1–2).

Q&A Why do I have documents and files in my list of results?

Any documents containing the words, Dreamweaver CS6, and any files that have been opened with Dreamweaver CS6 may appear in your list.

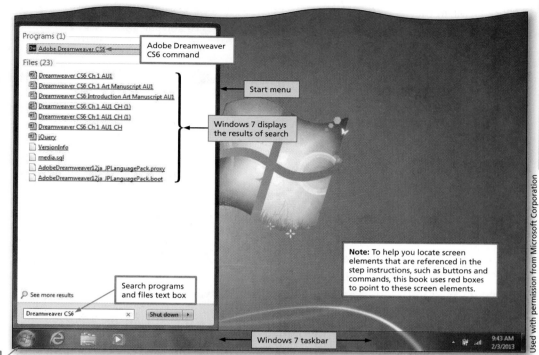

Figure 1–2

2

- Click Adobe Dreamweaver CS6 in the search results on the Start menu to start Dreamweaver and display the Welcome screen.

- If necessary, click the Workspace Switcher button on the Application bar, and then click Classic to switch to the Classic workspace (Figure 1–3).

Q&A What is the Classic workspace?

Eleven predefined workspace layouts designed for application developers, coders, and Web designers allow you to customize your workspace according to your role or target device. The Classic workspace provides all the tools necessary for a beginning Web designer's needs and omits features for advanced designers and programmers.

Figure 1–3

Q&A Why does the Application bar appear on two rows in Figure 1–3?

If your screen resolution is set to 1024 × 768, the Application bar appears on two rows. If you are using a higher screen resolution, the Application bar appears on one row at the top of the Dreamweaver window.

3

- Click HTML in the Create New list to create a blank HTML document.

- If the Dreamweaver window is not maximized, click the Maximize button next to the Close button on the Application bar to maximize the window.

Figure 1–4

- If the Design button is not selected, click the Design button on the Document toolbar to view the page design.

- If the Insert bar is not displayed, click Window on the Application bar and then click Insert to display the Insert panel (Figure 1–4).

Q&A What if a message is displayed regarding default file types?

If a message is displayed, click the Close button.

Q&A What is a maximized window?

A maximized window fills the entire screen. When you maximize a window, the Maximize button changes to a Restore Down button.

Other Ways

1. Double-click Dreamweaver icon on desktop, if one is present
2. Click Adobe Dreamweaver CS6 on Start menu
3. Click Adobe Dreamweaver icon on taskbar, if present

MAC For a detailed example of starting Dreamweaver using the Mac operating system, refer to the "To Start Adobe Dreamweaver CS6" steps in the For Mac Users appendix at the end of this book.

BTW

Q&As
For a complete list of the Q&As found in many of the step-by-step sequences in this book, visit the Dreamweaver CS6 Q&A chapter resource on the student companion site located at www.cengagebrain.com.

BTW

By the Way Boxes
For a complete list of the BTWs found in the margins of this book, visit the Dreamweaver BTW chapter resource on the student companion site located at www.cengagebrain.com.

Touring the Dreamweaver Window

With the Dreamweaver window open, take time to tour your new Web design environment. The Dreamweaver workspace lets you view documents and object properties. It provides toolbar buttons for the most common operations so that you quickly can make changes to your documents. In Dreamweaver, a document is an HTML file that is displayed in a browser as a Web page. Figure 1–4 shows how the Dreamweaver workspace looks the first time you start Dreamweaver after installation on most computers. To work efficiently, you should learn the basic terms and concepts of the Dreamweaver workspace, and understand how to choose options, use inspectors and panels, and set preferences that best fit your work style.

Dreamweaver Workspace

The **Dreamweaver workspace** is an integrated environment in which the Document window and panels are incorporated into one large application window. To create an efficient, customized workspace, Dreamweaver provides the Web site developer with 11 preset workspace layouts as shown in the Workspace Switcher list in Figure 1–5: App Developer, App Developer Plus, Business Catalyst, Classic, Coder, Coder Plus, Designer, Designer Compact, Dual Screen, Fluid Layout, and Mobile Applications. These workspaces provide different arrangements of panels: Depending on the workspace, some panels are hidden and some appear in different locations in the Dreamweaver window. Each workspace is designed for a different type of Dreamweaver user. For example, programmers who work primarily with HTML and other languages generally select the Coder or App Developer workspace. The Dual Screen option requires two monitors, with the Document window and Property inspector displayed on one monitor, and the panels displayed on a secondary monitor. The Classic workspace contains a visually integrated workspace and is ideal for beginners and nonprogrammers. Select the Mobile Applications view if you want to build an application intended for deployment on a tablet or smartphone device. The projects and exercises in this book use the Classic workspace.

Figure 1–5

In Classic view, the Application bar is at the top of the window, the Insert panel is displayed below the Application bar, the Document window is in the center with the panel dock and panels on the right, and the Property inspector is located at the bottom of the window as shown in Figure 1–5. The following list describes the components of the Dreamweaver workspace:

Application Bar The **Application bar** displays the Dreamweaver menu names and buttons for working with the window layout, extending Dreamweaver, managing sites, switching the workplace layout, searching for help, and manipulating the window. When you point to a menu name on the Application bar, the menu name is selected. When you click a menu name, the corresponding menu is displayed. Figure 1–6 on the next page shows the Edit menu.

Figure 1–6

The menus contain lists of common actions for performing tasks such as opening, saving, modifying, previewing, and inserting data in your Web page. The menus may display some commands that appear gray, or dimmed — which indicates they are not available for the current selection — instead of black.

Insert Bar Below the Application bar, the **Insert bar** (Figure 1–7), also called the **Insert panel**, allows quick access to frequently used commands.

Figure 1–7

You use the buttons on the Insert bar to insert various types of objects — such as images, tables, links, and dates — into a Web document. As you insert each object, a dialog box allows you to set and manipulate specific attributes of the object. The buttons on the Insert bar are organized into nine categories, such as Common and Layout, which you can access through tabs. Some categories also have buttons with pop-up menus. When you select an option from a pop-up menu, it becomes the default action for the button. When you start Dreamweaver, the category in which you last were working is displayed on the Insert bar.

Document Tab, Document Toolbar, and Document Window The **document tab** displays the Web page name, which is Untitled-1 for the first Web page you create in a Dreamweaver session, as shown in Figure 1–8. (The "X" is the Close button for the document tab.) The **Document toolbar** contains buttons that provide different views of the Document window (e.g., Code, Split, and Design), and some common operations, such as Preview/Debug in Browser, Refresh Design View, View Options, Visual Aids, and Check Browser Compatibility. The **Document window** displays the current document as you create and edit it.

Figure 1–8

When you make changes to a document, Dreamweaver places an asterisk following the file name in the document tab, indicating that the changes have not been saved. The asterisk is removed after the document is saved. The file path leading to the document's location is displayed to the far right of the document tab.

Status Bar The **status bar**, located below the Document window (Figure 1–9), provides additional information about the document you are creating.

Figure 1–9

The status bar displays the following options:

- **Tag selector:** Click any tag in the hierarchy to select that tag and all its contents.
- **Select tool:** Use the Select tool to return to default editing after using the Zoom or Hand tool.
- **Hand tool:** To pan a page after zooming, use the Hand tool to drag the page.
- **Zoom tool:** Available in Design view or Split view, you can use the Zoom tool to check the pixel accuracy of graphics or to better view the page.
- **Set magnification:** Use the Set magnification context menu to change the view from 6% to 6400%; default is 100%.
- **Mobile size:** Set the Document window to mobile size values, such as for smartphones.
- **Tablet size:** Set the Document window to tablet size values.
- **Desktop size:** Set the Document window to desktop size values.
- **Window size:** Set the Window size value, which includes the window's current dimensions (in pixels). Click this value to display the Window size pop-up menu.
- **Download size and download time:** Refer to this area for the size and estimated download time of the current page. Dreamweaver CS6 calculates the size based on the entire contents of the page, including all linked objects such as images and plug-ins.
- **Unicode (UTF-8):** Refer to this area for the type of text encoding. Unicode is an industry standard that allows computers to consistently represent and manipulate text expressed in most of the world's writing systems.

Property Inspector The **Property inspector**, docked at the bottom of the Document window, provides properties such as the color or font style of a selected object or text in the document. Figure 1–10 shows the default Property inspector when an object is not selected.

Figure 1–10

The Property inspector enables you to view and change a variety of properties for the selected object or text. The Property inspector is context sensitive, meaning it changes based on the selected object, which can include text, tables, images, and other objects. For example, to change the format of a selected heading, you click the Format button in the Property inspector and then select the new format in the list.

Panel Groups Within the panel dock shown in Figure 1–11 on the next page, related panels are displayed in a single panel group with individual tabs. A **panel dock** is a fixed area at the left or right edge of the workspace that hosts a panel group. A **panel** displays a collection of related tools, settings, and options. A **panel group** is a set of related panels docked together below one heading. A panel group typically contains three panels. Each panel provides a wide variety of tools to assist in developing and managing a Web site. For example, the Files panel is used to view and manage the files in your Dreamweaver site.

Figure 1–11

Displaying Document Views

The Document toolbar contains buttons that display different views of an active Web page.

Code View In **Code view**, the Document window displays the HTML, CSS, JavaScript, and other server-side (Web programming) language code within a Web page. Figure 1–12 shows the completed source code from the Small Business Incubator Plan Web site. The different parts of the code are associated with certain colors, making it easier to code by hand.

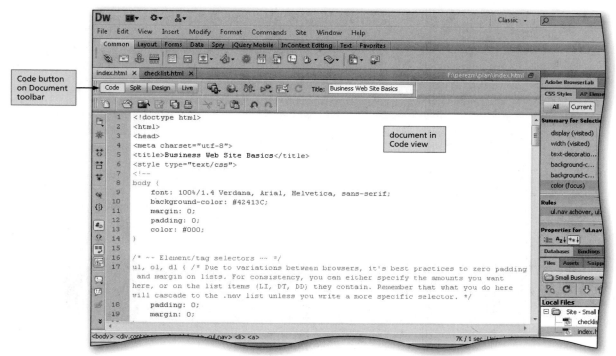

Figure 1–12

Split View **Split view** displays both the source code and the document design simultaneously. Figure 1–13 shows the completed chapter project Web page in Split view. If you add text in the document design pane, the source code is updated immediately.

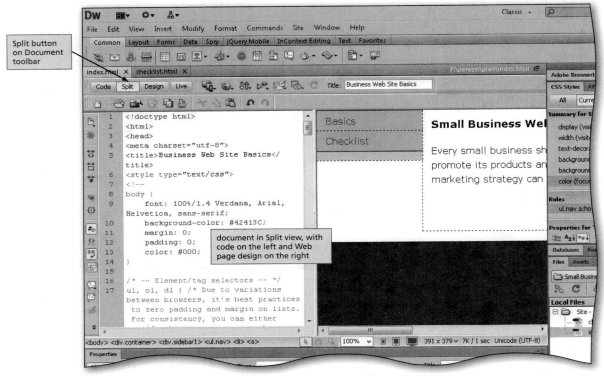

Figure 1–13

Design View The design environment, where you assemble your Web page elements and design your page, is called **Design view**, as shown in the completed project in Figure 1–14.

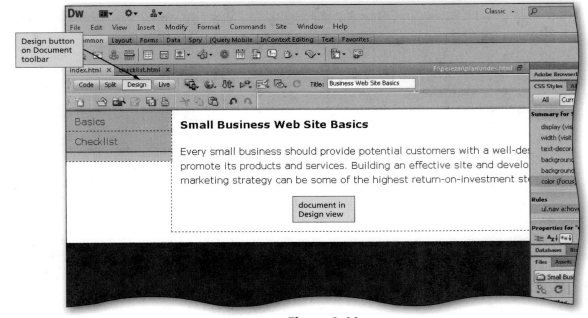

Figure 1–14

Live View **Live view** displays an interactive, browser-based view of the document. This view looks similar to the Design view except it does not support editing functions.

Opening and Closing Panels

The Dreamweaver panels help you organize and modify content using commands and functions. You can customize the workspace to display only the panels you want. Drag a panel by its title bar to move it from its default location and position it where you like, optimizing your Dreamweaver environment. Moving and hiding panels makes it easy to access the panels you need without cluttering your workspace. Each time you start Dreamweaver, the workspace is displayed in the same layout from the last time you used Dreamweaver.

Throughout the workspace, you can open and close the panel groups and display or hide other Dreamweaver features as needed, or move a panel to another location. You use the Window menu to open a panel and its group. Closing unused panels provides an uncluttered workspace in the Document window. You can use the panel options button or a panel's context menu (or shortcut menu) to close the panel or its group. You also can collapse a panel so it takes up less space in the panel dock by double-clicking the panel tab, or you can collapse the entire panel dock so it takes up less space in the Dreamweaver window. In either case, you can expand a panel, panel group, or panel dock to display one or more full panels again.

To Show, Hide, and Move Panels

The following steps show, hide, and move panels.

1

• Double-click the Properties tab below the Document window to collapse the Property inspector (Figure 1–15).

Figure 1–15

● Click the Collapse to Icons button in the panel dock to collapse all the panel groups (Figure 1–16).

Figure 1–16

● Click the Expand Panels button to expand the panel groups.

Q&A

What happened to the Collapse to Icons button?

The Collapse to Icons button and Expand Panels button are in the same location. After you collapse the panels, the button changes to the Expand Panels button so you can expand the panels again.

● Click the Properties tab to expand the Property inspector (Figure 1–17).

Q&A

What is the fastest way to open and close panels?

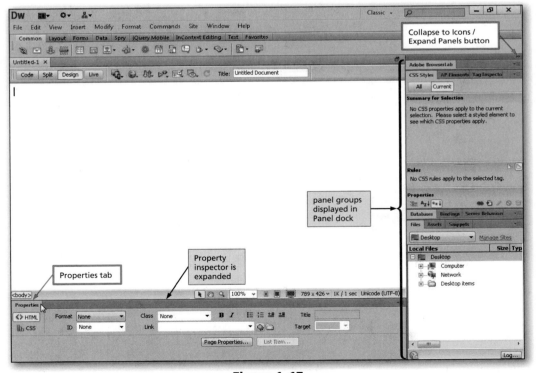

Figure 1–17

The fastest way to open and close panels in Dreamweaver is to use the F4 key, which opens or closes all panels and inspectors at one time.

4

- Drag the Adobe BrowserLab panel by its tab to the center of the screen to move the panel to a new location (Figure 1–18).

Figure 1–18

Other Ways

1. Click panel options button, click Close or click Close Tab Group

2. Right-click panel, click Close or click Close Tab Group

3. Right-click panel, click Minimize or click Expand Panel

4. Press F4

To Reset the Classic Workspace

After collapsing, expanding, and moving panels, you may want to return the workspace to its default settings. The default workspace, called Classic, displays commonly used panels. The following steps reset the Classic workspace.

1

- Click the Workspace Switcher button on the Application bar to display the Workspace Switcher menu (Figure 1–19).

Figure 1–19

- Click Reset 'Classic' to restore the workspace to its default settings (Figure 1–20).

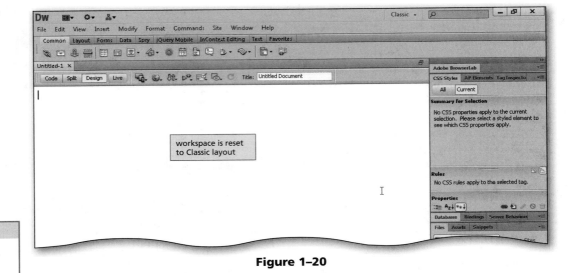

Figure 1–20

Other Ways

1. On Window menu, point to Workspace Layout, click Reset 'Classic'

To Display the Standard Toolbar

In the Classic workspace, Dreamweaver can display three toolbars: Style Rendering, Document, and Standard. You can choose to display or hide the toolbars by clicking View on the Application bar and then pointing to Toolbars. If a toolbar name has a check mark next to it, it is displayed in the window. To hide the toolbar, click the name of the toolbar so it no longer is displayed.

The Standard toolbar is not displayed by default in the Document window when Dreamweaver starts. As with other toolbars and panels, you can dock or undock and move the Standard toolbar so it can be displayed in a different location on your screen. Drag any toolbar by its selection handle to undock and move the toolbar.

The following steps display the Standard toolbar.

- Click View on the Application bar to display the View menu.

- If necessary, click the down-pointing arrow at the bottom of the View menu to scroll the menu.

- Point to Toolbars to display the Toolbars submenu (Figure 1–21).

Figure 1–21

2

- Click Standard on the Toolbars submenu to display the Standard toolbar (Figure 1–22).

Figure 1–22

Other Ways

1. Right-click blank area on toolbar, click Standard

To Access Preferences

In addition to creating a customized environment by selecting a workspace; collapsing, expanding, and moving the panels; and adding toolbars, you can further customize your environment by adjusting your preferences. Dreamweaver's work **preferences** are options that modify the appearance of the workspace, user interactions, accessibility features, and default settings such as font, file types, browsers, code coloring, and code hints. Dreamweaver offers you the flexibility to shape your Web page tools and your code output.

The following steps access Dreamweaver's preferences.

1

- Click Edit on the Application bar to display the Edit menu (Figure 1–23).

Figure 1–23

2

● Click Preferences to display the Preferences dialog box (Figure 1–24).

Q&A

How do I view the options within each category of preferences?

You can view each option by selecting the category in the left pane to display the options for that category in the main area of the dialog box.

3

● Click the OK button (Preferences dialog box) to close the dialog box.

Other Ways

1. Press CTRL+U

Figure 1–24

Understanding HTML5

Adobe Dreamweaver CS6 supports HTML5, the newest version of HTML. Enhanced features in HTML5 are streamlining Web site design and development so you can create more engaging Web sites, increase Web security, and deploy to multiple devices. You probably have viewed a Web site on a smartphone that was difficult to navigate because the site was not specifically designed for a mobile device. With Dreamweaver and HTML5, you can create an interactive site that will be rendered correctly on a variety of smartphones, tablets, and traditional computers. HTML5 includes native support of video without the use of a plug-in, such as Adobe Flash Player, so that videos play seamlessly on Apple devices, such as an iPad.

When a Dreamweaver page is created, an option called DocType is placed in the first line of HTML code. The **DocType** declaration is not a formatting tag, but rather an instruction to the Web browser indicating in what version of the markup language the page is written. The DocType declaration refers to a **Document Type Definition (DTD)**, which specifies the rules for the markup language so browsers can render the content correctly. For the projects in this book, the DocType will be set to HTML5 to access the latest features of HTML. The first line in an HTML5 document reads: <!DOCTYPE html>.

Understanding CSS3

Working hand in hand with HTML5, Dreamweaver CS6 also supports CSS3, Cascading Style Sheets. CSS3 is the new standard for Web site presentation. Web pages can be designed in two ways:

1. A Web page can contain layout and content information combined in a single HTML file. This option is not recommended because it is difficult to update and maintain such a Web page on larger sites.

2. A Web page can separate content from the layout in two separate files. The content information is coded in the HTML file, but the HTML file does not contain information about how that information is displayed. The appearance, or layout, is stored in a separate file called a CSS file.

A **CSS file** is a simple text file containing style rules that control the appearance of a Web page. Using CSS styles, you can control font size, font color, background, and many other attributes of a Web page, thus reducing a page's file size. In a large Web site that does not use CSS styles, making a formatting revision such as changing the font is very time consuming because each page must be changed individually to use the new font. By using CSS, you can change the font in one line of a CSS file and have the font automatically update throughout the entire site.

In this chapter, a simple text-only site about planning a Web site for a small business displays two basic pages created with a built-in Dreamweaver template that uses CSS. A **template** is a predesigned layout used to create pages with placeholder content. Dreamweaver templates provide a framework for designing a professional page that includes background colors, fonts, and a layout controlled by built-in CSS auto-generated code. In the chapter project, a predefined template with two fixed columns and a left sidebar displaying two vertical columns is used for the layout. Typically, the first vertical column displays a navigation menu while the second vertical column shows the main content of the page. Any predefined style within the template can be customized by changing the corresponding CSS settings.

> **Break Point:** If you wish to take a break, this is a good place to do so. You can quit Dreamweaver now. To resume at a later time, start Dreamweaver, and continue following the steps from this location forward.

Creating a New Site

After touring the Dreamweaver environment, you are ready to define a local site for the Small Business Incubator Web site. When you define a site, you create the folder that will contain the files and any subfolders for the site. The site consists of two pages of text that provide information on basic Web design best practices for small businesses that want to create a Web presence.

Defining a Local Site

Web design and Web site management are two important skills that a Web developer must possess and apply. Dreamweaver CS6 is a site creation and management tool. To use Dreamweaver effectively, you first must define the local site. After a Web site is developed within the local site location, the site can be published to a remote server for access by others on the Internet.

The general definition of a **site**, or Web site, is a set of linked documents with shared attributes, such as related topics, a similar design, or a shared purpose. In Dreamweaver, the term, site, can refer to any of the following:

• **Web site:** A set of pages on a server that are viewed through a Web browser by a site visitor

- **Remote site:** Files on the server that make up a Web site, from the author's point of view rather than a visitor's
- **Local site:** Files on your computer that correspond to the files on the remote site (You edit the files on your computer, often called the local computer, and then upload them to the remote site.)
- **Dreamweaver site definition:** A set of defining characteristics for a local site, plus information on how the local site corresponds to a remote site

All Dreamweaver Web sites begin with a local root folder. As you become familiar with Dreamweaver and complete the chapters in this book, you will find references to a **local site folder**, **local root folder**, **root folder**, and **root**. These terms are interchangeable. This folder is no different from any other folder on your computer's hard drive or other storage media, except in the way Dreamweaver views it. By default, Dreamweaver searches for Web pages, links, images, and other files in the designated root folder. Within the root folder, you can create additional folders and subfolders to organize images and other objects. A **subfolder** is a folder inside another folder. Dreamweaver displays only the files in the root folder and its subfolders when you preview the Web site in a Web browser.

Dreamweaver provides two options to define a site and create the hierarchy: You can create the root folder and any subfolders, or create the pages and then create the folders when saving the files. In this book, you create the root folder and subfolders, and then create the Web pages.

Plan Ahead

> **Determine the location for the local site**
> Before you create a Web site, you need to determine where you will save the site and its files.
>
> - If you plan to work on your Web site in various locations or on more than one computer, you should create your site on removable media, such as a USB flash drive. The Web sites in this book use a USB flash drive because these drives are portable and can store a lot of data.
> - If you always work on the same computer, you probably can create your site on the computer's hard drive. However, if you are working in a computer lab, your instructor or the lab supervisor might instruct you to save your site in a particular location on the hard drive or on removable media such as a USB flash drive. (This book assumes the Web site files are stored on a USB flash drive.)

Creating the Local Root Folder and Subfolders

You can use several options to create and manage your local root folder and subfolders, including Dreamweaver's Files panel, Dreamweaver's Site Setup feature, and Windows file management. In this book, you use the most common ways to manage files and folders: Dreamweaver's Site Setup feature to create the local root folder and subfolders, the Files panel to manage and edit your files and folders, and Windows file management to download and copy the data files.

To organize and create a Web site and understand how you access Web documents, you need to understand paths and folders. The term, path, sometimes is confusing for new users of the Web. It is, however, a simple concept: A **path** is the succession of folders that must be navigated to get from one folder to another. Because folders sometimes are referred to as **directories,** the two terms are often used interchangeably.

A typical path structure containing Web site files has a **master folder**, called the **root**, and is designated by the backslash symbol (\ ) in the path notation that appears in the Dreamweaver window. This root folder contains all of the other subfolders or nested folders. Further, each subfolder may contain additional subfolders or nested folders. On most sites, the root folder includes a subfolder for images.

For this book, you first will create a local root folder using your last name and first initial. Examples in this book use Mia Perez as the Web site author. Thus, Mia's local root folder is perezm and is located on drive F (a USB drive, which might have a different drive letter on your computer). Next, you will create a subfolder named plan for the Web site you create in this chapter. You will store related files and subfolders within the plan folder. When you navigate through this folder hierarchy, you are navigating along the path. The path to the Small Business Incubator Web site is F:\perezm\plan\. In all references to F:\perezm, substitute your last name and first initial and your drive location.

Using Site Setup to Create a Local Site

You create a local site using Dreamweaver's Site Setup dialog box, which provides four categories of settings. For the Web site you create in the chapter, you only need to work in the Site category, where you enter the name of your site and the path to the local site folder. For example, you will use Small Business Incubator Plan as the site name and F:\perezm\plan\ as the path to the local site. You can select the location of the local site folder instead of entering its path.

After you complete the site definition, the folder hierarchy structure is displayed in the Dreamweaver Local Files list on the Files panel. This hierarchy structure is similar to the Windows file organization. The **Local Files** list provides a view of the devices and folders on your computer, and shows how these devices and folders are organized.

To Quit and Restart Dreamweaver

The following step quits Dreamweaver and then restarts the program to display the Welcome screen.

1

- Click the Close button in the upper-right corner of the Dreamweaver window to quit Dreamweaver after touring the interface.

- Click the No button (Dreamweaver dialog box) if asked to save changes to Untitled-1.

- Click the Start button on the Windows 7 taskbar to display the Start menu.

- Type Dreamweaver CS6 in the 'Search programs and files' text box.

- Click Adobe Dreamweaver CS6 in the search results on the Start menu to start Dreamweaver and display the Welcome screen (Figure 1–25).

BTW

Dreamweaver Help
At any time while using Dreamweaver, you can find answers to questions and display information about various topics through Dreamweaver Help. Used properly, this form of assistance can increase your productivity and reduce your frustrations by minimizing the time you spend learning how to use Dreamweaver. For instruction about Dreamweaver Help and exercises that will help you gain confidence in using it, read the "Adobe Dreamweaver CS6 Help" appendix at the end of this book.

Figure 1–25

To Use Site Setup to Create a Local Site

The following steps define a local site by telling Dreamweaver where you plan to store local files. A USB drive is used for all projects and exercises in this book. If you are saving your sites in another location or on removable media, substitute that location for Removable Disk (F:).

1
- Click Dreamweaver Site in the Create New list to display the Site Setup dialog box (Figure 1–26).

Q&A

Should the name that appears in the Site Name text box be Unnamed Site 2?

Not necessarily. Your site number may be different.

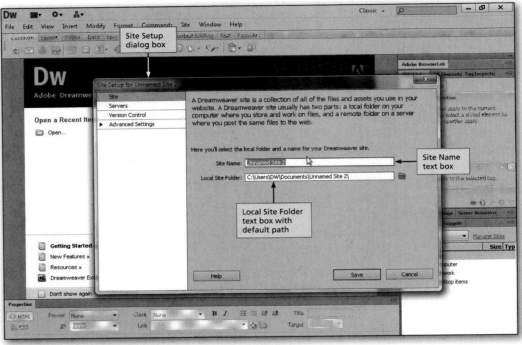

Figure 1–26

2
- Type Small Business Incubator Plan in the Site Name text box to name the site (Figure 1–27).

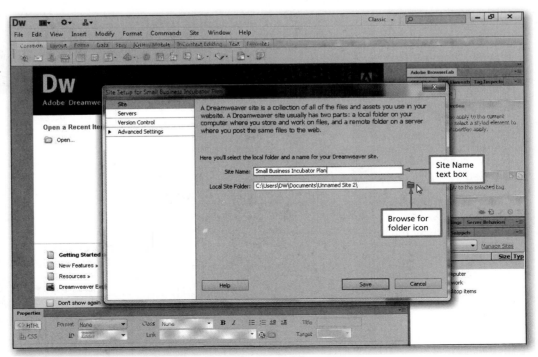

Figure 1–27

3

- Click the 'Browse for folder' icon to display the Choose Root Folder dialog box.

- Click the Select Box arrow to display locations on your system (Figure 1–28).

Q&A Do I have to save to a USB flash drive?

No. You can save to any device or folder. A folder is a specific location on a storage medium. You can save to the default folder or a different folder.

Figure 1–28

4

- Click Removable Disk (F:) in the list, or the name of your storage location.

Q&A What if my USB flash drive has a different name or letter?

It is very likely that your USB flash drive has a different name and drive letter, and is connected to a different port. Verify that the device in the Select text box is correct.

- Click the Create New Folder button to create a folder for your local site (Figure 1–29).

Figure 1–29

- For the root folder name, type your last name and first initial (with no spaces between your last name and initial) in the New folder text box. For example, type `perezm`.

- Press the ENTER key to rename the new folder (Figure 1–30).

Figure 1–30

- Click the Open button to open the root folder.

- Click the Create New Folder button in the Choose Root Folder dialog box to create a folder for the Small Business Incubator Plan site within the folder with your last name and first initial.

- Type `plan` as the name of the new folder, press the ENTER key, and then click the Open button to create the plan subfolder and open it.

- Click the Select button to select the plan folder for the new site and display the Site Setup dialog box (Figure 1–31).

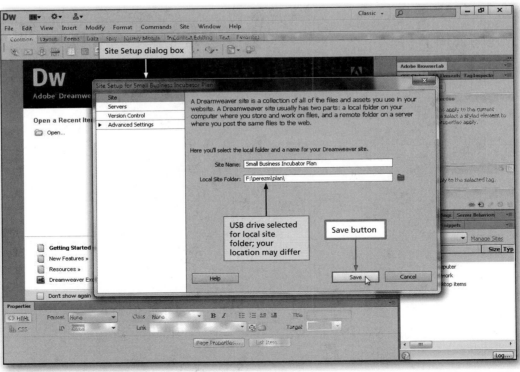

Figure 1–31

Q&A Why should I create a folder on the drive for my Web site?

Organizing your Web site folders now will save you time and prevent problems later.

Q&A Which files will I store in the plan folder?

The plan folder will contain all the files for the Small Business Incubator Plan site. In other words, the plan folder is the local root folder for the Web site.

7

- Click the Save button in the Site Setup dialog box to save the site settings and display the Small Business Incubator Plan site hierarchy on the Files panel (Figure 1–32).

Figure 1–32

Other Ways

1. Site menu, New Site

Selecting a Predefined Template

Dreamweaver CS6 provides templates with built-in layouts to help you quickly create a Web page. The layouts are predesigned pages with placeholder content. The placeholder content is replaced with your own formatted content.

Plan Ahead

Select the words and fonts for the text

Most informational Web pages start with a heading, include paragraphs of text and one or more lists, and then end with a closing line. Before you add text to a Web page, consider the following guidelines for organizing and formatting text:

- **Headings:** Start by identifying the headings you will use. Determine which headings are for main topics (Heading 1) and which are for subtopics (Heading 2 or 3).

- **Paragraphs:** For descriptions or other information, include short paragraphs of text. To emphasize important terms, format them as bold or italic.

- **Lists:** Use lists to organize key points, a sequence of steps, or other information you want to highlight. If amount or sequence matters, number each item in a list. Otherwise, use a bullet (a dot or other symbol that appears at the beginning of the paragraph).

- **Closing:** The closing is usually one sentence that provides information of interest to most Web page viewers, or that indicates where people can find more information about your topic.

The template used in the chapter project displays two fixed columns with an earth tone color design and a DocType defined as HTML5. Dreamweaver provides two types of predefined layouts: fixed and liquid. In a **fixed layout**, the values for the overall width, as well as any columns within the page, are written using pixel units in the CSS file. In a **liquid layout**, the values for the overall width, as well as any columns within the page, are written using percentages in the CSS file. A fixed layout offers a greater measure of control to align items within the fixed columns because the layout is not resized when the site visitor resizes his or her browser window.

To Select a Template Layout

The following steps create a two-column fixed layout with a left sidebar and a DocType defined as an HTML5 page.

1

- Click the More folder icon on the Welcome screen to display the New Document dialog box (Figure 1–33).

Q&A What if I do not see a Welcome screen?

Click File on the Application bar and select New to display the New Document dialog box.

Figure 1–33

2

- Click '2 column fixed, left sidebar' in the Layout column in the New Document dialog box to display a preview of a Web page with two columns.

- Click the DocType button, and then click HTML 5 to change the DocType to HTML 5 (Figure 1–34).

Q&A Do I need to select Blank Page in the left pane and HTML in the Page Type column?

No. Those options are selected by default in the New Document dialog box.

Figure 1–34

3

- Click the Create button to display the two-column fixed layout page in the Document window (Figure 1–35).

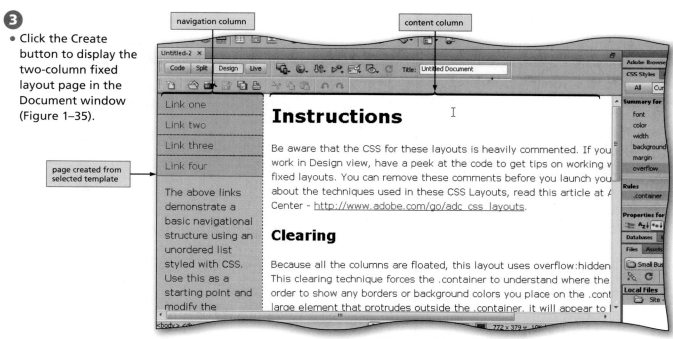

Figure 1–35

To Name and Save the Home Page

The **home page** is the starting point for a Web site. For most Web sites, the home page is named index. This name has special significance because most Web servers recognize index.html (or index.htm) as the default home page. If a folder contains multiple files, the browser determines that the first page to display on a site is the index file. Dreamweaver automatically adds the default extension .html to the file name. Documents with the .html or .htm extensions are displayed in Web browsers. If you have unsaved changes on a Web page, the document tab displays an asterisk after the html extension (index.html*). When you save the page, the asterisk disappears — confirming that your page is up to date in the saved file.

The following steps rename the untitled home page to index.html and then save it.

1

- Click File on the Application bar to display the File menu (Figure 1–36).

Figure 1–36

- Click Save As on the File menu to display the Save As dialog box (Figure 1–37).

Figure 1–37

- If necessary, select the text in the File Name text box, and then type index to name the home page (Figure 1–38).

Q&A

Is it necessary to type the extension .html after the file name?

No. By default, Dreamweaver saves an HTML file with the extension .html.

Figure 1–38

For a detailed example of saving a Web page using the Mac operating system, refer to the "To Save a File in Dreamweaver" steps in the For Mac Users appendix at the end of the book.

4

- Click the Save button (Save As dialog box) to save the home page as index.html and to display the new file name on the document tab (Figure 1–39).

Q&A What do the icons on the Files panel indicate?

A small device icon or folder icon is displayed next to each object listed on the Files panel. The device icon represents a device such as the Desktop or a disk

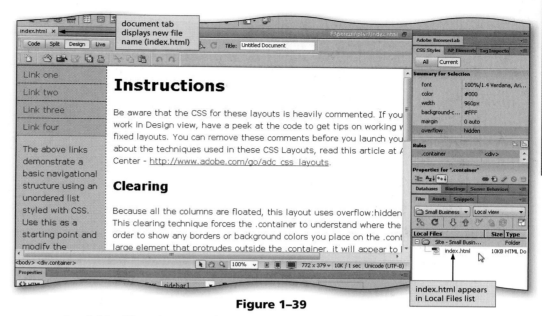

Figure 1–39

drive, and the folder icon represents a folder. These icons may have an expand (plus sign) or collapse (minus sign) next to them indicating whether the device or folder contains additional folders. You click these icons to expand or collapse the view of the file hierarchy.

To Edit Navigation Link Text

The two columns in the template contain placeholder text instead of an empty page so that you can view how the page will look when displayed in a browser. The left column includes links for navigating from one page to another. Both pages in the Small Business Incubator Plan Web site should display only two links: a Basics link used to display the home page, and a Checklist link used to display the checklist page. The following steps change the link text for the first two links and delete the remaining links in the navigation column.

1

- Drag to select the text, Link one, in the left column of index.html and type `Basics` to change the text for the first link.

- Drag to select the text, Link two, and type `Checklist` to change the text for the second link (Figure 1–40).

Figure 1–40

2

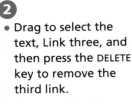

- Drag to select the text, Link three, and then press the DELETE key to remove the third link.

- Drag to select the text, Link four, and then press the DELETE key to remove the fourth link.

- Drag to select the paragraph below the links, and then press the DELETE key to remove the placeholder text (Figure 1–41).

placeholder text deleted from navigation pane

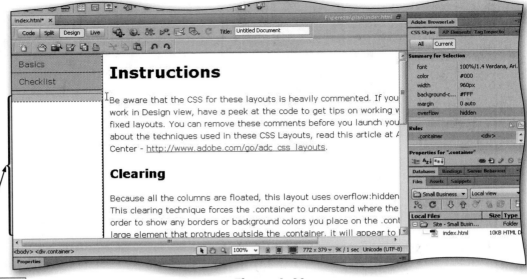

Figure 1–41

To Format Text Using Heading Styles

HTML defines a collection of font styles called **headings** to format the size of text. The advantage of using heading styles to format text that serves as a headline or title is that headings are displayed in relative sizes with Heading 1 <h1> being the largest heading and Heading 6 <h6> being the smallest heading. Any text formatted with Heading 1 is always larger than text formatted with Heading 2. **Formatting** involves setting heading styles, inserting special characters, and inserting or modifying other elements that enhance the appearance of the Web page. Dreamweaver provides three options for directly formatting text: the Format menu on the Application bar, the Text category on the Insert panel, and the Property inspector. In Chapter 2, you will format Web page text using CSS styles. To format the content title in the second column of the index page, you will use the text-related features of the Property inspector.

The Property inspector is one of the panels used most often when creating and formatting Web pages. Recall that it displays the properties, or characteristics, of the selected object. The object can be a table, text, an image, or some other item. The Property inspector is context sensitive, so its options change relative to the selected object.

The following steps edit the text and heading style in the content column.

1

- Drag to select the text, Instructions, in the right column of the index.html page, and then type `Small Business Web Site Basics` to change the content title (Figure 1–42).

updated title in content column

Figure 1–42

- Drag to select the paragraph below the new title, and then type `Every small business should provide potential customers with a well-designed Web site to promote its products and services. Building an effective site and developing an online marketing strategy can be some of the highest return-on-investment steps you can take.` to change the first paragraph.

- Drag to select the rest of the placeholder text in the content column, and then press the DELETE key to delete the text (Figure 1–43).

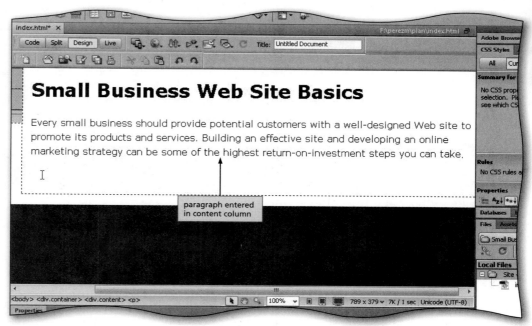

Figure 1–43

3

- Drag to select the content title, Small Business Web Site Basics.

- Click the Format button in the Property inspector to display styles to apply to the selected text (Figure 1–44).

Figure 1–44

4

- Click Heading 3 to apply the Heading 3 style to the content title text (Figure 1–45).

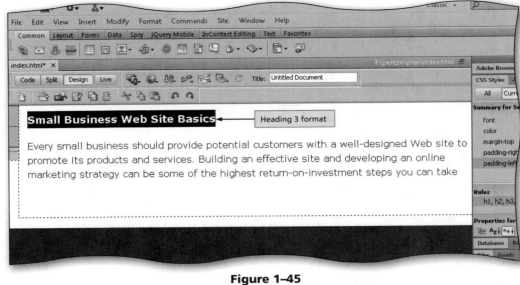

Other Ways

1. On Format menu, point to Paragraph Format, click Heading 3
2. Right-click selected text, point to Paragraph Format, click Heading 3

Figure 1–45

To Create a Link

Links allow users to move from page to page by clicking text or other objects. In the Property inspector, the Link box allows you to transform selected text or other objects into a hyperlink to a specified URL or Web page. You either can point to the hyperlink destination by dragging the Point to File button, or browse to a page in your Web site and select the file name. As you drag the Point to File button, Dreamweaver displays a line showing the connection between the Point to File button and the file link. In a browser, when the site visitor clicks the Basics link, the index page should open. The following steps create a hyperlink by dragging.

1

- Select the text, Basics, in the left column of index.html (Figure 1–46).

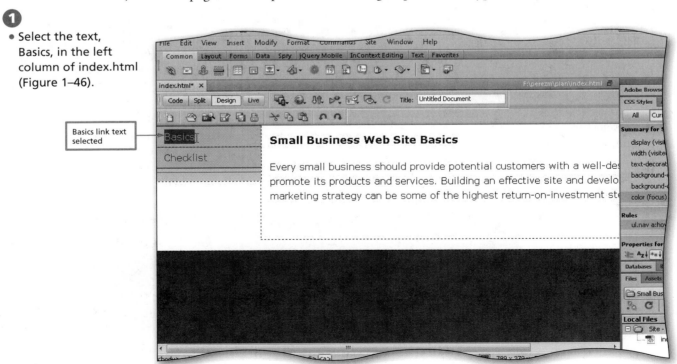

Figure 1–46

2
- Drag the Point to File button in the Property inspector to the index.html file on the Files panel to create a link to index.html (Figure 1–47).

3
- Release the mouse button to complete the link to index.html.

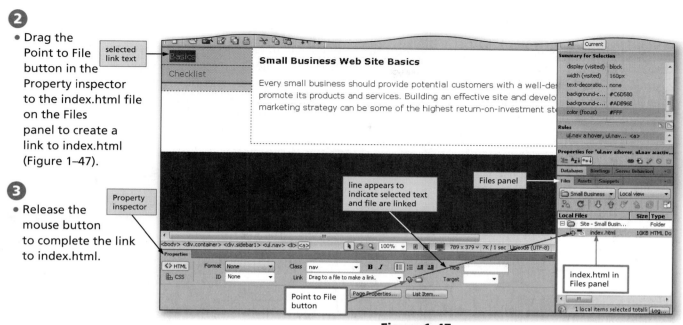

Figure 1–47

Other Ways	
1. Type URL or file name in Link box	2. Click Link arrow and select URL

To Save the Home Page

The following steps save the changes to the home page, index.html.

1
- Click File on the Application bar to display the File menu (Figure 1–48).

2
- Click Save on the File menu to save the document.

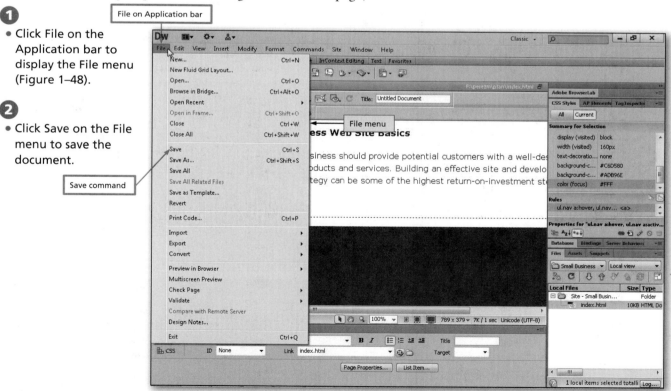

Figure 1–48

For a detailed example of saving a Web page using the Mac operating system, refer to the "To Save a File in Dreamweaver" steps in the For Mac Users appendix at the end of the book.

To Add a Second Page

The first page, index.html, is the model for the second page; in fact, a copy of the first page can serve as the second page. Creating a copy of the first page saves the design time of recreating the page.

The home page (index.html) and the second page (checklist.html) are identical except for the custom text in the content column of each page. As you add pages to your Web site, if your new page is similar to a previous page you created, first save the changes to the existing page, and then save the page again with the new page name, such as checklist.html. The following steps add a second page to the Web site.

- Click File on the Application bar to display the File menu.

- Click Save As on the File menu to display the Save As dialog box.

- Type checklist in File name text box to name the second page (Figure 1–49).

Figure 1–49

- Click the Save button in the Save As dialog box to save the second page as checklist.html (Figure 1–50).

Figure 1–50

To Create an Unordered List

Using lists is a convenient way to group and organize information. Web pages can have three types of lists: ordered (numbered), unordered (bulleted), and definition. **Ordered lists** contain text preceded by numbered steps. **Unordered lists** contain text preceded by bullets (dots or other symbols) or image bullets. You use an unordered list if the items need not be listed in any particular order. **Definition lists** do not use leading characters such as bullet points or numbers. Glossaries and descriptions often use this type of list.

You can type a new list or you can create a list from existing text. When you select existing text and add bullets, the blank lines between the list items are deleted. The following steps edit the checklist.html page to include a new title and a bulleted list of design best practices for a business Web site.

1

- Select the title text, Small Business Web Site Basics, in checklist.html, and then type `Web Site Planning Checklist` to change the title text (Figure 1–51).

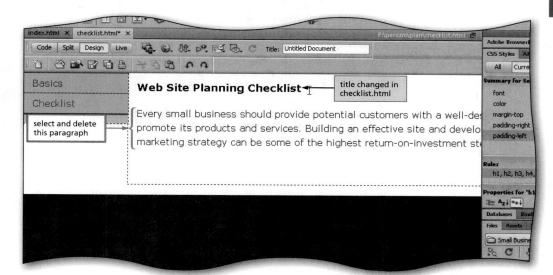

Figure 1–51

2

- Select the text in the paragraph below the title, and then press the DELETE key to delete the first paragraph.

- Type `The design and layout of a business Web site should be clean, simple, and professional` and then press the ENTER key to begin a new paragraph.

Figure 1–52

- Type `The navigation needs to be very simple with clear instructions for how to get to and how to buy your products/services` and then press the ENTER key to begin a new paragraph.

- Type `The site should include your business address, phone number, and e-mail address` (Figure 1–52).

3

- Drag to select the three checklist items (Figure 1–53).

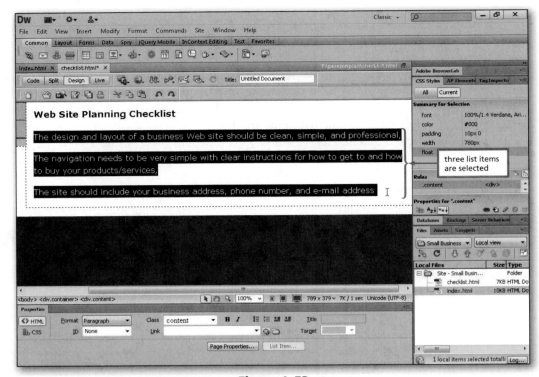

Figure 1–53

4

- In the Property inspector, click the Unordered List button to indent the text and add a bullet to each line.

- Click at the end of the third bulleted line to deselect the text (Figure 1–54).

Q&A

How do I start a list with a different number or letter?

In the Document window, click the list item you want to change, click Format on the Application bar, point to List, and then click Properties. In the List Properties dialog box, select the options you want to define.

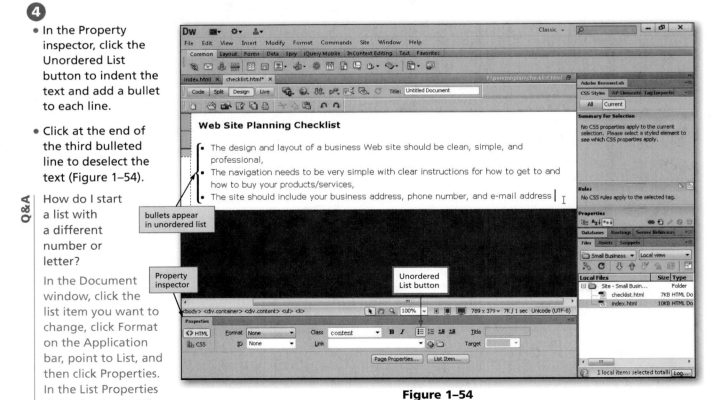

Figure 1–54

Other Ways

1. Format menu, point to List, click Unordered List
2. Right-click text, point to List, click Unordered List

To Add the Links to the Second Page

To complete the navigation, the text, Checklist, in the left column must be linked on both pages to checklist.html. The following steps link the navigation text to the second page.

- Drag the horizontal scroll bar at the bottom of the Document window to scroll to the left to display the left column.

- Select the text, Checklist, in the left column.

- Drag the Point to File button in the Property inspector to the checklist.html file on the Files panel to create a link to checklist.html (Figure 1–55).

Figure 1–55

- Click the index.html document tab to display the index page.

- Drag to select the text, Checklist, in the left column of index.html.

- Drag the Point to File button in the Property inspector to the checklist.html file on the Files panel to create a link to checklist.html (Figure 1–56).

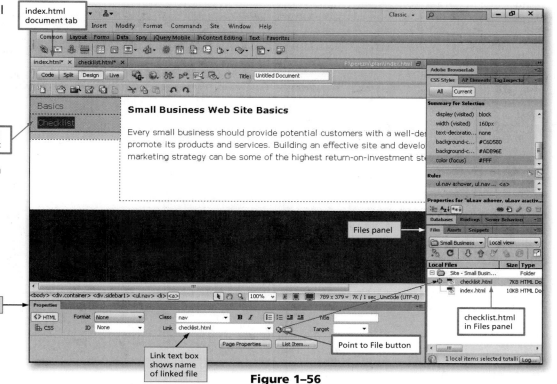

Figure 1–56

To Change the Web Page Title

A **Web page title** helps Web site visitors keep track of what they are viewing as they browse. It is important to give your Web page an appropriate title. When visitors to your Web page create bookmarks or add the Web page to their Favorites lists, they use the title for reference. If you do not title a page, the browser displays the page as Untitled Document in the browser tab, Favorites lists, and history lists. Because many search engines use the Web page title, you should create a descriptive and meaningful name. A document file name is not the same as the page title. The page title appears on the tab of the browser in Internet Explorer 7 and later versions.

The following steps change the Web page title of each page.

- With the index.html page still displayed, select the text, Untitled Document, in the Title text box on the Document toolbar to prepare to replace the text.

- Type Business Web Site Basics in the Title text box to enter a descriptive title for the Web page (Figure 1–57).

Figure 1–57

- Click the checklist. html document tab to display the checklist page.

- Select the text, Untitled Document, in the Title text box on the Document toolbar to prepare to replace the text.

- Type Business Web Site Checklist in the Title text box to enter a descriptive title for the Web page (Figure 1–58).

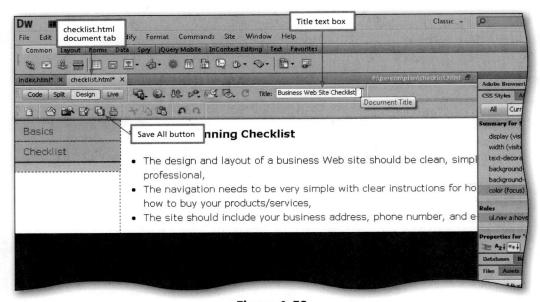

Figure 1–58

3
- Click the Save All button on the Standard toolbar to save both documents.

Q&A What is the difference between the Save button and the Save All button?

When you click the Save button, you save changes only in the displayed document. When you click the Save All button, you save changes in all the open documents.

To Check Spelling

After you create a Web page, you should inspect the page visually for spelling errors. In addition, you can use Dreamweaver's Check Spelling command to identify possible misspellings. The Check Spelling command ignores HTML tags.

The following steps use the Check Spelling command to check the spelling of your entire document. Your Web page may contain different misspelled words depending on the accuracy of your typing.

- Click the index.html document tab.

- Click at the beginning of the document in the right column to position the insertion point.

- Click Commands on the Application bar to display the Commands menu (Figure 1–59).

Figure 1–59

- Click Check Spelling to display the Check Spelling dialog box.

- If a misspelled word is highlighted, click the correct spelling of the word in the Suggestions list or type the correct spelling, and then click the Change button.

Q&A What should I do if Dreamweaver highlights a proper noun or correctly spelled word as being misspelled?

Click Ignore or click Ignore All if proper nouns are displayed as errors.

- If necessary, continue to check the spelling and, as necessary, correct any misspelled word.

- Click the OK button when you are finished checking spelling.

- Click the Save button on the Standard toolbar to save the document.

Other Ways

1. Press SHIFT+F7

Previewing a Web Page in a Browser

After you have created a Web page, it is a good practice to test your Web page by previewing it in Web browsers to ensure that it is displayed correctly. Using this strategy helps you catch errors so you will not copy or repeat them.

Review final tasks

Before completing a Web page, perform the following tasks to make sure it is ready for others to view:

- Give your Web page a title.

- Check the spelling and proofread the text.

- Preview the page in one or more browsers so you can see how it looks when others open it.

Plan Ahead

BTW

Quick Reference
For a table that lists how to complete the tasks covered in this book using the mouse, menus, context menus, and keyboard, see the Quick Reference Summary at the back of the book or visit the Dreamweaver student companion site located at www.cengagebrain.com.

As you create your Web page, you should be aware of the variety of available Web browsers. HTML5 can help create more consistency across browsers, but the pages should be tested in each browser platform even if you are using HTML5. Each browser may display text, images, and other Web page elements differently. For this reason, you should preview your Web pages in more than one browser to make sure the browsers display your Web pages as you designed them. Be aware that visitors viewing your Web page might have earlier versions of these browsers. Dreamweaver also provides an option called Preview in Adobe BrowserLab that provides a free online comparison of your page in multiple browsers. **Adobe BrowserLab** is an online service that helps ensure your Web content is displayed as intended.

The Preview/Debug in browser button on the Document toolbar provides a list of all Web browsers currently installed on your computer. You can select a primary browser in the Preferences dialog box. Before previewing a document, save the document; otherwise, the browser will not display your most recent changes.

To Choose a Browser and Preview the Web Site

To select the browser you want to use for the preview, use the Preview/Debug in browser button on the Document toolbar. The following steps preview the Small Business Incubator Plan Web site using Internet Explorer and Firefox.

1
- Click the Preview/ Debug in browser button on the Document toolbar to display a list of browsers installed on your computer (Figure 1–60).

Q&A Why do I have different browsers listed?

This list displays browsers that are installed on your local computer. If you want to test your page in other browsers, download and install multiple browsers.

Figure 1–60

2
- Click Preview in IExplore to display the index page in the Internet Explorer browser (Figure 1–61).

Q&A Which version of Internet Explorer does Dreamweaver use to preview the Web page?

Figure 1–61

Dreamweaver uses the version of Internet Explorer installed on your computer.

3

- Click the Close button on the Internet Explorer title bar to close the browser.

- If the Firefox browser is installed on your system, click the Preview/Debug in browser button again, and then click Preview in Firefox to display the Web page in the Firefox browser.

- Click the Close button on the Firefox title bar to close the browser.

Other Ways

1. On File menu, point to Preview in Browser, click browser of choice
2. Right-click document, click Preview in Browser, click browser
3. F12, CTRL+F12

Dreamweaver Help

The built-in Help feature in Dreamweaver provides reference materials and other forms of assistance. When the main Help page opens, it connects to the Adobe Web site.

To Access Dreamweaver Help

The following step accesses Dreamweaver Help. You must be connected to the Web to complete this step.

1

- With the Dreamweaver program open, click Help on the Application bar to display the Help menu.

- Click Dreamweaver Help to access Adobe Community Help online.

- If necessary, double-click the title bar to maximize the window (Figure 1–62).

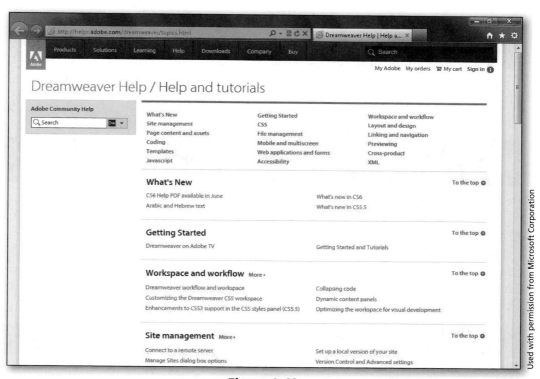

Figure 1–62

Used with permission from Microsoft Corporation

Other Ways

1. Press F1

To Quit Dreamweaver

The following step quits Dreamweaver and returns control to Windows.

1

- Click the Close button on the right side of the Application bar to close the window.

- If Dreamweaver displays a dialog box asking you to save changes, click the No button.

Other Ways

1. On File menu, click Exit
2. Press CTRL+Q

MAC For a detailed example of quitting Dreamweaver using the Mac operating system, refer to the "To Quit Dreamweaver" steps in the For Mac Users appendix at the end of this book.

Chapter Summary

In this chapter, you have learned how to start Dreamweaver, define a Web site, and create a Web page. You added a link and used Dreamweaver's Property inspector to connect to another page in the site. You also learned how to use an unordered list to organize information into a bulleted list. Once your Web page was completed, you learned how to save the Web page and preview it in a browser. To enhance your knowledge of Dreamweaver further, you learned the basics about Dreamweaver Help.

The following tasks are all the new Dreamweaver skills you learned, listed in the same order they were presented. For a list of keyboard commands for topics introduced in this chapter, see the Quick Reference for Windows at the back of this book. The list below includes all the new Dreamweaver skills you have learned in this chapter:

1. Start Dreamweaver (DW 28)
2. Show, Hide, and Move Panels (DW 37)
3. Reset the Classic Workspace (DW 39)
4. Display the Standard Toolbar (DW 40)
5. Access Preferences (DW 41)
6. Quit and Restart Dreamweaver (DW 45)
7. Use Site Setup to Create a Local Site (DW 46)
8. Select a Template Layout (DW 50)
9. Name and Save the Home Page (DW 51)
10. Edit Navigation Link Text (DW 53)
11. Format Text Using Heading Styles (DW 54)
12. Create a Link (DW 56)
13. Save the Home Page (DW 57)
14. Add a Second Page (DW 58)
15. Create an Unordered List (DW 59)
16. Add the Links to the Second Page (DW 61)
17. Change the Web Page Title (DW 62)
18. Check Spelling (DW 63)
19. Choose a Browser and Preview the Web Site (DW 64)
20. Access Dreamweaver Help (DW 65)
21. Quit Dreamweaver (DW 65)

Apply Your Knowledge

Reinforce the skills and apply the concepts you learned in this chapter.

Creating a New Web Page

Instructions: Start Dreamweaver. In this activity, you will define a local site, create a new Web page, and save the Web page. Next, you will give the page a title and then add text to the page. Finally, you will format the text and create an ordered list. The completed Web page is shown in Figure 1–63.

Web Site Development Steps, Easy as 1-2-3

1. The first step in developing a new Web site is to define a local site. A local site is defined in the Site Setup dialog box.
2. Once the new site is defined, a new HTML page is created and saved. The new page is typically the home page and the home page is named index.html.
3. Once the new HTML or home page is created, text is added to the page and then formatted.

Mia Perez

Figure 1–63

Perform the following tasks:

1. Use the Site Setup dialog box to define a new local site in the *your last name and first initial* folder (the F:\perezm folder, for example). Type `Apply` as the new site name.

2. Click the 'Browse for folder' icon and navigate to your USB flash drive. Create a new subfolder within the *your last name and first initial* folder and name it `Apply`. Open the folder, select it as the local site folder, and then save the Apply site.

3. Create a new HTML page. Save the new HTML page and type `apply1.html` as the file name.

4. Enter `Web Site Development` as the document title.

5. Type `Web Site Development Steps, Easy as 1-2-3` at the top of the page, and then press the ENTER key.

6. Type `The first step in developing a new Web site is to define a local site. A local site is defined in the Site Setup dialog box.` Press the ENTER key.

7. Type `Once the new site is defined, a new HTML page is created and saved. The new page is typically the home page and the home page is named index.html.` Press the ENTER key.

8. Type `Once the new HTML or home page is created, text is added to the page and then formatted.`

9. Press the ENTER key two times. Type your first and last names.

10. Apply the Heading 1 format to the first line of text.

11. Select paragraphs 2–4, and then click the Ordered List button in the Property inspector to make the text an ordered list.

12. Save your changes and then view your document in your browser. Compare your document to Figure 1–63. Make any necessary changes and then save your changes.

13. Submit the document in the format specified by your instructor.

Extend Your Knowledge

Extend the skills you learned in this chapter and experiment with new skills. You may need to use Help to complete the assignment.

Formatting a Web Page

Note: To complete this assignment, you will be required to use the Data Files for Students. Visit www.cengage.com/ct/studentdownload for detailed instructions, or contact your instructor for information about accessing the required files.

Instructions: Start Dreamweaver. A recreational soccer league wants to teach team managers how to create Web pages using Dreamweaver. The league president created a Web page and asks you to improve it. First, you will enhance the Web page by applying styles, aligning text, and indenting text. Finally, you will make the page more useful by adding links to text. The modified Web page is shown in Figure 1–64.

Continued >

Extend Your Knowledge *continued*

Figure 1–64

Perform the following tasks:

1. Use the Site Setup dialog box to define a new local site in the *your last name and first initial* folder (the F:\perezm folder, for example). Enter `Extend` as the new site name.

2. Click the 'Browse for folder' icon and navigate to your USB flash drive. Create a new subfolder within the *your last name and first initial* folder and name it `Extend`. Open the folder, select it as the local site folder, and then save the Extend site.

3. Using Windows Explorer, copy the extend1.html file from the Chapter 01\Extend folder into the *your last name and first initial*\Extend folder.

4. Return to Dreamweaver and then open the extend1.html document. (*Hint*: Click Open on the Welcome screen.)

5. Select the text in the first line, Customize Your Dreamweaver Interface, and apply the Heading 2 format.

6. Center-align the heading by using the Format menu on the Application bar.

7. Select the paragraph below the first line, starting with "You can customize" and ending with "customize your workspace." Use the Property inspector to apply italics to the text.

8. Select the three lines of text below the paragraph, starting with "Manage windows and panels" and ending with "Set general preferences for Dreamweaver". Indent these three lines of text by using the Blockquote button in the Property inspector or by using the Indent command on the Format menu.

9. In the last line of text, select "Dreamweaver Help". Using the Link text box in the Property inspector, link the following URL to the text: `http://helpx.adobe.com/ dreamweaver/topics.html`.

10. Place the insertion point at the end of the last sentence on the page. Press the ENTER key two times. Type your first and last names.

11. Save your changes and then view your document in your browser. Compare your document to Figure 1–64.

12. Click the Dreamweaver Help link to test your link. If the Adobe Dreamweaver Help site does not open, return to Dreamweaver and verify that you entered the correct URL in Step 9. Make any necessary changes and then save your changes.

13. Submit the document in the format specified by your instructor.

Make It Right

Analyze a Web page and correct all errors and/or improve the design.

Formatting and Checking the Spelling of a Web Page

Note: To complete this assignment, you will be required to use the Data Files for Students. Visit www.cengage.com/ct/studentdownload for detailed instructions, or contact your instructor for information about accessing the required files.

Instructions: Start Dreamweaver. You are working with a neighborhood association that wants to learn about Dreamweaver. An association member created a Web page and asks you to improve it. First, you will enhance the look of the Web page by applying styles, aligning text, and adding bullets. Next, you will make the Web page more useful by adding links to text and inserting a document title. Finally, you will check the spelling. The modified Web page is shown in Figure 1–65.

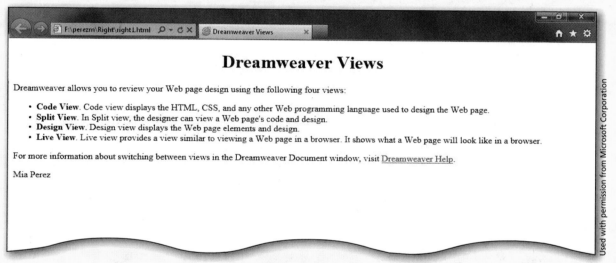

Figure 1–65

Perform the following tasks:

1. Use the Site Setup dialog box to define a new local site in the *your last name and first initial* folder (the F:\perezm folder, for example). Enter `Right` as the new site name and save it.

2. Click the 'Browse for folder' icon to navigate to your USB flash drive. Create a new subfolder within the *your last name and first initial* folder and name it `Right`. Open the folder and then select it as the local site folder. Save the Right site.

3. Using Windows Explorer, copy the right1.html file from the Chapter 01\Right folder into the *your last name and first initial*\Right folder.

4. Return to Dreamweaver and then open the right1.html document. (*Hint*: Click Open on the Welcome screen.)

5. Enter `Dreamweaver Views` as the Web page title.

6. Apply the Heading 1 format to the first line of text. Use the Format menu to center-align the heading on the page.

7. Apply bullets to the list of views, starting with "Code View" and ending with "Live View".

8. Bold each view name (Code View, Split View, Design View, and Live View).

9. Check the spelling using the Commands menu. Correct all misspelled words.

Continued >

Make It Right *continued*

10. In the last line of text, select "Dreamweaver Help". Using the Link text box in the Property inspector, link the following URL to the text: `http://helpx.adobe.com/dreamweaver/topics.html`.

11. Place the insertion point at the end of the last sentence on the page. Press the ENTER key two times. Type your first and last names.

12. Save your changes and then view your document in your browser. Compare your document to Figure 1–65.

13. Click the Dreamweaver Help link to test your link. If it did not open the Adobe Dreamweaver Help site, return to Dreamweaver and verify that you entered the correct URL in Step 10. Make any necessary changes and then save your work.

14. Submit the document in the format specified by your instructor.

In the Lab

Design and/or create a Web site using the guidelines, concepts, and skills presented in this chapter. Labs are listed in order of increasing difficulty.

Lab 1: Creating a Family Reunion Web Site

Problem: It has been more than 10 years since the entire Hydes family celebrated together. Janna Hydes has decided to coordinate a family reunion and requests your assistance in spreading the word by creating a Web site. Janna has provided you with all of the details about the event, and she asks you to share the information on the site.

Define a new Web site, and create and format a Web page for the Hydes Family Reunion. The Web page as it is displayed in a browser is shown in Figure 1–66. The text for the Web site is provided in Table 1–1.

Figure 1–66

Table 1–1 Hydes Family Reunion

Section	Text
Heading	Hydes 2014 Family Reunion
Invitation paragraph	Hydes Family, we've waited long enough. It's time to celebrate together Hydes style. Come one, come all to the Hydes 2014 Family Reunion.
Item 1	July 4, 2014 11:00 AM to 7:00 PM The Home of Steve and Janna Hydes 25743 Cherrylawn Court Beachtowne, FL 23289
Item 2	RSVP by June 25, 2014 to Janna at (683) 555-7425
Item 3	What to bring: Covered dish Bathing suit Towels Sunscreen Beach chairs Sand toys
Closing paragraph	Get ready for fun family games, prizes, great food, and plenty of laughter! This is going to be the best family reunion yet! We look forward to seeing everyone.

Perform the following tasks:

1. Start Dreamweaver. Click Dreamweaver Site in the Create New list to display the Site Setup dialog box. Define a new local site by typing `Reunion` in the Site name text box.

2. Click the 'Browse for folder' icon to display the Choose Root Folder dialog box. The current path should be F:*your last name and first initial*\ (substitute the drive letter as necessary). Create a new subfolder in the *your last name and first initial* folder. Type `Reunion` as the folder name, open and select the Reunion folder, and then save the site.

3. On the Welcome screen, click HTML in the Create New list to create a new HTML page. Save the page and type `index.html` as the file name.

4. Type `Hydes Family Reunion` in the Title text box.

5. Type the Web page text shown in Table 1–1. Press the ENTER key after typing the heading and invitation paragraph. For Item 1, press the SHIFT+ENTER keys to insert a line break after each line except the last line. Press the ENTER key after the last Item 1 line. Press the ENTER key after typing each line in Items 2 and 3. Type the closing paragraph.

6. Select the heading text and use the Property inspector to apply the Heading 1 format. Use the Format menu to center-align the heading.

7. Select the invitation paragraph and apply the Heading 3 format.

8. Select all the text for Item 1 and center-align it on the page.

9. Select the text for Item 2, use the Bold button in the Property inspector to apply the Bold style to the text, and then center-align it on the page.

10. Select all the items listed after "What to bring" and use the Unordered List button in the Property inspector to create an unordered bulleted list for the text.

11. Use the Italic button in the Property inspector to apply the Italic style to the closing paragraph.

12. Place the insertion point after the last sentence on the page. Press the ENTER key two times. Type your first and last names.

Continued >

In the Lab *continued*

13. Save your changes.

14. View your document in your browser and compare it to Figure 1–66. Make any necessary changes and then save your work.

15. Submit the document in the format specified by your instructor.

In the Lab

Lab 2: Creating a Recipe Web Site

Problem: Brooke Davis has acquired famous family recipes that have been passed down through generations. She wants to share recipes easily with other family members and friends. You talk to her about setting up a Web site to display the recipes. Because she likes the idea, she asks you to help her get started. You agree to develop the first two pages for her Web site.

Define a new Web site and use a fixed HTML layout to create two Web pages for Davis Family Recipes. The Web pages, as displayed in a browser, are shown in Figure 1–67. Text for the Web site recipe is provided in Table 1–2.

(a)

(b)

Used with permission from Microsoft Corporation

Figure 1–67

Table 1–2 Pork Tenderloin Recipe	
Section	**Text**
Heading	Timeless Pork Tenderloin
Ingredients section	Ingredients: 3-4 lb pork tenderloin 2 cloves garlic, chopped 1 teaspoon of kosher salt ¼ teaspoon of black pepper 1 tablespoon of olive oil
Directions section	Directions: Preheat the oven to 250 degrees. Cut numerous ½-inch slits on the top of the tenderloin. Rub the tenderloin with garlic and place garlic pieces into slits. In a small mixing bowl, combine salt, pepper, and olive oil. Rub the mixture on the tenderloin. Place the tenderloin in a shallow roasting pan and cook in the oven for 3 hours or until internal temperature reaches 160 degrees.

Perform the following tasks:

1. Start Dreamweaver. Use the Site Setup dialog box to define a new local site using `Davis Recipes` as the site name.

2. Click the 'Browse for folder' icon to display the Choose Root Folder dialog box. The current path should be F:*your last name and first initial*\\(substitute the drive letter as necessary). Create a new subfolder in the *your last name and first initial* folder. Enter `Recipes` as the folder name, open and select the Recipes folder, and then save the site.

3. On the Dreamweaver Welcome screen, click More in the Create New list. In the New Document dialog box, select Blank Page, Page Type: HTML, Layout: 2 column fixed, left sidebar. Set the DocType as HTML 5 and click the Create button. Save the new Web page using `index.html` as the file name.

4. Enter `Davis Family Recipes` as the Web page title.

5. Delete all of the text in the right column. Type `Davis Family Recipes` at the top of the right column. Press the ENTER key. (If the heading does not appear in the Heading 1 format, apply the Heading 1 format.)

6. Type `This site was created to share some famous family recipes that have been passed down over generations.` Press the ENTER key. Type `Click a recipe in the left navigation bar and start cooking!`

7. Press the ENTER key two times. Type your first and last names.

8. In the left navigation bar, replace the "Link one" text with `Home`. Replace the "Link two" text with `Timeless Pork Tenderloin`. Replace the "Link three" text with `Mom's Lasagna`. Replace the "Link four" text with `Mighty Meatballs`.

9. Delete all of the text below "Mighty Meatballs". Type `What are you hungry for tonight?` Use the Italic button in the Property inspector to apply italics to the text.

10. Save your changes.

11. To create a new document from the existing document, click File on the Application bar and then click Save As. Type `pork.html` as the file name and save the document.

12. Enter `Timeless Pork Tenderloin` as the Web page title.

13. Replace the text in the right column with the recipe text shown in Table 1–2. Press the ENTER key after typing each line or paragraph. (If the Timeless Pork heading does not appear in the Heading 1 format, apply the Heading 1 format.)

Continued >

In the Lab *continued*

14. Select the five items listed after "Ingredients" and use the Unordered List button in the Property inspector to create a bulleted list for the text.

15. Select the text, Home, in the upper-left column. Link it to the index.html page by dragging the Point to File button in the Property inspector to the index.html file in the Files panel.

16. Save your changes and close the pork.html file. The index.html document should be displayed. Select the "Timeless Pork Tenderloin" text in the left column. Link it to the pork.html page by dragging the Point to File button in the Property inspector to the pork.html file in the Files panel. Save your changes.

17. View the index.html page in your browser and compare it to Figure 1–67.

18. Test the link to Timeless Pork Tenderloin and the link to Home. If the links do not work, verify that you properly completed Steps 15 and 16. Make any necessary changes and then save your work.

19. Submit the documents in the format specified by your instructor.

In the Lab

Lab 3: Creating a Business Plan Tips Web Site

Problem: Tyler James is a business consultant who provides his clients with advice about starting their own businesses. He wants to create a Web site with tips for developing a solid business plan. He has hired you to develop his Web site.

Define a new Web site and use a liquid HTML layout to create a Business Plan Tips Web page. The Web page, as it is displayed in a browser, is shown in Figure 1–68. Text for the Web site is provided in Table 1–3.

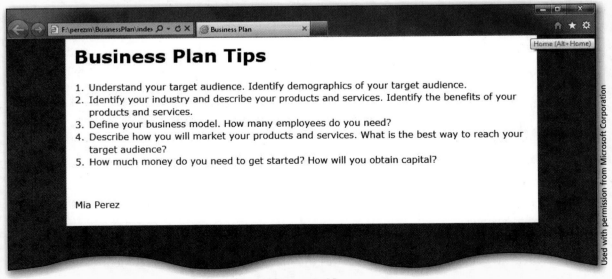

Figure 1–68

Table 1–3 Business Plan Tips

Section	Text
Heading	Business Plan Tips
Paragraph 1	Understand your target audience. Identify demographics of your target audience.
Paragraph 2	Identify your industry and describe your products and services. Identify the benefits of your products and services.
Paragraph 3	Define your business model. How many employees do you need?
Paragraph 4	Describe how you will market your products and services. What is the best way to reach your target audience?
Paragraph 5	How much money do you need to get started? How will you obtain capital?

1. Start Dreamweaver. Use the Site Setup dialog box to define a new local site using `BusinessPlan` as the site name.

2. Click the 'Browse for folder' icon and then create a new subfolder in the *your last name and first initial* folder named `BusinessPlan`. Open and select the BusinessPlan folder, and then save the site.

3. On the Dreamweaver Welcome screen, click More in the Create New list. Create a blank HTML page using the 1 column liquid, centered layout, and HTML5 as the DocType. Save the new Web page using `index.html` as the file name.

4. Enter `Business Plan` as the Web page title.

5. Delete all the text on the page, replacing it with the text shown in Table 1–3. Press the ENTER key after typing each line or paragraph.

6. Press the ENTER key two times after typing the last sentence. Type your first and last names.

7. Select all of the text below the heading and use the Ordered List button in the Property inspector to create a numbered list for the text.

8. Save your changes and then view your document in your browser. Compare your document to Figure 1–68. Make any necessary changes and then save your work.

9. Submit the document in the format specified by your instructor.

Cases and Places

Apply your creative thinking and problem solving skills to design and implement a solution.

1: Protecting Yourself from Identity Theft

Personal

You recently read an article about the growing trend of identity theft. The article has prompted you to create an educational Web site on how people can protect themselves from identity theft. Define a new local site in the *your last name and first initial* folder and name it Protect Yourself from Identity Theft. Name the new subfolder Theft. Create and save a new HTML Web page. Name the file protect. Use your browser to conduct some research on ways to protect yourself from identity theft. Create a heading for your Web page. Apply the Heading 1 format to the title and center-align the title on the page. Below the heading, create an unordered list of 10 different ways to protect yourself from identity theft. Title the document ID Theft. Check the spelling in the document. Include your name at the bottom of the page. Submit the document in the format specified by your instructor.

Continued >

Cases and Places *continued*

2: Creating a Web Site for a Literacy Promotion

Academic

You are in charge of the Literacy Committee at your university. Your mission is to promote reading for enjoyment to university students. You decide to create a Web site to inform students about the best-selling books. Define a new local site in the *your last name and first initial* folder and name it Reading for Fun. Name the new subfolder Read. Create and save a new HTML Web page. Name the file read. Use your browser to conduct some research on current best-selling books. Create a heading for your Web page. Apply the Heading 2 format to the title and center-align the title on the page. Below the heading, create an ordered list of the top 10 best-selling books. Bold three of the book titles. Title the document Reading for Fun. Check the spelling in the document. Include your name at the bottom of the page. Submit the document in the format specified by your instructor.

3: Creating a Web Site for an Accountant

Professional

Your friend is an accountant who wants to create a Web site to advertise his accountant services. You offer to help him develop a Web site. Define a new local site in the *your last name and first initial* folder and name it Accountant Services. Name the new subfolder Accountant. Create and save a new HTML Web page with a 2 column fixed, left sidebar layout. Be sure to select HTML 5 as the DocType. Name the file accountant. Delete the text in the right column. Create a heading for your Web page. Below the title, provide contact information for the accountant services. In the left column, provide links to Home, Services, Costs, and Schedule Appointment. Title the document Accountant Services. Check the spelling in the document. Delete the text below the links in the left column and type your name. Submit the document in the format specified by your instructor.

2 | Designing a Web Site Using a Template and CSS

Objectives

You will have mastered the material in this chapter when you can:

- Describe the anatomy of a style sheet
- Describe the types of style sheets
- Create a Dreamweaver Web site using a template and CSS
- Save the HTML template as a .dwt file
- Define the regions of a Web page
- Describe the CSS categories

- Create a CSS style sheet
- Create a CSS rule
- Apply CSS rule definitions
- Create an editable region within a template
- Create a new page from a template
- Preview a Web page using Live view

2 | Designing a Web Site Using a Template and CSS

Designing Web Pages with CSS

By designing a Web page from scratch, you can create a page customized to your exact needs and preferences. A Web site's design provides the first impression of the credibility of an organization. Content is an important part of any site. But if the presentation of that content is not consistent, easy to navigate, and aesthetically pleasing, the site visitor will quickly leave. **CSS**, or **Cascading Style Sheets**, provides the style and layout for HTML content. CSS is the means by which a Web site's presentation is defined, styled, and modified. The newest version presented in the chapter is the CSS3 standard.

To understand the concept of CSS, imagine a chef at a cooking school teaching dozens of students. If the chef spends an hour with each student privately teaching a new cooking technique, the amount of time required to teach this same lesson over and over means it would take days to teach everyone. It makes more sense for the chef to teach the entire class the new cooking technique at once. Similarly, if your Web site has dozens of pages, changing the background color of every single page individually would be very time consuming. But with CSS, you can make one adjustment in the CSS file to display the new background color on every page of the site. CSS allows complete and total control over the style of an entire Web site.

Project — Custom Template and Style Sheet

Designing a professional Web site that appeals to your target audience begins with a plan to define the style of the site, which should suit its purpose and audience. A local family photographer has launched a new Web site using the latest HTML5 and CSS3 standards to market the company's photography services, as shown in Figure 2–1. The Gallery Portrait and Family Photography business (called Gallery for short) requires a site that meets the goals described in its business mission statement: "Our mission is to capture cherished family moments while providing our clients with an unsurpassed photography experience." The Gallery specializes in artistic family and individual portrait photos that capture the different personalities of each subject. You begin the Gallery site in this chapter, and then expand it in subsequent chapters to include information about the company's services, portfolio, pricing, session details, and contact information.

To create a unique and memorable design for the Gallery site, follow the same process that professional Web designers follow when building a site. The Gallery site uses a custom template to establish the layout of the Web pages. Attached to the template is an external style sheet, which uses CSS3 to define the design for each area of the site, including the logo, navigation, main content, and footer areas. An external CSS3 style sheet is the professional standard for styling content throughout an entire Web site. Finally, you create a page based on the template, and then customize the content to suit the first page of the site, shown in Figure 2–1.

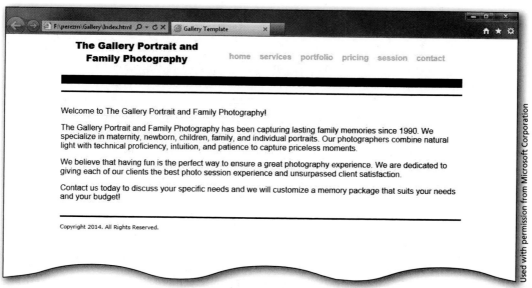

Figure 2–1

Overview

As you read this chapter, you will learn how to create the Web page project shown in Figure 2–1 by performing these general tasks:

- Create a new Dreamweaver HTML5 dynamic Web template.
- Add CSS and image folders.
- Create an external style sheet.
- Add CSS rules to the style sheet.
- Create an editable region in the template.
- Create a new page from the template.

Plan Ahead

General Project Guidelines

When creating a Dreamweaver Web site, the individual actions you perform and decisions you make will affect the appearance and characteristics of the entire Web site. When creating the opening page for a business Web site, as shown in Figure 2–1, you should follow these general guidelines:

1. **Create an HTML template.** Choose a blank HTML template so you can design a custom layout.

2. **Determine the layout and formatting of the Web site.** Before designing a CSS layout, carefully consider which site structure will convey your message effectively. Maintaining consistency in your page layout and design helps to ensure a productive user experience.

3. **Understand the anatomy of a CSS style sheet.** Recognize the elements of CSS styles.

4. **Create a CSS style sheet.** Define the element properties and values within the CSS style sheet.

More specific details about these guidelines are presented at appropriate points throughout the chapter. The chapter also identifies the actions performed and decisions made regarding these guidelines during the creation of the Web site home page shown in Figure 2–1.

Anatomy of a Style Sheet

The **World Wide Web Consortium (W3C)** — an international community where member organizations, a full-time staff, and the public work together to develop Web standards — mandates that CSS style sheets are the core of Web design. When you customize a Web site by creating, modifying, and applying CSS styles, all the Web pages in the site share a consistent look even as the content changes. A **style** is a rule that defines the appearance and position of text and graphics. A **style sheet** is a collection of styles that describes how to display the elements of an HTML document in a Web browser. You can develop CSS style sheets by entering code or by using Dreamweaver's CSS toolset. Designers typically define a style in the style sheet for a Web site and then apply the style to content in many locations throughout the site. Separating style from content means you can change a Web site's appearance easily. If you modify a CSS style, the site updates any content to which you applied that style to reflect the modifications.

A style sheet consists of **CSS rule definitions** that specify the layout and format properties that apply to an element, such as a heading, bullets, or a paragraph. For example, the heading at the top of each page could be defined in a CSS rule stating that this heading always appears as blue, 20-point, underlined text. The term, cascading, in Cascading Style Sheets refers to a sorting order that determines whether one style has precedence over another if two competing style rules affect the same content.

The CSS style sheet shown in Figure 2–2a lays the foundation for the design of the Web page in Figure 2–2b.

(a) Layout.css style sheet

(b) Home page for the Gallery Web site

Figure 2–2

Because a central style sheet provides the layout code for all pages within the site, style sheets originally were developed in the late 1990s to reduce the size of HTML files. In addition to smaller file sizes, CSS style sheets offer the following benefits, which have changed the architectural design of the Web:

- Faster download times because the styles are separated in a style sheet from the HTML code

- Reduced design expenses because one change in the style sheet updates the entire site

- Improved accessibility for site users who have disabilities

- Improved consistency in design and navigation throughout the site

Understanding the Structure of a Style

A style, also called a rule, uses CSS code to specify how to format an element or a section of a Web page. The anatomy of a style is shown in Figure 2–3. Although Dreamweaver automatically generates the CSS code you need after you make selections in the CSS rules dialog boxes, it is important to understand the elements of a style so you can make additional changes to the code.

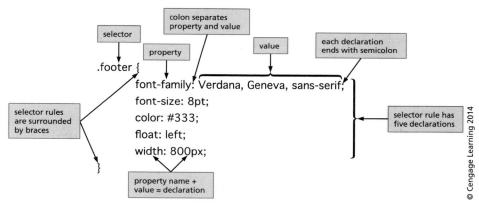

Figure 2–3

Selector Every CSS style begins with a **selector**, which is the name of the style. The selector informs the browser that a special class or element is styled a certain way. Class selectors begin with a period, as in .content, and ID selectors begin with a hash symbol, as in #right. A **class** identifies a particular region or division on a page, such as the footer, that can be customized. For example, the style shown in Figure 2–3 formats a special class named .footer according to the properties listed within the curly braces. A selector can have multiple properties.

Declaration Every CSS style also has a **declaration**, which defines the details of a style. In Figure 2–3, the first declaration indicates that the font-family for the .footer selector is Verdana, Geneva, sans-serif. A declaration includes a property and a value, and ends with a semicolon. The .footer selector has five declarations within the curly braces.

Property A **property** identifies the type of formatting to apply, such as the font family, color, or width. In Figure 2–3, the first declaration is for the font-family property.

Value   The **value** of a property specifies the exact formatting to apply. Separate the property and value with a colon. In Figure 2–3 on the previous page, the width property is set to 800 px, indicating that the footer element should be 800 pixels wide. The font-family property has three values: Verdana, Geneva, and sans-serif. The Web site uses the first value, Verdana, if that font is available on the visitor's browser. If Verdana is not installed on the visitor's browser, the Web site uses the next value, Geneva, if that font is available. If the first two fonts are not available, the Web site uses the next value, sans-serif, as a generic font to format the text. Separate multiple values for a property by commas. If a value contains more than one word, place quotation marks around the value.

Declaration Block   The CSS style code found between the two curly braces is considered a declaration block within the style sheet.

Identifying Types of Style Sheets

The single selector displayed in Figure 2–3 applies only to the footers throughout the Web site. To create a more comprehensive rule set, use a style sheet to specify a collection of CSS rules as shown in Figure 2–4.

Figure 2–4

The style sheet in Figure 2–4 is an external style sheet. However, you can define CSS rules in an external style sheet, in an internal style sheet, or as inline styles. **External style sheets**, the most commonly used type of style sheet, allow you to store the code for the site styles in a separate document. Dreamweaver takes care of linking the external style sheet to the HTML file by automatically creating code, but you will strengthen your Web designer skills if you understand what is happening under the hood. If you are coding a Web page manually, you need to place a link tag in the HTML code (the content of the page) to attach the external style sheet to the page and apply the style definitions. You typically place code similar to the following example in the HTML <head> section of the page:

```
<link href="CSS/layout.css" rel="style sheet" type="text/css">
<style type="text/css">
```

The **link tag** forms a relationship between the current document and an external style sheet, which is named layout.css in this case. External style sheets are text files with a .css file name extension. An external style sheet is a perfect way to format a large Web site because the styles are applied automatically to all pages in the site. Site management is simple when using an external style sheet because you can update the style in one place in the style sheet and then apply the change throughout the site. Separating the page content from presentation makes it much easier to maintain the appearance of your site.

Another type of style sheet, called an **internal style sheet**, applies formatting styles within an HTML document. In a multiple-page Web site, a single page may have a unique layout that differs from the layouts specified in the external style sheet. You can use an internal style sheet to create a distinct look for this one page only. You embed internal styles in the <head> tag using the <style> tag, as shown in the following HTML code:

```
<head>
<style type="text/css">
body {background-color:navy;}
</style>
</head>
```

This style rule sets the background color for body text to navy. Internal styles take precedence over external styles. If an external style sheet sets the background color of the entire site to light blue, the internal style sheet overrides that rule and displays the background color as navy on this page only. The internal style overrides the external style because the internal style is specific to this single page. HTML pages with internal styles can take longer to load, but the advantage of having one page with its own style rules makes it worthwhile.

The third approach to defining styles is to include inline styles within your Web site. **Inline styles** allow you to insert a style rule within an HTML tag in an HTML page. For example, suppose you want to display only one heading in red. Add an inline style within the heading tag to format the heading, as shown in the following code:

```
<h1 style="color: red;">The Photographer's Gallery</h1>
```

When the inline style code is placed within a tag, it affects that tag only. The other heading styles are not affected by this inline style. Inline styles override external and internal style coding styles. Excessive inline styles can create a slow-loading page that is also difficult to edit, so consider using inline styles very rarely in your site development.

Creating a Dreamweaver Web Template

The design of the Gallery Web site should have a consistent look and feel throughout every page. Instead of using a ready-made design template to create a page as you did in Chapter 1, in this chapter, you create a custom template from scratch. A custom template provides a basic layout for the entire site using design elements that you specify. Templates are best used when you are creating a large site where every page shares the same design characteristics such as the logo, background, font, and arrangement. When you save an HTML page as a Dreamweaver Web Template, Dreamweaver creates a template folder at the root level of the local root folder and generates a **.dwt** file that becomes the design source for all the pages that you generate from it. The .dwt extension stands for Dreamweaver Web Template and is associated with a special type of Web document that adds structure and layout to a page.

Dreamweaver templates have a number of design layout regions, or divisions; some can be edited and others cannot. By creating a Dreamweaver Web Template, you can include editable, unlocked regions for adding content to the page. An **editable region** on a Web page is an area where other Web page authors can change the content. For example, you would locate a calendar of upcoming events in an editable region of a page so that anyone designing the page could modify or update the calendar as necessary to keep it current. A template can also have **noneditable regions**, which are sections with static, unchanging content. By using noneditable regions in a template, you prevent changes to certain areas, such as a navigation bar, and preserve the consistent layout of each page based on the template.

Create an HTML template

Before you create a Web site, you must determine the look and feel of each page in the site. By creating a common template for the site that can be applied to each page of the site, the entire Web site maintains a cohesive, consistent presentation. After creating a template, you use it to create Web pages that share the same layout, style, and content. Place this unvarying content in the noneditable regions of the template. The template also should include editable regions for elements that vary from page to page, such as the page heading and descriptive text. Attach a style sheet to the template so that all the pages created from the template use the same CSS styles.

Organizing the Site Structure

Carefully organizing a business or personal Web site from the start can save you frustration and problems with navigation. You save the Gallery site in a root folder on your USB drive. Within the root folder, you can create additional folders and subfolders to organize images, CSS files, templates, and other objects for the site. In this chapter, you create two folders within the Gallery site to hold the CSS and image resources necessary for the design of the project. After you define a site using Dreamweaver's Site Setup feature, you can create the folder hierarchy shown in Figure 2–5.

In Figure 2–5, the root folder for the Gallery site contains a CSS folder, an Images folder, a Templates folder, and the index.html file, representing the home page that appears when you open the site. An external style sheet named layout.css resides within the CSS folder. When you add images to the Gallery site in Chapter 3, you place them in the Images folder so that when you want to insert an image into a page, you know where to find it. Dreamweaver automatically creates the Templates folder when you save an HTML page as a template file with the .dwt extension. In this case, the Dreamweaver Web Template is named Gallery Template and is stored in the Templates folder.

Gallery Web site in the perezm folder

© Cengage Learning 2014

Figure 2–5

To Start Dreamweaver

If you are stepping through this project on a computer and you want your screen to match the figures in this book, you should change your computer's resolution to 1024 × 768 and reset the Classic workspace. For more information about how to change the resolution on your computer, read the "Changing the Screen Resolution" appendix.

The following steps, which assume Windows 7 is running, start Dreamweaver based on a typical installation. You may need to ask your instructor how to start Dreamweaver for your system.

1 Click the Start button on the Windows 7 taskbar to display the Start menu and then type `Dreamweaver CS6` in the 'Search programs and files' box.

2 Click Adobe Dreamweaver CS6 in the list to start Dreamweaver and display the Welcome screen.

3 If the Dreamweaver window is not maximized, click the Maximize button next to the Close button on the Application bar to maximize the window (Figure 2–6).

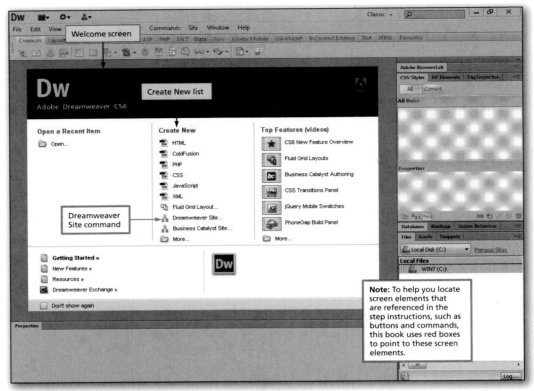

Figure 2–6

To Create a New Site

The following steps create a site named Gallery for the new photography studio Web site.

1

- Click Dreamweaver Site in the Create New list to display the Site Setup dialog box.

- Type `Gallery` in the Site name text box to name the site.

- Click the 'Browse for folder' icon to display the Choose Root Folder dialog box, and if necessary, navigate to your Removable Disk (F:) drive, click the root folder named with your last name and first initial (such as perezm), and then click the Open button to display the subfolders in the root folder.

- Click the Create New Folder button to create a folder, type `Gallery` as the name of the new folder, press the ENTER key, and then click the Open button to create the Gallery subfolder and open it.

- Click the Select button to display the Site Setup for Gallery dialog box (Figure 2–7).

Figure 2–7

2

• Click the Save button to save the site settings and display the Gallery root folder in the Files panel (Figure 2–8).

Figure 2–8

To Create Folders for the Image and CSS Files

The Gallery site uses an image file to display a background for the Web pages and a CSS file to set the Web page layout. To make it easy to manage files for a Web site, which can quickly grow to dozens of files, you should store the files in **resource folders**, which are subfolders in the root folder for the site. In each resource folder, store a single type of file. For example, store all the photos, line drawings, backgrounds, and other graphics in the Images folder. Store all the CSS style sheets in the CSS folder. The following steps create two resource folders for the image and CSS files.

1

• Right-click the Gallery root folder in the Files panel to display the folder's context menu (Figure 2–9).

Figure 2–9

- Click New Folder on the context menu to create a new folder.

- Type **CSS** to name the first resource folder in the Gallery site, and then press the ENTER key to create the CSS folder (Figure 2–10).

Figure 2–10

- Right-click the Gallery root folder in the Files panel to display the folder's context menu.

- Click New Folder on the context menu to create a new folder.

- Type **Images** to name the folder.

- Press the ENTER key to name the second resource folder (Figure 2–11).

Figure 2–11

To Create a Blank HTML Template

Dreamweaver CS6 provides a blank HTML template with no predefined layout for use in developing a template from scratch. After defining a site, the next step is to design a consistent layout of elements that appear on each page of the site. Save the HTML template as a Dreamweaver Web Template so you can use it to create pages for the site. If you modify the template, you immediately update the design of all pages attached to the template.

To begin a new HTML layout, you use the New Document dialog box, which provides options for creating blank pages, blank templates with liquid and fixed layouts, and blank templates without any predefined layout. After creating a template, you save it with a specific name. By default, Dreamweaver stores the new template in a folder named Templates in the root folder of your site. The following steps create a new blank HTML template.

1

- Click the More folder on the Welcome screen to display the New Document dialog box (Figure 2–12).

Q&A

What if I do not see a Welcome screen?

Instead of clicking the More folder on the Welcome screen, you can click File on the Application bar and then select New to display the New Document dialog box.

New Document dialog box

Figure 2–12

2

- Click Blank Template in the left pane to specify you are creating a blank template.

- Click HTML template in the Template Type list to select an HTML template.

- If necessary, click <none> in the Layout list to create a blank HTML template with no predefined layout.

- If necessary, click the DocType button and then click HTML 5 to set the DocType to HTML5 (Figure 2–13).

New Document dialog box

Template Type list Layout list

Blank Template

HTML template

<none>

HTML 5 DocType

Create button

Figure 2–13

- Click the Create button to display the blank HTML template in the Document window (Figure 2–14).

blank HTML template in Document window

Figure 2–14

To Save the HTML Page as a Template

When you create a template, Dreamweaver uses the name of the site followed by *Template.dwt* as the name of the template, such as Gallery Template.dwt. When saving the template, a dialog box appears reminding you that the template does not have any editable regions. Recall that an editable region is an area in a template that contains text or other objects users can edit. For example, if every Web page based on the template will have a different main heading, include the heading in an editable region. You define editable regions later in this chapter. The following steps save the blank HTML template as a Dreamweaver Web Template.

1

- Click File on the Application bar to display the File menu (Figure 2–15).

Figure 2–15

2

- Click Save on the File menu to display the Save As Template dialog box.

- If a warning dialog box is displayed, click the OK button to close the dialog box.

- If necessary, click the Site button to display the site list and then click Gallery to select the Gallery site.

- If necessary, select the placeholder text in the Save as text box, and then type `Gallery Template` to name the Dreamweaver Web template (Figure 2–16).

Q&A
Why is the Save As Template dialog box displayed when I select Save on the File menu?

Because this is the first time you are saving the template, Dreamweaver displays the Save As Template dialog box so you can specify a new name for the file.

Figure 2–16

Q&A
Will the template include editable regions?

Yes. You create the editable regions later in this chapter and in other chapters.

3

- Click the Save button to save the Dreamweaver Web template as Gallery Template.dwt in a folder named Templates in the Gallery file hierarchy.

- Click the expand icon for the Templates folder in the Files panel to expand the Templates folder and display the Gallery Template file (Figure 2–17).

Figure 2–17

Adding CSS Styles

The Gallery Web site will use CSS styles to structure the layout of the pages. Instead of cluttering each HTML page in the site with individual style tags for each element, CSS rules style an element with specified properties such as font type, size, and color throughout the site.

Before you can take advantage of the power of CSS styles, you should organize the content of the Web pages and identify the sections to which you will apply certain types of CSS styles. The most common way to organize content involves dividing the page into different regions, or divisions. Figure 2–18 shows each region of the page sketched during the planning phase of the Web site project. These six regions of the page are the building blocks of the Gallery site design.

The easiest way to format elements within a site is by using specific CSS styles within each region. You can apply positioning and formatting styles to text, images, tables, and other elements in each region. The formatting styles determine the appearance of individual elements by making text in the navigation region, for example, bold, orange, 12-point lowercase Arial text. The positioning styles create simple to complex layouts, arranging blocks of text, graphics, or images on the page. During the design phase of a Web site project, designers often use a wireframe to sketch the layout of the page as shown in Figure 2–18. A **wireframe** is a block diagram that shows the main elements of a Web page layout as boxes with brief descriptions.

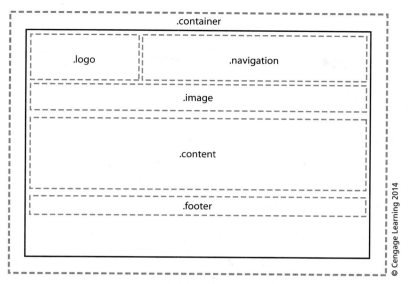

© Cengage Learning 2014

Figure 2–18

Each Dreamweaver CSS layout requires its own style sheet containing each region and the associated style rules necessary to make the layout work. An external style sheet declares style rules for each region, also called a class. Each class selector, identified with a beginning period, specifies a style for a group of elements.

Determine the layout and formatting of the Web site
When designing a Web site from scratch, you should consider the types of elements that you must format to create a consistent look across each page in the site. Consider each CSS rule that is needed to format every element:

- Determine the layout of the site, including the location of the logo, navigation, main content area, and footer.

- Plan the formatting necessary for each Web page element to determine the CSS rules for font styles, color, and heading size.

Plan Ahead

Recall that CSS is the current standard for formatting Web page elements. In addition, CSS is the standard for Web page layout. Instead of using HTML techniques, which involve tables or frames to structure content, CSS uses the **div tag**, an HTML tag that acts as a container for text, images, and other page elements. When laying out pages with CSS, you place the div tag around text, images, and other page elements to position the regions of content on the page. You can place other tags within a div tag.

BTW

Div Tags
To see examples of div tags used in CSS layouts, you can create a test page from a CSS layout listed in the New Document dialog box.

To Add a Div Tag

Because each region of the CSS layout is associated with a div tag, you need to insert a div tag for each region of content in the Web page or template. The Gallery site has six regions, so you insert six div tags. After naming a div tag, set the CSS rule definitions for the font, position, border, and other properties of that region. The outer region of the Web site, as shown in Figure 2–18, is called the .container class because it contains all the other regions. When adding a div tag, you specify where to store the CSS styles that apply to that region: in this document only, in an existing style sheet, or in a new style sheet. For the first div tag in a page or template, specify a new style sheet. Dreamweaver requests a name and location for the new .css file. In this case, name the new style sheet layout.css and store it in the CSS folder in the Gallery site. The following steps insert a div tag for the container region and save the CSS style sheet.

• On the Document toolbar, drag to select the text, Untitled Document, in the Title text box.

• Type `Gallery` as the title of the template page (Figure 2–19).

Figure 2–19

• Click the Document window, and then click the Insert Div Tag button on the Insert bar to display the Insert Div Tag dialog box (Figure 2–20).

Q&A What is the purpose of inserting a div tag?

You are inserting a div tag to create a division in the Gallery template.

Figure 2–20

• If necessary, click the Class text box and then type `container` to name the div tag (Figure 2–21).

Q&A Do I also enter a name in the ID text box?

No. You create a div tag as a class or an ID. You can apply a class div tag to any other tag on the page. You can apply an ID div tag only once on a page.

Q&A Should I type a period before the class name?

No. A period is not necessary because Dreamweaver automatically places a period before the class name in the next dialog box.

Figure 2–21

• Click the New CSS Rule button to display the New CSS Rule dialog box (Figure 2–22).

Q&A What is the purpose of the New CSS Rule dialog box?

Use this dialog box to add a CSS rule that defines the class you created; in this case, the container class.

Figure 2–22

• Click the Rule Definition button and then click (New Style Sheet File) in the Rule Definition list to select the location in which you want to define the rule, which is in a new style sheet file (Figure 2–23).

Q&A When (New Style Sheet File) is selected, where does Dreamweaver save the CSS style sheet?

When you determine that the rule definition should be saved in a new style sheet, click the OK button to display a dialog box requesting where to save the .css file.

Figure 2–23

6

• Click the OK button to create a new CSS rule for the container region and to display the Save Style Sheet File As dialog box (Figure 2–24).

Figure 2–24

- Double-click the CSS folder in the Save Style Sheet File As dialog box to select the file location for the style sheet.

- Click the File name text box and then type `layout` to name the CSS style sheet within the CSS folder (Figure 2–25).

 Which file type should I select when I save the style sheet?

Dreamweaver automatically selects .css as the default file type.

Figure 2–25

- Click the Save button to save the style sheet as layout.css and display the 'CSS Rule Definition for .container in layout.css' dialog box (Figure 2–26).

 Why is a CSS Rule Definition dialog box displayed after I save the style sheet?

You use this dialog box to specify the details of the styles to apply to the container region by selecting a formatting category and the appropriate value for each style rule.

Figure 2–26

Other Ways

1. Click style sheet on CSS Styles panel, click New Rule button

Setting CSS Rule Definitions

The layout.css style sheet contains the CSS rules that define the styles in the Gallery Web site. Instead of entering code by hand, Dreamweaver CS6 provides a CSS Rule Definition dialog box that allows Web designers to define styles easily and effectively for CSS element rules. The CSS Rule Definition dialog box appears when you are creating or modifying styles.

BTW

Creating CSS Rules
Besides using the New CSS Rule button on the CSS Styles panel, you can click the Targeted Rule button on the Property inspector and then click New CSS Rule to create a CSS rule.

Plan Ahead

> **Create a CSS style sheet**
> To create an external style sheet, you need to define which rules to set in each division, or region, of the site. Six div tags with detailed CSS rules change the default settings of the font, color, margins, and other CSS properties. By defining styles in an external style sheet, you can apply the styles in any page in the site connected to that style sheet. Because editing a style in the external style sheet updates all instances of that style throughout the site, external style sheets are the most powerful and flexible way to use styles.

The CSS Rule Definition dialog box in Figure 2–26 consists of nine categories of style rules. Table 2–1 describes each category.

Table 2–1 Categories in the CSS Rule Definition Dialog Box	
Category	**Purpose**
Type	Determines the appearance and format of text for the selected style
Background	Specifies the background color or background images to display as the page background
Block	Provides option styles to space and align text according to your custom settings
Box	Defines the spacing and placement of elements on a page, such as the location of an image within a defined region
Border	Specifies border styles, width, and color values for one or all edges of borders for text, images, and other Web elements
List	Defines list types, custom bullet images, and unique positioning selections
Positioning	Prescribes the placement of CSS elements within the page, which increases a designer's creative control over the appearance of a Web site
Extensions	Determines page breaks for printing and customizes the appearance of elements on the page
Transition	Enables animation changes in CSS values to occur smoothly over a specified duration

To Select CSS Rule Definitions

The .container class within the style sheet provides specifications for the width of the page and for the margin settings. The .container class is the default name for the large container that holds the other classes with the style sheet. In this case, you set the width of the page to 800px. **Pixels (px)** is the measurement unit for setting the dimensions of the container. The measurement value, such as 800, and the unit, such as px, typically are noted without a space between them. The **margin** determines the amount of space to maintain between the container region and the borders of the browser window. Here, you set the left and right margins to auto, which centers the container region horizontally within the browser window. The following steps define the CSS rule definitions for the .container class.

1

- Click Box in the Category list of the 'CSS Rule Definitions for .container in layout.css' dialog box to set the CSS rules for the layout of the container class (Figure 2–27).

Figure 2–27

2

- Click the Width box and then type 800 to set a width of 800 pixels for the .container class.

- Click Same for all in the Margin section to remove the check mark from the 'Same for all' check box.

- Click the Right box arrow in the Margin section, and then click auto to set the right margin to center automatically within the browser window.

- Click the Left box arrow in the Margin section, and then click auto to set the left margin to center automatically within the browser window (Figure 2–28).

Figure 2–28

3

- Click the Apply button to apply the CSS rules for the .container class within the layout.css file.

- Click the OK button (CSS Rule Definition dialog box) to define the CSS rules for the .container class.

- Click the OK button (Insert Div Tag dialog box) to close the Insert Div Tag dialog box.

- If necessary, select the text 'Content for class "container" Goes Here' in the Document window, and then press the DELETE key to delete the text from the container region (Figure 2–29).

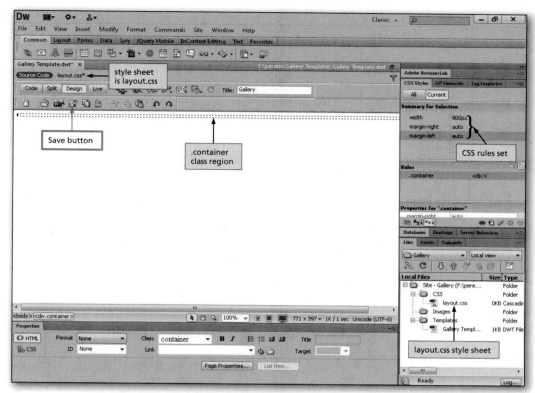

Figure 2–29

Q&A Why do I click the Apply button instead of the OK button in the CSS Rule Definition dialog box?

Click the Apply button to apply the styles in the current category. You can select another category and then set styles in that category. When you click the OK button, you apply all the selected styles in all the categories.

Q&A Why are dashed lines displayed in the Document window?

The dashed lines define the region set by the .container class. Later, you define other regions within the .container region.

Q&A Where are the classes listed for the style sheet?

The classes are listed on the CSS Styles panel on the right side of the Dreamweaver window.

4

- Click the Save button on the Standard toolbar to save your work.

Q&A What should I do if a dialog box notes that the template does not have any editable regions?

Click the OK button. You will add an editable region later in this chapter. Click the OK button each time this dialog box appears in this chapter.

Other Ways

1. Select class on CSS Styles panel, click Edit Rule button

Break Point: If you wish to take a break, this is a good place to do so. To resume at a later time, start Dreamweaver, if necessary, open the file called Gallery Template, and continue following the steps from this location forward.

To Add the Logo Div Tag and Define Its CSS Rules

A business typically uses its company logo, which can consist of an image and text, to create a recognizable reference to that business. In the Gallery site, the logo consists of the text, The Gallery Portrait and Family Photography, and an image. You add the image in the next chapter. Before you add the text, you define a layout region in the style sheet so you can control the placement and appearance of the region. In this case, you define a region named .logo in the layout.css style sheet to determine the custom arrangement of the Gallery logo. Next, you set the CSS rules for the region by defining the Type property such as font-family and font size, Block properties such as text alignment, and Box properties that set the size of the region. The **float property** determines where text and other objects should float around the region. In Chapter 3, you add an image to the template that should float to the left of the logo. The following steps define the CSS rule definitions for the .logo class.

1

- If necessary in the Gallery template, click within the container region.

- Click the Insert Div Tag button on the Insert bar to display the Insert Div Tag dialog box.

- If necessary, click the Class text box and then type logo to name the div tag (Figure 2–30).

Q&A

How can I tell if I am clicking within the container region?

If the insertion point is within the container region, <div.container> appears on the status bar.

Figure 2–30

2

- Click the New CSS Rule button to display the New CSS Rule dialog box for adding a new CSS rule that defines the logo class (Figure 2–31).

Figure 2–31

3

- Click the OK button to add the .logo selector to the layout.css style sheet and display the 'CSS Rule Definition for .logo in layout.css' dialog box (Figure 2–32).

Q&A Should I create another style sheet for the .logo class?

No. In this case, you save the six style classes within the same style sheet named layout.css.

Q&A How many classes can be added to the style sheet?

You can identify as many classes as you need to define the style of your site.

Figure 2–32

4

- If necessary, click Type in the Category list to display the Type options.

- Click the Font-family box arrow and then click 'Arial Black, Gadget, sans-serif' to set the font family for the .logo style.

- Click the Font-size box arrow and then click 14 to set the font size.

- Click the px button next to the Font-size box and then click pt to change the font size units from px to pt.

- Click the Color text box and then type #000 to change the font color to black (Figure 2–33).

Q&A Why is sans-serif or serif typically the last font listed in the Font-family font groupings?

The sans-serif and serif fonts are generic fonts that are displayed on any type of computer.

Q&A Are the px and pt font-size units basically the same?

The px unit measures fonts in pixels and the pt unit measures fonts in points. These units represent different sizes.

Figure 2–33

5

- Click the Apply button to apply the Type settings.

- Click Block in the Category list to display the Block options.

- Click the Text-align box arrow and then click center to set the text alignment for the .logo style (Figure 2–34).

Figure 2–34

6

- Click the Apply button to apply the Block settings.

- Click Box in the Category list to display the Box options.

- Click the Width text box and then type 300 to set the width of the region containing the .logo style.

- Click the Height text box and then type 75 to set the height of the region.

- Click the Float box arrow and then click left to specify that other elements float to the left of elements in the .logo style (Figure 2–35).

Figure 2–35

7

- Click the Apply button to apply the CSS rules for the .logo class within the layout.css file.

- Click the OK button (CSS Rule Definition dialog box) to define the CSS rules for the .logo class.

- Click the OK button (Insert Div Tag dialog box) to close the Insert Div Tag dialog box and display the .logo class region and its placeholder text (Figure 2–36).

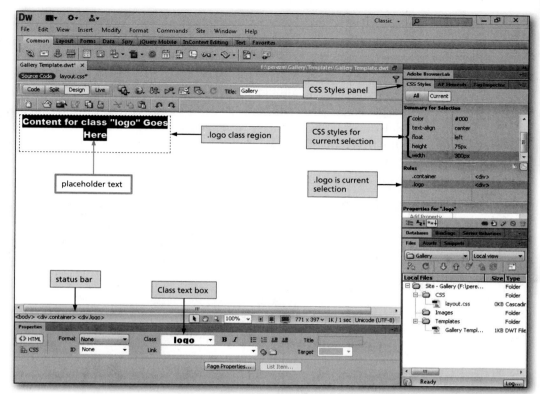

Figure 2–36

8

- If necessary, select the placeholder text 'Content for class "logo" Goes Here' in the Document window, and then type The Gallery Portrait and Family Photography to insert the logo text (Figure 2–37).

Figure 2–37

9

- Click the Save button on the Standard toolbar to save the template.

Q&A What should I do if a Dreamweaver dialog box indicates the template does not have any editable regions?

Click the 'Don't warn me again' check box to insert a check mark, and then click the OK button. You specify editable regions later in the chapter.

To Add the Navigation Div Tag and Define Its CSS Rules

Most Web pages have a navigation region that contains links to other pages in the site. Including the navigation region in the Web site template means the navigation links appear in the same place and style on each page, which makes it easy for site visitors to find the links and navigate the site. Web sites typically include navigation links either horizontally across the top or vertically along the left side of each page. Many site designers prefer a horizontal navigation bar at the top of the page because it uses the full width of the page for content instead of crowding the left edge of the page with links, but either design can be effective as long as the navigation provides a strong visual focus. The navigation region for the Gallery site is displayed in the upper-right corner of the page. Similar to defining the logo region, you define the format and position of the navigation region and its contents. The following steps define the CSS rule definitions for the .navigation class.

1

- Click to the right of the .logo region within the document to move the insertion point to the div.container region.

- Click the Insert Div Tag button on the Insert bar to display the Insert Div Tag dialog box.

- If necessary, click the Class text box and then type navigation to name the div tag (Figure 2–38).

Q&A Why does the status bar display <body> <div.container>?

The container region is now selected instead of the logo region.

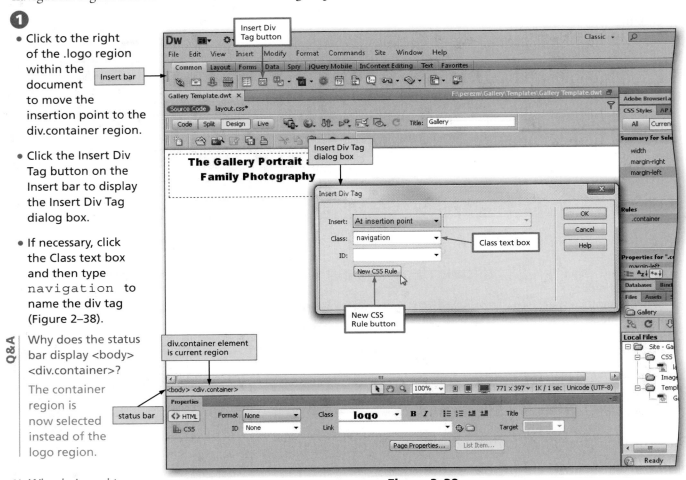

Figure 2–38

Q&A Why do I need to move the insertion point to the div.container region before creating the new navigation region?

You move the insertion point so you can create the new region in the div.container region, which you designed to hold all the other regions. Otherwise, you create the new navigation region in the logo region.

2

• Click the New CSS Rule button to display the New CSS Rule dialog box for adding a new CSS rule that defines the navigation class (Figure 2–39).

Figure 2–39

3

• Click the OK button to add the .navigation selector name to the layout.css file and display the 'CSS Rule Definition for .navigation in layout.css' dialog box.

• Click the Font-family box arrow and then click 'Arial, Helvetica, sans-serif' to set the font family for the .navigation style.

• Click the Font-size box arrow and then click 12 to set the font size for the .navigation style.

• Click the px button next to the Font-size box and then click pt to change the font size units from px to pt.

• Click the Line-height text box and then type 50 to set the line height to 50.

• Click the px button next to the Line-height box and then click pt to change the line height units from px to pt.

• Click the Font-weight box arrow and then click bolder to set the font to a bolder style.

• Click the Text-transform box arrow and then click lowercase to convert the text to lowercase letters.

• Click the Color text box and then type #F90 to change the style color to orange (Figure 2–40).

Figure 2–40

Q&A

What does the value, #F90, represent?

The value, #F90, is a hexadecimal number representing a color; in this case, orange. You can enter hexadecimal values in text boxes that request color values, or you can click the color palette button next to the text box to select a color.

4

- Click the Apply button to apply the Type settings.

- Click Block in the Category list to display the Block options.

- Click the Word-spacing text box, type 10, click the em button, and then click pt to change the word spacing in the .navigation style to 10 points.

- Click the Text-align box arrow and then click center to set the text alignment (Figure 2–41).

Figure 2–41

5

- Click the Apply button to apply the Block settings.

- Click Box in the Category list to display the Box options.

- Click the Width text box and then type 500 to set the width of the .navigation region.

- Click the Height text box and then type 75 to set the height of the .navigation region.

- Click the Float box arrow and then click left to change the float property (Figure 2–42).

Figure 2–42

6

- Click the Apply button to apply the CSS rules for the .navigation class within the layout.css style sheet.

- Click the OK button (CSS Rule Definition dialog box) to define the CSS rules for the .navigation class.

- Click the OK button (Insert Div Tag dialog box) to close the Insert Div Tag dialog box and display the .navigation class region and its placeholder text.

- If necessary, select the text 'Content for class "navigation" Goes Here' and then type home services portfolio pricing session contact to enter the navigation text (Figure 2–43).

Figure 2–43

Q&A Why does the navigation text appear in bold orange text?

The style rules you just set are applied automatically to the navigation text.

7

- Click the Save button on the Standard toolbar to save the template.

To Add the Image Div Tag and Define Its CSS Rules

Most Web pages display one or more images to increase the visual appeal of the page. If one image or a certain type of image appears on each page, include an image region in the template so the image appears in the same place and style throughout the site. The pages in the Gallery site eventually will include family and portrait images as samples of photography the company has produced. To display these images consistently on each page, you add an image region to the template and then set its properties. The image region serves as a placeholder for the main images that will be displayed in the Gallery site. The following steps define the CSS rules of the .image class.

1

- If necessary, scroll right and then click to the right of the .navigation div within the document to move the insertion point to the div.container element.

- Click the Insert Div Tag button on the Insert bar to display the Insert Div Tag dialog box.

- In the Class text box, type `image` to name the div tag (Figure 2–44).

Figure 2–44

2

- Click the New CSS Rule button to display the New CSS Rule dialog box for adding a new CSS rule that defines the image class (Figure 2–45).

Figure 2–45

- Click the OK button to add the .image selector name to the layout.css style sheet and display the 'CSS Rule Definition for .image in layout.css' dialog box.

- Click Background in the Category list to display the Background options.

- Click the Background-color text box and then type #000 to change the background color of the .image region to black (Figure 2–46).

Figure 2–46

- Click the Apply button to apply the Background settings.

- Click Box in the Category list to display the Box options.

- In the Width text box, type 800 to set the width of the image region to 800 pixels.

- Click the Float box arrow and then click left to set the value of the float property (Figure 2–47).

Figure 2–47

5

- Click the Apply button to apply the CSS rules for the .image class within the layout.css style sheet.

- Click the OK button (CSS Rule Definition dialog box) to define the CSS rules for the .image class.

- Click the OK button (Insert Div Tag dialog box) to close the Insert Div Tag dialog box and display the new image region (Figure 2–48).

Figure 2–48

To Add the Content Div Tag and Define Its CSS Rules

One way to create a consistent look for a Web site is to include a heading or other text in the same style and place on each page. To achieve this consistency, add a region for the text content to the template, and then specify the style and placement properties in the style sheet. Because each page in the Gallery site will include content such as a heading or other text below the logo and navigation regions, you can add a content region to the template. On the opening page, the content region displays welcome text, but other pages will display different content. For now, you insert the content region with placeholder text and specify the style properties for the region. One new property to enter is **padding**, which specifies the amount of space between the text and its border. The following steps define the CSS rules for the .content class.

- If necessary, scroll right and then click to the right of the .image div within the document to move the insertion point to the div.container element.

- Click the Insert Div Tag button on the Insert bar to display the Insert Div Tag dialog box.

- In the Class text box, type content to name the div tag.

- Click the New CSS Rule button to display the New CSS Rule dialog box for adding a new CSS rule that defines the content class (Figure 2–49).

Figure 2–49

- Click the OK button to add the .content selector to the layout.css style sheet and display the 'CSS Rule Definition for .content in layout.css' dialog box.

- Click the Font-family box arrow and then click 'Arial, Helvetica, sans-serif' to set the font family.

- Click the Font-size box arrow, click 12, click the px button, and then click pt to change the units to pt and the font size to 12 points.

- Click the Color text box and then type #000 to change the background color of the .content region to black (Figure 2–50).

Figure 2–50

3

- Click the Apply button to apply the Type settings.
- Click Box in the Category list to display the Box options.
- Click the Width text box and then type 800 to set the width of the .content region.
- Click the Float box arrow and then click left to set the value of the float property.
- Click 'Same for all' in the Padding section to remove the check mark from the 'Same for all' check box.
- Click the Top text box in the Padding section, type 10, click the px button, and then click pt to change the units to pt and set the top padding to 10 points above the text.
- Click the Bottom text box in the Padding section, type 10, click the px button, and then click pt to change the units to pt and set the bottom padding.
- Click 'Same for all' in the Margin section to remove the check mark from the 'Same for all' check box.
- Click the Top text box in the Margin section, type 10, click the px button, and then click pt to change the units to pt and set the top margin to 10 points.
- Click the Bottom text box in the Margin section, type 10, click the px button, and then click pt to change the units to pt and set the bottom margin (Figure 2–51).

Figure 2–51

4

- Click the Apply button to apply the Box settings.
- Click Border in the Category list to display the Border options.
- Click 'Same for all' in the Style section to remove the check mark from the 'Same for all' check box.
- Click the Top box arrow, click solid, click the Bottom box arrow, and then click solid to select a solid style for the top and bottom borders.
- Click 'Same for all' in the Width section to remove the check mark from the 'Same for all' check box.
- Click the Top box arrow, click medium, click the Bottom box arrow, and then click medium to select a medium width for the top and bottom borders.
- Click 'Same for all' in the Color section to remove the check mark from the 'Same for all' check box.
- Click the Top text box, type #000, click the Bottom text box, and then type #000 to set the color of the top and bottom borders to black (Figure 2–52).

Figure 2–52

5

- Click the Apply button to apply the CSS rules for the .content class within the layout.css style sheet.

- Click the OK button (CSS Rule Definition dialog box) to define the CSS rules for the .content class.

- Click the OK button (Insert Div Tag dialog box) to close the Insert Div Tag dialog box and display the new content region (Figure 2–53).

6

- Click the Save button on the Standard toolbar to save your work.

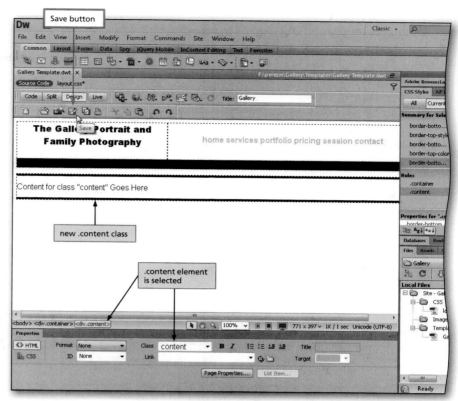

Figure 2–53

To Add the Footer Div Tag and Define Its CSS Rules

The footer of a site typically includes copyright or contact information. The Gallery site displays the year and the copyright information. The following steps define the CSS rules for the .footer class.

1

- If necessary, scroll right and then click to the right of the .content div within the document to move the insertion point to the div.container element.

- Click the Insert Div Tag button on the Insert bar to display the Insert Div Tag dialog box.

- In the Class text box, type `footer` to name the div tag.

- Click the New CSS Rule button to add a new CSS rule that defines the footer class (Figure 2–54).

Figure 2–54

2

- Click the OK button to add the .footer selector name to layout.css and display the 'CSS Rule Definition for .footer in layout.css' dialog box.

- Click the Font-family box arrow and click 'Verdana, Geneva, sans-serif' to set the font family.

- Click the Font-size text box, type 8, click the px button, and then click pt to change the units to pt and the font size to 8 points.

- Click the Color text box and type #333 to change the font color of the .footer div region to dark gray (Figure 2–55).

Figure 2–55

3

- Click the Apply button to apply the Type settings.

- Click Box in the Category list to display the Box options.

- Click the Width text box and then type 800 to set a width of 800 pixels for the .footer class.

- Click the Float box arrow and then click left to set the value of the float property (Figure 2–56).

Figure 2–56

4

- Click the Apply button to apply the CSS rules for the .footer class within the layout.css style sheet.

- Click the OK button (CSS Rule Definition dialog box) to define the CSS rules for the .footer class.

- Click the OK button (Insert Div Tag dialog box) to close the Insert Div Tag dialog box.

- If necessary, select the text 'Content for class "footer" Goes Here' and type Copyright 2014. All Rights Reserved. to enter the .footer class text (Figure 2–57).

Figure 2–57

5

- Click the Save button on the Standard toolbar to save your work.

Creating an Editable Region of a Template

Recall that the two types of regions you can include in a template are editable and noneditable regions. Noneditable regions, also called locked regions, are the sections of a template that have static, unchanging content, such as a logo or a navigation bar. An editable region on a Web page is an area where other Web page authors can edit the content. As a Web developer, you create editable regions in a template to allow other authors to add or remove information without worrying that they will alter the page layout. This gives you control over the layout of the pages and the template itself. For example, if an element, such as a navigation bar, is exactly the same across the entire site, it should be in a noneditable region of the template. Dreamweaver inserts an element as a noneditable region by default, meaning that no one can edit its content in a Web page based on the template. If a content area contains different information on each page, that content should be an editable region of the template. Because Dreamweaver templates contain no editable regions by default, the next step after creating a template typically is to specify some regions as editable regions so each page in the site can display different content.

To Create an Editable Region

In the Gallery site, the logo, navigation, and footer regions should display the same content on each page. Therefore, they can remain noneditable regions in the template. However, the content region of each page in the Gallery site contains different text. You need to specify that the content region is an editable region in the template so you can display different text on each page. The following steps create an editable region in the template.

1

- Select the text 'Content for class "content" Goes Here' in the content region, and then press the DELETE key to delete the placeholder text.

- Click an edge of the content region to select the region (Figure 2–58).

Figure 2–58

2

- Click Insert on the Application bar and then point to Template Objects to display the Template Objects submenu (Figure 2–59).

Figure 2–59

3

- Click Editable Region on the Template Objects submenu to display the New Editable Region dialog box.

- If necessary, select the text in the Name text box and then type `contentArea` to identify an editable region within the content region (Figure 2–60).

Figure 2–60

4

- Click the OK button to display the editable region.

- If necessary, click in the content region and then type `Insert page content here` to provide directions to add content to the editable region (Figure 2–61).

5

- Click the Save button on the Standard toolbar to save the completed template.

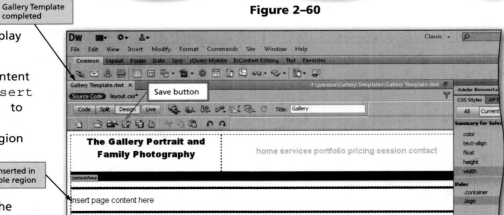

Figure 2–61

To Close the Template

The template is complete, so you can close it. The following steps close the template and display the Welcome screen again.

1

- Click File on the Application bar and then click Close to close the completed template and display the Welcome screen (Figure 2–62).

Q&A What should I do if an Adobe Dreamweaver CS6 dialog box is displayed?

Click the Yes button to save your changes to the style sheet.

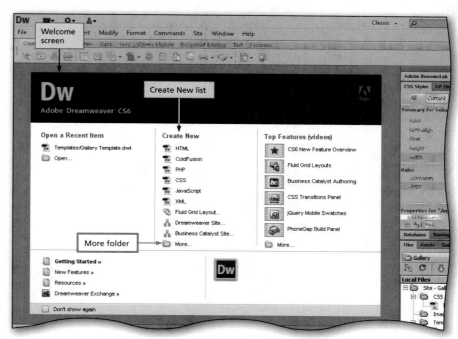

Figure 2–62

Other Ways

1. To add editable region, press CTRL+ALT+V

Creating a New Page from a Template

After creating and saving a template, you can use it to create Web pages on your site — just as you can create pages based on templates provided with Dreamweaver. To create a consistent site, be sure to associate each page with a template. As you create each new page of the site, you start with the template to establish the layout of the page. The noneditable regions of the template appear on the page as static, unchanging content. For example, if you add navigation, logo, and footer elements to a template, they appear on the Web page you create from the template and cannot be changed. Areas you specified as editable regions in the template appear on the Web page as content or areas you can change.

BTW

HTML and HTM File Extensions
Although Dreamweaver saves Web pages with a .html file extension by default, it can also save files with a .htm extension. Browsers recognize both file types as HTML files. You can set a preference to create pages using one extension or the other by clicking Edit on the Application bar, clicking Preferences, and then clicking the New Document category.

To Create a Page from a Template

To complete this assignment, you will be required to use the Data Files for Students. Visit www.cengage .com/ct/studentdownload for detailed instructions or contact your instructor for information about accessing the required files. The following steps open the Ch2_Home_Content file from the Data Files for Students.

The opening home page of the Gallery site is named index.html. In addition to the template elements, the index page uses the editable region of the template to display an opening message about the Gallery photography services. You add this message to the index.html page by copying text from a student data file named Ch2_Home_Page_Content.txt and pasting the text into index.html. The following steps create a new page from the template and add content to the editable region.

1

- Click More in the Create New list to display the New Document dialog box.

- Click Page from Template in the left pane of the New Document dialog box to create a page from the template.

- If necessary, click Gallery in the Site list to create a page for the Gallery site (Figure 2–63).

Figure 2–63

2

- Click the Create button to create a new page based on the template for the Gallery site.

- Click File on the Application bar and then click Save As to display the Save As dialog box.

- If necessary, select the text in the File name text box and then type index to name the new page created from the template (Figure 2–64).

Which folder should I select to save the index.html file?

Save the home page, index.html, in the root Gallery folder, which is the folder displayed by default in the Save As dialog box. When a browser is directed to the Gallery folder, the browser displays index.html as the opening page.

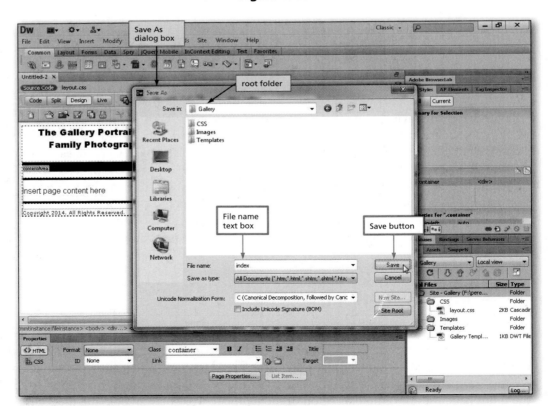

Figure 2–64

3

- Click the Save button to save and open index.html (Figure 2–65).

Q&A

When I move the mouse around the page, the pointer changes to a "not" symbol (circle with a line through it) over some parts of the page. What does this symbol represent in index.html?

The pointer displays a not symbol over the noneditable (locked) regions of the page.

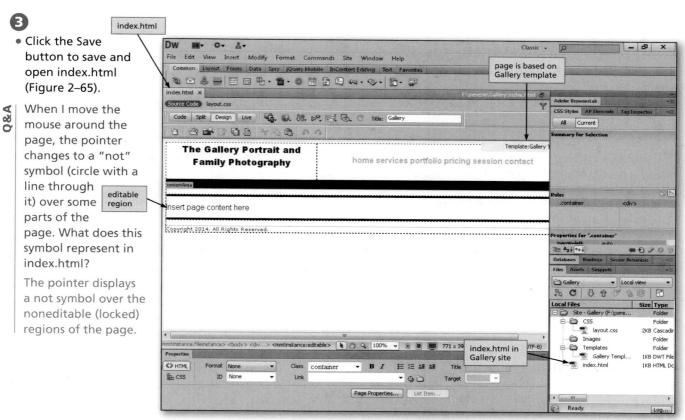

Figure 2–65

4

- If necessary, insert the drive containing your Data Files for Students into an available port. After a few seconds, if Windows displays a dialog box, click its Close button.

- With the Dreamweaver window open, click File on the Application bar, and then click Open to display the Open dialog box.

- In the Open dialog box, navigate to the storage location of the Data Files for Students.

- Click the Chapter 02 folder to display its contents, and then double-click the file, Ch2_Home_Page_Content, to open it.

- Select all the text in the file, click Edit on the Application bar, and then click Copy to copy the text.

- Click the index.html document tab, select the text, Insert page content here, on the index.html page, click Edit on the Application bar, and then click Paste to paste the text you copied (Figure 2–66).

5

- Close the Ch2_Home_Page_Content file.

- Click the Save All button on the Standard toolbar to save the site.

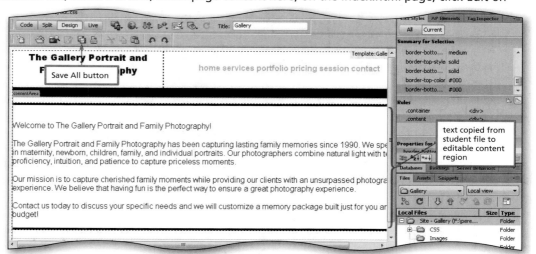

Figure 2–66

To View the Site in Live View

Live view provides a realistic rendering of what your page will look like in a browser, but lets you make any necessary changes without leaving Dreamweaver. The following steps display the page in Live view.

- Click the Live button on the Document toolbar to display a Live view of the site (Figure 2–67).

🔍 **Experiment**

- Click the Code, Split, and Design buttons to view the page in different views. When you are finished, click the Live button to return to Live view.

- Click the Live button again to return to Design view.

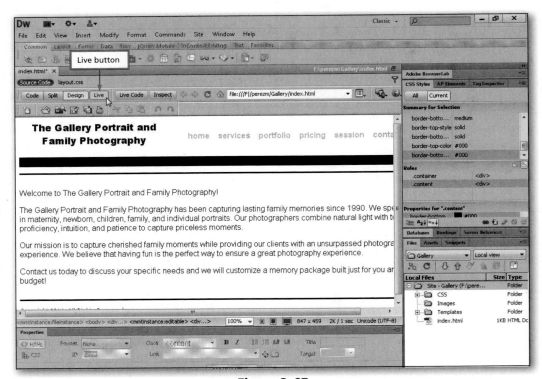

Figure 2–67

Other Ways
1. Press ALT+F11

To View the Site in the Browser

The following steps preview the Gallery Web site home page using Internet Explorer.

1 Click the 'Preview/Debug in browser' button on the Document toolbar.

2 Click Preview in IExplore in the Preview/Debug in browser list to display the Gallery Web site in the Internet Explorer browser.

3 Click the Internet Explorer Close button to close the browser.

To Quit Dreamweaver

The following steps quit Dreamweaver and return control to the operating system.

1 Click the Close button on the right side of the Application bar to close the window.

2 If Dreamweaver displays a dialog box asking you to save changes, click the No button.

Chapter Summary

In this chapter, you have learned how to create a Web site template using the design building blocks of CSS style sheets. You defined a new Web site, created a Dreamweaver Web Template, and defined regions of the page using a style sheet. You defined each region with CSS rules that provided consistent site formatting. You also learned how to create an editable region within a template. You added a page to the site based on the template and placed text in the editable region. You displayed the completed Web page in Live view and in a browser. The following tasks are all the new Dreamweaver skills you learned in this chapter:

1. Create a New Site (DW 86)
2. Create Folders for the Image and CSS Files (DW 87)
3. Create a Blank HTML Template (DW 88)
4. Save the HTML Page as a Template (DW 90)
5. Add a Div Tag (DW 93)
6. Select CSS Rule Definitions (DW 97)
7. Add the Logo Div Tag and Define Its CSS Rules (DW 100)
8. Add the Navigation Div Tag and Define Its CSS Rules (DW 104)
9. Add the Image Div Tag and Define Its CSS Rules (DW 107)
10. Add the Content Div Tag and Define Its CSS Rules (DW 109)
11. Add the Footer Div Tag and Define Its CSS Rules (DW 111)
12. Create an Editable Region (DW 113)
13. Close the Template (DW 115)
14. Create a Page from a Template (DW 115)
15. View the Site in Live View (DW 118)

Apply Your Knowledge

Reinforce the skills and apply the concepts you learned in this chapter.

Creating a New Web Page Template

Instructions: First, create a new HTML5 Web page template and save it. Next, insert div tags in the template and create a new external style sheet file. Finally, add new CSS rules so that the completed template in Live view looks like Figure 2–68. The CSS rule definitions for the template are provided in Table 2–2.

Figure 2–68

Continued >

Apply Your Knowledge *continued*

Perform the following tasks:

1. Use Windows Explorer to access your USB flash drive and create a new folder within the *your last name and first initial*\Apply folder (the folder named perezm\Apply, for example, which you created in Chapter 1). Name the folder `Templates`.

2. Start Dreamweaver. On the Dreamweaver Welcome screen, click the More folder. Create a new document as a blank template, HTML template, with no layout and DocType HTML5.

3. Save the new template in the Templates folder in the Apply root folder. Name the template `apply2_template.dwt`.

4. Insert a new div tag and name the class `container`.

5. Create a new CSS rule and specify that the rule definition will be defined in a new style sheet file. Name the style sheet file `apply2.css` and save it in a new folder named `CSS` in the root folder for the Apply site.

6. Define the CSS rule for the container class according to the settings provided in Table 2–2. Apply and accept your changes when you are finished.

7. Click after the placeholder text in the container and then press the ENTER key to insert a blank line.

8. Insert a div tag within the container. Name the class `header`. Refer to Table 2–2 to define the new CSS rule for the header in Apply2.css. Apply and accept your changes.

9. Replace text within the header div tag with `My Template Title`.

10. Insert a div tag below the header div tag but within the container div tag. Name the class `content`. Refer to Table 2–2 to define the new CSS rule for the content in apply2.css. Apply and accept your changes.

11. Delete the text within the content div tag and insert an editable region. Name the new editable region `Insert content here`.

12. Insert a div tag below the content div tag but within the container div tag. Name the class `footer`. Refer to Table 2–2 to define the new CSS rule for the footer in apply2.css. Apply and accept your changes.

13. Replace the text within the footer div tag with your name. Delete the placeholder text for the container region, and then press the BACKSPACE key to move the header to the top of the container.

14. Title the document `Apply2_Template`.

15. Save your changes and then view your document using Live view. Compare your document to Figure 2–68. Make any necessary changes and then save your changes.

16. Submit the document in the format specified by your instructor.

Table 2–2 CSS Rule Definitions for apply2_template

CSS Rule Definition for .container in apply2.css

Category	Property	Value
Box	Width	1000px
	Right Margin	auto
	Left Margin	auto

CSS Rule Definition for .header in apply2.css

Category	Property	Value
Type	Font-family	Verdana, Geneva, sans-serif
	Font-size	18pt
	Font-weight	bold
Background	Background-color	#9CC
Box	Width	1000px
	Height	75px

CSS Rule Definition for .content in apply2.css

Category	Property	Value
Type	Font-family	Arial, Helvetica, sans-serif
Box	Width	1000px
	Height	400px
Border	Style	solid, same for all
	Width	thin, same for all
	Color	#000, same for all

CSS Rule Definition for .footer in apply2.css

Category	Property	Value
Type	Font-family	Times New Roman, Times, serif
	Font-size	10pt
Box	Width	1000px

Extend Your Knowledge

Extend the skills you learned in this chapter and experiment with new skills. You may need to use Help to complete the assignment.

Attaching an External Style Sheet to a Web Page

Note: To complete this assignment, you will be required to use the Data Files for Students. Visit www.cengage.com/ct/studentdownload for detailed instructions or contact your instructor for information about accessing the required files.

Instructions: A volunteer service organization wants to create a Web site using style sheets. You are creating a Web page for the organization that explains the difference between internal and external style sheets. Apply styles to a page by attaching an external style sheet to an existing Web page. The completed Web page is shown in Figure 2–69.

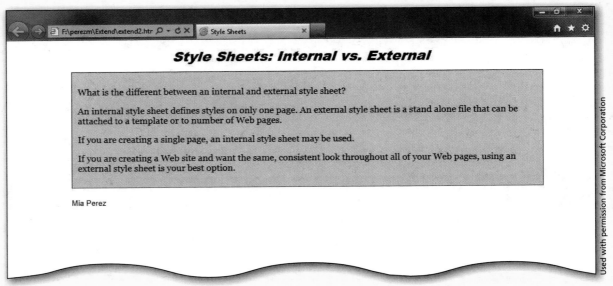

Figure 2–69

Perform the following tasks:

1. Use Windows Explorer to copy the CSS folder and the extend2.html file from the Chapter 02\Extend folder into the *your last name and first initial*\Extend folder (the folder named perezm\Extend, for example, which you created in Chapter 1).

2. Start Dreamweaver and open extend2.html.

3. On the CSS Styles panel, click the Attach Style Sheet button to display the Attach External Style Sheet dialog box. (*Hint*: Point to the buttons in the lower-right part of the CSS Styles panel to find the Attach Style Sheet button.) Click the Browse button in the Attach External Style Sheet dialog box, and then navigate to find and then select the extend2.css file located in the CSS folder in the Extend root folder. Add the CSS file as a link, and then accept your changes.

4. Replace the text, Your name here, with your name.

5. Title the document `Style Sheets`.

6. Save your changes and then view your document in your browser. Compare your document to Figure 2–69. Make any necessary changes and then save your changes.

7. Submit the document in the format specified by your instructor.

Make It Right

Analyze a Web page and correct all errors and/or improve the design.

Adding Div Tags and CSS Rule Definitions to a Web Page

Note: To complete this assignment, you will be required to use the Data Files for Students. Visit www.cengage.com/ct/studentdownload for detailed instructions or contact your instructor for information about accessing the required files.

Instructions: A bird-watching club is creating a Web site and wants to know the benefits of using CSS rules. You will create a Web page that lists these benefits. You also will create new div tags and add CSS rule definitions within an existing Web page. The CSS rule definitions for the Web page are provided in Table 2–3. The completed Web page is shown in Figure 2–70.

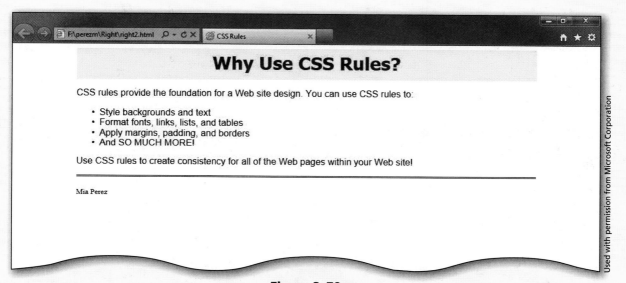

Figure 2–70

Perform the following tasks:

1.   Use Windows Explorer to copy the right2.html file from the Chapter 02\Right folder into the *your last name and first initial*\Right folder (the folder named perezm\Right, for example, which you created in Chapter 1).

2.   Open right2.html in your browser to view it and note that it currently has no design and no styles applied. Close your browser.

3.   Start Dreamweaver and open right2.html.

4.   Select all of the text on the page.

5.   Insert a new div tag and name the class `container`. Leave the insert type as the default 'Wrap around selection'.

6.   Refer to Table 2–3 to define the new CSS rule for the class container. The Rule Definition will be for this document only. Apply and accept your changes.

7.   Select the text, Why Use CSS Rules?

Continued >

Make It Right *continued*

Table 2–3 CSS Rule Definitions for right2.html

CSS Rule Definition for .container

Category	Property	Value
Box	Width	800px
	Right Margin	auto
	Left Margin	auto

CSS Rule Definition for .header

Category	Property	Value
Type	Font-family	Tahoma, Geneva, sans-serif
	Font-size	24pt
	Font-weight	bold
	Color	#030
Background	Background-color	#FFC
Block	Text-align	center
Box	Width	800px
	Height	50px
	Top Padding	5px

CSS Rule Definition for .content

Category	Property	Value
Type	Font-family	Arial, Helvetica, sans-serif
	Font-size	12pt
Box	Width	800px
Border	Bottom Style	double
	Bottom Width	medium
	Bottom Color	#000

CSS Rule Definition for .footer

Category	Property	Value
Type	Font-size	10pt
Box	Width	800px
	Top Margin	20px

8. Insert a new div tag and name the class `header`. Leave the insert type as the default 'Wrap around selection'.

9. Refer to Table 2–3 to define the new CSS rule for the class header in this document only. Apply and accept your changes.

10. Select the text below Why Use CSS Rules? beginning with "CSS rules provide" and ending with "within your Web site!"

11. Insert a new div tag and name the class `content`. Leave the insert type as the default 'Wrap around selection'.

12. Refer to Table 2–3 to define the new CSS rule for the class content in this document only. Apply and accept your changes.

13. Select the text, Your name here.

14. Insert a new div tag and name the class `footer`. Leave the insert type as the default 'Wrap around selection'.

15. Refer to Table 2–3 to define the new CSS rule for the class footer in this document only. Apply and accept your changes.

16. Replace the text, Your name here., with your name.

17. Title the document `CSS Rules`.

18. Save your changes and then view the Web page in your browser. Compare your page to Figure 2–70. Make any necessary changes and then save your changes.

19. Submit the document in the format specified by your instructor.

In the Lab

Design and/or create a Web document using the guidelines, concepts, and skills presented in this chapter. Labs are listed in order of increasing difficulty.

Lab 1: Designing a New Template for the Healthy Lifestyle Web Site

Note: To complete this assignment, you will be required to use the Data Files for Students. Visit www.cengage.com/ct/studentdownload for detailed instructions or contact your instructor for information about accessing the required files.

Problem: In an effort to reduce health insurance costs, your company wants to provide resources for living a healthy lifestyle. You have been asked to create an internal Web site for your company with information about how to live a healthy lifestyle. This Web site will be used as a resource by employees at your company. You thoughtfully have planned the design of the Web site and now are ready to create a template for the site.

Define a new Web site and create a new HTML5 template. Use div tags and CSS rules in your template design. The template in Live view is shown in Figure 2–71, and the final Web page is shown in Figure 2–72. The CSS rule definitions for the template are provided in Table 2–4.

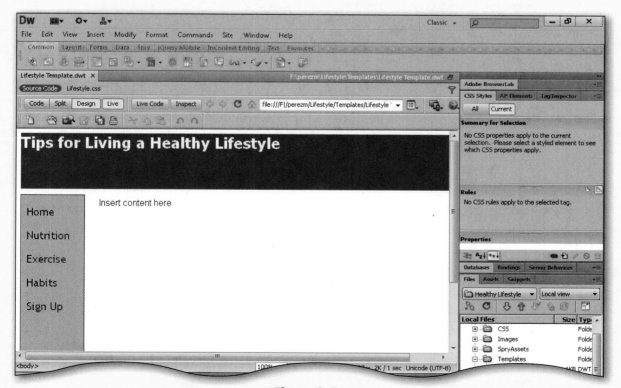

Figure 2–71

Continued >

In the Lab *continued*

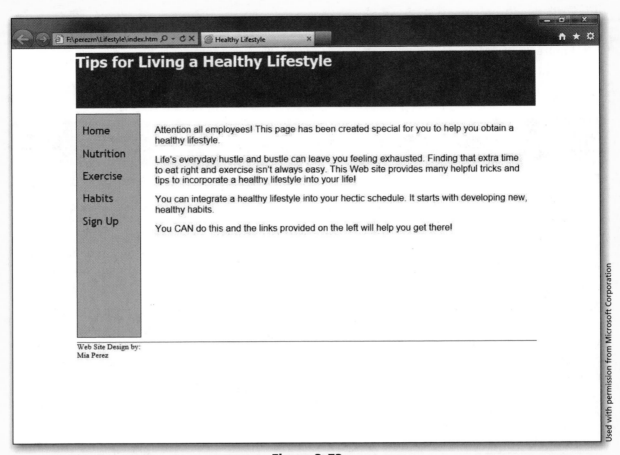

Figure 2–72

Perform the following tasks:

1. Start Dreamweaver. Click Dreamweaver Site in the Create New list of the Welcome screen to display the Site Setup dialog box. Type `Healthy Lifestyle` in the Site name text box.

2. Click the 'Browse for folder' icon to display the Choose Root Folder dialog box. Create a new subfolder in the *your last name and first initial* folder. Type `Lifestyle` as the folder name, select the folder, and then save the site.

3. On the Dreamweaver Welcome screen, click More in the Create New list. In the New Document dialog box, select Blank Template, Template Type: HTML template, Layout: <none>. Set the DocType to HTML5 and click the Create button. Save the new template using `Lifestyle Template` as the file name.

4. Use `Healthy Lifestyle` as the page title in the Title text box.

5. Insert a new div tag and name the class `container`.

6. Create a new CSS rule with a new style sheet file as the location for the rule definition. Name the style sheet file `Lifestyle.css`. Use the Create New Folder button in the Save Style Sheet File As dialog box to create a new folder and name it `CSS`. Save Lifestyle.css within the CSS folder.

7. Refer to Table 2–4 to define the CSS rule for the container. Apply and accept your changes.

8. Insert a blank line after the placeholder text in the container div tag.

9. Insert a div tag within the container. Name the class `header`.

Table 2–4 CSS Rule Definitions for Tips for Living a Healthy Lifestyle

CSS Rule Definition for .container in Lifestyle.css

Category	Property	Value
Box	Width	800px
	Right Margin	auto
	Left Margin	auto

CSS Rule Definition for .header in Lifestyle.css

Category	Property	Value
Type	Font-family	Tahoma, Geneva, sans-serif
	Font-size	20pt
	Font-weight	bold
	Color	#FFF
Background	Background-color	#039
Box	Width	800px
	Height	100px
	Bottom Margin	10px

CSS Rule Definition for .navigation in Lifestyle.css

Type	Font-family	Trebuchet MS, Arial, Helvetica, sans-serif
	Font-size	14pt
	Color	#333
Background	Background-color	#9CF
Box	Width	100px
	Height	400px
	Float	left
	Left Padding	10px
	Right Margin	10px
Border	Style	solid, same for all
	Width	thin, same for all
	Color	#003, same for all

CSS Rule Definition for .content in Lifestyle.css

Type	Font-family	Arial, Helvetica, sans-serif
	Font-size	12pt
Box	Width	650px
	Height	400px
	Float	left
	Padding	5px, same for all
	Left Margin	10px

CSS Rule Definition for .footer in Lifestyle.css

Type	Font-family	Times New Roman, Times, serif
	Font-size	10pt
Box	Width	800px
	Float	left
Border	Style	solid, same for all
	Width	thin, same for all
	Color	#333, same for all

Continued >

In the Lab *continued*

10. Create a new CSS rule. Refer to Table 2–4 to define the CSS rule for the header in Lifestyle. css. Apply and accept your changes.

11. Replace the text within the header div tag with `Tips for Living a Healthy Lifestyle`.

12. Insert a div tag after the header div tag but within the container div tag. Name the class `navigation`.

13. Create a new CSS rule. Refer to Table 2–4 to define the CSS rule for the navigation in Lifestyle.css. Apply and accept your changes.

14. Replace the text within the navigation div tag with the following list, pressing ENTER at the end of each line:

```
Home
Nutrition
Exercise
Habits
Sign Up
```

---

15. Insert a div tag to the right of the navigation div tag but within the container div tag. Name the class `content`.

16. Create a new CSS rule. Refer to Table 2–4 to define the CSS rule for the content in Lifestyle. css. Apply and accept your changes.

17. Delete the text within the content div tag and insert an editable region. Name the new editable region `Insert content here`.

18. Insert a div tag to the right of the content div tag but within the container div tag. Name the class `footer`.

19. Create a new CSS rule. Refer to Table 2–4 to define the CSS rule for the footer in Lifestyle.css. Apply and accept your changes.

20. Replace the text within the footer div tag with `Web Site Design by:`, press the SHIFT+ENTER keys, and then type your first and last names.

21. Delete the placeholder text for the container region, and then press the BACKSPACE key to move the header to the top of the container.

22. Save your changes and then view your template using Live view. Compare your template to Figure 2–71. Make any necessary changes and save your changes. Close the template.

23. Use the New Document dialog box to create a new Web page using the Lifestyle Template. Save the new page using `index` as the file name in the root folder of the Lifestyle site.

24. Replace the text, Insert content here, with text from the Lab1_Content.txt data file.

25. Save your changes and then view the Web page in your browser. Compare your page to Figure 2–72. Make any necessary changes and then save your changes.

26. Submit the documents in the format specified by your instructor.

In the Lab

Lab 2: Designing a New Template for Designs by Dolores

Note: To complete this assignment, you will be required to use the Data Files for Students. Visit www.cengage.com/ct/studentdownload for detailed instructions or contact your instructor for information about accessing the required files.

Problem: You are working as an intern for a Web site design company, Designs by Dolores. The owner, Dolores, is impressed with your Web site design knowledge and asks you to redesign her current site. You are excited about the opportunity to design your first Web site and begin by creating a template for the site.

Define a new Web site and create a new HTML5 template. Use div tags and CSS rules in your template design. The template in Live view is shown in Figure 2–73, and the final Web page is shown in Figure 2–74. The CSS rule definitions for the template are provided in Table 2–5.

Figure 2–73

Continued >

In the Lab *continued*

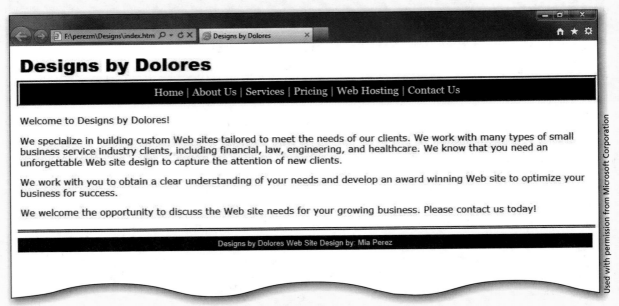

Figure 2–74

Perform the following tasks:

1. Start Dreamweaver. Click Dreamweaver Site in the Create New list to display the Site Setup dialog box. Type `Designs by Dolores` in the Site name text box.

2. Click the 'Browse for folder' icon to display the Choose Root Folder dialog box. Create a new subfolder in the *your last name and first initial* folder. Use `Designs` as the folder name, and then save the folder and the site.

3. On the Dreamweaver Welcome screen, click More in the Create New list. Create a blank HTML5 template with no layout. Set the DocType to HTML5. Save the new template as `Designs_Template` in the Designs by Dolores site.

4. Use `Designs by Dolores` as the page title.

5. Insert a new div tag and name the class `container`.

6. Create a new CSS rule with a new style sheet file as the rule definition. Name the style sheet file `Designs.css`. Save Designs.css in a new folder named `CSS`.

7. Refer to Table 2–5 for the container CSS rule definition.

8. Insert a blank line after the placeholder text in the container div tag.

9. Insert a div tag within the container. Name the class `header`.

10. Create a new CSS rule. Refer to Table 2–5 for the header CSS rule definition.

11. Replace the text within the header div tag with `Designs by Dolores`.

12. Insert a div tag below the header div tag but within the container div tag. Name the class `navigation`.

13. Create a new CSS rule. Refer to Table 2–5 for the navigation CSS rule definition.

14. Replace the text within the navigation div tag with `Home | About Us | Services | Pricing | Web Hosting | Contact Us.`

15. Insert a div tag below the navigation div tag but within the container div tag. Name the class `content`.

Table 2–5 CSS Rule Definitions for Designs by Dolores

CSS Rule Definition for .container in Designs.css

Category	Property	Value
Box	Width	1000px
	Right Margin	Auto
	Left Margin	Auto

CSS Rule Definition for .header in Designs.css

Category	Property	Value
Type	Font-family	Arial Black, Gadget, sans-serif
	Font-size	24pt
	Color	#303
Box	Width	1000px
	Top Padding	5px
	Bottom Padding	5px
	Left Padding	5px

CSS Rule Definition for .navigation in Designs.css

Category	Property	Value
Type	Font-family	Georgia, Times New Roman, Times, serif
	Font-size	14pt
	Color	#FFF
Background	Background-color	#303
Block	Text-align	center
Box	Width	1000px
	Top Padding	8px
	Bottom Padding	8px
Border	Style	groove, same for all
	Width	thick, same for all
	Color	#FFF, same for all

CSS Rule Definition for .content in Designs.css

Category	Property	Value
Type	Font-family	Verdana, Geneva, sans-serif
	Font-size	12pt
Box	Width	1000px
	Bottom Padding	5px
	Left Padding	5px
	Top Margin	10px
	Bottom Margin	10px
Border	Bottom Style	double
	Bottom Width	thick
	Bottom Color	#303

CSS Rule Definition for .footer in Designs.css

Category	Property	Value
Type	Font-family	Arial, Helvetica, sans-serif
	Font-size	10pt
	Color	#FFF
Background	Background-color	#333
Block	Text-align	center
Box	Width	1000px
	Top Padding	5px
	Bottom Padding	5px

Continued >

In the Lab *continued*

16. Create a new CSS rule. Refer to Table 2–5 for the content CSS rule definition.

17. Delete the text within the content div tag and insert an editable region. Name the new editable region `Insert content here`.

18. Insert a div tag below the content div tag but within the container div tag. Name the class `footer`.

19. Create a new CSS rule. Refer to Table 2–5 for the footer CSS rule definition.

20. Replace the text within the footer div tag with `Designs by Dolores Web Site Design by:` and then type your first and last names.

21. Delete the placeholder text for the container region, and then press the BACKSPACE key to move the header to the top of the container.

22. Save your changes and then view your template using Live view. Compare your template to Figure 2–73. Make and save any necessary changes, and then close the template.

23. Create a new Web page using the Designs Template. Save the new page using `index` as the file name in the root folder for the Designs site.

24. Replace the text, Insert content here, with text from the Lab2_Content.txt data file.

25. Save your changes and then view the Web page in your browser. Compare your page to Figure 2–74. Make any necessary changes and then save them.

26. Submit the documents in the format specified by your instructor.

In the Lab

Lab 3: Designing a New Template for Justin's Lawn Care Service

Note: To complete this assignment, you will be required to use the Data Files for Students. Visit www.cengage.com/ct/studentdownload for detailed instructions or contact your instructor for information about accessing the required files.

Problem: You have been hired to create a Web site for a new lawn care company, Justin's Lawn Care Service. You thoughtfully have planned the design of the Web site and now are ready to create a template for the site. You have met with Justin to discuss his needs for the Web site and are ready to start developing the site.

Define a new Web site and create a new HTML5 template. Use div tags and CSS rules in your template design. The template is shown in Figure 2–75, and the final Web page is shown in Figure 2–76. The CSS rule definitions for the template are provided in Table 2–6.

Figure 2–75

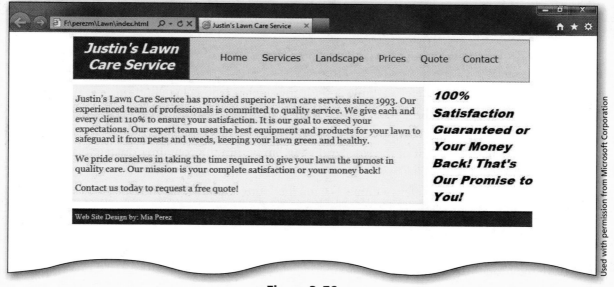

Figure 2–76

Perform the following tasks:

1. Start Dreamweaver. Use the Welcome screen to create a new site. Type `Justin's Lawn Care Service` as the site name.

2. Create a new subfolder named `Lawn` in the *your last name and first initial* folder, and then save the site.

Continued >

In the Lab *continued*

3. Create a blank HTML5 template with no layout. Save the new template as `Lawn_Template`.

4. Use `Justin's Lawn Care Service` as the page title.

5. Insert a new div tag and name the class `container`.

6. Create a new CSS rule with a new style sheet file named `Lawn.css`. Save Lawn.css in a new folder named `css`.

7. Refer to Table 2–6 for the container CSS rule definition.

8. Insert a blank line after the placeholder text in the container div tag.

9. Insert a div tag within the container. Name the class `header`.

10. Create a new CSS rule. Refer to Table 2–6 for the header CSS rule definition.

11. Replace the text within the header div tag with `Justin's Lawn Care Service`.

12. Insert a div tag to the right of the header div tag but within the container div tag. Name the class `navigation`.

13. Create a new CSS rule. Refer to Table 2–6 for the navigation CSS rule definition.

14. Replace the text within the navigation div tag with `Home Services Landscape Prices Quote Contact`.

15. Insert a div tag to the right of the navigation div tag but within the container div tag. Name the class `content`.

16. Create a new CSS rule. Refer to Table 2–6 for the content CSS rule definition.

17. Delete the text within the content div tag and insert an editable region. Name the new editable region `Insert content here`.

18. Insert a div tag to the right of the content div tag but within the container div tag. Name the class `sidebar`.

19. Create a new CSS rule. Refer to Table 2–6 for the sidebar CSS rule definition.

20. Replace the text within the sidebar div tag with `100% Satisfaction Guaranteed or Your Money Back! That's Our Promise to You!`.

21. Insert a div tag to the right of the sidebar div tag but within the container div tag. Name the class `footer`.

22. Create a new CSS rule. Refer to Table 2–6 for the footer CSS rule definition.

23. Replace the text within the footer div tag with `Web Site Design by:` and then type your first and last names.

24. Delete the placeholder text for the container region, and then press the BACKSPACE key to move the header to the top of the container.

25. Save your changes and then view the template using the Live view. Compare your template to Figure 2–75. Make and save any necessary changes, and then close the template.

26. Create a new Web page named `index` using the Lawn Template.

27. Replace the text, Insert content here, with text from the Lab3_content.txt data file.

28. Save your changes and then view the Web page in your browser. Compare your page to Figure 2–76. Make any necessary changes and then save your changes.

29. Submit the documents in the format specified by your instructor.

Table 2–6 CSS Rule Definitions for Justin's Lawn Care Service

CSS Rule Definition for .container in Lawn.css

Category	Property	Value
Box	Width	800px
	Right Margin	Auto
	Left Margin	Auto

CSS Rule Definition for .header in Lawn.css

Category	Property	Value
Type	Font-family	Tahoma, Geneva, sans-serif
	Font-size	18pt
	Font-weight	bold
	Font-style	italic
	Color	#FFF
Background	Background-color	#060
Block	Text-align	center
Box	Width	200px
	Float	left
	Height	70px
	Top Padding	5px
Border	Style	solid, same for all
	Width	thin, same for all
	Color	#960, same for all

CSS Rule Definition for .navigation in Lawn.css

Category	Property	Value
Type	Font-family	Verdana, Geneva, sans-serif
	Font-size	12pt
	Color	#030
Background	Background-color	#CFC
Block	Word-spacing	15pt
	Text-align	center
Box	Width	590px
	Float	left
	Height	50px
	Top Padding	25px
Border	Style	solid, same for all
	Width	thin, same for all
	Color	#960, same for all

CSS Rule Definition for .content in Lawn.css

Category	Property	Value
Type	Font-family	Georgia, Times New Roman, Times, serif
	Font-size	12pt
	Color	#360

Continued >

STUDENT ASSIGNMENTS

In the Lab *continued*

Table 2–6 CSS Rule Definitions for Justin's Lawn Care Service *(continued)*		
CSS Rule Definition for .content in Lawn.css *(continued)*		
Background	Background-color	#FFC
Box	Width	600px
	Float	left
	Right Padding	5px
	Left Padding	5px
	Top Margin	10px
	Right Margin	10px
	Bottom Margin	10px
CSS Rule Definition for .sidebar in Lawn.css		
Type	Font-family	Arial Black, Gadget, sans-serif
	Font-size	16pt
	Font-style	italic
	Color	#FFF
Box	Width	175px
	Float	right
	Top Margin	10px
	Bottom Margin	10px
CSS Rule Definition for .footer in Lawn.css		
Type	Font-family	Times New Roman, Times, serif
	Font-size	10pt
	Color	#FFF
Background	Background-color	#060
Box	Width	795px
	Float	left
	Top Padding	5px
	Bottom Padding	5px
	Left Padding	5px

Cases and Places

Apply your creative thinking and problem solving skills to design and implement a solution.

1: Creating a Web Site Template for Moving Tips

Personal

You recently moved out of your parents' home and, after realizing how much preparation is involved, you have decided to create a Web site with helpful tips and information about the moving process. Define a new local site in the *your last name and first initial* folder and name it

Moving Venture. Name the new subfolder Move. Create and save a new blank HTML template, layout none, and DocType HTML5. Name the file Move Template. Use a div tag to create a class container, and then insert the following class div tags within the container: header, navigation, content, and footer. Create a new CSS rule for each div tag and use a new style sheet file as the rule definition. Name the style sheet file move.css and save it to Removable Disk (F:)*your last name and first initial*\Move\CSS. The container box width should be between 800px and 1000px. Your CSS rule definitions for the other div tags should include a variety of category properties, such as font-family, font-weight, font-size, color, text-align, background, box width and height, and border style. Include a title in the header div tag. Make the navigation a left, vertical sidebar and include Home, Budget, Rentals, Tips, and Contact within the navigation bar. Include an editable region within the content div tag. Include your name in the footer. Title your document Moving Venture. Save the template. Create a new home page for the Web site using the template. Name the home page index. html. In the editable region, include a welcome paragraph that provides a mission statement and summary regarding the Web site's purpose. Submit the document in the format specified by your instructor.

2: Creating a Web Site Template for Student Campus Resources

Academic

You are a volunteer at your college campus library. The library provides print materials regarding various student activities, committees, and campus events. In an effort to reduce printing costs, the library has decided to develop a Web site with this information rather than printing numerous paper copies. You have been asked to design the Web site. Define a new local site in the *your last name and first initial* folder and name it Student Campus Resources. Name the new subfolder Campus. Create and save a new blank HTML template, layout none, and DocType HTML5. Name the file Campus Template. Use a div tag to create a class container, and then insert the following class div tags within the container: header, navigation, content, and footer. Create a new CSS rule for each div tag and use a new style sheet file as the rule definition. Name the style sheet file campus.css and save it to Removable Disk (F:)*your last name and first initial*\Campus\CSS. The container box width should be between 800px and 1000px. Your CSS rule definitions for the other div tags should include a variety of category properties, such as font-family, font-weight, font-size, color, text-align, background, box width and height, and border style. Include the text Student Campus Resources in the header div tag. Make the navigation horizontal, placed below the header, and include Home, Activities, Committees, Events, and Contact within the navigation bar. Include an editable region within the content div tag. Include your name in the footer. Title your document Student Campus Resources. Save the template. Create a new home page for the Web site using the template. Name the home page index.html. In the editable region, include a welcome paragraph that provides a mission statement and summary regarding the Web site purpose. Submit the document in the format specified by your instructor.

3: Creating a Web Site Template for French Villa Roast Café

Professional

You have been hired to design and develop a Web site for a local coffee shop, French Villa Roast Café. Define a new local site in the *your last name and first initial* folder and name it French Villa Roast Cafe. Name the new subfolder Cafe. Create and save a new blank HTML template, layout none, and DocType HTML5. Name the file Cafe Template. Use a div tag to create a class container, and then insert the following class div tags within the container: header, navigation, content, and footer. Create a new CSS rule for each div tag and use a new style sheet file as the rule definition. Name the style sheet file cafe.css and save it to Removable Disk (F:)*your last name and first initial*\Cafe\CSS. The container box width should be between 800px and 1000px. Your CSS

Continued >

Cases and Places *continued*

rule definitions for the other div tags should include a variety of category properties, such as font-family, font-weight, font-size, color, text-align, background, box width and height, and border style. Include the text, French Villa Roast Cafe, in the header div tag. Make the navigation horizontal, placed to the right of the header, and include Home, About, Menu, Rewards, and Contact within the navigation bar. Include an editable region within the content div tag. Include your name in the footer. Title your document French Villa Roast Cafe. Save the template. Create a new home page for the Web site using the template. Name the home page index.html. In the editable region, include a welcome paragraph that provides a mission statement and summary regarding the Web site purpose. Submit the document in the format specified by your instructor.

3 Adding Graphics and Links

Objectives

You will have mastered the material in this chapter when you can:

- Modify a Dreamweaver template
- Edit a CSS rule
- Add graphics to a template
- Describe image file formats
- Insert images on a Web page
- Describe Dreamweaver's image accessibility features
- Create a Facebook and Twitter presence on the site
- Add images to an HTML page

- Describe the different types of links
- Add a relative link to a template
- Add an absolute link to a template
- Create an e-mail link
- Format a rollover link
- Add a CSS rule to an existing style sheet
- Add an image placeholder and replace it with an image

3 | Adding Graphics and Links

Introduction

A Web page that captures the attention of visitors includes appealing images and easy-to-follow navigation links to other pages within the site. After establishing the initial layout of a site with style sheets, you can add content, including images and links to other pages. The content is the information provided in the Web site, and it should be engaging, relevant, and appropriate to the audience. Some people in the audience may need assistance viewing the site if they have limited vision or other visual impairments, so accessibility issues also should be addressed when developing the site.

By captivating your audience with graphics, you motivate each user to follow the navigation links and investigate the message of your business or topic on your Web pages. A well-designed site includes images that convey the professionalism and focus of the site. As you select each image for a site, remember that a picture truly is worth a thousand words.

Project — Promotional Images

The images displayed on the site for The Gallery Portrait and Family Photography and shown in Figure 3–1 not only are crucial to the design of the site, but also convey the studio's artistic style of photography. Besides increasing the appeal of the Web pages, the images market the Gallery as a business, so they serve as promotion images. Chapter 3 uses Dreamweaver to add pages to the Gallery site and then enhance those pages by including promotion images. The Gallery owners already market the Gallery online through their pages on the Facebook and Twitter social networking sites. Adding Facebook and Twitter image links on the Gallery's Web pages increases customer awareness and brand loyalty.

(a) Home Page

(b) Services Page

(c) Portfolio Page

(d) Pricing Page

(e) Session Page

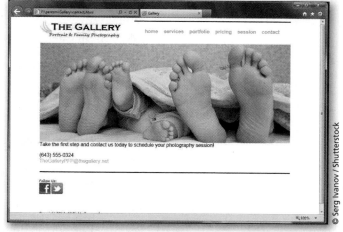

(f) Contact Page

Figure 3–1

Overview

As you read this chapter, you will learn how to create the Web page project shown in Figure 3–1 on the previous page by performing these general tasks:

- Modify a template.
- Add images to the site.
- Add pages to the site.
- Connect to social networks.
- Add relative, absolute, and e-mail links.
- Format links.
- Add a new CSS rule to an existing style sheet.
- Add an image placeholder.
- Replace an image placeholder.

Plan Ahead

General Project Guidelines

As you design any Web site, it is vital to consider several factors including the aesthetics of the graphics, the quality of the content, and the ease of the site's navigation. Web sites typically have a home page or an index page, but that does not necessarily mean that all visitors use it to enter the Web site. Generally, with most Web sites, the visitor can enter the site at any point that has a Web page address. This means each page requires links visitors can use to navigate to the other pages. As you modify the home page and add the pages shown in Figure 3–1 on the previous page, you should follow these general guidelines:

1. **Prepare images.** Select your images carefully to make sure they convey the look and feel of your site adequately. Each image placed on the Web must comply with copyright rules. Acquire and then organize your images within the Assets panel. Determine which image goes with which Web page.

2. **Consider accessibility.** Consider how people with accessibility concerns such as visual impairments can use the site and how the site can address these accessibility issues.

3. **Understand the use of social networking sites.** Recognize the value of marketing your site by linking to social networking sites such as Facebook and Twitter.

4. **Identify the navigation of the site.** Consider how each page is linked to other pages within the site. Links also can connect to outside sites and e-mail.

More specific details about these guidelines are presented at appropriate points throughout the chapter. The chapter also identifies the actions performed and decisions made regarding these guidelines during the development of the pages within the site shown in Figure 3–1.

To Start Dreamweaver and Open the Gallery Site

Each time you start Dreamweaver, it opens to the last site displayed when you closed the program. The following steps start Dreamweaver and open the Gallery Web site.

1 Click the Start button on the Windows 7 taskbar to display the Start menu, and then type `Dreamweaver CS6` in the 'Search programs and files' box.

2 Click Adobe Dreamweaver CS6 in the list to start Dreamweaver.

3 If the Dreamweaver window is not maximized, click the Maximize button next to the Close button on the Application bar to maximize the window.

④ If the Gallery site is not displayed in the Files panel, click the Sites button on the Files panel toolbar and then click Gallery to display the files and folders in the Gallery site.

Modifying a Template

The Gallery Dreamweaver Template created in Chapter 1 uses <div> tags to form a number of locked regions and one editable region identified as the content. Recall that Web page designers can edit locked regions only inside the template itself. Editable regions are placeholders for content unique to each page created from the template. The template and other design documents can serve as the Web site **prototype**, a realistic representation of how the new Web site will look and function when it is fully developed. Prototypes can range from a wireframe layout drawing to a working model of the site before it undergoes final development. (A **wireframe** is a sketch that illustrates the arrangement of content on each Web page.) It is best to show a prototype to your customer and ask for his or her approval early in the design process because it is much easier to make changes during the design stages rather than in the final stages of site development.

For the Gallery site, the owners of the studio reviewed the prototype, which you created in Chapter 2. It displays a single photograph with a black background on each page. The Gallery owners want to place unique images on each page of the site to showcase more of the studio's fine photography. They also want to remove the black background and increase the amount of space provided for the images. To meet these objectives, you need to modify the template and insert a second editable region within the image <div> tag. After designing a Dreamweaver template, you can modify any portion of the template to provide more flexibility when updating the site.

BTW

Adobe Tools for Prototypes
You can use Adobe Fireworks or Photoshop to create prototypes and wireframes, especially if you plan to show these mock-ups to clients or others on your Web site development team.

To Open the Gallery Template

Before modifying the Gallery Template file, you must open it in Dreamweaver. The following steps start Dreamweaver and open the Gallery Template.

① Start Dreamweaver as you usually do, and then click Open on the Dreamweaver Welcome screen to display the Open dialog box. If necessary, navigate to the Gallery site on Removable Disk (F:).

② Double-click the Templates folder in the Open dialog box to display the contents of the Templates folder (Figure 3–2).

③ Double-click Gallery Template to display the template in the Document window.

Figure 3–2

To Modify a Dreamweaver Template by Editing a CSS Rule

To edit the CSS rules established in a style sheet or document, you use the CSS Styles panel. You can display the CSS Styles panel in two modes. In **All mode**, the All Rules pane lists the CSS rules defined in the current document and in any style sheets attached to the document. Select a rule to display the CSS properties for that rule in the Properties pane. In **Current mode**, the CSS Styles panel shows style information for the current selection in the document, including CSS properties and rules. In either mode, the bottom of the CSS Styles panel contains buttons that allow you to alter the CSS rules. The button with a pencil icon is called the Edit Rule button, which you use to open a dialog box for editing the styles in the current document or the external style sheet. The layout.css style sheet defines all the styles in the Gallery Template. After opening the Gallery Template and selecting the image CSS rule in layout.css, you can use the CSS Styles panel to edit the background color and box height of the image container to meet the Gallery owner's objectives. The following steps modify the existing template to change CSS rules for the Gallery Web site.

1

- If necessary, click the All button on the CSS Styles panel to display the list of rules defined in layout.css (Figure 3–3).

Q&A What are the rules listed below layout.css in the CSS Styles panel?

These are the rules you defined in Chapter 2 to design and lay out the template for the Gallery Web site.

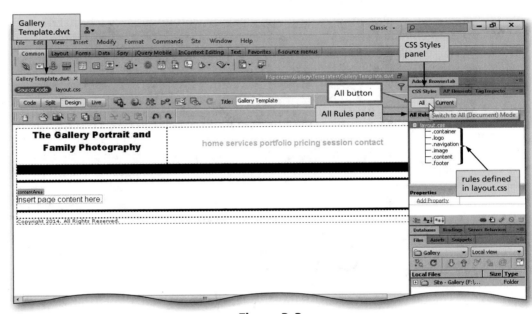

Figure 3–3

2

- Click .image in the All Rules pane to select the .image rule and display its properties in the Properties pane (Figure 3–4).

Q&A What part of the template does the .image rule format?

The .image rule determines the style of the image region, which is the area with the black background in Figure 3-4.

Figure 3–4

3

- Click the Edit Rule button on the CSS Styles panel to display the 'CSS Rule Definition for .image in layout.css' dialog box (Figure 3–5).

Figure 3–5

4

- If necessary, click Background in the Category list to display the Background options.

- Double-click the Background-color text box, delete #000, and then press the TAB key to remove the background color of the .image region (Figure 3–6).

Figure 3–6

- Click Box in the Category list to display the Box options.

- Click the Height text box and then type 325 to set the height of the image placeholder to 325 pixels (Figure 3–7).

- Click the Apply button in the 'CSS Rule Definition for .image in layout.css' dialog box to apply the CSS rules for .image in the layout.css file.

- Click the OK button in the 'CSS Rule Definition for .image in layout.css' dialog box to modify the CSS rules for .image.

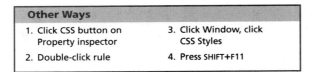

Figure 3–7

Other Ways	
1. Click CSS button on Property inspector	3. Click Window, click CSS Styles
2. Double-click rule	4. Press SHIFT+F11

To Modify a Dreamweaver Template by Adding an Editable Region

When you defined the regions of the Gallery Template in Chapter 2, Dreamweaver inserted them as noneditable, or locked, regions by default. You changed the content <div> container to an editable region so that each page in the Gallery site could include different text. Now that the Gallery owners want to display different images on each page as well, you need to define the image <div> container in the template as an editable region. In a document, Dreamweaver outlines each editable region in blue and displays a small blue tab identifying the region's name. You can determine which regions are not editable in a document by moving the pointer around the Document window. The pointer changes to a "not" symbol (a circle with a line through it) when you point to a locked region. The pointer does not change when you are working in a template because you can modify locked regions in templates. The following steps modify the template to add an editable image region for the Gallery Web site.

- Select the text, Content for class "image" Goes Here, in the Gallery Template, and then press the DELETE key to delete the text.

- Click Insert on the Application bar to display the Insert menu, and then point to Template Objects to display the Template Objects submenu (Figure 3–8).

Figure 3–8

 2

- Click Editable Region on the Template Objects submenu to display the New Editable Region dialog box.

- If necessary, select the text in the Name text box and then type `imageArea` to name the new editable region (Figure 3–9).

Figure 3–9

3

- Click the OK button in the New Editable Region dialog box to add the imageArea editable region to the template.

- Click the Save All button on the Standard toolbar to save the modified template and display the Update Template Files dialog box (Figure 3–10).

Q&A

What is the purpose of the Update Template Files dialog box?

When you modify and then save a template, Dreamweaver displays the Update Template Files dialog box so you also can update all of the documents attached to the template. In this case, when you modify the Gallery Template, you can update the index.html document with the same changes.

Figure 3–10

4

• Click the Update button to add the imageArea editable region to index.html and display the Update Pages dialog box (Figure 3–11).

5

• Click the Close button in the Update Pages dialog box to update the template and index.html.

Figure 3–11

Adding Graphics to the Web Site

The graphics that you select for a Web site have the power to create an emotional response in your audience. The best way to create interest in your Web site is to use images that complement the core message of the Web site. Images serve various purposes. For example, you can use photos to illustrate or support content, buttons to provide navigation, logos to identify a company or product, bullets to draw attention to text, mastheads to serve as title graphics, and drawings to add interest to a Web page background. The Gallery site should display photographs that represent the artistic family photography the studio provides. To include these photos in the Gallery site, you first must add the image files to the site's file structure.

Plan Ahead

Prepare images
Before you add images to a Web site, you must determine which images best support the site's mission to attract more traffic to your site. A personal Web site may include images of your friends, family members, or vacation settings taken with a digital camera. Business sites typically feature pictures of the products being sold. Keep the following guidelines in mind as you prepare images for a site:

• **Acquire the images.** To create your own images, you can take photos with a digital camera and store them in the JPEG format, use a scanner to scan your drawings and photos, or use a graphics editor such as Adobe Photoshop to create images. You also can download images from public domain Web sites, use clip art, or purchase images from stock photo collections. Be sure you have permission to reproduce the images you acquire from Web sites unless the images are clearly marked as being in the public domain.

• **Choose the right format.** Use JPEG files for photographic images and complicated graphics that contain color gradients and shadowing. Use GIF files for basic graphics, especially when you want to take advantage of transparency. You also can use PNG files for basic graphics, but not for photos.

(continued)

Prepare images (*continued*)

* **Keep the image file size small.** Use high-resolution images with an appropriate file size for faster loading. Because high-resolution image files are larger, and therefore take longer to download to a browser, use a graphics editor such as Adobe Photoshop to compress image files and reduce their file size without affecting quality. Background images in particular should have a small file size because they often appear on every page.

* **Check the dimensions.** Determine the dimensions of an image file in pixels. You can reduce the dimensions on the Web page by changing the width and height or by cropping the image. Enlarging images generally produces poor results.

As you select images, be aware of copyright laws. **Copyright** is the legal protection extended to the owners of original published and unpublished images and intellectual works. If you have not created the image yourself, you must obtain written authorization to use the image you intend to publish on your Web site unless the image is considered copyright-free. If you purchase images from stock photo collections, which are available at many Web sites, the rights to publish the images are included with your purchase. However, you should read the licensing agreement from each photo collection to determine under what conditions you can publish its images.

Understanding Image File Formats

Graphical images used on the Web fall into one of two broad categories: vector and bitmap. **Vector images** are composed of key points and paths that define shapes and coloring instructions, such as line and fill colors. A vector file contains a mathematical description of the image. The file describes the image to the computer, and the computer draws it. This type of image generally is associated with Adobe Flash, which is an animation program. One benefit of vector images is their small file size, particularly compared to the larger file sizes of bitmap images.

Bitmap images are the more common type of digital image file. A bitmap file maps, or plots, an image pixel by pixel. A **pixel**, or **picture element**, is the smallest point in a graphical image. Computer monitors display images by dividing the display screen into thousands (or millions) of pixels arranged in a **grid** of rows and columns. The pixels appear connected because they are so close together. This grid of pixels is a **bitmap**. The **bit-resolution** of an image is the number of bits used to represent each pixel. There are 8-bit images as well as 24- or 32-bit images, where each bit represents a pixel. An 8-bit image supports up to 256 colors, and a 24- or 32-bit image supports up to 16.7 million colors.

The three most common bitmap image file types that Web browsers support are JPEG, GIF, and PNG.

JPEG (.jpg) is an acronym for **Joint Photographic Experts Group**. JPEG files are the best format for photographic images because they can contain up to 16.7 million colors. **Progressive JPEG** is a new variation of the JPEG image format. This image format supports a gradually built display, which means the browser begins to build a low-resolution version of the full-sized JPEG image on the screen while the file is still downloading so visitors can view the image while the Web page downloads. Older browsers do not support progressive JPEG files.

GIF (.gif) is an acronym for **Graphics Interchange Format**. The GIF format uses 8-bit resolution, supports up to a maximum of 256 colors, and uses combinations of these 256 colors to simulate colors beyond that range. The GIF format is best for displaying images such as logos, icons, buttons, and other images with even colors and tones.

PNG (.png) stands for **Portable Network Graphics**. PNG, which is the native file format of Adobe Fireworks, is a GIF competitor and is used mostly for Web site images. All contemporary browsers support PNG files, though some older browsers do not support this format without a special plug-in.

When developing a Web site containing many pages, you should maintain a consistent, professional layout and design using images throughout all of the pages. The pages in a single site, for example, should use similar background colors or images, margins, and headings.

Adding Alt Text to Provide Accessibility

BTW

Alt Text and Screen Readers
People with visual impairments often use a screen reader to interact with Web pages. The screen reader recites the text provided as alt text to help users interpret the image.

People with visual impairments often use screen readers (speech synthesizers) that can read a text description aloud for each image and let users understand accompanying information about the images. Each image in a Web site should have **alternate text**, also called alt text, that assigns text to the image tag to describe the image. The **alt tag** is an HTML attribute that provides alternate text when nontextual elements, typically images, cannot be displayed. The alt text is considered an accessibility attribute because it provides access to everyone who visits your site. Alternate text always should describe the content of the image. For example, when the screen reader approaches a logo image, the alt tag text may be read as *Company image logo*.

Plan Ahead

Consider accessibility
After you select images for the site, consider what information the image is conveying as you create each alt tag (alternate text). The text should identify the same information that the image illustrates or communicates.

In addition to assisting people with visual impairments, alt tags can improve navigation when a graphics-intensive site is being viewed over a slow connection. Because the alt text appears before the page begins loading an image, site visitors can make navigation choices before graphics are fully rendered. Alt tags also determine how a search engine locates the content of your site. Search engines can only read text, so images with alt tags allow search engines to match the search description to the site's content, which may aid in search engine rankings. Alt tags are a required element for standards-based HTML coding.

To Copy Files into the Images Folder

Before adding an image to a site, you must add the image file to the file structure of the site. To complete this assignment, you will be required to use the Data Files for Students. Visit www.cengage.com/ct/student-download for detailed instructions or contact your instructor for information about accessing the required files. The following steps copy 12 files from the Data Files for Students to the Gallery site.

1

- If necessary, insert the drive containing your student data files into an available port. Use Windows Explorer to navigate to the storage location of the Data Files for Students.

- Double-click the Chapter 03 folder, and then double-click the Gallery folder to open the folders.

- Click the contact_image file, or the first file in the list, hold down the SHIFT key, and then click the twitter_image file, or the last file in the list, to select the images needed for the site (Figure 3–12).

Figure 3–12

2

- Right-click the selected files, click Copy on the context menu, and then navigate to the *your last name and first initial* folder on Removable Disk F: to prepare to copy the files.

- Double-click the Gallery folder, and then double-click the Images folder to open the Images folder.

- Right-click anywhere in the open window, and then click Paste on the context menu to copy the files into the Images folder. Verify that the folder now contains 12 images (Figure 3–13).

Figure 3–13

To Insert a Logo Image in the Template

Logos increase brand recognition and add visual appeal to any Web page. The Gallery's logo should appear in the upper-left corner of every page within the site to provide consistency to the layout. Instead of using a text logo, an image logo is available for the Gallery site. The following steps insert the Gallery logo into the Gallery Template.

1

- In Gallery Template.dwt, select the text, The Gallery Portrait and Family Photography, in the logo region and then press the DELETE key to delete the text.

- Click Insert on the Application bar to display the Insert menu (Figure 3–14).

Figure 3–14

2

- Click Image on the Insert menu to display the Select Image Source dialog box.

- Double-click the Images folder to display the image files available.

- Click gallery_logo to select the logo image (Figure 3–15).

Q&A

How long will this image take to load in a browser?

The Select Image Source dialog box lists the file size and approximate download time below the Image preview.

Figure 3–15

3

- Click the OK button in the Select Image Source dialog box to display the Image Tag Accessibility Attributes dialog box.

- In the Alternate text text box, type `Business logo` to add the alt tag necessary for accessibility (Figure 3–16).

Figure 3–16

4

- Click the OK button to display the Gallery logo image in the logo region (Figure 3–17).

Figure 3–17

Other Ways	
1. Drag image from Files panel or Assets panel	3. CTRL+ALT+I
2. Right-click image, click Insert	

Marketing a Site with Facebook and Twitter

A **social networking site** is an online community in which members share their interests, ideas, and files such as photos, music, and videos with other registered users. Some social networking sites are purely social, while others have a business focus.

Understand the use of social networking sites

Social networking sites offer a way to promote products and services over the Internet to a larger target audience. Before placing a link to a social networking site on your Web site, a Facebook page and Twitter presence must be established with professional, business-generating content. To establish a presence, join Facebook and Twitter, and then follow the directions on each Web site to post text, images, and links to showcase your organization.

Plan Ahead

Instead of advertising in a newspaper or magazine, many businesses target social networking sites, such as Facebook and Twitter, for their ads. **Facebook** is a social networking site that provides a platform to interact with customers and other businesses that are also members of Facebook. Visitors to a business-oriented Facebook page can engage with their favorite brands and receive product updates. Using Facebook, the Gallery site provides a more personalized, social experience. The Gallery owners have established the Facebook page shown in Figure 3–18.

Figure 3–18

Twitter is a social networking tool for posting very short updates, comments, or thoughts. If you want to receive posts, or tweets, from a Twitter member automatically, you can choose to become a follower of that member. Developing many followers is a goal of most business members. Using the Gallery's Twitter account, shown in Figure 3–19, the studio's owners can post information about special offers and photo packages, and links to the Gallery's Facebook page. Making a positive impression on your Twitter followers is invaluable when growing your business.

Figure 3–19

To Insert Social Networking Icons in the Template

Facebook and Twitter provide specific images for use as icons in other Web sites. Visitors to the Gallery Web site can click the Facebook icon to visit the Gallery's Facebook page, or they can click the Twitter icon to visit the Gallery's Twitter page. The following steps insert Facebook and Twitter icons in the footer of the Gallery Template.

1

- If necessary, scroll down in the Document window, and then click to the left of Copyright 2014 in the footer of the template to place the insertion point directly before the Copyright 2014 text.

- Type `Follow Us:` and then press the SHIFT+ENTER keys to add text to the footer (Figure 3–20).

Q&A What is the purpose of pressing the SHIFT+ENTER keys simultaneously?

Pressing the SHIFT+ENTER keys inserts a line break in the Web document. A line break starts a new line without adding blank space between the lines. Pressing the ENTER key creates a new paragraph. Browsers automatically add a blank line before and after a paragraph.

Figure 3–20

2

- Click Insert on the Application bar and then click Image on the Insert menu to display the Select Image Source dialog box.

- Click facebook_image in the Images folder to select the facebook_image file (Figure 3–21).

Q&A Does the Facebook icon automatically link to Facebook?

No. Later in this chapter, you add a link to the image to connect it to the Gallery's Facebook page.

Courtesy of Facebook

Figure 3–21

3

- Click the OK button in the Select Image Source dialog box to display the Image Tag Accessibility Attributes dialog box.

- In the Alternate text box, type `Facebook icon` to add the alt tag necessary for accessibility (Figure 3–22).

Figure 3–22

4

- Click the OK button to display the Facebook icon image in the footer region.

- Click to the right of the Facebook icon in the footer and then press the SPACEBAR to insert a space.

- Click Insert on the Application bar and then click Image to display the Select Image Source dialog box.

- Click twitter_image to select the Twitter icon in the Images folder (Figure 3–23).

Figure 3–23

5

- Click the OK button in the Select Image Source dialog box to open the Image Tag Accessibility Attributes dialog box.

- In the Alternate text text box, type `Twitter icon` to add the alt tag necessary for accessibility.

- Click the OK button to display the Twitter icon image in the footer region (Figure 3–24).

Figure 3–24

6

- Click to the left of the word, Copyright, in the footer to place the insertion point in front of that text.

- Press the ENTER key two times to create two blank lines between the Facebook and Twitter icons and the Copyright line.

- Click the Save All button on the Standard toolbar to save the template.

- Click Update in the Update Templates dialog box to add the icons to the Gallery Template and display the Update Pages dialog box.

- Click the Close button in the Update Pages dialog box to update the Gallery template and index.html (Figure 3–25).

7

- Click the Close button on the Gallery Template.dwt tab to close the template and display the Welcome screen.

Figure 3–25

Courtesy of Facebook; courtesy of Twitter

To Insert an Image on the Home Page

Because it is the first page most Web site visitors see, the home page must have enough visual interest to catch the attention of visitors and invite them to explore other pages. The following steps insert an image on index.html, the home page.

1

- Double-click index.html in the Files panel to open the index.html page.

- Select the text, imageArea, in the imageArea region and then press the DELETE key to delete the text (Figure 3–26).

Figure 3–26

2

- Click Insert on the Application bar and then click Image on the Insert menu to display the Select Image Source dialog box.

- Click index_image in the Images folder to select the image for index.html (Figure 3–27).

Figure 3–27

3

- Click the OK button in the Select Image Source dialog box to open the Image Tag Accessibility Attributes dialog box.

- In the Alternate text text box, type `Home family portrait` to add the alt tag necessary for accessibility.

- Click the OK button to display the index image in the imageArea region (Figure 3–28).

🔍 **Experiment**

- Click the Brightness and Contrast button in the Property inspector, and then click the OK button. Use the slider to change the brightness of the image. When you are finished, click the Cancel button to return the image to its original state.

Figure 3–28

4

- Click the Save button on the Standard toolbar to save your work.

Creating Additional Pages for the Site

After creating the template and home page, the next step is to create the other pages of the Gallery site to which the home page links. The plan for the Gallery site specifies that the site should contain six pages: index.html (the home page), services.html, portfolio.html, pricing.html, session.html, and contract.html. You can design each of these additional pages using the Gallery Template to set the standard structure of the page. If any design change is necessary, you only need to change the template. Dreamweaver then updates all of the pages automatically. The common elements such as the logo, navigation, and footer remain unchangeable, while the editable regions can display different pictures and content on each page.

To Create the Services Web Page

The Gallery specializes in portrait and family photography in a variety of beautiful natural settings throughout the Florida area. These services will be detailed in a page named services.html. The following steps create the services page using the Gallery Template.

1

- Click the Close button on the index.html tab to close the home page and display the Welcome screen.

- Click More in the Create New list to display the New Document dialog box.

- Click Page from Template in the left pane of the New Document dialog box to create a page from the template.

- If necessary, click Gallery in the Site list to create a page for the Gallery site (Figure 3–29).

Figure 3–29

2

- Click the Create button in the New Document dialog box to create a new page based on the template for the Gallery site.

- Click File on the Application bar and then click Save As to display the Save As dialog box.

- If necessary, select the text in the File name text box and then type `services.html` to name the new page (Figure 3–30).

Q&A

Which folder should I select when saving the services.html file?

Save the services.html page in the root Gallery folder, which is the folder displayed by default in the Save As dialog box.

Figure 3–30

3

- Click the Save button in the Save As dialog box to save the document as services.html.

- Select the text, imageArea, in the imageArea region and then press the DELETE key to delete the text.

- Click Insert on the Application bar and then click Image on the Insert menu to display the Select Image Source dialog box.

- If necessary, scroll down and click services_image to select the services image (Figure 3–31).

Figure 3–31

© .shock / Shutterstock

- Click the OK button in the Select Image Source dialog box to display the Image Tag Accessibility Attributes dialog box.

- In the Alternate text text box, type `Services family portrait` to add the alt tag necessary for accessibility (Figure 3–32).

Figure 3–32

- Click the OK button to display the services image in the imageArea region (Figure 3–33).

- Click the Save button on the Standard toolbar to save your work.

Figure 3–33

To Create the Portfolio Web Page

The portfolio page showcases portraits and family photos in which the personality of the subjects shines through. The following steps create the portfolio page using the Gallery Template.

- Click the Close button on the services.html tab to close the services page and display the Welcome screen.

- Click More in the Create New list to display the New Document dialog box.

- Click Page from Template in the left pane of the New Document dialog box to create a page from the template.

- If necessary, click Gallery in the Site list to create a page for the Gallery site (Figure 3–34).

Figure 3–34

- Click the Create button in the New Document dialog box to create a new page based on the template for the Gallery site.

- Click File on the Application bar and then click Save As to display the Save As dialog box.

- If necessary, select the text in the File name text box and then type `portfolio.html` to name the new page (Figure 3–35).

Figure 3–35

3

- Click the Save button in the Save As dialog box to save the document as portfolio.html.

- Select the text, imageArea, in the imageArea region and then press the DELETE key to delete the text.

- Click Insert on the Application bar and then click Image on the Insert menu to display the Select Image Source dialog box.

- Click portfolio_image to select the portfolio image in the Images folder (Figure 3–36).

Figure 3–36

4

- Click the OK button in the Select Image Source dialog box to open the Image Tag Accessibility Attributes dialog box.

- In the Alternate text text box, type `Portfolio family portrait` to add the alt tag necessary for accessibility (Figure 3–37).

Figure 3–37

5

- Click the OK button to display the Gallery portfolio image in the imageArea region (Figure 3–38).

6

- Click the Save button on the Standard toolbar to save your work.

Figure 3–38

To Create the Pricing Web Page

The package pricing information for the Gallery will be displayed on the pricing.html page. The following steps create the pricing page using the Gallery Template.

- Click the Close button on the portfolio.html tab to close the portfolio page and display the Welcome screen.

- Click More in the Create New list to display the New Document dialog box.

- Click Page from Template in the left pane of the New Document dialog box to create a page from the template. If necessary, click Gallery in the Site list, and then click the Create button to create a new page based on the template for the Gallery site.

- Click File on the Application bar and then click Save As to display the Save As dialog box.

- If necessary, select the text in the File name text box and then type pricing.html to name the new pricing page created from the template (Figure 3–39).

Figure 3–39

- Click the Save button in the Save As dialog box to save the document as pricing.html.

- Select the text, imageArea, and then press the DELETE key to delete the text.

- Click Insert on the Application bar and then click Image on the Insert menu to display the Select Image Source dialog box.

- Click pricing_image to select the pricing image in the Images folder (Figure 3–40).

Figure 3–40

- Click the OK button in the Select Image Source dialog box to open the Image Tag Accessibility Attributes dialog box.

- In the Alternate text text box, type `Pricing family portrait` to add the alt tag necessary for accessibility.

- Click the OK button in the Image Tag Accessibility Attributes dialog box to display the pricing image in the imageArea region (Figure 3–41).

Figure 3–41

© Monika Gniot / Shutterstock

❹
- Click the Save button on the Standard toolbar to save your work.

To Create the Session Web Page

Each photo shoot at the Gallery is a memorable experience. To prepare for a one-hour photography session at a selected venue, each client must decide what to wear and what to bring. The session.html page prepares each family for their special photo shoot. The following steps create the session page using the Gallery Template.

- Click the Close button on the pricing.html tab to close the pricing page and display the Welcome screen.

- Click More in the Create New list to display the New Document dialog box.

- Click Page from Template in the left pane of the New Document dialog box to create a page from the template. If necessary, click Gallery in the Site list, and then click the Create button to create a new page based on the template for the Gallery site.

- Click File on the Application bar and then click Save As to display the Save As dialog box. If necessary, select the text in the File name text box and then type `session.html` to name the session page (Figure 3–42).

Figure 3–42

- Click the Save button in the Save As dialog box to save the document as session.html.

- Select the text, imageArea, and press the DELETE key to delete the text.

- Click Insert on the Application bar and then click Image on the Insert menu to display the Select Image Source dialog box.

- Click session_image to select the session image in the Images folder (Figure 3–43).

Figure 3–43

- Click the OK button to open the Image Tag Accessibility Attributes dialog box.

- In the Alternate text text box, type `Session family portrait` to add the alt tag necessary for accessibility.

- Click the OK button to display the session image in the imageArea region (Figure 3–44).

4

- Click the Save button on the Standard toolbar to save your work.

Figure 3–44

To Create the Contact Web Page

Every business site should provide contact details such as location, phone numbers, and hours; and for a photography studio, possible session times also should be included. The following steps create the contact page using the Gallery Template.

1

- Click the Close button on the session.html tab to close the session page and display the Welcome screen.

- Click More in the Create New list to display the New Document dialog box.

- Click Page from Template in the left pane of the New Document dialog box to create a page from the template. If necessary, click Gallery in the Site list, and then click the Create button to create a new page based on the template for the Gallery site.

- Click File on the Application bar and then click Save As to display the Save As dialog box. If necessary, select the text in the File name text box and then type contact.html to name the contact page (Figure 3–45).

Figure 3–45

2

- Click the Save button in the Save As dialog box to save the document as contact.html.

- Select the text, imageArea, and then press the DELETE key to delete the text.

- Click Insert on the Application bar, click Image on the Insert menu to display the Select Image Source dialog box, and then click contact_image to select the contact image in the Images folder (Figure 3–46).

Figure 3–46

© Serg Ivanov / Shutterstock

- Click the OK button to display the Image Tag Accessibility Attributes dialog box.

- In the Alternate text text box, type `Contact family portrait` to add the alt tag necessary for accessibility.

- Click the OK button to display the contact image in the imageArea region (Figure 3–47).

- Click the Save button on the Standard toolbar to save your work.

- Click the Close button on the contact.html tab to close the contact page and display the Welcome screen.

Figure 3–47

Break Point: If you wish to take a break, this is a good place to do so. To resume at a later time, start Dreamweaver, and continue following the steps from this location forward.

Adding Links to the Gallery Site

Web site navigation is the pathway people take to visit the pages in a site. Web site navigation must be well constructed, easy to use, and intuitive. Thoughtful and effective navigation tools guide users to other pages on the site and contribute to the accessibility of each page. The fundamental tool for Web navigation is the link, which connects a Web page to another page or file. If you place the mouse pointer over a link in a browser, the Web address of the link appears in the status bar. This location is the Web page or file that opens when you click the link.

Plan Ahead

Identify the navigation of the site

Before you use links to create connections from one document to another on your Web site or within a document, keep the following guidelines in mind:

- **Prepare for links.** Some Web designers create links before creating the associated pages. Others prefer to create all of the files and pages first, and then create links. Choose a method that suits your work style, but be sure to test all of your links before publishing your Web site.

- **Link to text or images.** You can select any text or image on a page to create a link. When you do, visitors to your Web site can click the text or image to open another document or move to another place on the page.

- **Know the path or address.** To create relative links to pages in your site, the text files need to be stored in the same root folder or a subfolder in the root folder. To create absolute links, you need to know the URL of the Web page. To create e-mail links, you need to know the e-mail address.

- **Test the links.** Test all of the links on a Web page when you preview the page in a browser. Fix any broken links before publishing the page.

You can connect to another page using relative links or absolute links. A **relative link** connects Web pages within the site. For example, if a visitor begins on the home page of the Gallery site and clicks the link to the Contact page, the visitor is using a relative link. When you link text or an image to any file listed in the Files panel for the current site, you are creating a relative link. An **absolute link** means that the linked resource resides on another Web site outside of the current one, such as Facebook or Twitter. To create an absolute link, you provide the complete Web site address of the linked resource. For example, to include a link to the home page of the Professional Photographers of America (PPA) Web site, provide *http://www.ppa.com* as the complete Web address.

Another type of link in Dreamweaver is an **e-mail link**, which connects to a particular e-mail address. Clicking an e-mail link starts the user's default e-mail application and then opens a blank e-mail message containing the recipient's e-mail address.

BTW

Creating Links
To create links in Dreamweaver, you can use the Link box, the Browse For File button, or the Point to File button in the Property inspector. You also can use the Hyperlink button on the Insert bar.

To Open the Gallery Template Again

Add links to the Gallery Template so that any documents you create from the template will already contain the links to the other Web pages in the site. When you save the template with the links, Dreamweaver also updates all of the pages based on that template, which is a significant time-saver. The following steps reopen the Gallery Template.

1 On the Welcome screen, click Open to display the Open dialog box with the Gallery folder open.

2 Double-click the Templates folder in the Open dialog box and then click Gallery Template to select the Gallery Template (Figure 3–48).

3 Click the Open button to display the Gallery Template.

Figure 3–48

To Add Relative Links to the Gallery Template

Visitors can enter the Gallery site through any page within the site, not just the home page. Search engines, links from other Web sites, and bookmarks allow other pages to be used as entry points. Users must find their way around a Web site easily using relative links. You already have used the Point to File button to create links to other pages on the Gallery site. In fact, using the Point to File button is the easiest way to create a relative link. The following steps create relative links to each page within the site.

1

- Select the text, home, in the navigation region of the Gallery Template to select the link text (Figure 3–49).

Q&A

Why am I creating a relative link?

You use relative links when the linked documents are in the same site, such as those in your Gallery site.

Figure 3–49

2

- Drag the Point to File button in the Property inspector to the index.html file in the Files panel to display a link line (Figure 3–50).

Figure 3–50

3

- Release the mouse button to create the link to index.html.

- Select the text, services, in the navigation region to select the link text.

- Drag the Point to File button in the Property inspector to the services.html file in the Files panel to prepare to create a relative link to services.html (Figure 3–51).

Q&A

Why did the text link for home in the navigation region change to blue underlined text?

Figure 3–51

Dreamweaver changes all text links to blue and underlines them by default. Later in this chapter, you add a new CSS rule to change the color to yellow and prevent the underlining.

 4

- Release the mouse button to create the link to services.html.

- Select the text, portfolio, in the navigation region.

- Drag the Point to File button to the portfolio.html file to create a link.

- Select the text, pricing, in the navigation region, and then drag the Point to File button to the pricing.html file to create a link.

- Select the text, session, in the navigation region, and then drag the Point to File button to the session.html file to create a link.

- Select the text, contact, in the navigation region, and then drag the Point to File button to the contact.html file to create a link.

- Click a blank area of the page to deselect the text (Figure 3–52).

Q&A

Why does an icon of a ship's wheel appear from time to time?

Figure 3–52

That icon is the Code Navigator icon. It often appears when you select text or objects on a page. You can click it to display a list of code sources related to the selection. You don't need to use it in these steps, so you can ignore it for now.

Other Ways

1. Type file name in Link box

2. Click Browse For File button in Property inspector

3. On Insert menu, click Hyperlink

4. On Insert bar, click Hyperlink

5. Select text for linking, right-click selected text, click Make Link

6. SHIFT+drag to file

To Add Absolute Links to the Gallery Template

The Gallery site has a presence on Facebook and Twitter, which means the company has set up pages on Facebook and Twitter to promote its photography business. The Facebook and Twitter logos in the footer of the Gallery template each use an absolute link to open the Gallery's pages at Facebook and Twitter. These social networking sites are not part of the Gallery site, so each logo image uses an absolute link to connect to these outside sites. To create an image link, select the image, and then type the Web address in the Link text box. The following steps create absolute links to the Gallery's Facebook and Twitter pages.

1

- If necessary, scroll down in the Document window and then click the Facebook logo in the footer region to select the image (Figure 3–53).

Q&A Can I create links on a new page that doesn't contain any text or images yet?

No. You must select something on a page that becomes the link to another location, so you need to add text or images before creating links. If you want to create links on a new page, it's a good idea to save the page before making the links.

Figure 3–53

2

- Click the Link text box in the Property inspector and then type `https:// www.facebook.com/ TheGallery PortraitAndFamily Photography` to add an absolute link to the Gallery's Facebook page (Figure 3–54).

Q&A Why does the Facebook address in this step include https:// instead of http://?

A URL that begins with https:// identifies a secure Web site (Hypertext Transfer Protocol Secure). When a user connects to a Web site via HTTPS, the Web site encrypts the session with a digital certificate, which verifies the security of the connection.

Figure 3–54

3

- Click the Twitter logo in the footer region of the Gallery Template file to select the image.

- Click the Link text box and then type `https://twitter.com/TheGalleryPFP` to add an absolute link to the Gallery's Twitter page (Figure 3–55).

Figure 3–55

4

- Click the Save All button on the Standard toolbar to display the Update Template Files dialog box with six files listed for updating (Figure 3–56).

Q&A

Why does the Update Template Files dialog box appear at this point?

After changing the template (in this case, by adding six text links and two image links), Dreamweaver allows you to make the same changes to the documents based on the template.

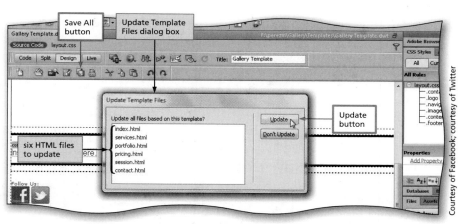

Figure 3–56

5

- Click the Update button to update all of the files based on this template and to open the Update Pages dialog box (Figure 3–57).

Q&A

Are all of the links ready to be tested?

The template now includes all of the necessary links to all pages within the Web site and is ready for testing.

6

- Click the Close button to update the HTML pages within the Gallery site.

Figure 3–57

To Add an E-mail Link to the Gallery Template

The Contact page of the Gallery site provides a contact phone number and e-mail address. When visitors click an e-mail link, the default e-mail program installed on their computer opens a new e-mail message. The e-mail address you specify is inserted in the To box of the e-mail message header. The following steps show how to use the Insert menu to create an e-mail link on the home page.

1

- Double-click contact.html in the Files panel to open the contact page.

- Select the text, Insert page content here, in the contentArea region, type `Take the`

`first step
and contact
us today to
schedule your
photography
session!`, and then press the ENTER key to add the contact text.

- Type `(643)
555-0324` and then press the SHIFT+ENTER keys to add the contact phone number and a line break.

- Type `TheGalleryPFP@
thegallery.net` to add the e-mail address (Figure 3–58).

Figure 3–58

2

- Select the text, TheGalleryPFP@ thegallery.net, to select the e-mail address.

- Click Insert on the Application bar to display the Insert menu (Figure 3–59).

Q&A

Will clicking the e-mail link open my Internet e-mail such as Gmail or Hotmail?

No. You can copy and paste an e-mail address from a Web site into your Internet e-mail. An e-mail link opens automatically only in a local e-mail program such as Outlook.

Figure 3–59

- Click Email Link on the Insert menu to display the Email Link dialog box (Figure 3–60).

Q&A

What information does the Email Link dialog box already contain?

The Text and Email text boxes in the Email Link dialog box already contain the display text (the text displayed on the Web page) and the e-mail address (the recipient of the e-mail the user creates).

Figure 3–60

- Click the OK button in the Email Link dialog box to create an e-mail link.
- Click a blank area of the page to deselect the text (Figure 3–61).

5

- Click the Save button on the Standard toolbar to save the contact.html page.
- Click the Close button on the contact.html tab to close the document.
- Click the Close button on the Gallery Template.dwt tab to close the template and display the Welcome screen.

Figure 3–61

Other Ways	
1. Click Email Link button on Insert bar	2. In Link box, type mailto: followed by e-mail address

Break Point: If you wish to take a break, this is a good place to do so. To resume at a later time, start Dreamweaver, and continue following the steps from this location forward.

Formatting Links

Dreamweaver refers to link text and its colors using the same terms that CSS uses. The color for link text is called the link color. The color of a link after it has been clicked is called the visited color. In the Gallery site, the link color of the text in the navigation region is blue. By default, link text is also underlined in the same color as the text. Adding relative links for the text in the navigation region made the links fully functional. Visitors can click each link to open the corresponding Web page.

To provide more interaction on the site, you can use CSS styles to format the links as rollover text instead of displaying the links in blue with underlining. A **rollover link** changes color when the mouse rolls over it. Rollover links in a Web site design allow you to change or highlight an image or text when the mouse points to it. This change in formatting provides an additional cue indicating that users can interact with the object by clicking it. When a mouse points to the orange links in the navigation area of the Gallery site, the rollover style can change the color to yellow, creating an interesting focal point to draw attention to the navigation links. CSS link styles are classified as page properties, which you can access using the Page Properties button in the Property inspector.

BTW

Rollover Images
Similar to rollover links, you can include rollover images that change when a user points to them on a Web page. To do so, you need two images: the original image, such as a button, and the rollover image, such as the button highlighted. Click Insert on the Application bar, point to Image Objects, and then click Rollover Image.

To Format a Link as Rollover Text

The following steps remove the blue underlining from text in the navigation region and add a rollover style to format the links.

1

- Open the Gallery Template file.

- If necessary, click a blank area of the Gallery Template to deselect any objects.

- Click the Page Properties button in the Property inspector to display the Page Properties dialog box (Figure 3–62).

Figure 3–62

2

- Click the Links (CSS) category to display the Links options.

- Click the Link color text box and then type #FF9900 to change the link color to orange.

- Click the Rollover links text box and then type #FFCC00 to change the rollover link text color to yellow.

- Click the Visited links text box and then type #FF9900 to change the visited link text color to orange.

- Click the Underline style button and then click Never underline on the Underline style list to remove the default underline for the link (Figure 3–63).

Figure 3–63

 Q&A

What is a visited link?

Before you visit a page, the link is displayed in a certain color by default. After you visit it, the link changes color. With Dreamweaver, you can set the visited link color to your preference.

- Click the Apply button in the Page Properties dialog box to change the link colors of the navigational controls.

- Click the OK button to close the Page Properties dialog box.

- Click the Save All button on the Standard toolbar to display the Update Template Files dialog box.

- Click the Update button to update all six HTML files based on this template and to open the Update Pages dialog box.

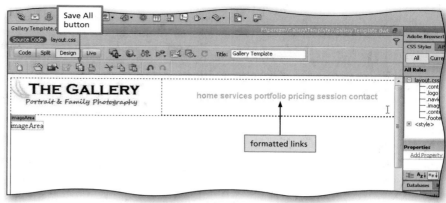

Figure 3–64

- Click the Close button in the Update Pages dialog box to close the Update Pages dialog box (Figure 3–64).

To Test the Rollover Links in a Browser

The following steps open and then preview the index.html page in Internet Explorer to test the rollover links.

1 Close the Gallery Template file.

2 Double-click index.html in the Files panel to open the index.html document.

3 Click the 'Preview/Debug in browser' button on the Document toolbar.

4 Click Preview in IExplore in the Preview/Debug in browser list to display the Gallery Web site in Internet Explorer (Figure 3–65).

Figure 3–65

5 Point to each link to view the rollover effect and then click each link to view the pages in the browser.

6 Click the Internet Explorer Close button to exit the browser.

7 Click the Close button on the index.html tab to close the index page and display the Welcome screen.

Other Ways

1. Press F12

Modifying the CSS Style Sheet

When testing the links in the Gallery Web pages, you may have noticed an orange border around the Facebook logo and the Twitter logo. When you changed the link color to orange, the two image links on the Gallery template also were set to include an orange border. As you design a Web site, you may create new CSS rules or change the initial CSS rules in the style sheet for the site. In this case, you can modify a CSS rule to remove the orange border from the image links.

Creating Compound Styles

A compound style applies to two or more tags, classes, or IDs. In Chapter 2, you added a class selector style to the style sheet to identify a region by providing a name that begins with a period such as .logo or .footer. Other selector styles include a tag selector, which redefines an HTML tag such as an h1 heading, and an ID selector, which begins with a # symbol to define a block element such as a paragraph. A **compound selector** is not a different type of selector, but is actually a combination of the different types of selector styles. For example, in the Gallery site, a compound selector style applies to an image element when it is used as a link because you are combining the styles for an image tag selector and for a link.

An **anchor tag** creates a link to another page or document, or to a location within the same page. The anchor tag is <a> and refers to a clickable hyperlink element. The most common use of the anchor tag is to make links to other pages. In the Gallery site, the selector name of the style assigned to the Facebook and Twitter image links includes references to an anchor and an image: a img. The *img* stands for image, and the *a* stands for anchor. The selector *a img* is a compound selector because it combines the anchor tag (a) and the image tag (img) to place (or anchor) an image link at a desired location. To remove the border from the image links, you can use the New CSS Rule button on the CSS Styles panel to add a new CSS rule for the *a img* compound selector.

To Add New CSS Rules with a Compound Selector

To remove the orange border from the Facebook and Twitter image links, you can add a new CSS rule using a compound selector within the layout.css file. The following steps modify the layout.css style sheet to add a new CSS rule for the Gallery Web site.

1

- On the Welcome screen, click Open to display the Open dialog box, double-click the Templates folder, and then double-click Gallery Template.dwt to display the Gallery Template (Figure 3–66).

Figure 3–66

- Click the New CSS Rule button at the bottom of the CSS Styles panel to display the New CSS Rule dialog box (Figure 3–67).

Figure 3–67

❸

- If necessary, click the Selector Type button and then click 'Compound (based on your selection)' to create a compound selector type.

- In the Selector Name text box, type a img to create a CSS rule that applies to anchor image elements displayed as links.

- If necessary, click the Rule Definition button and then click layout.css to add the new rule to the layout.css file (Figure 3–68).

Figure 3–68

❹

- Click the OK button in the New CSS Rule dialog box to display the 'CSS Rule Definition for a img in layout.css' dialog box.

- Click Border in the Category list to display the Border options.

- Click the Top box arrow in the Style section, and then click none to remove the default border around the image links (Figure 3–69).

Figure 3–69

5

- Click the Apply button in the 'CSS Rule Definition for a img in layout.css' dialog box to apply the CSS rules for a img within the layout.css style sheet.

- Click the OK button to define the new CSS rule for the image border.

- Click the Save All button on the Standard toolbar to save your work.

- Double-click index.html in the Files panel and then scroll down the page to view the Facebook and Twitter images (Figure 3–70).

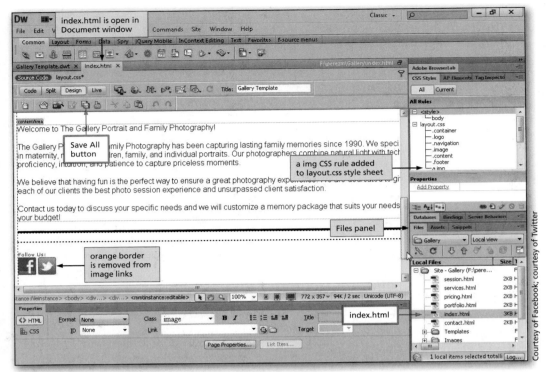

Figure 3–70

Courtesy of Facebook; courtesy of Twitter

Q&A

Why does the orange border no longer appear around the Facebook and Twitter images?

The new CSS rule removed the border from all image links in files attached to the layout.css style sheet.

6

- Close the index page.

Adding an Image Placeholder

After designing an initial Web site for a customer, you may not have access to the final images to complete the pages. For example, the customer might need to take photos of a product still being developed. In this case, you still can complete the design of the Web site. Dreamweaver contains a feature called an **image placeholder**, which reserves space on a Web page for an image during the design process by inserting a temporary photo in its place. A prototype of a Web site may contain image placeholders so the business owner can approve the prototype and the designers can continue working and complete the site. An image placeholder allows you to define the size and location of an image in your design without inserting the actual image. When you replace an image placeholder with the final graphic, the graphic uses the properties of the image placeholder, including the size, which saves you time and preserves the design of the page.

To Define an Image Placeholder

The portfolio page of the Gallery site contains portrait images taken by the photography studio to provide ideas for families to consider when planning their own photo sessions. To provide consistency in the photos, the portrait page can contain three image placeholders, each with a preset size of 150 pixels by 200 pixels. The following steps define an image placeholder on the portfolio page.

1

- In the Files panel, double-click portfolio.html to open the portfolio page.

- Scroll down and select the text, Insert page content here, in the contentArea region, type `Portraits`, and then press the SHIFT+ENTER keys to insert the text and a line break (Figure 3–71).

Figure 3–71

2

- Click Insert on the Application bar and then point to Image Objects on the Insert menu to display the Image Objects submenu (Figure 3–72).

Figure 3–72

- Click Image Placeholder on the Image Objects submenu to display the Image Placeholder dialog box.

- In the Name text box, type `Portrait` to name the image placeholder.

- Select the value in the Width text box and then type `150` to set the width of the image placeholder.

- Select the value in the Height text box and then type `200` to set the height of the image placeholder.

- Click the Alternate text text box and then type `Portrait picture` to set the alternate text of the image placeholder (Figure 3–73).

Figure 3–73

- Click the OK button in the Image Placeholder dialog box to create an image placeholder named Portrait (Figure 3–74).

Q&A

Does the image placeholder have to be gray?

No. You can set the color of the image placeholder using the Color button in the Image Placeholder dialog box.

Figure 3–74

Other Ways
1. On Insert bar, click Images button, click Image Placeholder

To Replace an Image Placeholder

The following steps replace the image placeholder with the actual image for the portfolio page.

- Double-click the Portrait image placeholder to display the Select Image Source dialog box.

- Click the image_portrait file in the Select Image Source dialog box to select the replacement for the image placeholder (Figure 3–75).

Q&A

Why did I insert an image placeholder if I immediately replace it with the actual image?

An image placeholder lets you set properties for an image so you can preserve the page design when you insert a photo or other image. When producing a Web site, you might not have the images as you design the pages. You immediately replace the image placeholder in these steps to practice the technique.

Figure 3–75

2

- Click the OK button in the Select Image Source dialog box to replace the image placeholder (Figure 3–76).

Figure 3–76

Other Ways

1. Select image placeholder, click Browse for File button on Property inspector

To Add Image Placeholders

The following steps add two other image placeholders and replacement images.

- Click to the right of the Portrait image to place the insertion point after the image.

- Press the ENTER key, type Family, and then press the SHIFT+ENTER keys to insert the text and a line break.

- Click Insert on the Application bar, point to Image Objects on the Insert menu, and then click Image Placeholder on the Image Objects submenu to display the Image Placeholder dialog box.

- In the Name text box, type Family to name the image placeholder.

- Select the value in the Width text box and then type 150 to set the width of the image placeholder.

- Select the value in the Height text box and then type 200 to set the height of the image placeholder.

- Click the Alternate text text box and then type Family picture to set the alternate text of the image placeholder (Figure 3–77).

Figure 3–77

© Phase4 Photography / Shutterstock

- Click the OK button in the Image Placeholder dialog box to create an image placeholder named Family.

- Double-click the Family image placeholder to display the Select Image Source dialog box, and then click the image_family file to select the replacement for the image placeholder.

- Click the OK button in the Select Image Source dialog box to replace the image placeholder (Figure 3–78).

Figure 3–78

- Click to the right of the Family image to place the insertion point after the image.

- Press the ENTER key, type Baby, and then press the SHIFT+ENTER keys to insert the text and a line break.

- Click Insert on the Application bar, point to Image Objects on the Insert menu, and then click Image Placeholder on the Image Objects submenu to display the Image Placeholder dialog box.

- In the Name text box, type `Baby` to name the image placeholder.

- Select the value in the Width text box and then type `150` to set the width of the image placeholder.

- Select the value in the Height text box and then type `200` to set the height of the image placeholder.

- Click the Alternate text text box and then type `Baby picture` to set the alternate text of the image placeholder (Figure 3–79).

Figure 3–79

- Click the OK button in the Image Placeholder dialog box to create an image placeholder named Baby.

- Double-click the Baby image placeholder to open the Select Image Source dialog box, and then click the image_baby file to select the replacement for the image placeholder.

- Click the OK button to replace the image placeholder (Figure 3–80).

- Click the Save All button on the Standard toolbar to save the Gallery Web site.

Figure 3–80

To View the Site in the Browser

The following steps preview the home page of the Gallery Web site using Internet Explorer.

1. Click the 'Preview/Debug in browser' button on the Document toolbar to display a list of browsers.

2. Click Preview in IExplore in the browser list to display the Gallery Web site in Internet Explorer.

3. Click each link on the page to test it. Scroll down as necessary to click the Facebook and Twitter image links. Click the Back button in the browser to return to the home page.

4. Click the Internet Explorer Close button to close the browser.

To Quit Dreamweaver

The following steps quit Dreamweaver and return control to the operating system.

1 Click the Close button on the right side of the Application bar to close the window.

2 If Dreamweaver displays a dialog box asking you to save changes, click the No button.

Chapter Summary

In this chapter, you were introduced to images and links and learned how to use placeholders. You began the chapter by modifying the Gallery template to add an editable region for images. Next, you added five new pages to the Gallery site and inserted graphics with alternate text on each page. You also used relative links to link the pages within the site, and you used absolute links connecting to Facebook and Twitter to provide a social networking presence for the site. In addition, you included an e-mail link that visitors can click to contact the owner of the Gallery photography studio. You modified a CSS rule to format all of the links as rollover links. Finally, you added image placeholders to a Web page and then replaced them with photos. The following tasks are all the new Dreamweaver skills you learned in this chapter:

1. Modify a Dreamweaver Template by Editing a CSS Rule (DW 144)
2. Modify a Dreamweaver Template by Adding an Editable Region (DW 146)
3. Copy Files into the Images Folder (DW 150)
4. Insert a Logo Image in the Template (DW 152)
5. Insert Social Networking Icons in the Template (DW 155)
6. Insert an Image on the Home Page (DW 157)
7. Create the Services Web Page (DW 159)
8. Create the Portfolio Web Page (DW 161)
9. Create the Pricing Web Page (DW 164)
10. Create the Session Web Page (DW 165)
11. Create the Contact Web Page (DW 166)
12. Add Relative Links to the Gallery Template (DW 170)
13. Add Absolute Links to the Gallery Template (DW 172)
14. Add an E-mail Link to the Gallery Template (DW 174)
15. Format a Link as Rollover Text (DW 176)
16. Add New CSS Rules with a Compound Selector (DW 178)
17. Define an Image Placeholder (DW 181)
18. Replace an Image Placeholder (DW 183)
19. Add Image Placeholders (DW 184)

Apply Your Knowledge

Reinforce the skills and apply the concepts you learned in this chapter.

Adding Images and a Link to a Web Page

Note: To complete this assignment, you will be required to use the Data Files for Students. Visit www.cengage.com/ct/studentdownload for detailed instructions on downloading the Data Files for Students or contact your instructor for information about accessing the required files.

Instructions: In this activity, you complete a Web page about the Mayan ruins of Tulum located on the Yucatán Peninsula in Mexico. To do so, you add images and a link to an existing Web page. The completed Web page is displayed in Figure 3–81.

Perform the following tasks:
1. Use Windows Explorer to copy the apply3.html file and the Images folder from the Chapter 03\Apply folder into the *your last name and first initial*\Apply folder.
2. Start Dreamweaver. Use the Sites button on the Files panel to display the Web sites created with Dreamweaver and the drives on your computer. Select the Apply site.
3. Open apply3.html. Select the word, Tulum, in the first sentence (not the main heading). Use the Link box on the Property inspector to insert a link to `http://en.wikipedia.org/wiki/Tulum`.

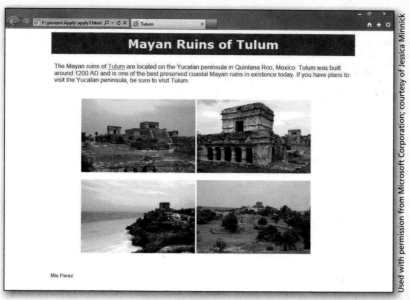

Used with permission from Microsoft Corporation; courtesy of Jessica Minnick

Figure 3–81

4. Double-click the image placeholder Tulum1 to display the Select Image Source dialog box, double-click the Images folder, and then click the tulum_image_1 file to select the replacement for the image placeholder. Click the OK button in the Select Image Source dialog box to replace the image placeholder.

5. Double-click the image placeholder Tulum2 to display the Select Image Source dialog box, and then click the tulum_image_2 file to select the replacement for the image placeholder. Click the OK button in the Select Image Source dialog box to replace the image placeholder.

6. Click to the right of Tulum_image_2, and then press the ENTER key. Use the Image command on the Insert menu to insert a new image, tulum_image_3.jpg. Enter `Tulum Picture 3` as the alternate text.

7. Place the insertion point after tulum_image_3.jpg and press the SPACEBAR. Use the Image command on the Insert menu to insert a new image, tulum_image_4.jpg. Enter `Tulum Picture 4` as the alternate text.

8. Replace the text, Your name here, with your first and last names.

9. Save your changes and then view your document in your browser. Compare your document to Figure 3–81. Make any necessary changes and then save your changes.

10. Submit the document in the format specified by your instructor.

Extend Your Knowledge

Extend the skills you learned in this chapter and experiment with new skills. You may need to use Help to complete the assignment.

Modifying Page Properties

Note: To complete this assignment, you will be required to use the Data Files for Students. Visit www.cengage.com/ct/studentdownload for detailed instructions on downloading the Data Files for Students or contact your instructor for information about accessing the required files.

Instructions: In this activity, you modify a Web page describing sites to visit on Maui. First you modify the page properties by selecting an image to use as a background. Then you establish link colors on the Web page. The page property changes are provided in Table 3–1. The completed Web page is displayed in Figure 3–82.

Continued >

Extend Your Knowledge *continued*

Table 3–1 Page Properties for Extend3.html		
Category	**Property**	**Value**
Appearance (CSS)	Background Image	Use the Browse button to navigate to Images/page_background
Links (CSS)	Link color	#60
	Rollover links	#F60
	Visited links	#009

Perform the following tasks:

1. Use Windows Explorer to copy the extend3.html file and the Images folder from the Chapter 03\ Extend folder into the *your last name and first initial*\Extend folder (the F:\perezm folder, for example).

2. Start Dreamweaver. Use the Sites button on the Files panel to select the Extend site.

3. Open extend3.html. Click the Page Properties button on the Property inspector, and then enter the page properties shown in Table 3–1.

4. Replace the text, Your name here, with your first and last names.

5. Save your changes and then view your document in your browser.

6. Point to the words, Maui and Haleakala National Park, to view the link changes. Click each link and then use your browser's Back button to return to the page to view the link color change.

7. Compare your document to Figure 3–82. Make any necessary changes and then save your changes.

8. Submit the document in the format specified by your instructor.

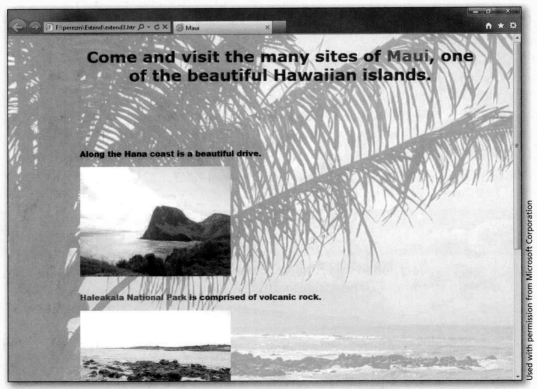

Figure 3–82

Make It Right

Analyze a Web site and suggest how to improve its design.

Editing CSS Rule Definitions on a Web Page

Note: To complete this assignment, you will be required to use the Data Files for Students. Visit www.cengage.com/ct/studentdownload for detailed instructions on downloading the Data Files for Students or contact your instructor for information about accessing the required files.

Instructions: The Learn HTML Web page provides tips for using HTML5. In this activity, you edit CSS rule definitions for four class selectors in the Learn HTML Web page. The CSS rule definitions for the page are provided in Table 3–2. The completed Web page is shown in Figure 3–83 on the next page.

Table 3–2 CSS Rule Definitions for right3.html		
CSS Rule Definition for .container		
Category	**Property**	**Value**
Box	Width	800px
	Right Margin	auto
	Left Margin	auto
CSS Rule Definition for .header		
Category	**Property**	**Value**
Type	Font-family	Verdana, Geneva, sans-serif
	Font-size	24pt
	Font-weight	bold
	Color	#C60
Background	Background-color	#FF9
Box	Bottom Margin	5px
CSS Rule Definition for .sidebar		
Category	**Property**	**Value**
Type	Font-family	Georgia, Times New Roman, Times, serif
	Font-size	14pt
	Font-style	italic
Background	Background-color	#F96
Box	Width	150px
	Height	500px
	Padding	15px, same for all
	Right Margin	10px
CSS Rule Definition for .content		
Category	**Property**	**Value**
Type	Font-family	Arial, Helvetica, sans-serif
Background	Background-color	#FFF
Box	Width	550px
	Height	500px
	Float	left

Continued >

Make It Right *continued*

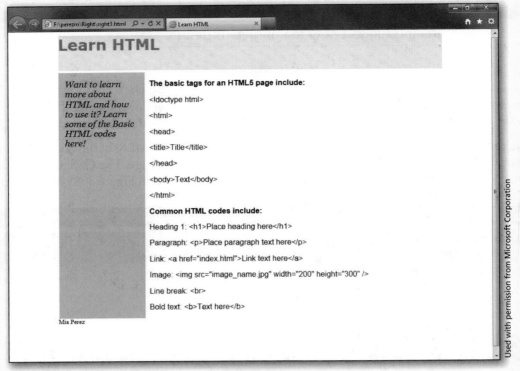

Figure 3–83

Perform the following tasks:

1. Use Windows Explorer to copy the right3.html file from the Chapter 03\Right folder into the *your last name and first initial*\Right folder (the F:\perezm folder, for example).

2. View right3.html in your browser to see its current design, and then close the browser.

3. Start Dreamweaver and open right3.html.

4. Edit the CSS rules for container, header, sidebar, and content. Refer to Table 3–2 to edit the CSS rules for each region. Apply and accept your changes.

5. Replace the text, Your name here, with your first and last names.

6. Save your changes and then view the Web page in your browser. Compare your page to Figure 3–83. Make any necessary changes and then save your changes.

7. Submit the document in the format specified by your instructor.

In the Lab

Design and/or create a document using the guidelines, concepts, and skills presented in this chapter. Labs are listed in order of increasing difficulty.

Lab 1: Adding Images and Links to the Healthy Lifestyle Web Site

Note: To complete this assignment, you will be required to use the Data Files for Students. Visit www.cengage.com/ct/studentdownload for detailed instructions on downloading the Data Files for Students or contact your instructor for information about accessing the required files.

Problem: You are creating an internal Web site for your company that features information about how to live a healthy lifestyle. Employees at your company will use this Web site as a resource for nutrition, exercise, and other health-related tips. In Chapter 2, you developed the template and home page for this Healthy Lifestyle Web site. Now you need to create other Web pages for the site and update the template with links to each page. You also need to modify CSS rules for the template header and navigation, and then adjust link colors and enhance the site with images.

First, use the Lifestyle Template to create Web pages for Nutrition, Exercise, Habits, and Sign Up. Update the Lifestyle Template with links to each page. Next, modify the Lifestyle CSS rule definitions to improve the formatting and design of the pages. Finally, add an image to the Home Web page, and then add images and text to the Nutrition Web page. The revised CSS rule definitions for the header and navigation are provided in Table 3–3. The page property values are provided in Table 3–4. The updated home page is shown in Figure 3–84, and the Nutrition page is shown in Figure 3–85.

Table 3–3 Modified CSS Rule Definitions for Lifestyle.css

CSS Rule Definition Updates for .header in Lifestyle.css

Category	Property	Value
Type	Color	#C30
Background	Background-color	Remove value
Block	Text-align	center
Box	Height	Remove value
	Top Padding	20px
	Bottom Padding	20px

CSS Rule Definition Updates for .navigation in Lifestyle.css

Category	Property	Value
Background	Background-image	Use the Browse button to select navigation_background in the Images folder
	Background color	Remove value
Box	Height	Remove value
Border	Style	Uncheck Same for all
	Top Style	dotted
	Right Style	Remove value
	Bottom Style	dotted
	Left Style	Remove value
	Width	Uncheck Same for all
	Top Width	medium
	Right Width	Remove value
	Bottom Width	medium
	Left Width	Remove value
	Color	Uncheck Same for all
	Top Color	#630
	Right Color	Remove value
	Bottom Color	#630

CSS Rule Definition Updates for .footer in Lifestyle.css

Category	Property	Value
Border	Top Width	thin
	Top Style	solid
	Top Color	#333

Continued >

In the Lab *continued*

Table 3–4 Page Properties for Healthy Lifestyle Pages		
Category	**Property**	**Value**
Links (CSS)	Link color	#C30
	Rollover links	#690
	Visited links	#C30
	Underline style	Show underline only on rollover

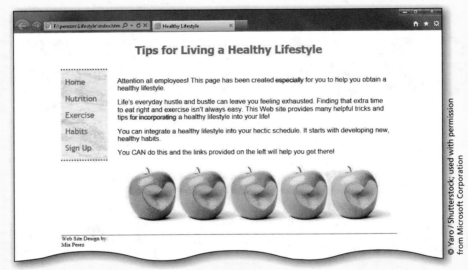

Figure 3–84

© Yaro / Shutterstock; used with permission from Microsoft Corporation

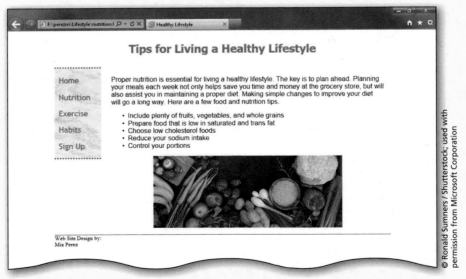

Figure 3–85

© Ronald Sumners / Shutterstock; used with permission from Microsoft Corporation

Perform the following tasks:

1. Use Windows Explorer to copy the Images folder and the nutrition.txt file from the Chapter 03\ Lab1 folder into the *your last name and first initial*\Lifestyle folder (the F:\perezm folder, for example).

2. Start Dreamweaver. Use the Sites button on the Files panel to select the Healthy Lifestyle site.

3. On the Dreamweaver Welcome screen, click More in the Create New list. In the New Document dialog box, select Page from Template, Site: Healthy Lifestyle, and Template for Site "Healthy Lifestyle": Lifestyle Template. Save the new Web page using `nutrition.html` as the file name. Close the file.

4. On the Dreamweaver Welcome screen, click More in the Create New list. In the New Document dialog box, select Page from Template, Site: Healthy Lifestyle, and Template for Site "Healthy Lifestyle": Lifestyle Template. Save the new Web page using `exercise.html` as the file name. Close the file.

5. Use the same method as in Steps 3 and 4 to create two more Web pages, using `habits.html` and `signup.html` as the file names. Close the files.

6. Open the Lifestyle Template.dwt file.

7. Select the word, Home, in the navigation bar. Use the Point to File button on the Property inspector to create a relative link to index.html. (*Hint*: You may need to use the scroll bar on the Files panel to scroll down and view the index.html file.)

8. Select the word, Nutrition, in the navigation bar. Use the Point to File button on the Property inspector to create a relative link to nutrition.html.

9. Select the word, Exercise, in the navigation bar. Use the Point to File button on the Property inspector to create a relative link to exercise.html.

10. Use the same method as in Steps 8 and 9 to create a link from the Habits text in the navigation bar to the habits.html file, and from the Sign Up text in the navigation bar to the signup.html file.

11. Use the Edit Rule button on the CSS Styles panel to edit the CSS rules for the header, navigation, and footer in Lifestyle.css. Refer to Table 3–3 for the updated values. Only update the values listed in the table; keep the other values the same. Apply and accept your changes.

12. Click the Page Properties button on the Property inspector and refer to Table 3–4 to change the page property values. Apply and accept your changes.

13. Click the Save All button on the Standard toolbar to save your changes. Click the Update button in the Update Template Files dialog box. Click the Close button in the Update Pages dialog box. Close the template.

14. Open index.html.

15. Place your insertion point after the last sentence in the content area and press the ENTER key. Use the Image command on the Insert menu to insert home_image. Use `Home image` as the alternate text.

16. Save your changes and view the document in your browser. Compare your document to Figure 3–84. Make any necessary changes, save your changes, and then close index.html.

17. Open nutrition.html.

18. Replace the text, Insert content here, with the text in the nutrition.txt file. Use the Unordered List button on the Property inspector to create an unordered list for the five lines of text below the paragraph, beginning with "Include plenty of…" and ending with "…your portions".

19. Place your insertion point after the last list item and press the ENTER key. Use the Unordered List button to remove the bullet. Use the Insert Image command on the Insert menu to insert the nutrition_image picture. Use `Nutrition image` as the alternate text.

20. Use the Format menu on the Application bar to center-align the picture.

21. Save your changes and view the document in your browser. Compare your document to Figure 3–85. Make any necessary changes and save your changes.

22. Click the links on the navigation bar to view the other pages, and to confirm that each item on the navigation bar is linked to the correct page. Make any necessary changes and then save your changes.

23. Submit the documents in the format specified by your instructor.

In the Lab

Lab 2: Adding Images and Links to the Designs by Dolores Web Site

Note: To complete this assignment, you will be required to use the Data Files for Students. Visit www.cengage.com/ct/studentdownload for detailed instructions on downloading the Data Files for Students or contact your instructor for information about accessing the required files.

Problem: You are creating a Web site for Designs by Dolores, a Web site design company. The site provides information about the company and its services. In Chapter 2, you developed the template and home page for the Designs by Dolores Web site. Now you need to create the Web pages for the site, insert a logo, and update the template with links to each page. You also need to modify the link colors and enhance the site with images.

First, use the Designs Template to create Web pages called About Us, Services, Pricing, Web Hosting, and Contact Us. Update the Design Template with links to each page. Next, modify the Lifestyle CSS rule definitions to improve the formatting and design of the pages. Finally, add text and an image to the About Us Web page. The revised CSS rule definitions for the header, navigation, content, and footer are provided in Table 3–5. The page property values are provided in Table 3–6. The updated home page is shown in Figure 3–86, and the About Us page is shown in Figure 3–87.

Table 3–5 CSS Rule Definition Updates for Designs by Dolores

CSS Rule Definition Updates for .header in Designs.css

Category	Property	Value
Type	Font-family	Remove value
	Font-size	Remove value
	Color	Remove value
Box	Top Padding	Remove value
	Bottom Padding	Remove value
	Left Padding	Remove value

CSS Rule Definition Updates for .navigation in Designs.css

Category	Property	Value
Background	Background-color	#036

CSS Rule Definition Updates for .content in Designs.css

Category	Property	Value
Box	Left Padding	Remove value
Border	Bottom Color	#036

CSS Rule Definition Updates for .footer in Designs.css

Category	Property	Value
Type	Color	#333
Background	Background-color	#FC0

Table 3–6 Page Properties

Category	Property	Value
Links (CSS)	Link color	#FFF
	Rollover links	#FF0
	Visited links	#FFF
	Underline style	Never underline

Figure 3–86

Figure 3–87

Continued >

In the Lab *continued*

Perform the following tasks:

1. Copy the Images folder and the about.txt file from the Chapter 03\Lab2 folder into the *your last name and first initial*\Designs folder (the F:\perezm folder, for example).

2. Start Dreamweaver. Use the Sites button on the Files panel to select the Designs by Dolores site.

3. Create a new Web page using the Designs Template. Save the new page in the root folder for the Designs site using `about.html` as the file name. Close the file.

4. Use the same method as in Step 3 to create four more Web pages and use `services.html`, `pricing.html`, `hosting.html`, and `contact.html` as the file names.

5. Close all open documents, and then open Designs Template.dwt.

6. Select the word, Home, in the navigation bar. Use the Point to File button on the Property inspector to create a relative link to index.html.

7. Select the words, About Us, in the navigation bar. Use the Point to File button to create a relative link to about.html.

8. Use the same method as in Steps 6 and 7 to create links for Services, Pricing, Web Hosting, and Contact Us.

9. Use the Edit Rule button on the CSS Styles panel to edit the CSS rules for the header, navigation, content, and footer in Lifestyle.css. Refer to Table 3–5 for the updated values. Only update the values listed in the table; keep the other values the same. Apply and accept your changes.

10. Delete the text, Designs by Dolores, in the header. Insert the designs_logo image in the header. Use `Business logo` as the alternate text.

11. Click a blank area of the page, and then click the Page Properties button on the Property inspector and refer to Table 3–6 to change the page property values. Apply and accept your changes.

12. Save your changes to the Designs Template and the Designs.css file. Update the files that use the template and then close the template.

13. Open index.html.

14. Place your insertion point to the left of the word, Welcome, in the content area. Insert the home_image image. Use `Home image` as the alternate text.

15. Right-click the image, point to Align on the shortcut menu, and then click Left to left-align the image.

16. Place your insertion point after the last sentence, Please contact us today!, and then press the ENTER key.

17. Save your changes and view the document in your browser. Compare your document to Figure 3–86. Make any necessary changes, save your changes, and then close index.html.

18. Open about.html.

19. Replace the text, Insert content here, with the text in about.txt.

20. Insert the about_image picture after the last paragraph, use `About image` as the alternate text, and then center-align the picture on the page.

21. Save your changes and view the document in your browser. Compare your document to Figure 3–87. Make any necessary changes and then save your changes.

22. Click the links on the navigation bar to view the other pages, and to confirm that each item on the navigation bar is linked to the correct page. Make any necessary changes and then save your changes.

23. Submit the documents in the format specified by your instructor.

In the Lab

Lab 3: Adding Images and Links to the Justin's Lawn Care Service Web Site

Note: To complete this assignment, you will be required to use the Data Files for Students. Visit www.cengage.com/ct/studentdownload for detailed instructions on downloading the Data Files for Students or contact your instructor for information about accessing the required files.

Problem: You are creating a Web site for a new lawn care company, Justin's Lawn Care Service. The Web site will provide information to customers, including descriptions of services and pricing. In Chapter 2, you developed the template and home page for the Justin's Lawn Care Service site. Now you need to create the Web pages for the site, add a logo to the template, update the template with links to each page, modify the link colors, and enhance the site with images. You also will modify the CSS rule definitions.

First, use the Lawn Template to create Web pages for Services, Landscape, Prices, Quote, and Contact. Update the Design Template with links to each page. Next, modify the Lawn CSS rule definitions to improve the format and design of the pages. Add a logo and an image to the template, and then set an image as the page background. Finally, add images to the Landscape Web page. The revised CSS rule definitions for the header, navigation, content, and footer are provided in Table 3–7. The page property values are provided in Table 3–8. The Landscape page is shown in Figure 3–88, and the Contact page is shown in Figure 3–89.

Table 3–7 Updated CSS Rule Definitions for Justin's Lawn Care Service

CSS Rule Definition for .header in Lawn.css

Category	Property	Value
Type	Font-family	Remove value
	Font-size	Remove value
	Font-weight	Remove value
	Font-style	Remove value
	Color	Remove value
Background	Background-color	Remove value
Box	Top Padding	Remove value

CSS Rule Definition for .navigation in Lawn.css

Category	Property	Value
Type	Font-weight	bold
Background	Background-color	Remove value
Border	Style	Remove value (keep Same for all box checked)
	Width	Remove value (keep Same for all box checked)
	Color	Remove value (keep Same for all box checked)

Table 3–8 Page Properties

Category	Property	Value
Appearance (CSS)	Background image	Use the Browse button to select background_image in the Images folder
Links (CSS)	Link color	#030
	Rollover links	#090
	Visited links	#030
	Underline style	Show underline only on rollover

Continued >

In the Lab *continued*

Figure 3–88

Figure 3–89

Used with permission from Microsoft Corporation

Perform the following tasks:

1. Start Dreamweaver. Use the Sites button on the Files panel to select the Justin's Lawn Care Service site.

2. Use the Lawn_Template to create the following Web pages: `services.html`, `landscape.html`, `prices.html`, `quote.html`, and `contact.html`. Save and close each new Web page.

3. Open Lawn_Template.dwt. Add the appropriate relative links to Home, Services, Landscape, Prices, Quote, and Contact in the navigation bar.

4. Edit the CSS rules for the header and navigation in Lawn.css. Refer to Table 3–7 to modify the values. Apply and accept your changes.

5. Replace the text in the header with the lawn_logo image. Use `Business logo` as the alternate text.

6. Replace the text in the sidebar with the sidebar_image. image. Use `Sidebar image` as the alternate text.

7. Add page properties as specified in Table 3–8. Apply and accept your changes.

8. Save your changes to the Lawn Template and the Lawn.css file. Update files and then close the template file.

9. Open landscape.html.

10. Replace the text, Insert content here, with `Landscaping Ideas.`

11. Press the ENTER key and then insert the landscape1 and landscape2 images. Press the SHIFT+ENTER keys and then insert the landscape3 and landscape4 images. Press the SPACEBAR to separate the images that appear on one line. Use `Landscape image 1`, `Landscape image 2`, `Landscape image 3`, and `Landscape image 4` for the alternate text, respectively.

12. Click to the right of Landscape image 4, press the ENTER key, and then type `Plants and Flowers` below the landscape images.

13. Press the ENTER key and then insert the plant1, plant2, plant3, plant4, and plant5 images. Press the SPACEBAR to separate the images. Use `Plant image 1`, `Plant image 2`, `Plant image 3`, `Plant image 4`, and `Plant image 5` for the alternate text, respectively.

14. Save your changes and view the document in your browser. Compare your document to Figure 3–88. Make any necessary changes and save your changes.

15. Open contact.html.

16. Replace the text, Insert content here, with `For additional information about our services, please contact us at (777) 555-2629 or e-mail us at JustinsLCS@justin.net.`

17. Add an e-mail link, `JustinsLCS@justin.net`, to the e-mail text.

18. Save your changes and view the document in your browser. Compare your document to Figure 3–89. Make any necessary changes and save your changes.

19. Click the links on the navigation bar to view the other pages, and to confirm that each item on the navigation bar is linked to the correct page. Make any necessary changes and save your changes.

20. Submit the documents in the format specified by your instructor.

Cases and Places

Apply your creative thinking and problem solving skills to design and implement a solution.

1: Adding Web Pages and Links for Moving Venture Tips

Personal

You have created the home page for Moving Venture Tips and now need to create the other Web pages for the site. After creating the pages, you will add links to the pages from the navigation bar on the Move Template. You have decided to modify the font color and background color for the

Continued >

Cases and Places *continued*

header and navigation. You also want to modify the page properties by adding link colors. You also will add an image to the Rentals page. Use the Move Template to create Web pages for Budget, Rentals, Tips, and Contact. After creating these pages, link the text in the navigation bar to each page in the site. Modify the CSS rules for the header by changing the type color and background-color. Modify the CSS rules for the navigation by changing the background-color, border style, and box width. Add page properties for Links (CSS) by defining a color for the link color, rollover links, and visited links. Add text about rental information to the Rentals page. Create an Images folder and save it within the Move root folder. Add an image to the Rentals page. Check the spelling using the Commands menu and correct all misspelled words. Submit the document in the format specified by your instructor.

2: Adding Web Pages, Images, and Links for Student Campus Resources

Academic

You have created the home page for Student Campus Resources and now need to create the other Web pages for the site. After creating the pages, you will add links to the pages from the navigation bar on the Campus Template. You have decided to modify the font color and background color for the navigation. You also want to modify page properties by adding a background color and link colors. You also will add text and an image to the Activities page. Use the Campus Template to create Web pages for Activities, Committees, Events, and Contact. After creating these pages, link the text in the navigation bar to each page in the site. Modify the CSS rules for the navigation by changing the type color, background-color, and border colors (if you have borders). Modify the CSS rules for the content by changing or removing the box height. Modify the CSS rules for the footer by changing the font-family and color (in the Type category). Add page properties for Appearance (CSS) by defining a background color. Add page properties for Links (CSS) by defining a color for the link color, rollover links, and visited links. Add text describing student activities information to the Activities page. Create an Images folder and save it within the Campus root folder. Add an image to the Activities page and center-align the image on the page. Check the spelling using the Commands menu and correct all misspelled words. Submit the document in the format specified by your instructor.

3: Adding Web Pages, Images, and Links for French Villa Roast Café

Professional

You have created the home page for French Villa Roast Café and now need to create the other Web pages for the site. After creating the pages, you will add links to the pages from the navigation on the Cafe Template. You have decided to modify the font color for the navigation, and the background color and padding for the content. You also want to modify the page properties by adding a background image and link colors. You also will add an image to the Home and About pages. Use the Cafe Template to create Web pages for About, Menu, Rewards, and Contact. After creating these pages, link the text in the navigation bar to each page in the site. Modify the CSS rules for the navigation by changing the type color. Modify the CSS rules for the content by changing the background color and adjusting the box padding. Add page properties for Appearance (CSS) by defining a background image. Add page properties for Links (CSS) by defining a color for the link color, rollover links, and visited links. Add text to the About page. Add text to the Contact page and include an e-mail link. Create an Images folder and save it within the Cafe root folder. Add an image to the Home page and right-align the image on the page. Add an image to the About page and center-align the image on the page. Check the spelling using the Commands menu and correct all misspelled words. Submit the document in the format specified by your instructor.

4 | Exploring Tables and Forms

Objectives

You will have mastered the material in this chapter when you can:

- Design a Web page using tables
- Insert a table
- Format text in a table
- Modify a table structure
- Design a Web page using forms
- Insert a table into a form

- Describe and add text fields
- Add input tag accessibility attributes
- Describe and add a menu and a radio group
- Describe and add buttons
- View and test a form

4 | Exploring Tables and Forms

Introduction

To structure text, images, links, and forms into a grid pattern that contains rows and columns, Web designers employ tables. Web pages use tables to organize information. Dreamweaver's tables are very similar to the table feature in word processing programs such as Microsoft Word. A table allows you to add vertical and horizontal structure to a Web page by creating columns of text and laying out tabular data. You can delete, split, and merge rows and columns; modify table, row, or cell properties to add color and adjust alignment; and copy, paste, and delete cells in the table structure.

Tables also enable the Web site designer to lay out and create forms in a structured format. Web page forms can provide visitors with dynamic information as well as request and process information and feedback they provide. Web forms are highly versatile tools for conducting surveys, requesting job applications, and providing order forms, tests, automated responses, user questions, and online reservations.

Project — Formatted Tables and Forms

Continuing the design of the Gallery site, a table in the Services page provides information about the different types of photo services, and a table in the Pricing page itemizes session fees. The Services table, shown in Figure 4–1a, highlights the services the Gallery offers, including those for portrait, family, children, newborn, and maternity photography in a natural, relaxed setting. The Pricing Information table, shown in Figure 4–1b, is intended to answer customer questions about the costs for a photography portrait session as well as product offerings.

In addition to structuring information, a table also can be used to create a form. In this chapter, you add a form to the Contact page of the Gallery site. The Contact form, shown in Figure 4–1c, contains a request to schedule or inquire about a photography session. The form provides descriptive labels and Form objects, such as a text box, list menu, and radio buttons, allowing users to submit their information to the Gallery photography studio. As you complete the activities in this chapter, you will find that forms are one of the more important sources of interactivity on the Web and a standard tool for the Web page designer.

(a) Table on Services page

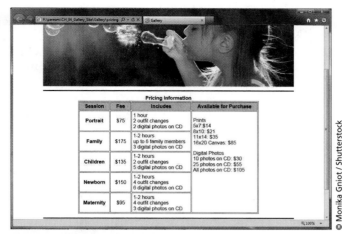

(b) Table on Pricing page

(c) Table and form on Contact page

Figure 4–1

Overview

As you read this chapter, you will learn how to create the Web page project shown in Figure 4–1 by performing these general tasks:

- Insert a table into a Dreamweaver Web page.
- Format the table.
- Merge cells.
- Add accessibility attributes.
- Insert a form into a Dreamweaver Web page.
- Add labels, text fields, menus, and radio buttons to a form.
- Add a Submit button and a Reset button.

Plan Ahead

General Project Guidelines

When adding content to pages within a Web site, consider if the information would best be organized logically within a table format using rows and columns. If you intend to collect information from your site's visitors, a form can provide feedback. As you add two tables as shown in Figure 4–1a and Figure 4–1b, and a form in a Web page as shown in Figure 4–1c, you should follow these general guidelines:

1. **Determine what to insert into tables.** Create and organize the new content for the Web pages on your site. Consider whether you can organize and format some content in tables.

2. **Consider table layout.** Define the caption for the table, number of rows and columns, table width, border size, and cell padding. Determine whether cells within the table need to be merged to provide a better layout. If so, determine which cells need to be merged.

3. **Plan the format of the form pages.** Determine the purpose of the form. Consider the layout of the form.

4. **Consider the data you will collect.** Use the data to determine rows and columns that will be included as part of the form. Decide what the labels should state within the form. Consider the audience that will use the form and what is the best way to collect the data.

5. **Determine the types of controls you will add to the form.** The controls you add will determine and affect the type of data you can collect.

More specific details about these guidelines are presented at appropriate points throughout the chapter as necessary. The chapter also identifies the actions performed and decisions made regarding these guidelines during the development of the pages within the site shown in Figure 4–1.

To Start Dreamweaver and Open the Gallery Site

Each time you start Dreamweaver, it opens to the last site displayed when the program closed. The following steps start Dreamweaver and open the Gallery Web site.

1 Click the Start button on the Windows 7 taskbar to display the Start menu, and then type `Dreamweaver CS6` in the 'Search programs and files' box.

2 Click Adobe Dreamweaver CS6 in the list to start Dreamweaver.

3 If the Dreamweaver window is not maximized, click the Maximize button next to the Close button on the Application bar to maximize the window.

4 If the Gallery site is not displayed in the Files panel, click the Sites button on the Files panel toolbar and then click Gallery to display the files and folders in the Gallery site.

Understanding Tables

Web designers use tables to present large amounts of detailed information that can be uniformly structured into rows and columns. If a paragraph becomes cumbersome and repetitive within a Web page, consider using a table instead to format the information in an easy-to-follow layout. A table consists of **rows**, which extend horizontally from left to right; **columns**, which extend vertically from top to bottom; and **cells**, which define the area where a row and a column intersect. Each cell in the table can contain any standard element you use on a Web page, including text, images, and other objects.

Plan
Ahead

> **Determine what to insert into tables.**
> Readability is a key factor on any Web site because it enhances the user experience. Visitors prefer not to read lengthy paragraphs online. By taking advantage of simple tables to structure content, you can allow users to find the information they need in a few seconds.

Designing Table Layouts

Creating a table in Dreamweaver is a simple three-step process that begins with inserting a table, configuring the table layout, and finally adding the content, such as the text or images. After you insert a table, a Table dialog box opens that requests the number of rows and columns, table width, and other property settings as shown in Table 4–1.

Table 4–1 Table Dialog Box Settings		
Attribute	**Default**	**Description**
Rows	3	Determines the number of rows in the table
Columns	3	Determines the number of columns in the table
Table width	200 pixels	Specifies the width of the table in pixels or as a percentage of the browser window's width
Border thickness	1	Specifies the border width in pixels
Cell padding	None	Specifies the number of pixels between a cell's border and its contents
Cell spacing	None	Specifies the number of pixels between adjacent table cells
Header	None	Specifies whether the top row or first column is designated as a header row or column
Caption	None	Provides a table heading
Summary	None	Provides a table description; used by screen readers

Plan
Ahead

> **Consider table layout.**
>
> **Choose a caption for the table.** A caption provides a table heading. For a simple table, the caption should act as an adequate summary of the table's contents.
>
> **Determine the number of rows and columns.** Analyze the information that will be placed in the table structure to determine how many row and column elements are necessary.
>
> **Format the table.** Format a Web page table by setting various properties within the table. In Dreamweaver, you set the format properties entering text into the table structure. You set table properties — such as the width of the table, the width of the table's border, and the cell padding that determines the number of pixels between a cell's content and the cell boundaries — in the Table dialog box or Property inspector. Before formatting the table, determine if you need to merge cells together to provide a larger single cell or if you need to split a cell into two or more cells. You also can change the properties of a certain cell or selection of cells instead of the whole table.

The Services Web page highlights the Gallery's specialization of photography services in portrait, family, children, newborn, and maternity photos to capture memorable personal moments. By adding a table to display these services, as shown in Figure 4–2, customers can quickly evaluate if the Gallery's services match their photography needs. The Services table contains an opening caption, five horizontal rows and two vertical columns, a table width of 800 pixels, a 0-pixel border around the contents of the table, a cell padding of 8 pixels, and a left header. The left header appears centered and in a bold text. By default, the contents of the column or row that you designate as a header are displayed in a bold font and centered. The default is to create a table with no headers — that is, all rows and columns look the same. The Caption option displays a title outside of the table. If you specify a caption, the Align Caption option indicates where the table caption appears in relation to the table.

Figure 4–2

BTW

Providing a Table Summary
Summaries are especially useful in tables of data, such as a bus schedule or price list, where the content of a cell is meaningless without a column or row heading. For data tables, summaries should describe the layout of the table.

Adding a Summary to Provide Accessibility

When you create a table in Dreamweaver, the Summary option provides a table description for use in accessible content. Accessibility refers to making Web tables usable for people with visual, auditory, motor, and other disabilities. Summary text is similar to the alt text you added for images in Chapter 3. You add Summary text to the tables you create in this chapter. Screen readers recite the summary text to indicate the primary purpose of the table, but the text does not appear in the user's browser. The Summary text box is optional, and serves to improve the accessibility of your table.

To Insert a Table into the Services Page

The following steps insert a table with five rows and two columns into the Services Web page.

1

- Double-click the services.html file in the Files panel to display the contents of the Services page.

- Scroll down the page and select the placeholder text, Insert page content here, in the contentArea region, and then press the DELETE key to delete the placeholder text.

- Click Insert on the Application bar to display the Insert menu (Figure 4–3).

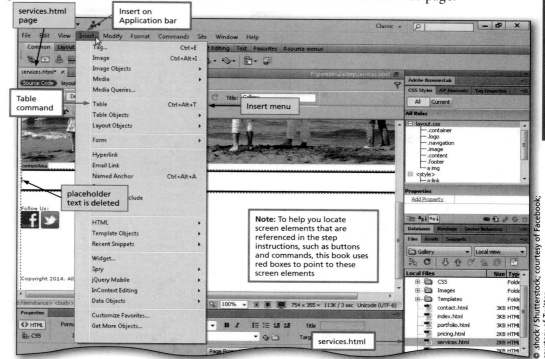

Note: To help you locate screen elements that are referenced in the step instructions, such as buttons and commands, this book uses red boxes to point to these screen elements

Figure 4–3

2

- Click Table on the Insert menu to display the Table dialog box (Figure 4–4).

Figure 4–4

3

- In the Rows text box, type 5 to change the number of rows.

- Double-click the Columns text box and then type 2 to change the number of columns.

- Double-click the Table width text box and then type 800 to set the width to 800 pixels.

- Double-click the Border thickness text box and then type 0 to set the border thickness.

- Click the Cell padding text box and then type 8 to set the number of cell padding pixels (Figure 4–5).

Figure 4–5

4

- Click Left in the Header area to create a left header in the table.

- Click the Caption text box and then type About Our Services to display a caption at the top of the table.

- Click the Summary text box and then type This table provides information about our portrait, family, children, newborn, and maternity photography services. to provide accessibility summary text (Figure 4–6).

Figure 4–6

5

- Click the OK button in the Table dialog box to create a table in the Services page (Figure 4–7).

Figure 4–7

Other Ways
1. Click Table button on Insert bar

To Add Text to the Table

After you use the Table dialog box to create the structure of the table, the entire table is selected automatically. Therefore, be careful not to type anything when the table is selected or that text will replace the whole table. Instead, click a cell in the table before starting to enter content. In the table you just inserted, all of the cells are equal in width, but they expand as you add the text shown in Table 4–2 to describe the services provided by the Gallery photography studio.

Table 4–2 About Our Services	
Service	**Description**
Portrait	Whether you are looking for a professional studio head shot or a candid photo, we can provide just what you need for your individual portrait session.
Family	Family photos are important pieces for your home. Let us capture fun-filled family moments that you can proudly display throughout your house.
Children	We believe that children's photography should be fun and relaxed. Play time at a park or near water is the perfect setting to capture fun expressions while your children are having a good time.
Newborn	Nothing is more precious than a newborn baby. We work around your infant to capture memorable moments in your baby's life.
Maternity	Pregnancy is a special time for expecting parents. Preserving it with classy, creative pictures is the perfect way to remember your beautiful baby bump.

The following steps add text to the table displayed on the Services page.

1

- Click in row 1, column 1 and then type `Portrait` to add text to the first row of the table.

- Click in row 2, column 1 and then type `Family` to add text to the second row.

- Click in row 3, column 1 and then type `Children` to add text to the third row.

- Click in row 4, column 1 and then type `Newborn` to add text to the fourth row.

- Click in row 5, column 1 and then type `Maternity` to add text to the fifth row (Figure 4–8).

Q&A

Why is the text centered within the cells?

When you enter text in a cell, Dreamweaver aligns the text in the center of each cell by default.

Figure 4–8

2

- Click in row 1, column 2 and then type `Whether you are looking for a professional studio head shot or a candid photo, we can provide just what you need for your individual portrait session` to add a description to the first row of the table.

- Enter the remaining descriptions for the services shown in Table 4–2 in rows 2, 3, 4, and 5 to finish entering the text descriptions in the table (Figure 4–9).

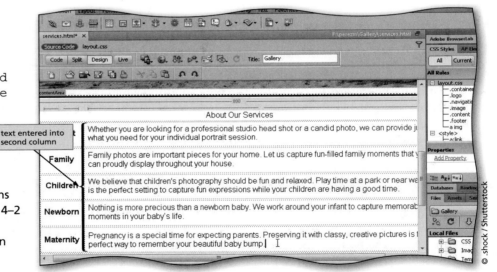

Figure 4–9

Formatting Tables

Each table within a Web page can be formatted to meet the design needs of the site. You use the Property inspector to format table attributes such as merging cells or setting the width of a table column. The Property inspector options change depending on the selected object within the table. When a table is selected, the Property inspector displays table properties, as shown in Figure 4–10. When another table element — a row, column, or cell — is selected, the Property inspector displays properties for the selected element. Table 4–3 describes the table elements in the Property inspector.

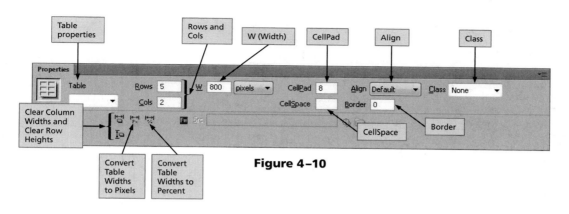

Figure 4–10

Table 4–3 Table Properties	
Table Element	**Description**
Table	Specifies the table ID, an identifier used for Cascading Style Sheets, scripting, and accessibility. A table ID is not required; however, it always is a good idea to add this identifier.
Rows and Cols	The number of rows and columns in the table.
W	Specifies the minimum width of the table in either pixels or percent. If a size is not specified, the size can vary depending on the monitor and browser settings. A table width specified in pixels is displayed as the same size in all browsers. A table width specified in percent is altered in appearance based on the user's monitor resolution and browser window size.
CellPad	The number of pixels between the cell border and the cell content.
CellSpace	The number of pixels between adjacent table cells.
Align	Determines where the table appears, relative to other elements in the same paragraph such as text or images. The default alignment is to the left.
Class	An attribute used with Cascading Style Sheets.
Border	Specifies the border width in pixels.
Clear Column Widths and Clear Row Heights	Delete all specified row height or column width values from the table.
Convert Table Widths to Pixels	Sets the width of each column in the table to its current width expressed as pixels.
Convert Table Widths to Percent	Sets the width of the table and each column in the table to their current widths expressed as percentages of the Document window's width.

Setting Cell, Row, and Column Properties

When you select a cell, row, or column, the properties in the upper pane of the Property inspector are the same as the standard properties for text. You can use these properties to include standard HTML formatting tags within a cell, row, or column. The part of the table you select determines which properties are displayed in the lower pane of the Property inspector. The properties for cells, rows, and columns are the same except for one element — the icon displayed in the upper-left corner of the Property inspector. On the next page, Figure 4–11 shows the cell properties, Figure 4–12 shows the row properties, and Figure 4–13 shows the column properties of the Property inspector. Table 4–4 on the next page describes the Property inspector elements for the cell, row, and column properties.

Figure 4–11

Figure 4–12

Figure 4–13

Table 4–4 Cell, Row, and Column Properties

Table Element	Description
Horz	Specifies the horizontal alignment of the contents of a cell, row, or column. The contents can be aligned to the left, right, or center of the cells.
Vert	Specifies the vertical alignment of the contents of a cell, row, or column. The contents can be aligned to the top, middle, bottom, or baseline of the cells.
W and H	Specifies the width and height of selected cells in pixels or as a percentage of the entire table's width or height.
No wrap	Prevents line wrapping, keeping all text in a given cell on a single line. If No wrap is enabled, cells widen to accommodate all data as it is typed or pasted into a cell.
Bg (Background color)	Sets the background color of a cell, row, or column selected from the color picker (use the Bg button) or specified as a hexadecimal number (use the Bg text box).
Header	Formats the selected cells as table header cells. The contents of table header cells are bold and centered by default.
Merges selected cells using spans	Combines selected cells, rows, or columns into one cell (available when two or more cells, rows, or columns are selected).
Splits cell into rows or columns	Divides a cell, creating two or more cells (available when a single cell is selected).

Selecting Table Elements

Dreamweaver can change the format of the text of an entire table, a specific row or column, or an individual cell within a table. You can select the entire table by clicking the outermost edge of the table and then apply the format changes to all of the text within the table, such as selecting a new font or font size. The pointer changes to an arrow with a table grid icon when you select the table. When a table is selected, sizing handles appear on the table's lower and right edges, as shown in Figure 4–14. You can resize the table by dragging its sizing handles.

Figure 4–14

To select a single row or column to format the contents of the cells, position the insertion point to the left edge of a row or the top edge of a column. A small black selection arrow appears, as shown in Figure 4–15, indicating the row or column that you are about to select. In addition, the cells in the row or column are outlined in red. Click to select the row or column of cells. You then can apply formatting options to customize the table so it matches the design and layout of your site.

Figure 4–15

To Format Table Text

You can modify the appearance of text within the table, such as changing text alignment, by first selecting the entire table, a row or a column, or an individual cell and then applying the format. The following steps change the alignment of text within a column of the Services table.

1

• Point to the top of the left column in the table until a selection arrow appears (Figure 4–16).

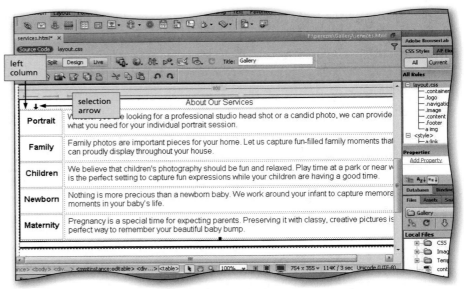

Figure 4–16

2

• Click to select the first column of cells.

• Click Format on the Application bar and then point to Align to display the Align submenu (Figure 4–17).

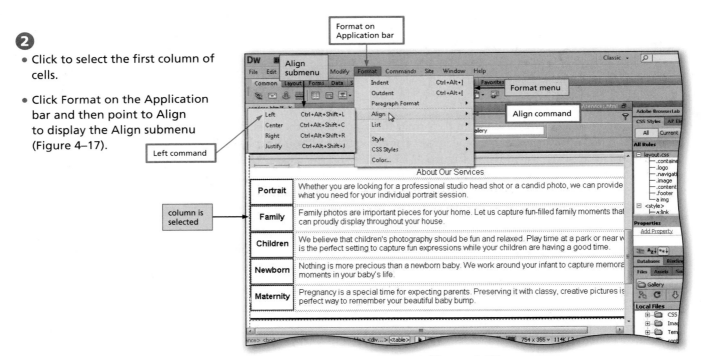

Figure 4–17

Dreamweaver Chapter 4

3

- Click Left on the Align submenu to left-align the text in the first column of the table (Figure 4–18).

Figure 4–18

Other Ways
1. Click panel options button, click Close or click Close Tab Group	2. To align, right-click text, point to Align, click alignment command

To Format the Table Caption

The caption, which displays a description of the contents of the table, appears outside the table. After selecting the caption, you can use the Property inspector to apply a format such as Bold to the selected text. The following steps bold the text caption and view the finished table in a browser.

1

- Select the text, About Our Services, to select the caption for formatting (Figure 4–19).

Figure 4–19

2

- In the Property inspector, click the Bold button to bold the selected text, and then click outside the caption to view the bold text (Figure 4–20).

Q&A

Can I use the Property inspector to format text within a table?

Yes. You can use the Property inspector to format every element within the table structure.

Figure 4–20

3

- Click the Save button on the Standard toolbar to save your work.

- Click the 'Preview/ Debug in browser' button on the Document toolbar to display a list of browsers.

- Click Preview in IExplore in the list to display the Services page in Internet Explorer (Figure 4–21).

4

- Click the Internet Explorer Close button to close the browser.

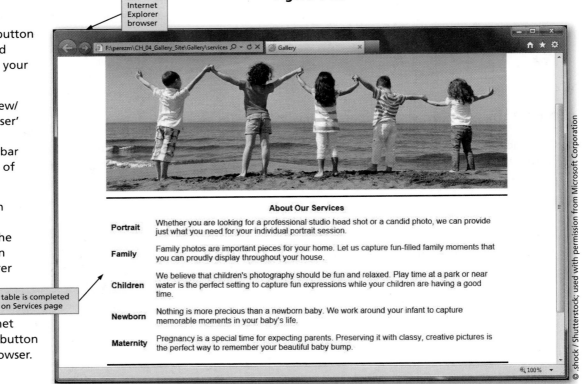

Figure 4–21

Understanding the HTML Structure of a Table

As you work with and become more familiar with tables, it is helpful to have a basic understanding of the HTML structure of a table. For example, suppose you have a table with two rows and two columns, displaying a total of four cells, such as the following:

First cell	Second cell
Third cell	Fourth cell

The general syntax of the table is:

```
<table>
  <tr>
    <td> First cell </td>
    <td> Second cell </td>
  </tr>
  <tr>
    <td> Third cell </td>
    <td> Fourth cell </td>
  </tr>
</table>
```

When you click in a table in Dreamweaver, the tag selector displays the <table>, <td>, and <tr> tags. The <table> tag indicates the whole table. Clicking the <table> tag in the tag selector selects the whole table. The <td> tag indicates **table data**. Clicking the <td> tag in the tag selector selects the cell containing the insertion point. The <tr> tag indicates **table row**. Clicking the <tr> tag in the tag selector selects the row containing the insertion point.

To Insert a Table into the Pricing Page

A primary reason for visiting the Gallery site is to identify the pricing for a photography session and photo costs. Pricing information tables play an important role for every company that offers products or services. A pricing table must be simple, but at the same time clearly differentiate between features and prices of different products and services. The Gallery studio carefully examined its product portfolio and selected the most important features to present in its pricing plan. The following steps insert a table with six rows and four columns into the Pricing Web page.

1

• Click the Close button on the services.html tab to close the Services page.

• In the Files panel, double-click pricing.html to display the Pricing page.

• Select the text, Insert page content here, in the contentArea region and then press the DELETE key to delete the placeholder text.

• Click Insert on the Application bar to display the Insert menu (Figure 4–22).

Figure 4–22

2

- Click Table on the Insert menu to display the Table dialog box (Figure 4–23).

Figure 4–23

3

- In the Rows text box, type 6 to change the number of rows.

- Double-click the Columns text box and then type 4 to change the number of columns.

- Double-click the Table width text box and then type 650 to set the width.

- Double-click the Border thickness text box and then type 1 to set the border thickness.

- Double-click the Cell padding text box and then type 4 to set the cell padding.

- Click Both in the Header area to create top and left headers in the table.

- Click the Caption text box and then type Pricing Information to display a caption at the top of the table.

Figure 4–24

- Click the Summary text box and type This table provides pricing information for photography services. to provide accessibility summary text (Figure 4–24).

4

- Click the OK button in the Table dialog box and scroll down to view the table in the Services page (Figure 4–25).

© Monika Gniot / Shutterstock

© Monika Gniot / Shutterstock

Figure 4–25

Other Ways
1. Click Table button on Insert bar

Merging and Splitting Cells in a Table

You can create a cell that spans two or more other cells by **merging** cells. You should be familiar with the concept of merging cells if you have worked with spreadsheets or word processing tables. Using HTML, merging cells is a more complicated process. Dreamweaver, however, simplifies the process of merging cells by hiding some complex HTML table restructuring code behind an easy-to-use interface in the Property inspector. By merging and splitting cells, you can set alignments that are more complex than straight rows and columns.

To merge two or more cells, select the cells and then click the 'Merges selected cells using spans' button in the Property inspector. The selected cells must be contiguous and in the shape of a line or a rectangle. You can merge any number of adjacent cells as long as the entire selection is a line or a rectangle. To split a cell, click the cell and then click the 'Splits cell into rows or columns' button in the Property inspector to display the Split Cell dialog box. In the Split Cell dialog box, specify how to split the cell and then click the OK button. You can split a cell into any number of rows or columns, regardless of whether it was merged previously. When you split a cell into two rows, the other cells in the same row as the split cell are not split. If you split a cell into two or more columns, the other cells in the same column are not split. To select a cell quickly, click in the cell and then click the <td> tag on the tag selector.

BTW

Deleting a Row or Column
Select a row or column and then press the DELETE key. You also can delete a row or column by clicking a cell, clicking Modify on the Application bar, pointing to Table, and then clicking Delete Row or Delete Column on the submenu. Or click a cell within a row or column, right-click to display the context menu, point to Table, and then click Delete Row or Delete Column.

To Merge Cells in a Table

You can use the Property inspector to merge cells before or after text is added to the cell. The last column in the Pricing Information table should have a header with the text, Available for Purchase. The five current cells should be merged into one cell to list the prices for the photo prints and digital photos. The following steps merge multiple cells in a table.

1

- Click in row 2, column 4 of the Pricing Information table and then drag to select the next four cells in the last column to select a total of five cells (Figure 4–26).

Q&A

When you select multiple cells to merge, must the selection be shaped as a rectangle?

Yes. A merged cell selection must be in a contiguous line and in the shape of a rectangle.

Figure 4–26

2

- In the Property inspector, click the 'Merges selected cells using spans' button to merge the five selected cells in the last column into one cell (Figure 4–27).

Figure 4–27

Other Ways	
1. Right-click selected cells, click Merge Cells	2. On Modify menu, point to Table, click Merge Cells

To Add Text to the Pricing Table

After inserting the table in the Pricing page, you are ready to enter and format the pricing text. Table 4–5 lists the Gallery's pricing options. Notice that several cells in Table 4–5 contain more than one line of text. To add multiple lines of text within the same cell, press the SHIFT+ENTER keys at the end of a line to insert a line break.

Table 4–5 Pricing Information Table

Session	Fee	Includes		Available for Purchase
Portrait	$75	1 hour 2 outfit changes 2 digital photos on CD		Prints 5x7: $14 8x10: $21
Family	$175	1-2 hours up to 6 family members 3 digital photos on CD		11x14: $35 16x20 Canvas: $85
Children	$135	1-2 hours 2 outfit changes 5 digital photos on CD		Digital Photos 10 photos on CD: $30 25 photos on CD: $55 All photos on CD: $105
Newborn	$150	1-2 hours 4 outfit changes 6 digital photos on CD		
Maternity	$95	1-2 hours 4 outfit changes 3 digital photos on CD		

The following steps add text to the table displayed on the Pricing page.

1

- Click in row 1, column 1 and then type `Session` to add text to the first row of the table.

- Click in row 2, column 1 and then type `Portrait` to add text to the second row.

- Enter the remaining text for the first column shown in Table 4–5 to complete the text for the first column (Figure 4–28).

Q&A

Why was the text in the first column in the table automatically bolded?

In the Table dialog box, the Header was set to Both. The first column and first row of this table are each headers, which are displayed in bold automatically.

Figure 4–28

2

- Click in row 1, column 2 and then type Fee to add text to the second column.

- Enter the remaining descriptions for the fees shown in Table 4–5 to finish entering the text for the second column (Figure 4–29).

Q&A

Why were the fees not displayed in bold text in the table?

The Fee column is not a header. When you select Both as the header option, Dreamweaver bolds the text in the first row and first column.

Figure 4–29

© Monika Gniot / Shutterstock

3

- Click in row 1, column 3 and then type Includes to add text to the third column.

- Click in row 2, column 3, type 1 hour, and then press the SHIFT+ENTER keys to create a line break.

- On the next line in the same cell, type 2 outfit changes and then press the SHIFT+ENTER keys to create a line break.

- On the next line in the same cell, type 2 digital photos on CD to complete the cell text.

- Enter the remaining text for the third column shown in Table 4–5 to complete the text for the third column, pressing the SHIFT+ENTER keys to create line breaks between each line of text within a cell (Figure 4–30).

Figure 4–30

- Click in row 1, column 4 and then type `Available for Purchase` to add text to the last column.

- In the merged cell, type the text shown in Table 4–5 to complete the table, pressing the SHIFT+ENTER keys to create line breaks between each line of text within the cell except before the text, Digital Photos, where you insert two line breaks (Figure 4–31).

- Click the Save All button on the Standard toolbar to save your work.

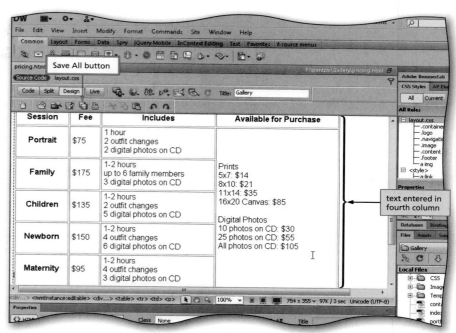

Figure 4–31

To Align the Table

When you insert a table, Dreamweaver adds the table to the page with the default left alignment. You can set the alignment of a table to Left, Center, or Right. With the table selected, you can use the Align property in the Property inspector to change the alignment of the Pricing Information table to Center. The following steps align a table in the center of the page.

1

- Click the outermost edge of the Pricing Information table to select the entire table (Figure 4–32).

Q&A Why does the table have a red border and black handles?

The border and handles indicate that the table is selected.

Figure 4–32

2

- Click the Align button in the Property inspector and then click Center to center the table on the page (Figure 4–33).

Figure 4–33

To Adjust the Table Width

If you overestimate or underestimate the table width when first inserting a table into the Document window, you can adjust the table width using the Property inspector.

The Pricing Information table is too wide for the text it contains and needs to be adjusted. You change the table width by selecting the table and then changing the width in the Property inspector. The following steps adjust the width of the table.

1

- With the Pricing Information table selected, double-click the W box in the Property inspector to select the width value (Figure 4–34).

Figure 4–34

2

- Type 575 in the W box to adjust the width of the table and then scroll up to display the size (Figure 4–35).

Q&A

What is the visual feedback displayed above the table?

Visual feedback is the green ruler above the table. It displays the number of pixels for the table width.

© Monika Gniot / Shutterstock

Figure 4–35

To Adjust the Column Width

In addition to changing the width of the entire table, Dreamweaver assists you in setting properties for column width or row height. When you change the width of a single cell in Dreamweaver, the remaining cells in that column are adjusted automatically to match the newly defined cell width. You also can change the row height of a single cell to define the height of the entire row. To change the width of a column row, you can adjust the width of the column by dragging the divider between the columns to the specified width or by entering the value in the W box (the Column Width property) in the Property inspector.

To create a custom fit for the text within each column in the Pricing Information table, you can set the four column widths to 90, 60, 200, and 225 pixels, respectively. Set the first two columns by dragging the right border of the column you want to change to the correct width measurement. As you drag the right border of the column, visual feedback above the table displays the exact number of pixels in each table column. Use the W box in the Property inspector to set the appropriate pixel measurements in the third and fourth columns. The following steps adjust the column width of multiple columns.

1

- Click the right border of the first column in the table and drag to the right until the pixel size is displayed in the visual feedback as 90 pixels (Figure 4–36).

© Monika Gniot / Shutterstock

Figure 4–36

2

- Click the right border of the second column and drag to the right until the pixel size is displayed in the visual feedback as 60 pixels (Figure 4–37).

Figure 4–37

3

- Point to the top edge of the third column to display a selection arrow and then click to select the column (Figure 4–38).

Figure 4–38

④

- Click the W box in the Property inspector and then type 200 to enter a width value.

- Press the ENTER key to resize the third column (Figure 4–39).

Q&A

Two numbers appear for each column width. What do both of these values mean?

The first number in the column width specifies the value placed in the code. The second value in parentheses represents the width of the column in the window size indicated on the status bar.

Figure 4–39

⑤

- Point to the top edge of the fourth column to display a selection arrow, and then click to select the column.

- Click the W box in the Property inspector, type 225, and then press the ENTER key to resize the fourth column (Figure 4–40).

⑥

- Click the Save button on the Standard toolbar to save your work.

Figure 4–40

Changing the Default Cell Alignment

The default horizontal cell alignment for text is left. When you enter text in a cell, it appears along the left margin of the cell. You can change the horizontal alignment using the Horz button in the Property inspector by clicking the cell and then changing the Horz setting to Center or Right. The default vertical cell alignment is Middle, which aligns the cell content in the middle of the cell. You change the vertical alignment using the Vert button in the Property inspector. Table 4–6 describes the cell alignment options.

BTW

Table Formatting Conflicts
When a property, such as alignment, is set to one value for the whole table and another value for individual cells, cell formatting takes precedence over row formatting; this in turn takes precedence over table formatting. The order of precedence for table formatting is cells, rows, and table.

Table 4–6 Cell Alignment Options

Alignment	Description
Default	Specifies a baseline alignment; default may vary depending on the user's browser
Baseline	Aligns the cell content at the bottom of the cell (same as Bottom)
Top	Aligns the cell content at the top of the cell
Bottom	Aligns the cell content at the bottom of the cell
TextTop	Aligns the top of the image with the top of the tallest character in the text line
Absolute Middle	Aligns the middle of the image with the middle of the text in the current line
Absolute Bottom	Aligns the bottom of the image with the bottom of the line of text
Left	Places the selected image on the left margin, wrapping text around it to the right; if left-aligned text precedes the object on the line, it generally forces left-aligned objects to wrap to a new line
Middle	Aligns the middle of the image with the baseline of the current line
Right	Places the image on the right margin, wrapping text around the object to the left; if right-aligned text precedes the object on the line, it generally forces right-aligned objects to wrap to a new line

To Align Text within a Table Cell

Alignment properties can be applied to a single cell, to multiple cells, or to the entire table. The following steps align the text within the table cells.

1

- Point to the top edge of the second column to display the selection arrow and then click to select the column.

- Click the Horz button in the Property inspector and then click Center to center the text horizontally in the second column (Figure 4–41).

Figure 4–41

© Monika Gniot / Shutterstock

2

- Click the merged cell in the fourth column to select the cell.

- Click the Vert button in the Property inspector and then click Top to top-align the text in the cell (Figure 4–42).

Figure 4–42

To Set the Background Color of Cells in a Table

You can apply background color to an entire table or to individual cells. If a background color is not specified, the table uses the same background color as the Web page. To set the background color of a table or its cells, you click the Bg (Background color) button in the Property inspector to display a color palette, also called a color picker. You can enter a hexadecimal color preceded by a number sign (#), such as #0000FF, in the Bg text box if you know the hexadecimal code.

To follow the color design of the page and to emphasize the header row, you can apply an orange background color to the first row of the Pricing Information table. The following steps set the background color of the cells in a table.

1

- Point to the left edge of the first row to display a selection arrow and then click to select the row.

- Click the Bg button in the Property inspector to display the color picker, and then point to the #FF9900 orange box to display its hexadecimal number (Figure 4–43).

Figure 4–43

2

- Click the #FF9900 orange box to change the background color of the selected row (Figure 4–44).

Can I type the hexadecimal code for the background color instead of using the color picker?

Yes. You can type the hexadecimal color in the Bg text box to identify the background color.

Figure 4–44

3

- Click the Save button on the Standard toolbar to save your work.

- Click the 'Preview/ Debug in browser' button on the Document toolbar to display a list of browsers.

- Click Preview in IExplore in the list to display the Pricing page in Internet Explorer. Scroll down the page to view the table (Figure 4–45).

4

- Click the Internet Explorer Close button to close the browser.

Figure 4–45

Break Point: If you wish to take a break, this is a good place to do so. To resume at a later time, start Dreamweaver and continue following the steps from this location forward.

Understanding How Forms Work

Forms are interactive elements that provide a way for a Web site visitor to interact with the site. Users complete forms to give feedback, submit an order for merchandise or services, request information, make reservations, and so on. The Gallery photography studio has requested that its Web site use a form to collect information from customers who are interested in scheduling a photography session. Dreamweaver provides a number of Form objects to collect input including text boxes, list boxes, menus, radio buttons, and buttons. After a user enters information into the form elements, Dreamweaver's validation ensures that the information is filled in and properly formatted.

Plan Ahead

Plan the format of the form pages.
To integrate a form page into your Web site, format it the same way you format other pages on the site. Use the same background image, for example, and the same font and styles for the text. To minimize the amount of scrolling users must do to complete the form, sketch the form and plan where to insert the controls such as text boxes and labels. If you are converting a paper-based form into a Web form, identify how you can condense the form to fit the screen and what types of electronic controls you will use where users enter information on the printed form.

Creating a Form

To insert a form on a Web page, you can use the Form button on the Forms tab of the Insert bar. Dreamweaver creates the JavaScript necessary for processing the form, inserts the beginning <form> and ending </form> tags into the source code, and then displays a dotted red outline to represent the form in Design view. Unlike a table, you cannot resize a form by dragging the borders. Rather, the form expands as you insert objects. When viewed in a browser, the form outline is not displayed; therefore, no visible border exists to turn on or off.

Plan Ahead

Consider the data you will collect.
Use familiar labels that clearly describe the data users should enter. For example, if you are requesting a date, consider that your audience may be unsure which date format to use. Provide a sample or layout of the date such as mm/dd/yyyy. If necessary, include simple, clear instructions about what information users should provide. Consider providing radio button options instead of expecting the user to write a narrative answer. Finally, organize the input fields so the order is logical and predictable to users.

Form Processing

A form provides an effective way to collect data from a Web site visitor. Forms, however, do not process data. Typically, forms contain objects that users interact with by entering or selecting information, for example. After providing the requested information, users click a button to submit the data to a server for processing or to e-mail it to a designated e-mail address. This chapter covers the insertion of tables and forms, but form processing is beyond the scope of this text.

Dreamweaver **behaviors** are ways to add scripting events to the elements on your Web page. Dreamweaver writes the JavaScript and the event attribute for you. You can create behaviors to validate form information. In Chapter 5, you add Spry form validation to the form created in this chapter to provide a Dreamweaver behavior that checks the user's entries into the form.

To submit a form, a Web site must run a script to process the form input data. A script is a text file that is executed within an application and usually is written in Perl, VBScript, JavaScript, Java, or C++. These scripts reside on a server. Therefore, they are called server-side scripts. Other server-side technologies include Adobe ColdFusion, ASP.NET, PHP, and JavaServer Pages (JSP). Some types of database applications support these technologies. A common way to process form data is through a Common Gateway Interface (CGI) script. When a browser collects data, it sends the data to a Hypertext Transfer Protocol (HTTP) server (a gateway) specified in the HTML form. The server starts a program (which also is specified in the HTML form) that can process the collected data. The gateway can process the data as you specify. It may return customized HTML based on the user's entries, log the data to a file, or e-mail the data to someone.

To Insert a Form into a Web Page

Using a form, the Contact page in the Gallery site collects the customer's name, e-mail address, and phone number, the type of session, the preferred session date, and how the customer heard about the photography studio. The following steps insert a form into the Contact page.

1

- Click the Close button on the pricing.html tab to close the Pricing page.

- In the Files panel, double-click contact.html to display the Contact page.

- Scroll down, click after the e-mail address, TheGalleryPFP@thegallery. net, and then press the ENTER key to move the insertion point to the next line.

- Type You may complete the form below to schedule your photography session. and then press the ENTER key to enter text that introduces the form (Figure 4–46).

Figure 4–46

2

- Click Insert on the Application bar to display the Insert menu, and then point to Form to display the Form submenu (Figure 4–47).

Figure 4–47

3

- Click Form on the Form submenu to insert a form outlined by a dotted red line (Figure 4–48).

Q&A Will the dotted red outline of the form appear on the Web page?

No. The form outline is a guide to help you select the form and insert text and form objects. When the form is displayed on a Web page, the outline does not appear.

Figure 4–48

© Serg Ivanov / Shutterstock

4

- Click the Form ID text box in the Property inspector and then type contact to name the form (Figure 4–49).

Q&A

Why should I name the form?

Although a form does not need a name to work, a name is helpful if you use Dreamweaver behavior or JavaScript to interact with the form.

Figure 4–49

Other Ways

1. Click Form button on Forms tab of Insert bar
2. Click Form button on Insert bar

Using the Form Property Inspector

As you have seen, the Property inspector options change depending on the selected object. Figure 4–50 shows the Property inspector for a selected form. Table 4–7 lists the form elements and descriptions.

Figure 4–50

Table 4–7 Form Elements

Form Element	Description
Form ID	Naming a form makes it possible to reference or control the form with a behavior.
Action	Contains the mailto address where the form results can be e-mailed or specifies the URL to the dynamic page or script that will process the form.
Target	Specifies the window or frame in which to display the data after processing if a script specifies that a new page should be displayed. The four targets are _blank, _parent, _self, and _top. The _blank target opens the referenced link (or processed data) in a new browser window, leaving the current window untouched. The **_blank target** is the one most often used with a jump menu, which is discussed later in this chapter. The **_self-target** opens the destination document in the same window as the one in which the form was submitted. The two other targets mostly are used with frames.
Method	Indicates the method by which the form data is transferred to the server. The three options are **POST**, which embeds the form data in the HTTP request; **GET**, which appends the form data to the URL requesting the page; and **Default**, which uses the browser's default setting to send the form data to the server.
Enctype	Specifies a **MIME** (Multipurpose Internet Mail Extensions) type for the data being submitted to the server so the server software will know how to interpret the data.
Class	Sets style sheet attributes and/or attaches a style sheet to the current document.

To Insert a Table to Design the Form

The first step in building a Web form is to create the table structure to assist with the layout of the form elements. The table structure dictates how the form appears on the Web page. Although a table is not required to build a form, using one helps to organize the layout of a form.

The form on the Contact page of the Gallery site should contain seven rows and two columns. The following steps insert a table to design the form.

- If necessary, click within the dotted red form area to place the insertion point within the Form object.

- Click Insert on the Application bar and then click Table on the Insert menu to display the Table dialog box.

- In the Rows text box, type 7 to change the number of rows.

- Double-click the Columns text box and then type 2 to change the number of columns.

- Double-click the Table width text box and then type 325 to set the width to 325 pixels.

- Double-click the Border thickness text box and then type 0 to set the border thickness.

- Double-click the Cell padding text box and then type 4 to set the number of cell padding pixels.

- Click None in the Header area to create a table without a header (Figure 4–51).

Figure 4–51

- Click the OK button in the Table dialog box to create a table in the Contact page (Figure 4–52).

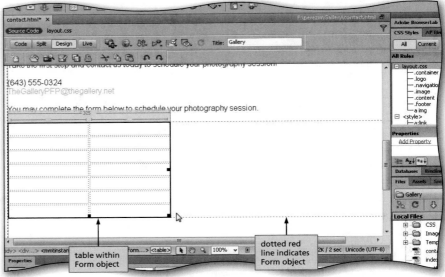

Figure 4–52

To Add Labels to the Table

Labels identify the type of data users should enter into a form. The first column in the table displays the labels of the requested information for the form. The second column displays the form elements such as text boxes and radio buttons to collect the user's information. The following steps add labels to the table structure displayed in the form.

- Click in row 1, column 1 and then type `First Name:` to add a label to the first row of the table.

- Click in row 2, column 1 and then type `Last Name:` to add a label to the second row.

- Click in row 3, column 1 and then type `E-mail:` to add a label to the third row.

- Click in row 4, column 1 and then type `Phone Number:` to add a label to the fourth row.

- Click in row 5, column 1 and then type `Type of Session:` to add a label to the fifth row.

- Click in row 6, column 1 and then type `Preferred Session Date:` to add a label to the sixth row.

- Click in row 7, column 1 and then type `How did you hear about us?` to add a label to the last row (Figure 4–53).

Figure 4–53

- Click the W box in the Property inspector and then type 125 to enter a column width.

- Press the ENTER key to adjust the column width of the first column (Figure 4–54).

Experiment

- Type 200 in the H box in the Property inspector to change the row height. When you are finished, click the Edit menu and then click Undo to return the row to its original state.

Figure 4–54

Adding Form Objects

In Dreamweaver, users enter data in forms using form objects such as text fields, check boxes, and radio buttons. Each form object should have a unique name — except radio buttons within the same group, which should share the same name. To insert a form field in a Web page, first add the field and any descriptive labels, and then modify the properties of the field. All Dreamweaver form objects are available on the Forms tab of the Insert bar (Figure 4–55). Table 4–8 on the next page lists the names and descriptions of buttons on the Forms tab.

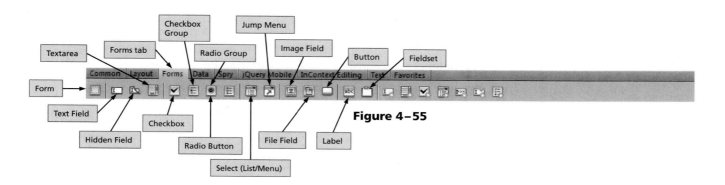

Figure 4–55

Table 4–8 Forms Tab on Insert Bar	
Button Name	**Description**
Form	Inserts a form into the Document window
Text Field	Accepts any type of alphanumeric text entry
Hidden Field	Stores information entered by a user and then uses that data within the site database
Textarea	Provides a multiline text entry field
Checkbox	Represents a selection
Checkbox Group	Allows multiple responses in a single group of options, letting the user select as many options as apply
Radio Button	Represents an exclusive choice; only one item in a group of buttons can be selected
Radio Group	Represents a group of radio buttons
Select (List/Menu)	List displays option values within a scrolling list that allows users to select multiple options; Menu displays the option values in a pop-up menu that allows users to select only a single item
Jump Menu	A special form of a pop-up menu that lets the viewer link to another document or file
Image Field	Creates a custom, graphical button
File Field	Allows users to browse to a file on their computers and upload the file as form data
Button	Performs actions when clicked; Submit and Reset buttons send data to the server and clear the form fields, respectively
Label	Provides a way to associate the text label for a field with the field structurally
Fieldset	Inserts a container tag for a logical group of form elements

Plan Ahead

Determine the types of controls you will add to the form.
After creating a form and inserting a table to align the form contents, you add objects that users select to enter information into the form. Select objects based on the type of information you want to collect: Text Fields and Textareas for text entries such as addresses, Checkboxes, Radio Buttons, and List/Menus for options users select, and Buttons for submitting and resetting the form.

BTW

Text Fields and Text Areas
When you insert a text field, you can use the Property inspector to set its type as Single-line, Multi-line, or Password. Inserting a multi-line text field is the same as inserting a Text Area object.

Adding Text Fields

A **Text Field** is a form object in which users enter a response. Forms support three types of Text Field objects: single-line, multiple-line, and password. Data entered into a Text Field object can consist of alphanumeric and punctuation characters. When you insert a text field into a form, the Input Tag Accessibility Attributes dialog box opens (Figure 4–56). Table 4–9 contains a description of the options in this dialog box. By setting accessibility attributes for each form object, visitors can complete the form even if they use a screen reader.

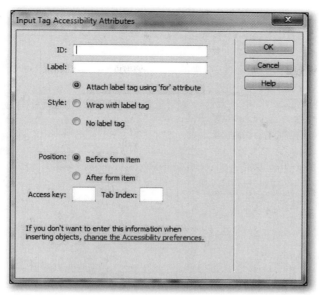

Figure 4–56

Table 4–9 Options in the Input Tag Accessibility Attributes Dialog Box

Attribute Name	Description
ID	Assigns an ID value that can be used to refer to a field from JavaScript and also used as an attribute value.
Label	The descriptive text that identifies the form object.
Style	Provides three options for the <label> tag: Attach label tag using 'for' attribute allows the user to associate a label with a form element, even if the two are in different table cells. 'Wrap with label tag' wraps a label tag around the form item. 'No label tag' turns off the Accessibility option.
Position	Determines the placement of the label text in relation to the form object — before or after the form object.
Access key	Selects the form object in the browser using a keyboard shortcut (one letter). This key is used in combination with the CTRL key (Windows) to access the object.
Tab Index	Specifies the order in which the form objects are selected when pressing the TAB key. The tab order goes from the lowest to highest number.

To Add Text Fields to a Form

The user enters his or her information in the First Name, Last Name, E-mail, and Phone Number Text Field objects in the form on the Contact page. The following steps add several Text Fields to a form.

1

• Click the Forms tab on the Insert bar to display the Form buttons (Figure 4–57).

Figure 4–57

2

- In the table, click row 1, column 2 and then click the Text Field button on the Forms tab to insert a Text Field object and display the Input Tag Accessibility Attributes dialog box (Figure 4–58).

Figure 4–58

3

- In the ID text box, type `fname` to assign a name to the First Name text field.

- Click the Access key text box and then type `F` to set the access key.

- Click the Tab Index text box and then type `1` to set the tab position (Figure 4–59).

Q&A How does the Access key work?

When the page opens in the browser, you can press the ALT+F keys as a keyboard shortcut to access this field.

Q&A What is the purpose of the tab index?

When you press the TAB key, you progress from one form item to another in the order specified by the tab index.

Figure 4–59

- Click the OK button in the Input Tag Accessibility Attributes dialog box to add the First Name text field (Figure 4–60).

Text Field inserted

Figure 4–60

5

- Click row 2, column 2 and then click the Text Field button on the Forms tab to insert a Text Field object and display the Input Tag Accessibility Attributes dialog box.

- In the ID text box, type `lname` to assign a name to the Last Name text field.

- Click the Access key text box and then type `L` to set the access key.

- Click the Tab Index text box and then type `2` to set the tab position (Figure 4–61).

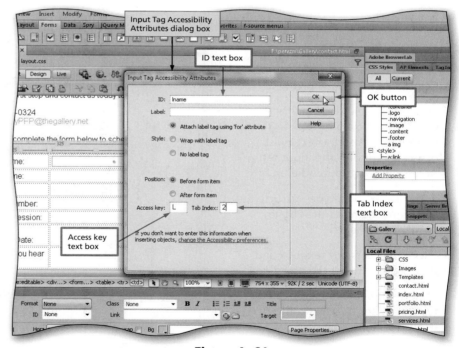

Input Tag Accessibility Attributes dialog box

ID text box

OK button

Tab Index text box

Access key text box

Figure 4–61

- Click the OK button in the Input Tag Accessibility Attributes dialog box to add the Last Name text field.

- Click row 3, column 2 and then click the Text Field button on the Forms tab to insert a Text Field object and display the Input Tag Accessibility Attributes dialog box.

- In the ID text box, type email to assign a name to the E-mail text field.

- Click the Access key text box and then type E to set the access key.

- Click the Tab Index text box and then type 3 to set the tab position (Figure 4–62).

Figure 4–62

- Click the OK button in the Input Tag Accessibility Attributes dialog box to add the E-mail text field.

- Click row 4, column 2 and then click the Text Field button on the Forms tab to insert a Text Field object and display the Input Tag Accessibility Attributes dialog box.

- In the ID text box, type phone to assign a name to the Phone Number text field.

- Click the Access key text box and then type P to set the access key.

- Click the Tab Index text box and type 4 to set the tab position (Figure 4–63).

8

- Click the OK button in the Input Tag Accessibility Attributes dialog box to add the Phone Number text field.

Figure 4–63

Other Ways

1. On Insert menu, point to Form, click Text Field

Adding a Menu

Another way to provide form field options for your Web site visitors is to use the Select (List/Menu) button on the Forms bar to include lists and menus. These objects let users select one or more options from many choices within a limited space. A **list** provides a scroll bar with up and down arrows enabling users to scroll the list, whereas a menu displays a pop-up list. Multiple selections can be made from a list, while users can select only one item from a menu.

You also can offer your Web site visitors a range of choices by using a pop-up menu. This type of menu (also called a drop-down menu) allows a user to select a single item from a list. A pop-up menu is useful when you have a limited amount of space because it occupies only a single line in the form. Only one option is visible when the menu is displayed in the browser. Clicking an arrow button displays the entire list. The user then clicks one of the menu items to make a selection.

To Add a Menu to a Form

As customers fill out the Contact form, they request a type of photography session: Portrait, Family, Children, Newborn, and Maternity. To allow this selection, you can insert a Select object in the form and then set the five session types as list values. By default, a Select object uses Menu as its Type property, which means users click the menu's arrow button to display all the list values. The following steps add a menu to the form on the Contact page.

1

- Click row 5, column 2 to select the cell (Figure 4–64).

Figure 4–64

2

- Click the Select (List/Menu) button on the Forms tab to insert a Select object and display the Input Tag Accessibility Attributes dialog box.

- In the ID text box, type `type` to assign a name to the Select object.

- Click the Access key text box and type `T` to set the access key.

- Click the Tab Index text box and type `5` to set the tab position (Figure 4–65).

Figure 4–65

3

- Click the OK button in the Input Tag Accessibility Attributes dialog box to add the Select object to the form.

- If necessary, click the Select object to display its properties in the Property inspector (Figure 4–66).

Figure 4–66

● Click the List Values button
in the Property inspector to
display the List Values dialog box
(Figure 4–67).

Figure 4–67

⑤

● In the text box for entering an
Item Label, type `Portrait` to
enter an Item Label for the first
menu item (Figure 4–68).

Q&A

What is an Item Label?

An Item Label is the text that
appears on a menu. Users click this
text to select the menu item.

Figure 4–68

● Click the plus button and then type
`Family` to enter an Item Label
for the second menu item.

● Click the plus button and then type
`Children` to enter an Item Label
for the third menu item.

● Click the plus button and then type
`Newborn` to enter an Item Label
for the fourth menu item.

● Click the plus button and then
type `Maternity` to enter an
Item Label for the fifth menu item
(Figure 4–69).

Figure 4–69

- Click the OK button in List Values dialog box to update the Select object in the form.

- In the Initially selected list box, click Portrait to select the initial value to display in the Select object (Figure 4–70).

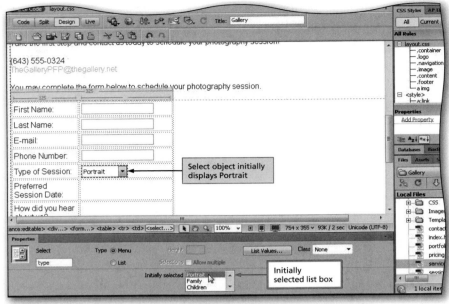

Figure 4–70

Text Field Properties

When you select a Text Field within a form, the Property inspector displays the properties of that field, as shown in Figure 4–71. Table 4–10 lists the attribute names and descriptions for a single-line text field.

Figure 4–71

Table 4–10 Properties for a Single-Line Text Field	
Attribute Name	**Description**
TextField	Assigns a unique name to the Form object
Char width	Specifies the width of the field in characters
Max chars	Specifies the maximum number of characters that can be entered into the field
Type	Designates the field as a single-line, multiple-line, or password field
Init val	Assigns the value that is displayed in the field when the form first loads
Class	Establishes an attribute used with Cascading Style Sheets
Disabled	Disables the text area
Read-only	Lets users read but not change the value in the field

To Add an Initial Value to a Text Field

When the Contact page opens in a browser, the Preferred Session Date Text Field in the form requests a date in a format such as 11/18/2014. However, the date format can differ depending on the locale of the user. To clarify the format users should follow when entering the date, specify an initial value such as mm/dd/yyyy to identify the month, day, and year order. To do so, use the Init val property in the Text Field Property inspector. An **Init val** displays an initial value such as a number, text, or a note to the Web site visitor to identify the correct format for entering a value. The following steps add a Text Field object with an initial value to the form on the Contact page.

- Click row 6, column 2 to place the insertion point in the cell.

- Click the Text Field button on the Forms tab to insert a Text Field object and display the Input Tag Accessibility Attributes dialog box.

- In the ID text box, type date to assign a name to the Text Field object.

- Click the Access key text box and type D to set the access key.

- Click the Tab Index text box and type 6 to set the tab position (Figure 4–72).

Figure 4–72

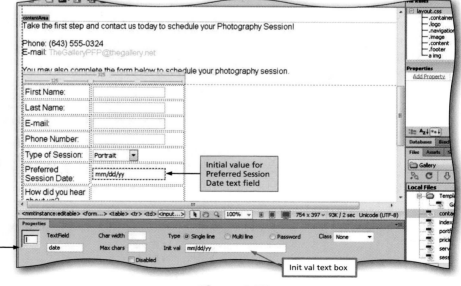

- Click the OK button in the Input Tag Accessibility Attributes dialog box to add the Text Field object to the form.

- Click the Text Field object you just added to display its properties in the Property inspector.

- Click the Init val text box in the Property inspector, type mm/dd/yy and then press the ENTER key to display an initial value for the Text Field object (Figure 4–73).

Figure 4–73

Other Ways
1. On Insert menu, point to Form, click Text Field

Adding Radio Buttons in a Radio Group

In addition to Text Field and Select objects, you can use radio buttons to collect user information on a form. A Radio Button object includes the button and a descriptive label. For example, you might insert a New Customer radio button on a form that users click if they are new customers. Use the Radio Button Property inspector shown in Figure 4–74 to specify the Checked value, which is the value you want to send to the server-side script or application when a user selects this radio button. For the Initial state, select Checked if you want an option to appear selected when the form first loads in the browser.

Figure 4–74

A **Radio Group** object includes two or more related radio buttons and allows a user to select only one radio button in the group. If one button is already selected in the group and the user clicks a different radio button, the previously selected button is deselected. When you insert a Radio Group object, you use the Radio Group dialog box to name the object and to provide labels and values for each radio button in the group, which streamlines the process of adding a set of radio buttons to a form.

To Add a Radio Group

The last request on the Gallery Contact form asks "How did you hear about us?" For reporting purposes, instead of asking an open-ended question that leads to a variety of answers, provide a predefined set of responses in a Radio Group object so the responses are easier to interpret. In addition, it is less time consuming for customers to choose one of five choices than typing a response. The following steps add a Radio Group object to the Contact form.

- Click row 7, column 2 to place the insertion point in the cell (Figure 4–75).

Figure 4–75

2

- Click the Radio Group button on the Forms tab to insert a Radio Group object and display the Radio Group dialog box.

- In the Name text box, type `referral` to name the Radio Group object.

- Click the first Radio label and then type `Google` to provide a descriptive label for the first radio button in the group (Figure 4–76).

Q&A Why does the radio group already have two default buttons?

Every radio group includes at least two radio buttons.

Figure 4–76

3

- Click the second Radio label and then type `Magazine Ad` to provide a descriptive label for the second radio button in the group.

- Click the plus button, click the third Radio label, and then type `Newspaper` to provide a descriptive label for the third radio button.

- Click the plus button, scroll down, click the fourth Radio label, and then type `Friend` to provide a descriptive label for the fourth radio button.

- Click the plus button, scroll down, click the fifth Radio label, and then type `Other` to provide a descriptive label for the fifth radio button (Figure 4–77).

Figure 4–77

4

- Click the OK button in the Radio Group dialog box to add the Radio Group object to the form.

- Click outside the form to deselect the Radio Group object (Figure 4–78).

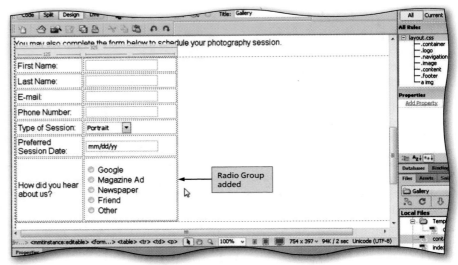

Figure 4–78

Other Ways

1. On Insert menu, point to Form, click Radio Group

To Add Submit and Reset Buttons to a Form

Each Web form needs at least one button for submitting the data to a server or application. The most common button on a Web form is a Submit button, which sends data from the completed form to the processing application. Most Web forms also include a Reset button, which clears all the fields in the form. When you add a button to a form, Dreamweaver automatically assigns it properties suitable for a Submit button.

The following steps add Submit and Reset buttons to a form.

1

- If necessary, click to the right of the table and then press the ENTER key to place the insertion point on the line below the table (Figure 4–79).

Q&A

Does it matter where the Submit button is placed on the Web page?

Yes. The Submit button must be placed on the form, which is indicated by the dotted red outline in Dreamweaver. Otherwise, the button is not considered part of the Form object.

Figure 4–79

2

- Click the Button button on the Forms tab to insert a Button object and display the Input Tag Accessibility Attributes dialog box.

- In the ID text box, type submit to assign a name to the Button object.

- Click the Access key text box and type S to set the access key.

- Click the Tab Index text box and type 7 to set the tab position (Figure 4–80).

Figure 4–80

3

- Click the OK button in the Input Tag Accessibility Attributes dialog box to add the button to the form.

- If necessary, click the Submit form option button in the Property inspector to select the Submit form action (Figure 4–81).

Figure 4–81

- Click to the right of the Submit button and press the ENTER key to place the insertion point on the line below the Button object.

- Click the Button button on the Forms tab to open the Input Tag Accessibility Attributes dialog box.

- In the ID text box, type reset to assign a name to the Button object.

- Click the Access key text box and type R to set the access key.

- Click the Tab Index text box and type 8 to set the tab position (Figure 4–82).

Figure 4–82

- Click the OK button in the Input Tag Accessibility Attributes dialog box to add the button to the form.

- Click the Reset form option button in the Property inspector to select the Reset form action and change the text from Submit to Reset on the second Button object (Figure 4–83).

Q&A

Does the Reset button clear the form in the browser?

Yes. Users click the Reset button to clear information from the form.

- Click the Save All button on the Standard toolbar to save your work.

Figure 4–83

Other Ways

1. On Insert menu, point to Form, click Button

To View and Test the Site in the Browser

When you test the form on the Contact page, keep in mind that clicking the Submit button does not send the form data to a server. However, clicking the Reset button clears the data from the form. The following steps preview and test the table and Form objects on the Contact page using Internet Explorer.

1 Click the 'Preview/Debug in browser' button on the Document toolbar to display a list of browsers.

2 Click Preview in IExplore in the list to display the Gallery Web site in Internet Explorer.

3 Open the Services page to view the first table, and then open the Pricing page to view the second table.

4 Open the Contact page and enter your information into the Web form.

5 Click the Internet Explorer Close button to close the browser.

To Quit Dreamweaver

The following steps quit Dreamweaver and return control to the operating system.

1 Click the Close button on the right side of the Application bar to close the window.

2 If Dreamweaver displays a dialog box asking you to save changes, click the No button.

Chapter Summary

In this chapter, you learned how to add tables and a form to the Gallery site that provide detailed information to your customers about photography services. You formatted the table by changing alignment, setting column width, merging cells, applying bold, and specifying cell background color. You added a text field, a radio group, and Submit and Reset buttons to the Contact form. Finally, you viewed and tested the tables and the form in your browser. The following tasks are all the new Dreamweaver skills you learned in this chapter:

1. Insert a Table into the Services page (DW 207)
2. Add Text to the Table (DW 209)
3. Format Table Text (DW 214)
4. Format the Table Caption (DW 215)
5. Merge Cells in a Table (DW 220)
6. Align the Table (DW 223)
7. Adjust the Table Width (DW 224)
8. Adjust the Column Width (DW 225)
9. Align Text within a Table Cell (DW 228)
10. Set the Background Color of Cells in a Table (DW 229)
11. Insert a Form into a Web Page (DW 232)
12. Insert a Table to Design the Form (DW 235)
13. Add Text Fields to a Form (DW 239)
14. Add a Menu to a Form (DW 243)
15. Add an Initial Value to a Text Field (DW 247)
16. Add a Radio Group (DW 248)
17. Add Submit and Reset Buttons to a Form (DW 250)

Apply Your Knowledge

Reinforce the skills and apply the concepts you learned in this chapter.

Adding a Table to a Web Page

Instructions: In this activity, you create a table with six rows and four columns that contains information about a training schedule. The completed Web page is displayed in Figure 4–84.

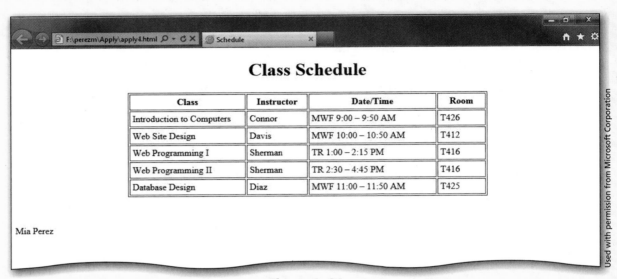

Class Schedule

Class	Instructor	Date/Time	Room
Introduction to Computers	Connor	MWF 9:00 – 9:50 AM	T426
Web Site Design	Davis	MWF 10:00 – 10:50 AM	T412
Web Programming I	Sherman	TR 1:00 – 2:15 PM	T416
Web Programming II	Sherman	TR 2:30 – 4:45 PM	T416
Database Design	Diaz	MWF 11:00 – 11:50 AM	T425

Mia Perez

Figure 4–84

Perform the following tasks:

1. Start Dreamweaver. Use the Sites button on the Files panel to select the Apply site.
2. Create a new HTML document, and then save it as `apply4.html`.
3. Enter `Schedule` as the document title.
4. Use `Class Schedule` as the document heading. Select the document heading and use Heading 1 as the format in the Property inspector. Center the heading on the page.
5. After the Class Schedule heading, press the ENTER key. Insert a table, enter the following values in the Table dialog box, and then click the OK button:
   - Rows: `6`
   - Columns: `4`
   - Table width: `620`
   - Border thickness: `1` pixel
   - Cell padding: `4`
   - Header: `Top`
   - Summary: `This table provides class schedule information.`
6. Enter the text as shown in Table 4–11.
7. Change the width of the first column to `190`, the width of the second column to `95`, the width of the third column to `210`, and the width of the fourth column to `73`.
8. Center-align the table on the page.
9. Click to the right of the table. Press the ENTER key twice. Type your first and last names.

10. Save your changes and then view your document in your browser. Compare your document to Figure 4–84. Make any necessary changes, and then save your changes.

11. Submit the document in the format specified by your instructor.

Table 4–11 Class Schedule

Column 1	Column 2	Column 3	Column 4
Class	Instructor	Date/Time	Room
Introduction to Computers	Connor	MWF 9:00 – 9:50 AM	T426
Web Site Design	Davis	MWF 10:00 – 10:50 AM	T412
Web Programming I	Sherman	TR 1:00 – 2:15 PM	T416
Web Programming II	Sherman	TR 2:30 – 4:45 PM	T416
Database Design	Diaz	MWF 11:00 – 11:50 AM	T425

Extend Your Knowledge

Extend the skills you learned in this chapter and experiment with new skills. You may need to use Help to complete the assignment.

Creating a Form

Note: To complete this assignment, you will be required to use the Data Files for Students. Visit www.cengage.com/ct/studentdownload for detailed instructions or contact your instructor for information about accessing the required files.

Instructions: In this activity, you create a form using a table layout and add two buttons. First, you insert four Text Fields. Next, you insert a Text Area and a Checkbox Group with three check box options. Finally, you insert the Submit and Reset buttons. The completed Web page is displayed in Figure 4–85.

Figure 4–85

Continued >

Extend Your Knowledge *continued*

Perform the following tasks:

1. Use Windows Explorer to copy the extend4.html file from the Chapter 04\Extend folder into the *your last name and first initial*\Extend folder.

2. Start Dreamweaver. Use the Sites button on the Files panel to select the Extend site. Open extend4.html.

3. In the first row, second column of the table, insert a Text Field object for First Name. Use `fname` for the ID, use `F` for the Access key, and set the Tab Index to `1`.

4. In the second row, second column of the table, insert a Text Field object for Last Name. Use `lname` for the ID, use `L` for the Access key, and set the Tab Index to `2`.

5. In the third row, second column of the table, insert a Text Field object for E-mail. Use `email` for the ID, use `E` for the Access key, and set the Tab Index to `3`.

6. In the fourth row, second column of the table, insert a Text Field object for Phone Number. Use `phone` for the ID, use `P` for the Access key, and set the Tab Index to `4`.

7. In the fifth row, second column of the table, insert a Text Area object for Address. (*Hint*: Point to the buttons on the Form bar to identify the TextArea button.) Use `address` for the ID, use `A` for the Access key, and set the Tab Index to `5`.

8. In the second column, last row of the table, insert a Checkbox Group object. Use `contact` for the Checkbox Group name. Use `E-mail`, `Phone`, and `Mail` as the labels for the check boxes.

9. Insert a button below the table. Use `submit` for the ID, use `S` for the Access key, and set the Tab Index to `6`. Confirm that the Submit form option button is selected in the Property inspector.

10. Click after the Submit button and then press the ENTER key. Insert another button. Use `reset` for the ID, use `R` for the Access key, and set the Tab Index to `7`. In the Property inspector, select the Reset form option button.

11. Replace the text, Your name here, with your first and last names.

12. Save your changes and then view your document in your browser.

13. Compare your document to Figure 4–85. Make any necessary changes and then save your changes.

14. Submit the document in the format specified by your instructor.

Make It Right

Analyze a Web page and suggest how to improve its design.

Creating a Table to Lay Out Content

Note: To complete this assignment, you will be required to use the Data Files for Students. Visit www.cengage.com/ct/studentdownload for detailed instructions or contact your instructor for information about accessing the required files.

Instructions: The Local Library Events Web page provides a list of events at local libraries. In this activity, you modify the list by making it into a table. First, you insert a table with six rows and four columns. Next, you move the content into the table and modify the column widths. Finally, you center-align the table on the page. The modified Web page is shown in Figure 4–86.

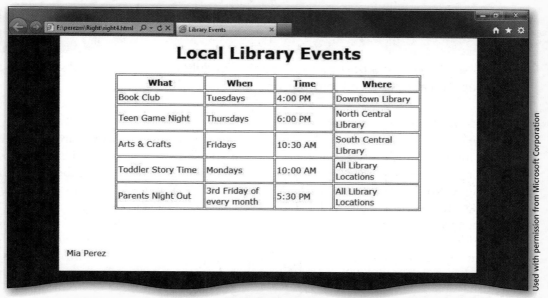

Used with permission from Microsoft Corporation

Figure 4–86

Perform the following tasks:

1. Use Windows Explorer to copy the right4.html file from the Chapter 04\Right folder into the *your last name and first initial*\Right folder.

2. Open right4.html in your browser to view its contents and then close the browser.

3. Start Dreamweaver. Use the Sites button on the Files panel to select the Right site. Open right4.html.

4. Insert a table below the page heading. Enter the following values in the Table dialog box and then click the OK button:
   - Rows: 6
   - Columns: 4
   - Table width: 600
   - Border thickness: 1 pixel
   - Cell padding: 2
   - Header: Top
   - Summary: This table contains library event information.

5. Use What, When, Time, and Where as the table headings in the first row.

6. Move the Book Club event information into the second row. Move the Teen Game Night event information into the third row. Move the Arts & Crafts event information into the fourth row. Move the Toddler Story Time event information into the fifth row. Move the Parents Night Out event information into the sixth row.

7. Change the width of the first column to 165, the width of the second column to 130, the width of the third column to 108, and the width of the fourth column to 161.

8. Center-align the table on the page.

9. Delete any remaining event text below the table.

10. Replace the text, Your name here, with your first and last names.

11. Save your changes and then view the Web page in your browser. Compare your page to Figure 4–86. Make any necessary changes and then save your changes.

12. Submit the document in the format specified by your instructor.

In the Lab

Design and/or create a document using the guidelines, concepts, and skills presented in this chapter. Labs are listed in order of increasing difficulty.

Lab 1: Adding Table and Form Elements to the Healthy Lifestyle Web Site

Problem: You are creating an internal Web site for your company that features information about how to live a healthy lifestyle. Employees at your company will use this Web site as a resource for nutrition, exercise, and other health-related tips. In Chapter 2, you created the Habits and Sign Up Web pages. Now you need to add content to these pages. You need to add a table with information about how to change a habit on the Habits Web page. You need to create a form on the Sign Up Web page where employees can sign up to receive weekly e-mail tips.

First, insert a table and add content to the table on the Habits page. Then, add a form, a table, and form elements to the Sign Up page. The Habits page is shown in Figure 4–87. The Sign Up page is shown in Figure 4–88.

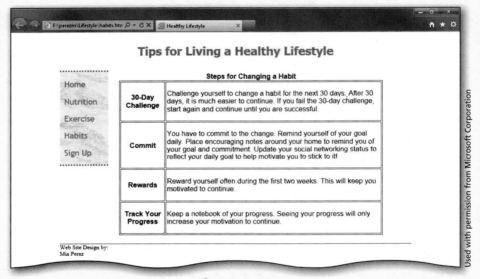

Figure 4–87

Figure 4–88

Perform the following tasks:

1. Start Dreamweaver. Use the Sites button on the Files panel to select the Healthy Lifestyle site. Open habits.html.

2. Delete the text, Insert content here, in the editable region. Insert a table. Enter the following values in the Table dialog box and then click the OK button:
   - Rows: `4`
   - Columns: `2`
   - Table width: `600`
   - Border thickness: `1` pixel
   - Cell padding: `2`
   - Header: `Left`
   - Caption: `Steps for Changing a Habit`
   - Summary: `This table provides information about how to change a habit.`

3. Enter the text as shown in Table 4–12 on the next page.

4. Bold the table caption, Steps for Changing a Habit.

5. Save your changes and view the document in your browser. Compare your document to Figure 4–87. Make any necessary changes and save your changes. Close habits.html.

6. Open signup.html.

7. Delete the text, Insert content here, in the editable region. Insert a table. Enter the following values in the Table dialog box and then click the OK button:
   - Rows: `4`
   - Columns: `2`
   - Table width: `500`
   - Border thickness: `0` pixels
   - Cell padding: `5`
   - Header: `None`
   - Summary: `This table is a form to enable employees to sign up to receive weekly e-mail tips.`

8. Type `First Name:` in the first row, first column. Insert a Text Field in the first row, second column. Use `fname` for the ID, `F` for the Access key, and `1` for the Tab Index.

9. Type `Last Name:` in the second row, first column. Insert a Text Field in the second row, second column. Use `lname` for the ID, `L` for the Access key, and `2` for the Tab Index.

10. Type `E-mail:` in the third row, first column. Insert a Text Field in the third row, second column. Use `email` for the ID, `E` for the Access key, and `3` for the Tab Index.

11. Type `I would like to receive tips for:` in the fourth row, first column. Insert a Radio Group in the fourth row, second column. Use `tips` for the name. Use `Dinner`, `Exercise,` and `Both` as the radio button labels.

12. Insert a button below the table. Use `submit` for the ID, use `S` for the Access key, and set the Tab Index to `4`. Confirm that the Submit form option button is selected in the Property inspector.

Continued >

In the Lab *continued*

13. Click after the Submit button and then press the ENTER key. Insert another button. Use `reset` for the ID, use `R` for the Access key, and set the Tab Index to `5`. In the Property inspector, select the Reset form option button.

14. Save your changes and view the document in your browser. Compare your document to Figure 4–88. Make any necessary changes and save your changes.

15. Submit the documents in the format specified by your instructor.

Table 4–12 Steps for Changing a Habit	
Column 1	**Column 2**
30-Day Challenge	Challenge yourself to change a habit for the next 30 days. After 30 days, it is much easier to continue. If you fail the 30-day challenge, start again and continue until you are successful.
Commit	You have to commit to the change. Remind yourself of your goal daily. Place encouraging notes around your home to remind you of your goal and commitment. Update your social networking status to reflect your daily goal to help motivate you to stick to it!
Rewards	Reward yourself often during the first two weeks. This will keep you motivated to continue.
Track Your Progress	Keep a notebook of your progress. Seeing your progress will only increase your motivation to continue.

In the Lab

Lab 2: Adding Table and Form Elements to the Designs by Dolores Web Site

Problem: You are creating a Web site for Designs by Dolores, a Web site design company. The site provides information about the company and its services. In Chapter 2, you created the Services, Pricing, and Contact Us pages. Now you need to add content to the Services and Pricing pages. Additionally, you need to create a form on the Contact Us page.

First, insert a table on the Services Web page and add content. Next, insert a table on the Pricing Web page and add content. Finally, create a form on the Contact Us Web page. The Services page is shown in Figure 4–89. The Pricing page is shown in Figure 4–90. The Contact Us page is shown in Figure 4–91.

Figure 4–89

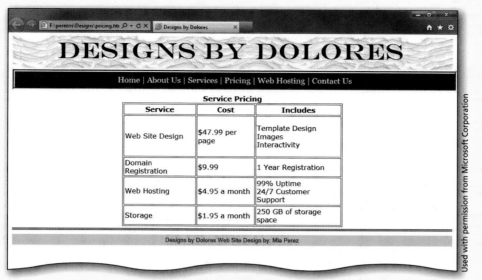

Figure 4–90

Figure 4–91

Perform the following tasks:

1. Start Dreamweaver. Use the Sites button on the Files panel to select the Designs by Dolores site. Open services.html.

2. Delete the text, Insert content here, in the editable region. Insert a table. Enter the following values in the Table dialog box and then click the OK button:

- Rows: 4
- Columns: 2
- Table width: 800
- Border thickness: 0   pixels
- Cell padding: 5

Continued >

- Header: `Left`
- Caption: `Our Services`
- Summary: `This table contains information about the services offered by Designs by Dolores.`

3. Enter the text as shown in Table 4–13.

4. Bold the table caption, Our Services. Center-align the table on the page.

5. Save your changes and view the document in your browser. Compare your document to Figure 4–89. Make any necessary changes and save your changes. Close services.html.

6. Open pricing.html.

7. Delete the text, Insert content here, in the editable region. Insert a table. Enter the following values in the Table dialog box and then click the OK button:

- Rows: `5`
- Columns: `3`
- Table width: `500`
- Border thickness: `1` pixel
- Cell padding: `2`
- Header: `Top`
- Caption: `Service Pricing`
- Summary: `This table contains service pricing information.`

8. Enter the text as shown in Table 4–14.

9. Bold the table caption, Service Pricing. Center-align the table on the page.

10. Save your changes and view the document in your browser. Compare your document to Figure 4–90. Make any necessary changes and save your changes. Close pricing.html.

11. Open contact.html.

12. Replace the text, Insert content here, with `Need a Web site? Please complete the form below and one of our professionals will be in touch with you soon.`

13. Press the ENTER key. Insert a form and then insert a table within the form. Enter the following values in the Table dialog box and then click the OK button:

- Rows: `5`
- Columns: `2`
- Table width: `600`
- Border thickness: `0` pixels
- Cell padding: `5`
- Header: `None`
- Summary: `This table contains the contact form.`

14. Type `First Name:` in the first row, first column. Insert a Text Field in the first row, second column. Use `fname` for the ID, `F` for the Access key, and `1` for the Tab Index.

15. Type `Last Name:` in the second row, first column. Insert a Text Field in the second row, second column. Use `lname` for the ID, `L` for the Access key, and `2` for the Tab Index.

16. Type `E-mail:` in the third row, first column. Insert a Text Field in the third row, second column. Use `email` for the ID, `E` for the Access key, and `3` for the Tab Index.

17. Type `Phone Number:` in the fourth row, first column. Insert a Text Field in the third row, second column. Use `phone` for the ID, `P` for the Access key, and `4` for the Tab Index.

18. Type `Business Industry:` in the fifth row, first column. Insert a Select (List/Menu) object in the fifth row, second column. Use `industry` for the name, `I` for the Access key, and `5` for the Tab Index.

19. Click the List Values button in the Property inspector and use `Financial, Law, Retail, Government, Engineering, Education,` and `Other` as the radio button labels. Use Other for the Initially selected value.

20. Insert a button below the table. Use `submit` for the ID, use `S` for the Access key, and set the Tab Index to `6`. Confirm that the Submit form option button is selected in the Property inspector.

21. Click after the Submit button and then press the ENTER key. Insert another button. Use `reset` for the ID, use `R` for the Access key, and set the Tab Index to `7`. In the Property inspector, select the Reset form option button.

22. Save your changes and view the document in your browser. Compare your document to Figure 4–91. Make any necessary changes and save your changes.

23. Submit the documents in the format specified by your instructor.

Table 4–13 Our Services	
Column 1	**Column 2**
Web Site Design	Whether you are a new business needing an online presence or an existing business that needs to revamp your current Web site, our design experts are here to make your business shine online.
Domain Registration	Finding and registering a domain name can be complicated. Let us simplify this daunting task and help you acquire a domain name that suits your needs. Registering multiple domain names assures traffic to your site and helps save you money.
Web Hosting	Let us host your Web site. Our Web hosting services provide you with unlimited disk space, 99% uptime guarantee, and superior 24/7 customer service.
Storage	Backing up your files is critical to restoring operations in the event of a disaster. We provide affordable and secure storage for your business needs.

Table 4–14 Service Pricing		
Column 1	**Column 2**	**Column 3**
Service	Cost	Includes
Web Site Design	$47.99 per page	Template Design Images Interactivity
Domain Registration	$9.99	1 Year Registration
Web Hosting	$4.95 a month	99% Uptime 24/7 Customer Support
Storage	$1.95 a month	250 GB of storage space

In the Lab

Lab 3: Adding Tables and Form Elements to the Justin's Lawn Care Service Web Site

Problem: You are creating a Web site for a new lawn care company, Justin's Lawn Care Service. The Web site will provide information to customers, including descriptions of services and pricing. In Chapter 2, you created the Services, Prices, and Quote Web pages. Now you need to add content to the Services and Prices page. You also need to create a form on the Quote page.

First, insert a table on the Services Web page and add content. Next, insert a table on the Prices Web page and add content. Finally, create a form on the Quote Web page. The Services page is shown in Figure 4–92. The Prices page is shown in Figure 4–93. The Quote page is shown in Figure 4–94.

Figure 4–92

Figure 4–93

Used with permission from Microsoft Corporation

Figure 4–94

Perform the following tasks:

1. Start Dreamweaver. Use the Sites button on the Files panel to select the Justin's Lawn Care Service site. Open services.html.

2. Delete the text, Insert content here, in the editable region. Insert a table. Enter the following values in the Table dialog box and then click the OK button:
   - Rows: 4
   - Columns: 2
   - Table width: 550
   - Border thickness: 0 pixels
   - Cell padding: 4
   - Header: None
   - Caption: Our Services
   - Summary: This table contains service pricing information.

3. Enter the text as shown in Table 4–15 on page 267.

4. Bold the table caption, Our Services. Center-align the table on the page.

5. Save your changes and view the document in your browser. Compare your document to Figure 4–92. Make any necessary changes and save your changes. Close services.html.

6. Open prices.html.

7. Delete the text, Insert content here, in the editable region. Insert a table. Enter the following values in the Table dialog box and then click the OK button:
   - Rows: 4
   - Columns: 3
   - Table width: 550
   - Border thickness: 1 pixel
   - Cell padding: 4

Continued >

In the Lab *continued*

- Header: `Top`
- Caption: `Our Prices`
- Summary: `This table contains price information.`

8. Enter the text as shown in Table 4–16.

9. Bold the table caption, Our Prices. Center-align the table on the page.

10. Save your changes and view the document in your browser. Compare your document to Figure 4–93. Make any necessary changes and save your changes. Close prices.html.

11. Open quote.html.

12. Replace the text, Insert content here, with `For a free estimate of services for your lawn care needs, please complete the form below.`

13. Press the ENTER key. Insert a form, and then insert a table. Enter the following values in the Table dialog box and then click the OK button:
    - Rows: `5`
    - Columns: `2`
    - Table width: `600`
    - Border thickness: `0` pixels
    - Cell padding: `5`
    - Summary: `This table contains the quote form.`

14. Type `First Name:` in the first row, first column. Insert a Text Field in the first row, second column. Use `fname` for the ID, `F` for the Access key, and `1` for the Tab Index.

15. Type `Last Name:` in the second row, first column. Insert a Text Field in the second row, second column. Use `lname` for the ID, `L` for the Access key, and `2` for the Tab Index.

16. Type `Phone Number:` in the third row, first column. Insert a Text Field in the third row, second column. Use `phone` for the ID, `P` for the Access key, and `3` for the Tab Index.

17. Type `E-mail:` in the fourth row, first column. Insert a Text Field in the fourth row, second column. Use `email` for the ID, `E` for the Access key, and `4` for the Tab Index.

18. Type `Service Interests:` in the fifth row, first column. Insert a Checkbox Group in the fifth row, second column. Use `services` for the name. Use `Lawn Maintenance`, `Trimming`, `Seasonal Planting`, and `Landscape Design` as the check box labels.

19. Insert a button below the table. Use `submit` for the ID, use `S` for the Access key, and set the Tab Index to `5`. Confirm that the Submit form option button is selected in the Property inspector.

20. Click after the Submit button and then press the ENTER key. Insert another button. Use `reset` for the ID, use `R` for the Access key, and set the Tab Index to `6`. In the Property inspector, select the Reset form option button.

21. Save your changes and view the document in your browser. Compare your document to Figure 4–94. Make any necessary changes and save your changes.

22. Submit the documents in the format specified by your instructor.

Table 4–15 Our Services

Column 1	Column 2
Lawn Maintenance	Our standard lawn care service includes mowing the lawn and clipping around all trees, posts, and fencing. We also edge all sidewalks, patios, and driveways, and fertilize your lawn in the spring and fall.
Trimming	Trimming is a crucial part of a neat and clean landscape. We assess the needs of your hedges, shrubs, and low trees, and then trim them according to a personalized schedule.
Seasonal Planting	We can plant your annuals and perennials to suit your taste and property needs. We can replant your favorite types of plants up to five times a year.
Landscape Design	Landscaping is the first thing you notice when you look at a property. From arranging plantings to building paths and patios, we design and create outdoor living spaces for you to enjoy. We will listen to your ideas and work with you to achieve the design you want. Visit our Landscape page for ideas and then contact us to schedule an appointment.

Table 4–16 Our Prices

Column 1	Column 2	Column 3
Service	Cost	Includes
Monthly Lawn Care Maintenance	$42.99 per month	Mowing, edging, and trimming
Seasonal Planting	$7.99 & up	The purchase and planting of seasonal plants
Landscape Design	$52.95 & up	Custom landscape design recommendation and creation

Cases and Places

Apply your creative thinking and problem solving skills to design and implement a solution.

1: Adding Tables and a Form to the Moving Venture Tips Web Site

Personal

You have created all of the pages for Moving Venture Tips and now need to add a table to the Budget page, and a table and a form to the Contact page. You have decided to provide an example budget on the Budget page. Use a table with a minimum of five rows and two columns to create a sample budget on the Budget page. Use Expense, Budget, January, February, and March as the column headings and then include budget information for each row and column. Insert a form on the Contact page, and then insert a table with four rows and two columns. Use First Name, Last Name, E-mail, and I would like to receive more information about as labels in the first column. Insert text fields for First Name, Last Name, and E-mail in the second column. Insert a Radio Group in the last row, second column of the table. Use Moving Tips, Budgeting, and Rentals as labels. Insert a Submit button and a Reset button below the table. Check the spelling using the Commands menu and correct all misspelled words. Submit the document in the format specified by your instructor.

2: Adding Tables and a Form to Student Campus Resources

Academic

You have created all of the pages for Student Campus Resources and now need to add a table to the Events page, and a table and a form to the Contact page. Use a table with a minimum of six rows and four columns to list campus events on the Events page. Use Event Name, Date, Time, Location as your column headings and then complete the table by listing at least four different events. Insert a form on the Contact page, and then insert a table with four rows and two columns. Use First

Name, Last Name, E-mail, and I would like to receive weekly e-mails about as labels in the first column. Insert text fields for First Name, Last Name, and E-mail in the second column, and insert a Select (List/Menu) in the last row, second column. Use Activities, Committees, Events, and All of the above as the list values. Insert a Submit button and a Reset button below the table. Check the spelling using the Commands menu and correct all misspelled words. Submit the document in the format specified by your instructor.

3: Adding Web Pages, Images, and Links for French Villa Roast Café

Professional

You have created all of the pages for French Villa Roast Café and now need to add a table to the Menu page, and a table and a form to the Contact page. Use a table with a minimum of six rows and four columns to create a menu on the Menu page. Create column headings for the menu and then fill out the table by listing at least five different menu items. Insert a form on the Rewards page, and then insert a table with five rows and two columns. Use First Name, Last Name, E-mail, Phone Number, and How many times a month do you purchase coffee from us? as labels in the first column. Insert text fields for First Name, Last Name, and E-mail in the second column. Insert a Radio Group in the last row, second column. Use 1-3, 4-9, and 10+ as labels. Insert a Submit button and a Reset button below the table. Check the spelling using the Commands menu and correct all misspelled words. Submit the document in the format specified by your instructor.

5 | Creating Interactive Web Pages with Spry and Adobe Widgets

Objectives

You will have mastered the material in this chapter when you can:

- Describe the Spry framework
- Identify Spry widgets
- Apply Spry validation to a text field
- Edit a Web page form with Spry validation
- Test a Web page form with Spry validation
- Add the Spry Collapsible Panel to a Web page
- Install Adobe AIR

- Create an Adobe account
- Use the Adobe Dreamweaver Widget Browser
- Review widgets in Adobe Exchange and save a widget to My Widget
- Add a LightBox Gallery widget to a collapsible panel within a Web page
- Review the LightBox Gallery widget in a browser

5 | Creating Interactive Web Pages with Spry and Adobe Widgets

Introduction

Interactive Web pages enhance a visitor's experience by providing a more memorable Web site experience. This helps attract new customers and retain current customers. A Web site can offer interactivity in many ways, such as an interactive navigational menu bar, validation for form fields, an image slide show viewer, or collapsible panels that organize large amounts of information on a page. Providing interactivity normally would require coding knowledge and time to create the interactive objects. Fortunately, Adobe Dreamweaver CS6 tools can provide interactivity without requiring coding knowledge.

Interactive objects make it easier to use a Web site and can provide stunning visual appeal for visitors to your Web site. For example, a Web form allows you to enter personal information. But if you leave several contact fields blank, the correct information will not be forwarded to the site owner. A feature within Dreamweaver, called **Spry validation**, allows you to check for valid entries in Web forms. The form can verify each entry using conditions that you specify, such as requiring users to fill in a form text field or enter an e-mail address in a valid format.

As a Web designer, you can use Dreamweaver to add powerful Spry elements, such as a collapsible panel, directly into a Web page. Spry Collapsible Panels have at least one tab and a content area. The content area is displayed or hidden when you click the corresponding tab. Other Adobe widgets beyond the installed Spry widgets are also available for download, such as the LightBox Gallery, which allows a visitor to click a thumbnail image from a gallery to display a larger version, dimming the page content behind it, so the gallery acts as a slide show. Interactive widgets introduce a realm of engagement and interactivity well beyond a static page.

Project — Interactive Web Pages

In Chapter 4, you created a form on the Contact Web page to acquire potential customer information for the Gallery Portrait and Family Photography studio. The form contained fields for customers to enter their contact information. Currently, the form fields do not contain any type of validation, so a visitor does not have to complete each field properly. Adding Spry validation widgets, as shown in Figure 5–1a, to the Gallery's Contact page verifies that the information entered into the form meets specified conditions. Additionally, the Gallery owners are interested in showcasing more of their work on the Web site. In Chapter 5, you create a visually appealing, streamlined Portfolio Web page (Figures 5–1b, 5–1c, 5–1d) with an animated slide show using a LightBox Gallery widget within a Spry Collapsible Panel.

(a) Spry validation on the Contact page

(b) Portfolio page with Spry Collapsible Panels

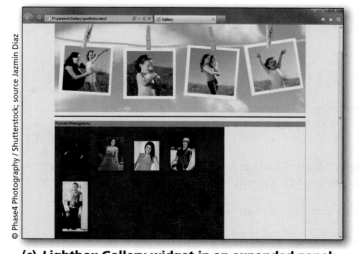

(c) Lightbox Gallery widget in an expanded panel

(d) Zoom effect on Portfolio page

Figure 5–1

Overview

As you read this chapter, you will learn how to create interactive Web pages by performing these general tasks:

- Explore Spry options and how they work.
- Modify a form with Spry validation.
- Test a Spry validation Web page.
- Add the Spry Collapsible Panel widget to a Web page.
- Add headings to a collapsible panel.
- Create an Adobe account to access Adobe Exchange.
- Explore the Adobe Widget Browser.
- Add the LightBox Gallery widget within the Spry Collapsible Panel.

Plan
Ahead

General Project Guidelines

When adding Spry widgets to a Web site, consider the appearance and the characteristics of the completed site. As you add Spry widgets, you should follow these general guidelines:

1. **Review what you need to publish a Web site that uses Spry widgets.** A Web page containing a Spry widget needs support files that specify the formatting and behavior of the widget. Dreamweaver creates the support files for you automatically. You need to upload these files to the server when you publish the site.

2. **Select Spry widgets.** Determine which Spry widgets you will use, the page(s) in which they will be used, and where they will be placed on a page.

3. **Edit and format Spry widgets.** Change the content and format of the widgets to match the design of your Web site.

4. **Add custom content to a widget.** After adding a widget to a Web page and then customizing it to fit the page, add text or images as necessary to suit the purpose of the widget.

More specific details about these guidelines are presented at appropriate points throughout the chapter.

To Start Dreamweaver and Open the Gallery Site

Each time you start Dreamweaver, it opens to the last site displayed when you closed the program. The following steps start Dreamweaver and open the Gallery Web site.

1 Click the Start button on the Windows 7 taskbar to display the Start menu, and then type `Dreamweaver CS6` in the 'Search programs and files' box.

2 Click Adobe Dreamweaver CS6 in the list to start Dreamweaver.

3 If the Dreamweaver window is not maximized, click the Maximize button next to the Close button on the Application bar to maximize the window.

4 If the Gallery site is not displayed in the Files panel, click the Sites button on the Files panel toolbar and then click Gallery to display the files and folders in the Gallery site.

Understanding the Spry Framework

Dreamweaver's Spry tools provide additional Web page customization options to create a rich, interactive user experience. The **Spry framework for AJAX** is a JavaScript library that supports a set of reusable widgets. **AJAX (Asynchronous JavaScript and XML)** combines several Web technologies to develop a Web application that efficiently works with a Web browser to process and transfer customer data to a Web server. A **Spry widget** is an element containing HTML, CSS, and JavaScript code to facilitate interaction with a user. Examples of a Spry widget include form validation, collapsible panels, and a menu bar.

A Spry widget consists of three parts: structure, behavior, and styling. HTML code defines the **widget structure**. The **widget behavior** is determined by the JavaScript code and controls how the widget responds to a user when an event begins. CSS code controls the **widget styling**, which defines the appearance of the widget.

Review what you need to publish a Web site that uses Spry widgets.
When you insert Spry widgets into a Web page, Dreamweaver automatically creates a SpryAssets folder within the Web site root folder, and stores the JavaScript and CSS files related to the Spry widget within this folder. Each time you insert a Spry widget, Dreamweaver adds a corresponding JavaScript file and CSS file to the SpryAssets folder. The JavaScript file contains the code related to the widget's behavior. The CSS file contains the styling information related to the widget. These files are named with the type of Spry widget inserted. For example, if a Spry Validation Text Field is added to a Web page, the JavaScript file is named SpryValidationTextField.js (the extension .js represents a JavaScript file) and the CSS file is named SpryValidationTextField.css. You must upload the SpryAssets folder to the Web server so that the Web pages containing the Spry widgets work properly.

Plan Ahead

The use of Dreamweaver's Spry widgets allows you to integrate interactivity into your Web pages without needing to know how to code in HTML, CSS, or JavaScript. Additionally, you can edit a widget's style to suit your needs.

Spry Widget Options

You can add many Spry widget options to a Web page. To locate the Spry Widget category on the Insert bar, click the Spry tab. The Spry category on the Insert bar is shown in Figure 5–2. Table 5–1 describes the Spry widgets available through Adobe Dreamweaver CS6.

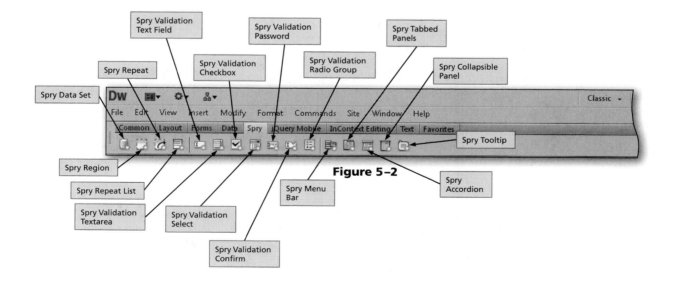

Figure 5–2

Table 5–1 Spry Widgets	
Command	**Description**
Spry Data Set	JavaScript object containing pointers to XML data sources
Spry Region	JavaScript object used to enclose data objects, which includes two types of regions: the Spry Region wraps around data objects, such as tables; and the Spry Detail Region works with a master table object to allow dynamic updating of data
Spry Repeat	Data structure that displays repeating data such as a set of photograph thumbnails
Spry Repeat List	Data structure that displays data as an ordered list, an unordered or a bulleted list, a definition list, or a drop-down list
Spry Validation Text Field	Data structure that displays valid or invalid data when a site visitor enters text
Spry Validation Textarea	Widget that validates the text entered into a Textarea field
Spry Validation Checkbox	Widget that displays valid or invalid states when the user selects or fails to select a check box
Spry Validation Select	Drop-down menu that displays valid or invalid states when the user makes a selection
Spry Validation Password	Widget that validates password input
Spry Validation Confirm	Widget that confirms valid data was entered
Spry Validation Radio Group	Widget that validates an option is selected within the radio group
Spry Menu Bar	Widget that provides a set of navigational menu items that display submenus or links when a site visitor points to the item
Spry Tabbed Panels	Widget used to organize content into panels; users can access panels by clicking a tab at the top of the panel
Spry Accordion	Widget that resembles a standard vertical menu bar; the panels collapse and expand to display or hide content panels
Spry Collapsible Panel	Widget that stores content in a compact space; users can hide or reveal the content by clicking a tab
Spry Tooltip	Widget that displays an on-screen tip when users point to forms and other data

BTW

Getting More Widgets
The Adobe Exchange offers more widgets than the built-in Spry widgets included with Dreamweaver. Click the Extend Dreamweaver button on the Application bar and then click Browse for Web Widgets.

Adding Spry to a Web Page

Dreamweaver provides various Spry options, as described in Table 5–1, including Spry validation widgets, which you will integrate into the form on the Contact Web page. On the Portfolio Web page, you will add a Spry Collapsible Panel widget to display many sample photos in a compact space. Each page should also contain a Submit button so users can submit their form information to the server for processing, and a Reset button so users can clear the form and re-enter data as necessary.

Plan Ahead

Select Spry widgets.
Although Dreamweaver provides 15 Spry widgets for adding interactivity to Web sites, this chapter uses the Spry Validation Text Field, Spry Validation Radio Group, and Spry Collapsible Panel widgets. Consider incorporating these widgets in the following circumstances:

- **Spry Validation Text Field.** Determine which fields require validation in the Web form such as required fields or e-mail format fields. Use this type of Spry widget when your Web site includes a form and you want to make sure you capture data from the user.

- **Spry Validation Radio Group.** Use this type of Spry widget when you want to require users to make a selection from a group.

- **Spry Collapsible Panel.** Use this type of Spry widget when you want to organize large amounts of information on a page in a compact space.

Using Spry Validation Widgets

The form created on the Contact page in Chapter 4 contains fields for user entry. Currently, these fields do not contain rules to require or validate that users complete the form. For example, all e-mail addresses have a prescribed format starting with a unique name followed by an @ symbol and a domain name. An e-mail address should not contain a blank space. Dreamweaver includes a built-in Spry validation widget that tests the e-mail address a user enters to determine whether the address matches the format.

After the user completes the form and clicks the Submit button, Spry validation confirms that users filled in the required text fields in the specified format. The form displays an error message if a required text field is blank or the text field is not in the prescribed format. In Dreamweaver, you use the Preview states property of a widget to view its message options. These options vary depending on the widget. The following states are some of the general options available.

Initial state. Determines how the text field is displayed in a browser before the user clicks the Submit button; does not include a message

Required state. Specifies the error message to display if the user does not enter text into the text field

Valid state. Determines that the user entered the text in the correct format; does not include a message

Invalid state. Specifies the error message to display if the user does not enter the text in the specified format

To Open the Contact Web Page and Select the Spry Category on the Insert Bar

Before adding Spry widgets to the Contact Web page, you must open the page in Dreamweaver and display the Spry category on the Insert bar. The following steps open the Contact Web page and display the Spry category on the Insert bar.

1

- Double-click contact.html in the Files panel to display the Contact page in the Document window (Figure 5–3).

Note: To help you locate screen elements that are referenced in the step instructions, such as buttons and commands, this book uses red boxes to point to these screen elements.

© Serg Ivanov / Shutterstock

Figure 5–3

- Click the Spry tab on the Insert bar to display the Spry options (Figure 5–4).

Figure 5–4

To Add Spry Validation to a Required Text Field

If a visitor submits a partially completed form, the Gallery might not have enough information to contact this new customer. Add Spry validation to the form to make certain that visitors complete the required text fields on the form. To confirm that the user does not leave a form text field blank, use the Spry Validation Text Field widget to verify that the text box contains text. You can add the Spry Validation Text Field widget using the Insert menu on the Application bar or using the Spry Validation Text Field button on the Insert bar. After adding the Spry Validation Text Field, you use the Property inspector to modify the Spry TextField name and the Preview states setting. Recall that the Preview states property determines the error message to display if the user does not enter information or enters invalid information. The following steps apply Spry validation to the First Name text field.

- If necessary, scroll down the page and click the First Name text field to select the field.

- Click the Spry Validation Text Field button on the Insert bar to change the text field to a Spry Validation Text Field, and to display the properties of the First Name text field on the Property inspector (Figure 5–5).

Q&A Why do dashed lines appear around the text field?

The dashed lines indicate that the text field is selected.

Q&A Does clicking the Spry Validation Text Field button create a second text field for the First Name field?

No. Clicking this button applies Spry validation to the selected text field.

Q&A Why does the Property inspector change after I click the Spry Validation Text Field button?

Now that you have applied Spry validation to the text field, the Property inspector displays validation properties for the selected text field.

Figure 5–5

2

- Double-click the Spry TextField text box on the Property inspector and then type `firstName` to rename the field (Figure 5–6).

Q&A The Required check box on the Property inspector is checked, though I did not click it. Is this box supposed to be checked?

Yes. By default, the Required check box is checked. Because Spry validation is designed to require text input from the user, Required is the default setting of a Spry Validation Text Field.

Property inspector

Spry TextField box

Figure 5–6

3

- Click the Preview states button to display the list of Preview states.

- Click Required to select the setting and to display the A value is required error message next to the firstName Spry Validation Text Field (Figure 5–7).

Q&A What is the Preview states required error message?

If a user does not enter text in the firstName field, the Required Preview states sets an error message to appear after the text field, advising the user that the field is required.

Figure 5–7

4

- Select the text, A value is required, next to the firstName Spry Validation Text Field to prepare to replace it (Figure 5–8).

Q&A Should I also select the period at the end of the message?

No. Delete all the text except for the period. A period should appear at the end of the replacement text.

Figure 5–8

5

- Type Please provide your first name to change the required error message (Figure 5–9).

Q&A Does the error message appear on the Contact page when I view it in my browser?

No. This text appears only if the user clicks the Submit button without entering text into the firstName field.

Figure 5–9

6

- Click the Save button on the Standard toolbar to save your work and display the Copy Dependent Files dialog box (Figure 5–10).

Q&A Why is the Copy Dependent Files dialog box displayed?

When you insert a Spry widget, Dreamweaver creates dependent asset files that you need to include the widget on the Web page. Be sure to copy the files to your site so the widget works properly.

Q&A On the contact.html page tab, what do SpryValidationTextField.js and SpryValidationTextField.css refer to?

SpryValidationTextField.js indicates that a JavaScript (.js) file named SpryValidationTextField.

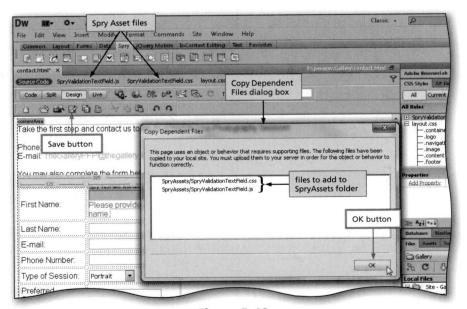

Figure 5–10

js is attached to the Contact page. This file is contained within the SpryAssets folder. SpryValidationTextField.css indicates that another CSS file is attached to the Contact page. The rules for SpryValidationTextField.css appear in the CSS Styles panel. This file is also contained within the SpryAssets folder.

7

- Click the OK button to save the Spry Asset files and to create the SpryAssets folder in the Files panel (Figure 5–11).

Q&A What is the SpryAssets folder?

The SpryAssets folder contains the Spry widget files associated with the Web site.

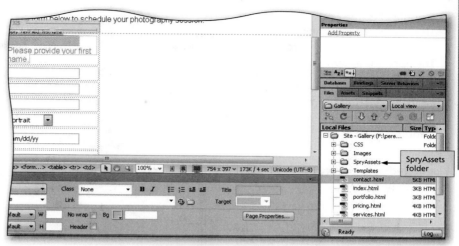

Figure 5–11

Other Ways

1. On Application bar, click Insert, point to Spry, click Spry Validation Text Field

---

To Add Spry Validation to Another Required Text Field

In addition to entering text in the First Name field, users also should be required to enter text in the Last Name field so the form contains complete contact information when users submit it. The following steps apply Spry Validation to the Last Name text field.

1

- Click the Last Name text field to select the field.

- Click the Spry Validation Text Field button on the Insert bar to change the text field to a Spry Validation Text Field (Figure 5–12).

Figure 5–12

2

- Double-click the Spry TextField text box on the Property inspector and then type `lastName` to rename the Spry Validation Text Field.

- Click the Preview states button and then click Required to display the A value is required error message (Figure 5–13).

Q&A

Why is the Spry TextField value entered as one word, as in lastName?

The name cannot include any spaces, so to use a descriptive name containing two words, you remove the space but capitalize the first letter of the second word to make the name easy to read.

Figure 5–13

3

- Select the text, A value is required, next to the lastName Spry Validation Text Field, and then type `Please provide your last name` to change the required error message (Figure 5–14).

4

- Click the Save button on the Standard toolbar to save your work.

Figure 5–14

To Add Spry Validation to an E-mail Text Field

You want to make the E-mail text field a required text field and add validation to confirm that the text matches the format of an e-mail address, as in myname@email.com. If the e-mail address entered is missing the @ symbol or the domain, it does not pass the validation test. The following steps apply Spry validation to an e-mail text field.

- Click the E-mail text field to select the field.

- Click the Spry Validation Text Field button on the Insert bar to change the text field to a Spry Validation Text Field (Figure 5–15).

Figure 5–15

- Double-click the Spry TextField text box on the Property inspector and then type `e-mail` to rename the Spry Validation Text Field (Figure 5–16).

Figure 5–16

- Click the Type button and then click Email Address to select the type of Spry validation widget.

- Click the Preview states button, and then click Required to select the setting and to view the **A value is required** error message (Figure 5–17).

Q&A

How does the Email Address type validate the E-mail text field?

The Email Address type reviews the text to confirm that it is in the proper e-mail format, such as myname@email.com. If the e-mail address is not in the proper format, the form displays the Invalid format error message.

Figure 5–17

- Select the text, A value is required, next to the e-mail Spry Validation Text Field to prepare to replace it.

- Type `Please provide your`, press ENTER, and then type `e-mail address` to change the required error message for the e-mail Spry Validation Text Field (Figure 5–18).

- Click the Save button on the Standard toolbar to save your work.

Figure 5–18

To Add Spry Validation to a Phone Number Text Field

You want to make the Phone Number text field a required text field and add validation to confirm that the text entered is a phone number. The validation test checks that the phone number entered is in the proper format: (999) 999-9999. If the phone number entered is missing a number or is not in the required format, it will not pass the validation test. The following steps apply Spry validation to a phone number text field.

1

- If necessary, scroll down the page, and then click the Phone Number text field to select the field.

- Click the Spry Validation Text Field button on the Insert bar to change the text field to a Spry Validation Text Field (Figure 5–19).

Figure 5–19

2

- Double-click the Spry TextField text box on the Property inspector and then type `phoneNumber` to rename the field.

- Click the Type button and then click Phone Number to select the type of Spry validation widget (Figure 5–20).

Q&A

How does the Phone Number type validate the Phone Number text field?

The Phone Number type only allows numbers and phone number formatting characters, such as parentheses ( ) and a hyphen (-). If the phone number entered is not within the specified pattern, such as (999) 999-9999, the Web page displays the Invalid format error message.

Figure 5–20

- If necessary, click the Format button on the Property inspector, and then click US/Canada to select the phone number format.

- Click the Hint text box and then Type (999) .999-9999 to provide a reminder for users about the valid format.

- Click the Enforce pattern check box to select it (Figure 5–21).

Q&A | What is the US/Canada format?

The US/Canada format is a specific phone number pattern that includes parentheses ( ) and a hyphen (-), such as (999) 999-9999.

Q&A | What is the Hint property?

When the browser displays the form, (999) 999-9999 appears in the Phone Number field to show the desired format. When the user moves the insertion point to the Phone Number text field, the hint disappears, allowing the user to type a phone number.

Q&A | What happens to the Phone Number text field when the Enforce pattern check box is selected?

As a user enters a phone number into the field, the parentheses ( ) and hyphen (-) are inserted automatically.

Figure 5–21

- Click the Save button on the Standard toolbar to save your work.

To Add Spry Validation to Another Required Text Field

Next, you can make the Preferred Session Date text field a required text field and add validation to confirm that the text entered is a date. The validation test checks that the date entered is in the specified date format, such as mm/dd/yy. If the user enters a date in a different format, it will not pass the validation test. The following steps apply Spry validation to the Preferred Session Date text field.

1

- Click the Preferred Session Date text field to select the field.

- Click the Spry Validation Text Field button on the Insert bar to change the text field to a Spry Validation Text Field (Figure 5–22).

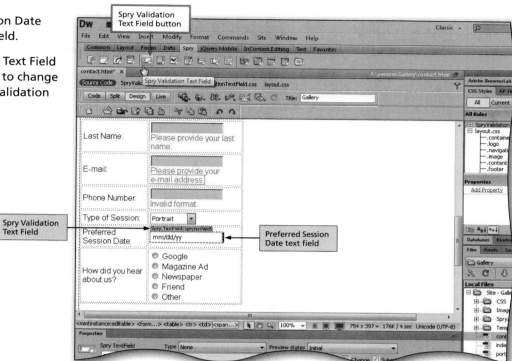

Figure 5–22

2

- Double-click the Spry TextField text box and then type sessionDate to rename the Spry Validation Text Field.

- Click the Type button and then click Date to select the type of Spry validation widget (Figure 5–23).

Q&A

How does the Date type validate the Date text field?

The Date type reviews the text the user enters to confirm it is a date in the specified date format, such as mm/dd/yy. If the user enters a date in a different format, the Web page displays the Invalid format error message.

Figure 5–23

- If necessary, click the Format button on the Property inspector, and then click mm/dd/yy to select a date format.

- Click the Hint text box and then type `mm/dd/yy` to provide a reminder for users about the valid format.

- Click the Enforce pattern check box to select it (Figure 5–24).

Q&A

What happens to the Preferred Session Date text field when the Enforce pattern check box is selected?

As a user types a date into the field, the form inserts forward slashes (/) automatically where appropriate.

Figure 5–24

- Click the Preferred Session Date text field to select the field.

- Double-click the value in the Init val text box and then press the DELETE key to delete the value (Figure 5–25).

Q&A

Why do I need to delete the initial value?

Deleting the initial value means the user does not need to delete it before typing a date. The Hint property displays mm/dd/yy in the Preferred Session Date text field until the user clicks the text box so the user can enter a date.

- Click the Save button on the Standard toolbar to save your work.

Figure 5–25

To Add Spry Validation to a Radio Group

You want to make the 'How did you hear about us?' Radio Group a required response. To complete this task, first delete the existing Radio Group and then insert the Spry Validation Radio Group widget. Inserting the Spry Validation Radio Group widget adds two files to the SpryAssets folder: SpryValidationRadioGroup.js and SpryValidationRadioGroup.css. The following steps delete the existing Radio Group and insert a Spry Validation Radio Group widget.

1

- Select the 'How did you hear about us?' Radio Group to select it and then press the DELETE key to delete it (Figure 5–26).

Figure 5–26

2

- Click the Spry Validation Radio Group button on the Insert bar to insert a Spry Validation Radio Group widget and to open the Spry Validation Radio Group dialog box.

- In the Name text box, replace the text RadioGroup1 with Referral to provide a unique name (Figure 5–27).

Figure 5–27

3

• Click the first Radio label in the Label list and then type `Google` to replace the text.

• Click the second Radio label in the Label list and then type `Magazine Ad` to replace the text (Figure 5–28).

Figure 5–28

4

• Click the plus button to add another label and value to the list.

• Click the third Radio label in the Label list and then type `Newspaper` to replace the text (Figure 5–29).

Figure 5–29

5

• Click the plus button to add another label and value to the list.

• If necessary, use the vertical scroll bar to scroll down and click the fourth Radio label in the Label list, and then type `Friend` to replace the text (Figure 5–30).

Figure 5–30

- Click the plus button to add another label and value to the list.

- Click the fifth Radio label in the Label list and then type `Other` to replace the text (Figure 5–31).

Figure 5–31

7

- Click the OK button to insert the Spry Validation Radio Group.

- Double-click the text in the Spry Radio Group text box on the Property inspector and then type `referral` to rename the Spry Radio Group (Figure 5–32).

Figure 5–32

- Click the Save button on the Standard toolbar to save your work and display the Copy Dependent Files dialog box (Figure 5–33).

9

- Click the OK button to save the Spry Asset files to the SpryAssets folder.

Figure 5–33

DW 290 Dreamweaver Chapter 5 Creating Interactive Web Pages with Spry and Adobe Widgets

To Test the Spry Validation Form in a Browser

The following steps open and then preview the contact.html page in Internet Explorer to test the form.

1

- Click the 'Preview/ Debug in browser' button on the Document toolbar to display a list of browsers.

- Click Preview in IExplore in the 'Preview/Debug in browser' list to display the Gallery Web site in Internet Explorer (Figure 5–34).

Figure 5–34

2

- If a security message appears regarding ActiveX controls, click the 'Allow blocked content' button to allow the Spry validation form to work properly.

- Click the Submit button to test the form (Figure 5–35).

Q&A

What should happen after I click the Submit button?

Each field should display a required validation message, except for the Type of Session field.

Figure 5–35

- Click the First Name text field, type your first name, click the Last Name text field, and then type your last name to test those fields.

- Click the E-mail text box, and then type the beginning part of your e-mail address, such as perezm, to test the field.

- Click the Submit button again to submit the form (Figure 5–36).

Q&A

Should I include the @ symbol or domain when I type my e-mail address?

No. You are testing the E-mail field to make sure it shows the Invalid format error message.

Figure 5–36

- Click the E-mail text box and then type your complete e-mail address to test the field again.

- Click the Phone Number text box and then type your phone number to enter a phone number.

- Click the Type of Session box arrow and then click Family to select a session type.

- Click the Preferred Session Date text box and then type today's date to enter a date.

- Click the Friend option button to select an option in the 'How did you hear about us?' Radio Group (Figure 5–37).

5

- Click the Submit button to submit the form, and then close Internet Explorer.

- Close the contact.html page.

Figure 5–37

Other Ways
1. Press ALT+S

Break Point: If you wish to take a break, this is a good place to do so. To resume at a later time, start Dreamweaver and continue following the steps from this location forward.

Spry CSS Files
You can view the Spry CSS files for each Spry widget in the CSS Styles panel. You can modify the default styling for each type of Spry widget used within a Web site.

Using Spry Collapsible Panels

The Portfolio Web page showcases the Gallery's photography work. Eventually, many images will be included on the page. To maximize space and minimize the length of the page, you can use Spry Collapsible Panel widgets to organize and store the images. You will add three Spry Collapsible Panels to the Portfolio Web page. The first Spry Collapsible Panel is for showcasing the Gallery's portrait photography. The second Spry Collapsible Panel is for family photography, and the third Spry Collapsible Panel is for baby photography.

To Add Spry Collapsible Panels to a Web Page

The following steps open the Portfolio Web page and insert Spry Collapsible Panel widgets.

1

- Double-click portfolio.html in the Files panel to display the Portfolio page in the Document window.

- Select the text and images within the editable region (Figure 5–38).

Figure 5–38

© Source: Jazmin Diaz

2

- Press the DELETE key to delete the selected text and images.

- Click the Spry Collapsible Panel button on the Insert bar to insert a Spry Collapsible Panel and to display the properties of the Spry Collapsible Panel on the Property inspector (Figure 5–39).

Figure 5–39

3

- Double-click the Collapsible panel text box on the Property inspector and then type `portraitPanel` to rename the collapsible panel.

- Click the Default state button and then click Closed to set the Default state of the panel.

- Click the Display button and then click Closed to set the Display state of the panel (Figure 5–40).

Q&A

What does it mean to set the Default state to Closed for the Spry Collapsible Panel?

Selecting Closed as the Default state means the collapsible panel will be closed when the Portfolio Web page is displayed in a browser. Users can click the collapsible panel to view its content. Setting the Default state to Closed saves space on the Web page when it opens.

Figure 5–40

4

- Click below the Content line in the portraitPanel to deselect the panel.

- Click the Spry Collapsible Panel button on the Insert bar to insert a second Spry Collapsible Panel (Figure 5–41).

Figure 5–41

5

- Double-click the Collapsible panel text box on the Property inspector and then type `familyPanel` to rename the collapsible panel.

- Click the Default state button and then click Closed to set the Default state of the panel.

- Click the Display button and then click Closed to set the Display state of the panel (Figure 5–42).

Figure 5–42

6

- Click below the Content line in the familyPanel to place the insertion point.

- Click the Spry Collapsible Panel button on the Insert bar to insert a third Spry Collapsible Panel (Figure 5–43).

Spry Collapsible Panel button

third Spry Collapsible Panel

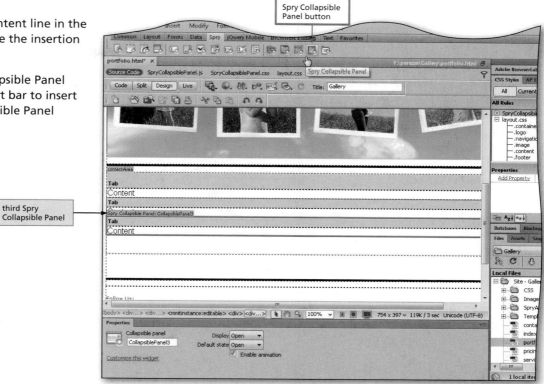

Figure 5–43

© Phase4 Photography / Shutterstock

7

- Double-click the Collapsible panel text box on the Property inspector and then type `babyPanel` to rename the collapsible panel.

- Click the Default state button and then click Closed to set the Default state of the panel.

- Click the Display button and then click Closed to set the Display state of the panel (Figure 5–44).

third Spry Collapsible Panel is named babyPanel

Display button

Default state button

Collapsible panel text box

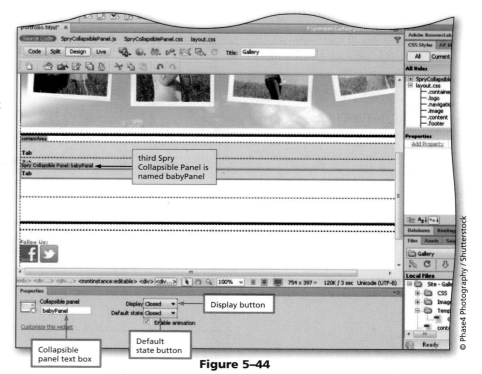

Figure 5–44

© Phase4 Photography / Shutterstock

• Click below the babyPanel to deselect it.

• Click the Save button on the Standard toolbar to save your work and display the Copy Dependent Files dialog box (Figure 5–45).

Q&A

Why does the text, SpryCollapsiblePanel.js and SpryCollapsiblePanel.css, appear on the portfolio.html page tab?

These are the files the browser needs to display the Spry Collapsible Panel widgets. The JavaScript and CSS files are contained within the SpryAssets folder in the Files panel.

• Click the OK button to save the Spry Asset files in the SpryAssets folder.

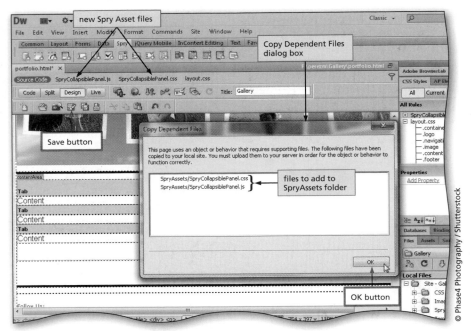

Figure 5–45

To Add Panel Headings

Tab is the default name for each Collapsible Panel widget. The following steps rename each tab to identify the type of images each tab will contain.

1

• Delete the text, Tab, in the portraitPanel Collapsible Panel widget and then type `Portrait Photography` to rename the tab (Figure 5–46).

Figure 5–46

- Delete the text, Tab, in the familyPanel Collapsible Panel widget and then type `Family Photography` to rename the tab.

- Delete the text, Tab, in the babyPanel Collapsible Panel widget and then type `Baby Photography` to rename the tab (Figure 5–47).

Q&A Why is it important to name each tab?

The tab title is always displayed on the Web page, even if the panel is closed. Naming each tab identifies the contents within each panel.

❸

- Click the Save button on the Standard toolbar to save your work.

Figure 5–47

© Phase4 Photography / Shutterstock

Using the Adobe Widget Browser

In addition to Spry widgets, Adobe provides a resource for other widgets through the Adobe Widget Browser. The **Adobe Widget Browser** is an Adobe AIR application that allows Web site designers to access a library of online widgets in Adobe Exchange. **Adobe Integrated Runtime (AIR)** applications allow Web site developers access to Web resources. **Adobe Exchange** provides many types of Web tags, scripts, and other custom Web items available for download. Widget designers can upload their custom-built widgets to Adobe Exchange to share widgets that they create.

In Adobe Exchange, you can select widgets to use in your Dreamweaver Web site and add them to a personal list of available widgets called My Widgets in the Adobe Widget Browser. You can add the widgets stored in My Widgets to your Web pages. You must accept terms and conditions before using some widgets.

One widget available in the Adobe Widget Browser is called the LightBox Gallery widget. You can use this widget to enhance the Gallery Web site. The LightBox Gallery widget can display sample portrait, family, and baby photography, and let visitors select and view a larger version of a photo. When a visitor clicks a photo, the widget animates the photo so it grows larger on the Web page to create an engaging effect.

Before you can access the widgets in the Adobe Widget Browser, you must install Adobe AIR and create an Adobe account. You do not need to pay a fee to download and install Adobe AIR or create an Adobe account. In addition, you do not need an Adobe account to create a My Widgets folder and store widgets in it.

BTW

Adobe Widget Browser Help
To find help when using the Adobe Widget Browser, open the Dreamweaver Help file and then search for Widget Browser.

To Check Your Computer for the Adobe AIR Application

Before you can use the Adobe Widget Browser, make sure Adobe AIR is installed on your computer. The following steps check to see if Adobe AIR is installed on your computer.

1

• Click the Extend Dreamweaver button on the title bar to display the Extend Dreamweaver options (Figure 5–48).

Figure 5–48

2

• Click Widget Browser to select it, and then click the Accept button in the End User License Agreement dialog box to display the Adobe Widget Browser window, which confirms Adobe AIR is installed on your computer (Figure 5–49).

Q&A

What does it mean if the Adobe Widget Browser window is not displayed?

That means Adobe AIR is not installed on your computer. Complete the steps in the "To Download and Install Adobe AIR" section.

Figure 5–49

To Download and Install Adobe AIR

If Adobe AIR is not installed on your computer, you can download the program and install it free of charge. The following steps download and install the Adobe AIR application.

1
- Open your browser and type `http://get.adobe.com/air/` in the Address bar to open the Adobe AIR page on the Adobe Web site (Figure 5–50).

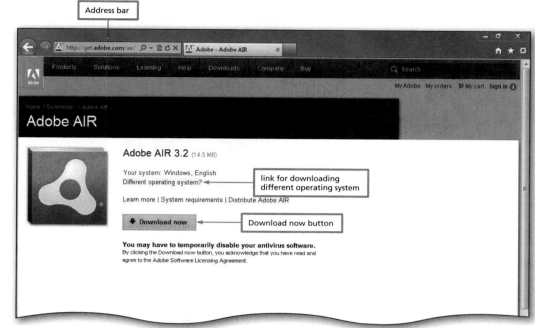

Figure 5–50

2
- If the Adobe AIR page shows your correct operating system, click the Download now button to begin downloading Adobe AIR.

- If the Adobe AIR page shows the incorrect operating system, click the 'Different operating system?' link, use the arrow buttons for Steps 1 and 2 to select your operating system and version, and then download the application (Figure 5–51).

Figure 5–51

 Why does this Web site provide a download for a different version of Adobe AIR?

Adobe may have released a newer version of Adobe AIR. Continue with the installation.

3

- On the Information bar, click the Run button to start installing Adobe AIR and display the Adobe AIR Setup dialog box (Figure 5–52).

Q&A

What should I do if a User Account Control dialog box appears asking if I want to allow this program to make changes to my computer?

Click the OK or Allow button to install the software.

Adobe AIR Setup dialog box

I Agree button

Figure 5–52

4

- Click the I Agree button in the Adobe AIR Setup dialog box to accept the license terms and to display the Installation completed message in the Adobe AIR Setup dialog box (Figure 5–53).

Adobe AIR Setup dialog box

Finish button

Figure 5–53

5

- Click the Finish button in the Adobe AIR Setup dialog box to finish installing the software.

- Close your browser.

To Create an Adobe Account

If you do not have an Adobe account, you must create one so you can view and select widgets to use in your Web sites. The following steps create an Adobe account if you do not already have one.

1

- If necessary, click the Extend Dreamweaver button on the title bar, and then click Widget Browser to display the Adobe Widget Browser window (Figure 5–54).

Adobe Widget Browser window

Sign In button

Figure 5–54

2

- Click the Sign In button to display the Sign In dialog box (Figure 5–55).

I have a Sign Out button, not a Sign In button. What should I do?

You are already signed in to your Adobe account. Skip ahead to the "To View and Add Widgets from Adobe Exchange to My Widgets" section.

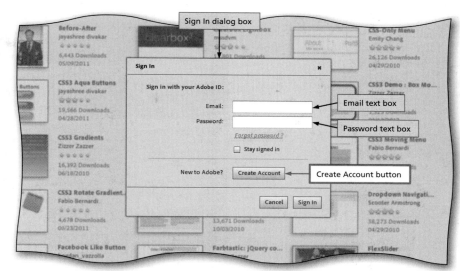

Figure 5–55

3

- If you need to create an account, click the Create Account button to visit the Adobe Web site (Figure 5–56).

I already have an Adobe account. Do I need to create another one?

No. If you already have an Adobe account, enter your e-mail address and password in the Sign In dialog box or the 'Returning members sign in' section of the Adobe Sign In page.

Figure 5–56

4

- If you need to create an account, click the Create an Adobe Account button to display the Join Adobe page (Figure 5–57).

Q&A What should I do if I do not need to create an account?

Skip ahead to Step 2 in the next section, "To Sign in to the Adobe Widget Browser."

Account Details form

Figure 5–57

5

- Complete the Account Details form to create an Adobe account.

- Click the Continue button at the bottom of the form to display the Thank You page (Figure 5–58).

6

- Click the Continue button and then close your browser to finish creating an Adobe account.

Thank You page

Continue button

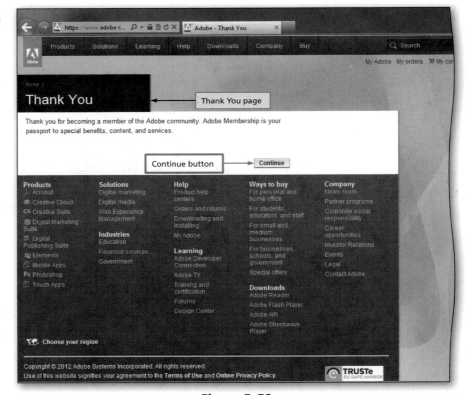

Figure 5–58

To Sign in to the Adobe Widget Browser

Once you have established an Adobe account, you need to sign in to access Adobe Exchange using the Adobe Widget Browser window so you can review the widgets available in Adobe Exchange. The following steps sign you in to your Adobe account through the Adobe Widget Browser.

1 If necessary, open the Adobe Widget Browser.

2 Click the Sign In button to display the Sign In dialog box.

3 Enter the e-mail address and password used to create your Adobe account to sign in.

4 Click the Sign In button to finish signing in to your Adobe account and display the Adobe Widget Browser (Figure 5–59).

Figure 5–59

To View and Add Widgets from Adobe Exchange to My Widgets

Once you have signed in to the Adobe Widget Browser, you can review the widgets available in Adobe Exchange and add them to My Widgets. My Widgets is the location where you store saved widgets from Adobe Exchange. The following steps view widgets and add them to My Widgets.

1

- Scroll down to view all of the widgets available through Adobe Exchange (Figure 5–60).

Figure 5–60

2

- Scroll to the top of the window, click the Filter text box, and then type `light` to search for the LightBox Gallery Widget (Figure 5–61).

Figure 5–61

3

- Click the LightBox Gallery Widget to select it.

- Review the information provided in the window to learn more about this widget (Figure 5–62).

Figure 5–62

- Click the Preview button to see a live view of the widget.

- If necessary, click the <default> option in the Widget Presets list to select the default developer preset.

- On the Live View tab, click the first sample image to view it (Figure 5–63).

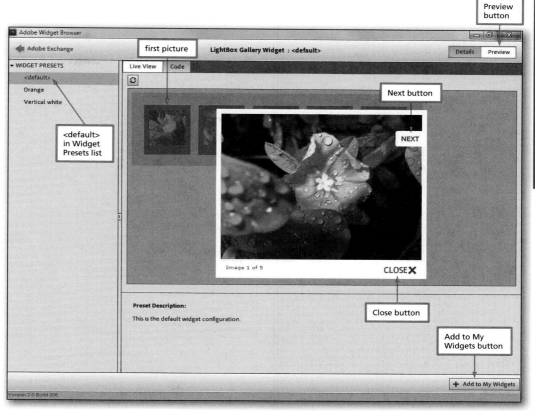

Figure 5–63

5

- Point to an image and then click the Next button to view all of the images.

- Click the Close button when you are finished viewing the images.

- Click the Add to My Widgets button to add the LightBox Gallery widget to My Widgets and to display the Widget Added dialog box (Figure 5–64).

Figure 5–64

6

● Click the Go to My Widgets button in the Widget Added dialog box to view the widget in My Widgets (Figure 5–65).

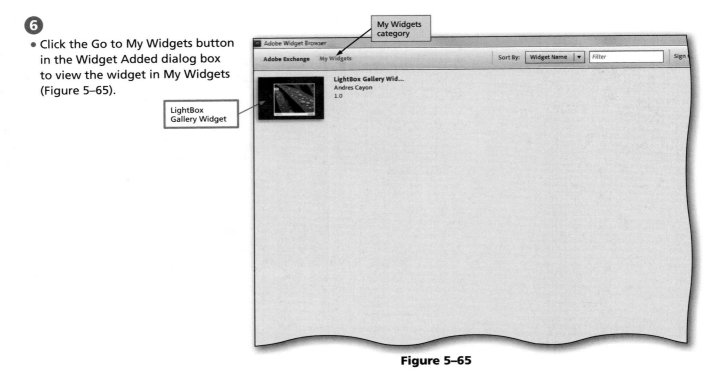

Figure 5–65

Editing and Formatting Widgets

After you add the LightBox Gallery widget to My Widgets, you can create a preset for the widget to modify the widget's formatting and properties. A **preset** is a set of predefined properties for the widget. You create a preset to specify the background color, size, text color, margins, padding, and other properties of the widget. The preset you create provides custom properties specifically designed for the Gallery Web site.

Plan Ahead

> **Edit and format Spry widgets.**
> After you add Spry widgets and widgets from other sources to a Web page, typically you need to edit and format the widgets. Consider what you must change to have the widget fit the design of your Web page. For example, you might need to change properties such as background color to match the style of the Web page. You also might need to modify widget controls so they work for your Web site.

To Create a Widget Preset for the LightBox Gallery Widget

The LightBox Gallery widget gives a rich, interactive look and feel to the Gallery Web site. The widget includes buttons for navigation. Before anyone can use the buttons, you need to update the file path for the widget's buttons to associate them with the Gallery site. Otherwise, the widget will not display the buttons. In addition, you can format the widget to match the design of the Gallery site. To do so, you create presets using the Adobe Widget Browser. The following steps create a preset for the LightBox Gallery widget.

- In My Widgets, click the LightBox Gallery widget to select it and display options for modifying the widget (Figure 5–66).

Figure 5–66

- If necessary, click <default> in the Developer Presets list to select it.

- Click the Configure button to create a new preset (Figure 5–67).

Figure 5–67

- Click the Gallery panel to display the Gallery preset options.

- Double-click the Width text box and then type 800 to modify the widget width (Figure 5–68).

Figure 5–68

- Click the Icons panel to display the file paths for the loading icon and navigation buttons.

- Click in the Loading text box before the text, /images/lightbox/lightbox-ico-loading.gif, and then type /your last name and first initial/ Gallery to define the location of the Loading icon within the Gallery Web site.

- Click in the Previous Button text box before the text, /images/lightbox/lightbox-btn-prev.gif, and then type /your last name and first initial/Gallery to define the location of the Previous Button within the Gallery Web site.

Figure 5–69

- Click in the Next Button text box before the text, /images/lightbox/lightbox-btn-next.gif, and then type /your last name and first initial/Gallery to define the location of the Next Button within the Gallery Web site.

- Click in the Close Button text box before the text, /images/lightbox/lightbox-btn-close.gif, and then type /your last name and first initial/Gallery to define the location of the Close Button within the Gallery Web site.

- Select the text in the Name text box and then type Portfolio to name the preset (Figure 5–69).

Q&A

What is the purpose of changing the file paths on the Icons panel?

The Icons panel lists properties for the buttons in the LightBox Gallery widget. The file path of the buttons must be updated to include the file path of the Gallery Web site otherwise they will not be displayed.

5

- Click the Save Preset button to save the preset and display the Portfolio preset in the My Presets list (Figure 5–70).

What does it mean when the Portfolio preset is displayed in the My Presets list?

Now that you have defined the Portfolio preset, the widget width will be adjusted as you specified when you add the widget to the Gallery site. Additionally, the widget will include loading icon and navigation buttons.

Figure 5–70

6

- Click the Close button to close the Adobe Widget Browser.

Adding an Adobe Widget to a Web Page

To enhance the appearance of the Gallery Web site, you can insert the LightBox Gallery widget within each collapsible panel on the Portfolio page. You then can replace the default images in the widget with images from your data files.

Plan Ahead

Add custom content to a widget.
You add a widget to a Web page to enhance the page. Spry widgets and widgets you add from other sources might contain default content that needs to be replaced to fit the purpose of your Web page. For example, you can add images to each tab in a Spry Collapsible Panel widget. When you plan the Web page, determine what content should appear in widgets and what purpose it serves to include them in widgets. If inserting content in widgets does not enhance the page, add the content to the page as you usually do.

The LightBox Gallery widget is an interactive way to showcase images on a Web site. Two image files are linked to each image within the widget; one image is the thumbnail image and the other is the full-size image. A **thumbnail image** is a smaller version of an image. Web pages typically display thumbnail images to conserve file size. The Portfolio page will use the LightBox Gallery widget to display thumbnails of sample portrait, family, and baby photography. Visitors can click a thumbnail image to display a full-size version of the photo.

To Copy Files to a New Lightbox Folder

Before adding images to the LightBox Gallery widget, you must create a Lightbox folder in the Images folder for the Gallery site. To complete this assignment, you will be required to use the Data Files for Students. Visit www.cengage.com/ct/studentdownload for detailed instructions or contact your instructor for information about accessing the required files. The following steps create the Lightbox folder and copy 30 files from the Data Files for Students to the Gallery site.

1 If necessary, insert the USB flash drive containing your student data files, and then use Windows Explorer to open a window displaying the contents of the drive containing the Data Files for Students.

2 Double-click the Chapter 05 folder and then double-click the Gallery folder to open it.

3 Click the baby_1a_thumb file, or the first file in the list, hold down the SHIFT key, and then click the portrait_5b file, or the last file in the list, to select the images needed for the site.

4 Right-click the selected files, click Copy on the context menu, and then navigate to the *your last name and first initial* folder on Removable Disk F: to prepare to copy the files.

5 Double-click the Gallery folder, and then double-click the Images folder to open the Images folder.

6 Create a new folder named Lightbox, and then double-click the Lightbox folder to open it.

7 Right-click a blank spot in the open window, and then click Paste on the context menu to copy the 30 image files into the Lightbox folder (Figure 5–71).

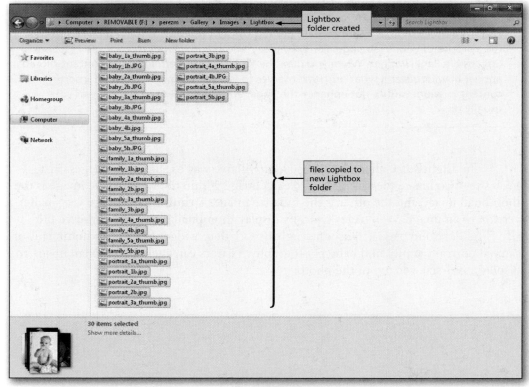

Figure 5–71

To Add the LightBox Gallery Widget to a Web Page

The image files you copied into the Lightbox folder include thumbnail images and full-size images of the photos to display on the Portfolio page. First, you insert a LightBox Gallery widget within each collapsible panel on the Portfolio page. Then you can link each image to a thumbnail image file and a full-size image file. Each collapsible panel will use a LightBox Gallery widget to showcase the Gallery's photography. The following steps add the LightBox Gallery widget within a Collapsible Panel widget on the Portfolio Web page.

1

- In portfolio.html, scroll to view the right edge of the portraitPanel (Figure 5–72).

Figure 5–72

2

- Point to the panel and then click the 'Click to show panel content' button to display the portraitPanel content.

- Delete the text, Content, below the Portrait Photography panel name to create space for the LightBox Gallery widget.

- Click Insert on the Application bar to display the Insert menu (Figure 5–73).

Q&A

Why don't I see the panel below the Portrait Photography panel name now?

The panel is now empty, so it looks like it has been removed. However, it is still part of the page.

Figure 5–73

- Click Widget on the Insert menu to display the Widget dialog box.

- If necessary, click the Widget button and then click LightBox Gallery Widget (1.0) to select the widget.

- Click the Preset button and then click Portfolio to select the page for the widget (Figure 5–74).

Figure 5–74

- Click the OK button in the Widget dialog box to insert the LightBox Gallery widget (Figure 5–75).

Figure 5–75

5

- If necessary, scroll to the right and then click the 'Click to show panel content' button on the familyPanel to display the familyPanel content.

- Delete the text, Content, below the Family Photography panel name.

- Click Insert on the Application bar, and then click Widget to display the Widget dialog box.

- Confirm that the Widget button displays LightBox Gallery Widget (1.0) and the Preset button displays Portfolio to select the widget and the preset.

- Click the OK button in the Widget dialog box to insert the LightBox Gallery widget (Figure 5–76).

second LightBox Gallery widget

icons for thumbnails on familyPanel

Figure 5–76

© Phase4 Photography / Shutterstock

6

- If necessary, scroll to the right and click the 'Click to show panel content' button on the babyPanel to display the babyPanel content.

- Delete the text, Content, below the Baby Photography panel name.

- Click Insert on the Application bar to display the Insert menu and then click Widget to display the Widget dialog box.

- Confirm that the Widget button displays LightBox Gallery Widget (1.0) and the Preset button displays Portfolio to select the widget and the preset.

- Click the OK button in the Widget dialog box to insert the LightBox Gallery widget (Figure 5–77).

third LightBox Gallery widget

icons for thumbnails on babyPanel

Figure 5–77

- Click below the widget to deselect it, and then click the Save button on the Standard toolbar to save your work and display the Copy Dependent Files dialog box (Figure 5–78).

- Click the OK button in the Copy Dependent Files dialog box to save the Spry Asset and image files.

Q&A I noticed that image files are being saved to the Images folder. What are these image files?

The LightBox Gallery widget contains default image files. You will replace them shortly.

Figure 5–78

To Add Images to the Portrait Photography LightBox Gallery Widget

The Portrait Photography LightBox Gallery widget is now ready for the images to display on the Portfolio page. The following steps replace the default images in the LightBox Gallery widget with images to showcase the Gallery's portrait photography.

- In the Files panel, expand the Images folder and then expand the Lightbox folder to view the image files contained in the folder (Figure 5–79).

Figure 5–79

2

- If necessary, scroll to display the portrait image files.

- Click the first image on the Portrait Photography tab to select the image.

- Click the Point to File button next to the Src text box, and then drag the pointer to portrait_1a_thumb .jpg in the Files panel to select the image.

- Click the Point to File button next to the Link text box, and then drag the pointer to portrait_1b.jpg in the Files panel to link to the image (Figure 5–80).

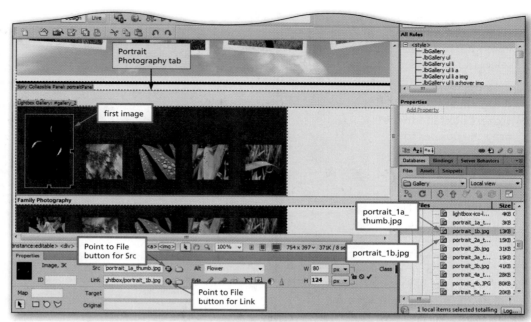

Figure 5–80

Q&A

Why do I need to select one file in the Src text box and a different file in the Link text box?

Because the LightBox Gallery widget accommodates a thumbnail image and a full-size image, you must select a source file for the thumbnail. You also link to the file containing the full-size image so that when the thumbnail is clicked, the full-size image opens.

3

- Click the second image on the Portrait Photography tab to select the image.

- Click the Point to File button next to the Src text box, and then drag the pointer to portrait_2a_thumb. jpg in the Files panel to select the image.

- Click the Point to File button next to the Link text box, and then drag the pointer to portrait_2b.jpg in the Files panel to link to the image (Figure 5–81).

Figure 5–81

• Click the third image on the Portrait Photography tab to select the image.

• Click the Point to File button next to the Src text box, and then drag the pointer to portrait_3a_thumb.jpg in the Files panel to select the image.

• Click the Point to File button next to the Link text box, and then drag the pointer to portrait_3b.jpg in the Files panel to link to the image (Figure 5–82).

Figure 5–82

• Click the fourth image on the Portrait Photography tab to select the image.

• Click the Point to File button next to the Src text box, and then drag the pointer to portrait_4a_thumb.jpg in the Files panel to select the image.

• Click the Point to File button next to the Link text box, and then drag the pointer to portrait_4b.jpg in the Files panel to link to the image.

• Click the fifth image on the Portrait Photography tab to select the image.

Figure 5–83

• Click the Point to File button next to the Src text box, and then drag the pointer to portrait_5a_thumb.jpg in the Files panel to select the image.

• Click the Point to File button next to the Link text box, and then drag the pointer to portrait_5b.jpg in the Files panel to link to the image (Figure 5–83).

6

• Click outside of the widget to deselect it and then click the Save button on the Standard toolbar to save your work.

To Add Images to the Family Photography LightBox Gallery Widget

The Family Photography LightBox Gallery widget is ready for images. The following steps show you how to replace the current images in the LightBox Gallery widget with images to showcase the Gallery's family photography.

1

- If necessary, scroll to display the family files in the Files panel.

- Click the first image on the Family Photography tab to select it.

- Click the Point to File button next to the Src text box, and then drag the pointer to family_1a_thumb.jpg in the Files panel to select the image.

- Click the Point to File button next to the Link text box, and then drag the pointer to family_1b.jpg in the Files panel to link to the image (Figure 5–84).

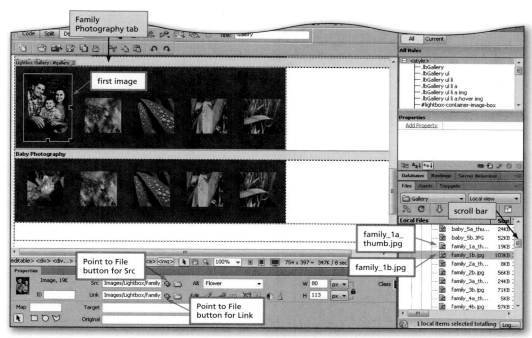

Figure 5–84

2

- Click the second image on the Family Photography tab to select the image.

- Click the Point to File button next to the Src text box, and then drag the pointer to family_2a_thumb.jpg in the Files panel to select the image.

- Click the Point to File button next to the Link text box, and then drag the pointer to family_2b.jpg in the Files panel to link to the image (Figure 5–85).

Figure 5–85

- Click the third image on the Family Photography tab to select the image.

- Click the Point to File button next to the Src text box, and then drag the pointer to family_3a_thumb.jpg in the Files panel to select the image.

- Click the Point to File button next to the Link text box, and then drag the pointer to family_3b.jpg in the Files panel to link to the image (Figure 5–86).

Figure 5–86

- Click the fourth image on the Family Photography tab to select the image.

- Click the Point to File button next to the Src text box, and then drag the pointer to family_4a_thumb.jpg in the Files panel to select the image.

- Click the Point to File button next to the Link text box, and then drag the pointer to family_4b.jpg in the Files panel to link to the image.

- Click the fifth image on the Family Photography tab to select the image.

Figure 5–87

- Click the Point to File button next to the Src text box, and then drag the pointer to family_5a_thumb.jpg in the Files panel to select the image.

- Click the Point to File button next to the Link text box, and then drag the pointer to family_5b.jpg in the Files panel to link to the image (Figure 5–87).

5

- Click outside of the widget to deselect the widget and then click the Save button on the Standard toolbar to save your work.

To Add Images to the Baby Photography LightBox Gallery Widget

The Baby Photography LightBox Gallery widget is ready for images. The following steps show you how to replace the current images in the LightBox Gallery widget with images to showcase the Gallery's baby photography.

1

- If necessary, scroll to display the baby files in the Files panel.

- Click the first image on the Baby Photography tab to select it.

- Click the Point to File button next to the Src text box, and then drag the pointer to baby_1a_thumb.jpg in the Files panel to select the image.

- Click the Point to File button next to the Link text box, and then drag the pointer to baby_1b.jpg in the Files panel to link to the image (Figure 5–88).

Figure 5–88

2

- Click the second image on the Baby Photography tab to select the image.

- Click the Point to File button next to the Src text box, and then drag the pointer to baby_2a_thumb.jpg in the Files panel to select the image.

- Click the Point to File button next to the Link text box, and then drag the pointer to baby_2b .jpg in the Files panel to link to the image (Figure 5–89).

Figure 5–89

- Click the third image on the Baby Photography tab to select the image.

- Click the Point to File button next to the Src text box, and then drag the pointer to baby_3a_thumb.jpg in the Files panel to select the image.

- Click the Point to File button next to the Link text box, and then drag the pointer to baby_3b.jpg in the Files panel to link to the image.

- Click the fourth image on the Baby Photography tab to select the image.

Figure 5–90

- Click the Point to File button next to the Src text box, and then drag the pointer to baby_4a_thumb.jpg in the Files panel to select the image.

- Click the Point to File button next to the Link text box, and then drag the pointer to baby_4b.jpg in the Files panel to link to the image.

- Click the fifth image on the Baby Photography tab to select the image.

- Click the Point to File button next to the Src text box, and then drag the pointer to baby_5a_thumb.jpg in the Files panel to select the image.

- Click the Point to File button next to the Link text box, and then drag the pointer to baby_5b.jpg in the Files panel to link to the image (Figure 5–90).

- Click outside of the widget to deselect it and then click the Save button on the Standard toolbar to save your work.

To View the Collapsible Panels and LightBox Gallery Widget in a Browser

The following steps open the portfolio.html page in Internet Explorer to view the collapsible panels and LightBox Gallery widgets.

1. Click the 'Preview/Debug in browser' button on the Document toolbar to display a list of browsers.

2. Click Preview in IExplore in the 'Preview/Debug in browser' list to display the Gallery Web site in Internet Explorer.

3. If necessary, click the 'Allow blocked content' button to allow the widgets to work properly.

4 Click the Portrait Photography tab to display the first LightBox Gallery widget.

5 Click the first thumbnail on the Portrait Photography tab to display the full-size image (Figure 5–91).

Figure 5–91

6 Click each image to advance to the next image, and then click the last image to close it.

7 Click the Portrait Photography tab to close the Portrait Photography collapsible panel.

8 Click the Family Photography tab to display the second LightBox Gallery widget.

9 Click the first thumbnail on the Family Photography tab to display the full-size image, and then click each image to display it.

10 Click the Family Photography tab to close the Family Photography collapsible panel.

11 Click the Baby Photography tab to display the third LightBox Gallery widget.

12 Click the first thumbnail on the Baby Photography tab to display the full-size image, and then click each image to display it.

13 Close your browser, and then close Dreamweaver.

Chapter Summary

In this chapter, you applied Spry validation to a form on the Contact page using Dreamweaver's Spry validation widgets. You also used Spry to insert Collapsible Panel widgets. You used the Adobe Widget Browser to view widgets within Adobe Exchange and then saved a widget to My Widgets. You added LightBox Gallery widgets to the Spry Collapsible Panels. You also learned how to replace images in the LightBox Gallery widget. You displayed the updated Web pages in a browser and tested the form validation, the collapsible panels, and the LightBox Gallery widget. The following tasks are all the new Dreamweaver skills you learned in this chapter:

1. Open the Contact Web Page and Select the Spry Category on the Insert Bar (DW 275)
2. Add Spry Validation to a Required Text Field (DW 276)
3. Add Spry Validation to Another Required Text Field (DW 279)
4. Add Spry Validation to an E-mail Text Field (DW 281)
5. Add Spry Validation to a Phone Number Text Field (DW 283)
6. Add Spry Validation to Another Required Text Field (DW 284)
7. Add Spry Validation to a Radio Group (DW 287)
8. Test the Spry Validation Form in a Browser (DW 290)
9. Add Spry Collapsible Panels to a Web Page (DW 292)
10. Add Panel Headings (DW 296)
11. Check Your Computer for the Adobe AIR Application (DW 298)
12. Download and Install Adobe AIR (DW 299)
13. Create an Adobe Account (DW 300)
14. View and Add Widgets from Adobe Exchange to My Widgets (DW 303)
15. Create a Widget Preset for the LightBox Gallery Widget (DW 306)
16. Add the LightBox Gallery Widget to a Web Page (DW 311)
17. Add Images to the Portrait Photography Light-Box Gallery Widget (DW 314)
18. Add Images to the Family Photography LightBox Gallery Widget (DW 317)
19. Add Images to the Baby Photography LightBox Gallery Widget (DW 319)

Apply Your Knowledge

Reinforce the skills and apply the concepts you learned in this chapter.

Adding Spry Collapsible Panels to a Web Page

Instructions: In this activity, you create a new Web page that contains information about Spry widgets. You add three Spry Collapsible Panels, change the tab headings, and add content to each tab. The completed Web page is shown in Figure 5–92.

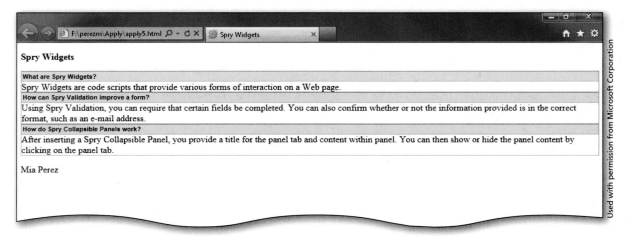

Figure 5–92

Perform the following tasks:

1. Start Dreamweaver. Use the Sites button on the Files panel to display the Web sites created with Dreamweaver and the drives on your computer. Select the Apply site.

2. Create a new HTML file and name it `apply5.html`.

3. Title the document `Spry Widgets`.

4. Type `Spry Widgets` at the top of the page and bold the heading.

5. Press the ENTER key and insert a Spry Collapsible Panel widget.

6. Use `spryPanel1` as the Collapsible panel name on the Property inspector, set the Default state to Closed and set the Display to Closed.

7. Replace the Tab name, Tab, with `What are Spry Widgets?`. Answer this question, using your own words, in the content area of spryPanel1.

8. Click below spryPanel1 and insert another Spry Collapsible Panel widget.

9. Use `spryPanel2` as the Collapsible panel name and set the Default state to Closed.

10. Replace the Tab name, Tab, with `How can Spry Validation improve a form?`. Answer this question, using your own words, in the content area of spryPanel2.

11. Click below spryPanel2 and insert another Spry Collapsible Panel widget.

12. Use `spryPanel3` as the Collapsible panel name and set the Default state to Closed.

13. Replace the Tab name, Tab, with `How do Spry Collapsible Panels work?`. Answer this question, using your own words, in the content area of spryPanel3.

14. Include your name below the third panel.

15. Save your changes and copy dependent files. View your document in your browser and click each panel to view its content.

16. Compare your document to Figure 5–92. Make any necessary changes and then save your changes.

17. Submit the document in the format specified by your instructor.

Extend Your Knowledge

Extend the skills you learned in this chapter and experiment with new skills. You may need to use Help to complete the assignment.

Adding Spry Tabbed Panels

Instructions: In this activity, you create a new Web page with information about Spry Tabbed Panels. You add Spry Tabbed Panels, change the tab headings, and add content to each tab. The completed Web page is shown in Figure 5–93.

Used with permission from Microsoft Corporation

Figure 5–93

Continued >

STUDENT ASSIGNMENTS

Extend Your Knowledge *continued*

Perform the following tasks:

1. Start Dreamweaver. Use the Sites button on the Files panel to select the Extend site.
2. Create a new HTML file and name it `extend5.html`.
3. Title the document `Spry Tabbed Panels`.
4. Type `Using Spry Tabbed Panels` at the top of the page and bold the heading.
5. Press the ENTER key and use the Insert bar to insert a Spry Tabbed Panels widget.
6. Replace the Tab name, Tab 1, with `Step 1`. In the content area of the Step 1 tab, replace the text, Content 1, with `Place your insertion point where you want to insert the Spry Tabbed Panels and then click the Spry Tabbed Panels button on the Insert bar` to describe how to insert the widget.
7. Replace the Tab name, Tab 2, with `Step 2`.
8. Click the eye-open button to show panel content on the Step 2 tab. In the content area of the Step 2 tab, replace the text, Content 2, with `Rename each tab and insert content within the content area of each tab. If necessary, use the Property inspector to add additional tabbed panels` to insert the Step 2 text.
9. Include your name below the panels.
10. Save your changes and copy dependent files. View your document in your browser and click each panel to view its content.
11. Compare your document to Figure 5–93. Make any necessary changes and then save your changes.
12. Submit the document in the format specified by your instructor.

Make It Right

Analyze a Web page and suggest how to improve its design.

Adding Spry Validation to a Web Page Form

Note: To complete this assignment, you will be required to use the Data Files for Students. Visit www.cengage.com/ct/studentdownload for detailed instructions or contact your instructor for information about accessing the required files.

Instructions: In this activity, you modify a Web page form using Spry Validation widgets. You apply Spry validation to four text fields and change the validation properties for each text field. The completed Web page is shown in Figure 5–94.

Figure 5–94

Perform the following tasks:

1. Use Windows Explorer to copy the right5.html file from the Chapter 05\Right folder provided with your data files into the *your last name and first initial*\Right folder.

2. Start Dreamweaver and open right3.html. If necessary, click the Spry tab on the Insert bar.

3. Click the Last Name text field and use the Spry Validation Text Field button to add validation to this field.

4. In the Property inspector, identify the Spry TextField as `lastName`. Set the Preview states as Required.

5. Select the text, A value is required, that was inserted after the lastName Spry Validation Text Field and then type `Required field`.

6. Click the First Name text field and use the Spry Validation Text Field button to add validation to this field.

7. In the Property inspector, identify the Spry TextField as `firstName`. Set the Preview states as Required.

8. Select the text, A value is required, that was inserted after the firstName Spry Validation Text Field and delete it. Type `Required field`.

9. Click the E-mail Address text field and use the Spry Validation Text Field button to add validation to this field.

10. In the Property inspector, identify the Spry TextField as `Email`. Set the Type to Email Address.

11. Click the Phone Number text field and use the Spry Validation Text Field button to add validation to this field.

12. In the Property inspector, identify the Spry TextField as `phoneNumber`. Set the Type to Phone Number. If necessary, set the Format as US/Canada and then click the Enforce pattern check box.

13. Include your name below the form.

14. Save your changes and copy dependent files. View the document in your browser and click the Submit button to test the Spry validation.

15. Compare your document to Figure 5–94. Make any necessary changes, and then save your changes.

16. Submit the document in the format specified by your instructor.

In the Lab

Design and/or create a document using the guidelines, concepts, and skills presented in this chapter. Labs are listed in order of increasing difficulty.

Lab 1: Modifying the Sign Up Form with Spry Validation

Problem: You are creating an internal Web site for your company that features information about how to live a healthy lifestyle. Employees at your company will use this Web site as a resource for nutrition, exercise, and other health-related tips. You have created a form on the Sign Up Web page where employees will enter information to sign up for weekly health tips. Now you need to modify the form with Spry validation.

First, modify the First Name, Last Name, and E-mail text fields with Spry Validation Text Fields. Next, format the properties for each field. Finally, remove the current Radio Group and replace it with a Spry Validation Radio Group. The updated Sign Up page is shown in Figure 5–95.

Continued >

In the Lab *continued*

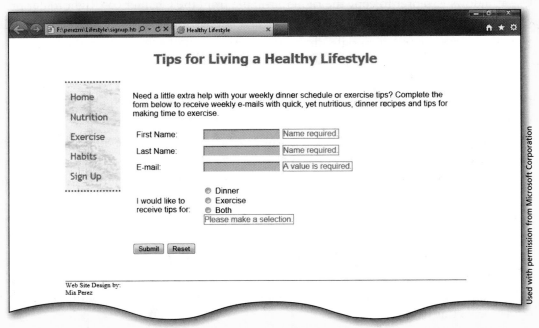

Figure 5–95

Perform the following tasks:

1. Start Dreamweaver. Use the Sites button on the Files panel to select the Healthy Lifestyle site. Open signup.html.

2. Click the First Name text field and use the Spry Validation Text Field button to add validation to this field.

3. In the Property inspector, identify the Spry TextField as `firstName`.

4. Click the Preview states box arrow and then select Required. Select the text, A value is required, that was inserted after the firstName Spry Validation Text Field and delete it. Type `Name required`.

5. Click the Last Name text field and use the Spry Validation Text Field button to add validation to this field.

6. In the Property inspector, identify the Spry TextField as `lastName`.

7. Click the Preview states box arrow and then select Required. Select the text, A value is required, that was inserted after the lastName Spry Validation Text Field and delete it. Type `Name required`.

8. Click the E-mail Address text field and use the Spry Validation Text Field button to add validation to this field.

9. In the Property inspector, identify the Spry TextField as `Email`. Click the Type box arrow and then select Email Address.

10. Delete the current Radio Group and insert a Spry Validation Radio Group.

11. Use `Tips` as the Radio Group name. Use `Dinner` and `Exercise` as the first two Labels. Add one more radio button and use `Both` for the Label name.

12. Save your changes and copy dependent files. View the document in your browser and click the Submit button to test the Spry validation.

13. Compare your document to Figure 5–95. Make any necessary changes, and then save your changes.

14. Submit the document in the format specified by your instructor.

In the Lab

Lab 2: Modifying the Contact Us Form with Spry Validation

Problem: You are creating a Web site for Designs by Dolores, a Web site design company. The site provides information about the company and its services. In Chapter 4, you created a form on the Contact Us page for the Designs by Dolores Web site. Now you need to modify the form by adding Spry validation.

First, modify the First Name, Last Name, E-mail, and Phone Number text fields by applying Spry Validation Text Fields. Next, format the properties for each field. The updated Contact Us page is shown in Figure 5–96.

Figure 5–96

Perform the following tasks:

1. Start Dreamweaver. Use the Sites button on the Files panel to select the Designs by Dolores site. Open contact.html.

2. Modify the First Name text field by applying a Spry Validation Text Field.

3. In the Property inspector, identify the Spry TextField as `firstName`.

4. Select Required for the Preview states. Select the text, A value is required, that was inserted after the firstName Spry Validation Text Field and delete it. Type `Please provide your first name.`

5. Modify the Last Name text field by applying a Spry Validation Text Field.

6. In the Property inspector, identify the Spry TextField as `lastName`.

7. Select Required for the Preview states. Select the text, A value is required, that was inserted after the lastName Spry Validation Text Field and delete it. Type `Please provide your last name.`

8. Modify the E-mail text field by applying a Spry Validation Text Field.

9. In the Property inspector, identify the Spry TextField as `Email`. Use Email Address for the Type.

Continued >

In the Lab *continued*

10. Modify the Phone Number text field by applying a Spry Validation Text Field.

11. In the Property inspector, identify the Spry TextField as `phoneNumber`. Use Phone Number for the Type. Click the Enforce pattern check box.

12. Save your changes and copy dependent files. View the document in your browser and click the Submit button to test the Spry validation.

13. Compare your document to Figure 5–96. Make any necessary changes, and then save your changes.

14. Submit the document in the format specified by your instructor.

In the Lab

Lab 3: Modifying the Quote Form with Spry Validation and Adding a Calendar Widget

Problem: You are creating a Web site for a new lawn care company, Justin's Lawn Care Service. The Web site will provide information to customers, including descriptions of services and pricing. In Chapter 4, you developed a form for the Quote page. Now you need to modify the form by adding Spry Validation.

First, modify the First Name, Last Name, Phone Number, and E-mail text fields by applying Spry Validation Text Fields. Next, format the properties for each field. The updated Quote page is shown in Figure 5–97.

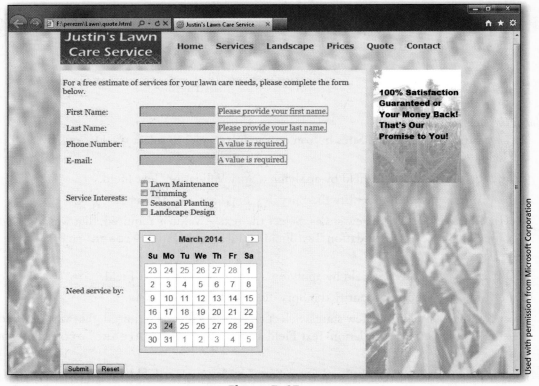

Used with permission from Microsoft Corporation

Figure 5–97

Perform the following tasks:

1. Start Dreamweaver. Use the Sites button on the Files panel to select the Justin's Lawn Care Service site. Open quote.html.

2. Modify the First Name text field by applying a Spry Validation Text Field. Use `firstName` as the Spry TextField.

3. Select Required for the Preview states and use `Please provide your first name` as the Required text.

4. Modify the Last Name text field by applying a Spry Validation Text Field. Use `lastName` as the Spry TextField.

5. Select Required for the Preview states and use `Please provide your last name` as the Required text.

6. Modify the Phone Number text field by applying a Spry Validation Text Field. Use `phoneNumber` as the Spry TextField.

7. Use Phone Number for the Type and enforce the pattern.

8. Modify the E-mail text field by applying a Spry Validation Text Field. Use `Email` as the Spry TextField.

9. Select Email Address for the Type.

10. Add a row below Service Interests. (*Hint*: On the Insert menu, select Table Objects, and then select Insert Row Below.)

11. Type `Need Service by:` in the first column of the new row.

12. Open the Adobe Widget Browser. Browse Adobe Exchange for the YUI Calendar for Widget Browser. If this widget is not available on Adobe Exchange, select a different calendar widget. Add the widget to My Widgets.

13. Add the YUI Calendar for Widget Browser in the second column of the last row.

14. Save your changes and copy dependent files. View the document in your browser and click the Submit button to test the Spry validation. Click a date on the calendar to test the widget.

15. Compare your document to Figure 5–97. Make any necessary changes, and then save your changes.

16. Submit the document in the format specified by your instructor.

Cases and Places

Apply your creative thinking and problem solving skills to design and implement a solution.

1: Adding Spry Validation to the Contact Page for Moving Venture Tips

Personal

You have created a form on the Contact page for Moving Venture Tips and now need to add Spry validation to the form fields. Review the form elements added to the Contact page and determine which Spry validation widgets should be integrated. Update text fields to Spry Validation Text Fields and update the property type for e-mail to Email Address. Remove the existing Radio Group and add a Spry Validation Radio Group. Check the spelling using the Commands menu, and correct all misspelled words. Save and open the Contact page in your Web browser to test the Spry validation fields. Submit the document in the format specified by your instructor.

Continued >

Cases and Places *continued*

2: Adding Spry Validation to the Contact Page for Student Campus Resources

Academic

You have created a form on the Contact page for Student Campus Resources and now need to add Spry validation to the form fields. You also have created the Committees page and now need to add Spry Collapsible Panels and content. Review the form elements added to the Contact page and determine which Spry validation widgets should be integrated. Update text fields to Spry Validation Text Fields and update the property type for e-mail to Email Address. Save and open the Contact page in your Web browser to test the Spry validation fields. Add four Spry Collapsible Panels to the Committees page. Give each panel heading a committee name and provide content about the committee within each panel content area. Name each Spry Collapsible Panel on the Property inspector and set the Default state to Closed. Save and open the Committees page in your Web browser to review the panels. Check the spelling using the Commands menu, and correct all misspelled words. Submit the document in the format specified by your instructor.

3: Adding Web Pages, Images, and Links for French Villa Roast Café

Professional

You have created a form on the Rewards page for French Villa Roast Café and now need to add Spry validation to the form fields. You also have created the Contact page and now need to add a widget to the page. Review the form elements added to the Rewards page and determine which Spry validation widgets should be integrated. Update text fields to Spry Validation Text Fields. Update the property type for e-mail to Email Address. Update the property type for phone number to Phone Number and enforce the pattern. Remove the existing Radio Group and add a Spry Validation Radio Group. Save and open the Rewards page in your Web browser to test the Spry validation fields. Add the Facebook Like Button widget to the Contact page below the contact information. Save and open the Contact page in your Web browser to view the widget. Check the spelling using the Commands menu, and correct all misspelled words. Submit the document in the format specified by your instructor.

6 | Enhancing Web Pages with Audio and Video

Objectives

You will have mastered the material in this chapter when you can:

- Describe how to add multimedia using plug-ins and HTML5
- Explain audio codecs
- Embed a sound file in a Web page
- Set the parameters of an audio file
- Add HTML5 code to play an audio file

- Describe video formats
- Embed a video file in a Web page
- Set the parameters of a video file
- Add HTML5 code to play a video file

6 | Enhancing Web Pages with Audio and Video

Introduction

A captivating Web site is about more than text and information; it is also a medium for expressing artistic creativity and optimizing the presentation of information. Web pages can include media objects, also called multimedia and interactive media, to enhance the experience for users. On multimedia Web pages, users can play audio files such as music, sound effects, or speech and video files to augment the content on the page. HTML5 adds multimedia capabilities such as audio and video to basic HTML pages.

Listening to music on the Web is a popular pastime. Audio files can include a podcast of a breaking news story posted to a Web site, a broadcast of an Internet radio station, background music that sets a mood for the Web page, or a song downloaded from the latest album of a hot new music group. The Web also includes video files that showcase product demos, professional broadcasts, music videos, prerecorded television clips, and marketing videos, such as one that provides a tour of a scenic vacation destination.

In this chapter, you learn how to add interactive media to a Web page. Interactive media is not suitable for all Web sites. You most likely have visited Web sites that contained so many bits and pieces of multimedia that, instead of being a constructive part of the site, distracted you from the experience the Web designers intended. Therefore, when adding media elements to your Web page, you need to consider the value of each element and how it will enhance or detract from your site.

Project — Web Pages with Multimedia

The Gallery photography studio has decided to follow the current trend in digital marketing by adding multimedia elements to enhance the visual material on its site. Adding audio and video to a Web page can be accomplished in two ways in most modern browsers. Older browsers use plug-ins to play audio and video files. Newer browsers use HTML5, which supports video and audio tags that allow users to play video and audio files without an external plug-in or player. The chapter project adds audio and video files using both the plug-in and HTML5 methods.

The Portfolio page of the Gallery site shown in Figure 6–1a plays an audio file with soft background music to create a mood that can enhance a visitor's browsing experience. To bring the Gallery's photos to life, a video slide show plays in the Session page, as shown in Figure 6–1b. Professional, polished multimedia in small doses adds entertainment value to the Gallery site while showcasing additional photos in the video.

(a) The Portfolio page plays an audio file

© Phase4 Photography / Shutterstock; courtesy of Facebook; courtesy of Twitter

(b) The Session page plays a video file

© Flashon Studio / Shutterstock; Rocketclips / Getty Images

Figure 6–1

Overview

As you read this chapter, you will learn how to create the Web page project shown in Figure 6–1 by performing these general tasks:

- Add sound to a Web page using a plug-in.
- Set parameters for the audio plug-in.
- Add sound to a Web page using HTML5 code.
- Add video to a Web page using a plug-in.
- Set parameters for the video plug-in.
- Add video to a Web page using HTML5 code.

<table>
<tr><td>Plan
Ahead</td><td>

General Project Guidelines

When adding interactive multimedia to a Web site, consider the purpose and audience of the site. As you create the Web pages shown in Figure 6–1, you should follow these general guidelines:

1. **Consider adding multimedia files to a Web page.** Web pages can be more engaging and useful with multimedia elements such as audio and video.

2. **Add sound to a Web page.** If spoken language or music will add an entertainment or instructional value, consider adding sound to a Web page, such as the splash page, which is the page that opens when most visitors enter your site. You can use sound elements to guide visitors through your site, especially if you use interactive media controls.

3. **Determine how to embed multimedia files.** Dreamweaver allows you to embed multimedia files using plug-ins or HTML5 code. Select the method that is most appropriate for the purpose and audience of your Web page.

4. **Play video on a Web page.** Video is especially effective for training visitors, displaying demonstrations, or marketing a service.

More specific details about these guidelines are presented at appropriate points throughout the chapter. The chapter also identifies the actions performed and decisions made regarding these guidelines during the development of the pages within the site shown in Figure 6–1.

</td></tr>
</table>

To Start Dreamweaver and Open the Gallery Site

Each time you start Dreamweaver, it opens to the last site displayed when you closed the program. The following steps start Dreamweaver and open the Gallery Web site.

1 Click the Start button on the Windows 7 taskbar to display the Start menu, and then type `Dreamweaver CS6` in the 'Search programs and files' box.

2 Click Adobe Dreamweaver CS6 in the list to start Dreamweaver.

3 If the Dreamweaver window is not maximized, click the Maximize button next to the Close button on the Application bar to maximize the window.

4 If the Gallery site is not displayed in the Files panel, click the Sites button on the Files panel toolbar and then click Gallery to display the files and folders in the Gallery site.

Adding Multimedia with Plug-ins or HTML5

Recently, the computing world has changed from one in which people use a single device — primarily a PC — to one in which they use several platforms such as Web-enabled tablets and smartphones. Now that the user experience spans many devices, Web standards play a more important role than ever, for both users and developers.

HTML5 Web standards within the newest browsers are replacing older technologies that did not support mobile devices with limited resources. For example, an iPhone or iPad does not support Web pages that display Flash animation, which requires a plug-in. A **plug-in** is a piece of software that acts as an add-on to a Web browser and provides additional functionality to the browser. Plug-ins can allow a browser to display additional content it was not originally designed to display. Recent browsers that run on traditional computers and mobile devices do not support legacy plug-ins, but instead rely on the new HTML5 Web technology to play audio and video elements. Plug-ins provide support for particular data types, which allows the site visitor to view specific documents, watch animation, or play multimedia files within a Web browser without opening an outside program.

Consider adding multimedia files to a Web page.

Multimedia files can enhance Web pages by providing engaging experiences. Visitors can listen to music that highlights the mood of the page or play a speech related to the Web page content. In addition to audio content, visitors can watch videos that inform, instruct, or entertain them.

To add multimedia files using Dreamweaver, you can insert a link to an audio or video file, or you can embed an audio or video file in the Web page. If you link to a multimedia file, you reduce the bandwidth your Web site must manage. (Video files in particular use more bandwidth than other types of files.) Embedding a multimedia file offers the advantage of letting visitors play the file without leaving the Web page. Web designers also can specify how the embedded multimedia file plays in the browser: automatically when the page opens, or only when the user clicks the Play button in the playback controls.

Plan Ahead

Older browsers require users to install a plug-in before the browsers can display media objects. For instance, the Flash Player is required to view Flash files. The Flash Player is available as an add-on for Firefox and as an ActiveX control for Microsoft Internet Explorer. Adobe provides this player as a free download at the Adobe Web site. Other popular plug-ins include QuickTime Player to play movie files and Acrobat Reader to display PDF files.

In this chapter, you add an audio file and a video file as plug-ins for legacy browsers, and then use HTML5 code to play multimedia files on newer browsers for cross-platform functionality. Developers face the possibility that many users are still using legacy browsers while others are using the most recent browsers. Quickly, HTML5 is becoming the prominent Web standard as the next wave of innovation pushes the boundary toward a world without plug-ins. This chapter provides instruction for adding media objects using plug-ins and HTML5 to meet the needs of your varied audience.

Adding Sound

Adding sound to your Web page can add interest and set a mood. Background music can enhance your theme. Attaching audio to objects, such as the sound of clicking buttons, can provide valuable feedback to the Web site visitor. Sound, however, can be expensive in terms of the Web site size and download time, particularly for those visitors with slower access. Another consideration is that adding sound to a Web page can be a challenging and confusing task. Most computers today have some type of sound card and some type of sound-capable plug-in that works with the browser. The difficult part, though, is generating desirable sounds.

As you work with sound, you will discover that the Web supports several popular sound file formats, along with their corresponding plug-ins, but has not settled on a standard audio file format. The trick is to find a widely used audio file format that most browsers handle in the same way. Some factors to consider before deciding on a format and method for adding sound are the sound's purpose, your audience, the file size, the sound quality you want, and the differences between browsers.

<table>
<tr><td>Plan
Ahead</td><td>

Add sound to a Web page.
As with any other technology, you first determine what you want to accomplish by adding a sound. Your sound should serve a clear and useful purpose or have an entertaining or instructional value. In most instances, when you add a background sound, keep the sound short, do not loop the sound, and provide your visitor with an option to stop the sound. Based on which browser you are using, a sound file is placed within a Web page using two methods:

- **Add sound using a plug-in.** Sound embedded into a Web page that supports plug-ins can be set to play automatically as the page loads, or a user can click on audio controls to start the audio file on command.
- **Add sound using HTML5 code.** HTML5 defines a new element for modern and mobile browsers that specifies a standard way to embed an audio file in a Web page: the <audio> element. The audio HTML5 element allows you to deliver audio files directly through the browser, without the need for a plug-in.

</td></tr>
</table>

Understanding Audio Codecs

A **codec** is a program that allows you to read and save media files, often compressing them to reduce file size. For example, a codec can compress large audio files such as WAV files into a much smaller MP3 audio file type. All codecs involve a trade-off between the amount of compression and the resulting quality. If you compress a media file too much, the quality of the sound or video becomes poor and unusable. If you do not compress a media file enough, the file may take too long to download into a browser. To play an MP3 file that has been compressed with the MP3 codec, a computer must use the codec to also decompress the file locally to play the audio file.

Table 6–1 lists and describes the commonly used sound file formats.

Table 6–1 Common Sound File Formats	
File Name Extension	**Description**
.aif (Audio Interchange File Format, or AIFF)	The AIFF format can be played by most browsers and does not require a plug-in; you also can record AIFF files from a CD, tape, microphone, and so on. The large file size, however, limits the length of sound clips that you can use on your Web pages.
.midi (Musical Instrument Digital Interface, or MIDI)	The MIDI format is for instrumental music. MIDI files are supported by many browsers and do not require a plug-in. The sound quality is good, but it can vary depending on a visitor's sound card. A small MIDI file can provide a long sound clip. MIDI files cannot be recorded and must be synthesized on a computer with special hardware and software.
.mp3 (Moving Picture Experts Group Audio, or MPEG Audio Layer-3, or MP3)	The MP3 format is a compressed format that allows for small sound files with very good sound quality. You can stream an MP3 file so that a visitor does not have to wait for the entire file to download before hearing it. To play MP3 files, visitors must download and install a plug-in such as QuickTime, Windows Media Player, or RealPlayer.
.ogg, .ogv, .oga, .ogx, .spx (Ogg container format)	The Ogg multimedia framework supports audio, video, text, and metadata. The Ogg file type is primarily associated with the Ogg Vorbis software by the Xiph.Org Foundation. Ogg is an open and standardized format designed for streaming and manipulating media files. Ogg's various codecs have been incorporated into many free and proprietary media players.
.qt, .qtm, .mov (QuickTime)	These formats are designed for audio and video files by Apple. QuickTime is included with the Mac operating system, and most Mac applications can use files in these formats. PCs also can play media in the QuickTime format, though they need a QuickTime driver to do so.
.ra, .ram, .rpm (RealAudio)	The RealAudio format has a very high degree of compression, with smaller file sizes than the MP3 format. Whole song files can be downloaded in a reasonable amount of time. The files also can be streamed, so visitors can begin listening to the sound before the file has been downloaded completely. The sound quality is poorer than that of MP3 files. Visitors must download and install the RealPlayer helper application or plug-in to play these files.
.wav (Waveform Audio File Format, or WAV)	WAV-formatted files have good sound quality, are supported by many browsers, and do not require a plug-in. The large file size, however, severely limits the length of sound clips that you can use on your Web pages.

To Copy the Audio and Video Folders

Before adding an audio or video file to a site, you must add the multimedia files to the file structure of the site. To complete the following steps, you will be required to use the Data Files for Students. Visit www.cengage.com/ct/studentdownload for detailed instructions or contact your instructor for information about accessing the required files. The following steps show how to copy files from the Data Files for Students to the Gallery site.

1 Use Windows Explorer to navigate to the storage location of the Data Files for Students.

2 Double-click the Chapter 06 folder, and then double-click the Gallery folder to open the folders.

3 Click the Audio folder, hold down the shift key, and then click the Video folder to select both folders (Figure 6–2).

4 Right-click the selected folders, click Copy on the context menu, and then navigate to the *your last name and first initial* folder on Removable Disk F: to prepare to copy the files.

5 Double-click the Gallery folder, right-click anywhere in the open window, and then click Paste on the context menu to copy the folders into the Gallery site.

6 Click the background of the window to deselect the folders. Verify that the Gallery site now contains an Audio folder and a Video folder (Figure 6–3).

Figure 6–2

Figure 6–3

Embedding a Sound File Using a Plug-In

To incorporate a background sound file directly into a Web page, you can embed the audio file using Dreamweaver. However, the sound plays only if visitors to your site have the appropriate plug-in. **Embedding** a sound file means that the music plays in a browser with an installed plug-in that supports the codec of the audio file. Audio files can be played on legacy browsers and some present-day browsers using third-party browser plug-ins such as Flash, QuickTime, and Silverlight.

To Embed a Background Sound Using a Plug-In

When the Portfolio page opens in the Gallery site, the photographer has requested that a soft background song set the mood as the visitor views the photographs within the collapsible panels. The portfolio_audio.mp3 song can begin automatically when the page is launched and play one time for 1 minute and 37 seconds (the length of the music file). The following steps embed a song that plays using a browser plug-in.

1

- In the Files panel, double-click portfolio.html to open the Portfolio page.

- Click below the Baby Photography Collapsible Panel to place the insertion point below the Collapsible Panel (Figure 6–4).

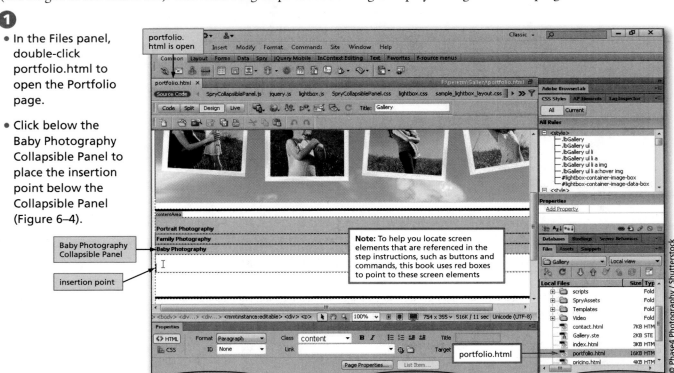

Figure 6–4

2

- If necessary, click the Common tab on the Insert bar to display the Common category of buttons.

- Click the Media button arrow on the Insert bar to display the Media menu (Figure 6–5).

Figure 6–5

© Phase4 Photography / Shutterstock

3

- Click Plugin to display the Select File dialog box.

- Double-click the Audio folder to display the audio files.

- Click portfolio_audio.mp3 to select the sound file for the Portfolio page (Figure 6–6).

Why does the appearance of the Media button change after I select Plugin?

The Media button displays an icon for the last media object you selected. For example, after you select Plugin, the Media button displays a Plugin icon. If you want to insert another Plugin object, you can click the Media button instead of the Media button arrow.

Figure 6–6

- Click the OK button to insert a placeholder for the background sound file (Figure 6–7).

Why does Dreamweaver insert a placeholder for the sound file?

When you add a background sound to a page, Dreamweaver inserts a placeholder as a cue that the page includes a media object.

placeholder for background sound

Figure 6–7

© Phase4 Photography / Shutterstock

Other Ways

1. Insert menu, point to Media, click Plugin

Setting the Parameters of a Sound File

After embedding an audio file as a plug-in file, you can define parameters to play the file automatically when the site loads, display a controller that provides a stop button, or loop the song continuously. (A parameter is similar to a property; it defines the characteristics of an object.) You also can define the default volume of the sound or the music so that it plays softly in the background, and determine how long to play the song. You set the parameters of embedded sound files in the Property inspector. Table 6–2 lists frequently used parameters for the audio plug-in.

Table 6–2 Audio Plug-In Parameters	
Parameter	**Description**
autoplay	Defines whether the player should start automatically
hidden	Informs the browser not to display the audio controls
loop	Informs the browser to play the audio file continuously

To Set the Parameters of a Sound File

When sound is integrated into the Portfolio page, you can determine how the song plays within the browser. Set the parameters of the plug-in in the Property inspector to specify the source file, set the background sound to play automatically, and hide the audio controls. The following steps set the parameters of the audio plug-in object.

- If necessary, select the sound placeholder.

- Click the Parameters button in the Property inspector to display the Parameters dialog box (Figure 6–8).

Figure 6–8

© Phase4 Photography / Shutterstock

- Type `id` to enter the name of the first audio parameter.

- Press the TAB key twice to move the insertion point to the Value column.

- Type `portfolio_audio` in the Value column to specify the file name of the embedded sound object (Figure 6–9).

Figure 6–9

© Phase4 Photography / Shutterstock

3

- Click the plus button and then type `hidden` to enter the name of the second parameter.

- Press the TAB key twice to move the insertion point to the Value column.

- Type `true` in the Value column to specify that the audio controls are hidden in the Web page (Figure 6–10).

Figure 6–10

4

- Click the plus button and then type `autoplay` to enter the name of the third parameter.

- Press the TAB key twice to move the insertion point to the Value column.

- Type `true` in the Value column to specify that the audio automatically plays when the Web page opens (Figure 6–11).

Figure 6–11

5

- Click the plus button and then type `loop` to enter the name of the fourth parameter.

- Press the TAB key twice to move the insertion point to the Value column.

- Type `false` in the Value column to specify that the sound file plays one time only (Figure 6–12).

Figure 6–12

6

- Click the OK button to apply the parameters to the background sound file.

- Click the Save button on the Standard toolbar to save your changes.

- Click the 'Preview/ Debug in browser' button on the Document toolbar and then click Preview in IExplore in the browser list to display the Portfolio page in Internet Explorer.

- If necessary, click the 'Allow blocked content' button to play the audio file (Figure 6–13).

Portfolio page plays background music when it is displayed in the browser

Figure 6–13

Q&A What should happen when I open the Portfolio page in a browser?

The music file should automatically play one time.

Q&A The audio file seems to play, but I don't hear any sound. What is the problem?

Check to see if the volume on your speakers is muted in the notification area on a Windows computer. On a Mac, click the Volume icon on the menu bar and then drag the slider.

7

- Click the Internet Explorer Close button to close the browser.

Adding an Audio File with HTML5 Code

When you design a Web site, you cannot control which browser visitors use to view your site. Browsers translate the HTML5 code, allowing you to read text, view images, play videos, and listen to audio clips on Web sites, though each browser renders the Web page content in a different way.

A typical browser supports multiple audio file types, regardless of the operating system running it, but no universal audio or video file type is supported by all browsers. As an HTML5 developer, you need to make sure that audio content is created in different formats that each browser supports. Table 6–3 displays the audio formats supported by the major browsers using HTML5 code.

Table 6–3 HTML5 Audio Formats	
Browser	**Supported Audio Format**
Apple Safari	MP3, WAV
Google Chrome	MP3, OGG, WAV
Microsoft Internet Explorer	MP3
Mozilla Firefox	MP3, WAV
Opera	OGG, WAV

Because one audio file type is not supported by all browsers, you should develop your audio content in at least two formats such as OGG and MP3 in order to cover the major browser types. The browser listing shown in Table 6–3 may change as HTML5 gains popularity and more software development companies use it.

Coding HTML5 Audio

BTW

Audio and Video Controls
Each browser renders audio and video controls with a different visual layout, but the usual controls, such as play/pause button, position slider, current track position indicator, and volume control, are all present.

HTML5 media tags for audio and video media elements aim to standardize elements on a page and to reduce the use of plug-ins. To embed sounds, music, and other audio on a Web page, Web developers can use the HTML5 audio element, which is supported by Internet Explorer 9 and 10, Firefox, Opera, Chrome, and Safari. In the audio element, you can include the *controls* attribute to display a control bar that viewers use to play the sound or the music file. Following the audio element, use the HTML5 source element to list more than one format for the audio file so it plays in multiple browsers. Three audio formats are compatible with the audio element: .mp3, .wav, and .ogg. To play one audio file, include three source elements: one for each audio format. The first source element typically specifies the file in the MP3 format.

To add HTML5 audio code to a Web page, you can work in Code view. By typing the following HTML5 code in Code view, a modern browser can play the portfolio_audio.mp3, portfolio_audio.wav, or portfolio_audio.ogg audio file stored in the Audio folder without using plug-ins or without a third-party service hosting the audio files.

```
<audio controls autoplay="autoplay" loop>
<source src="Audio/portfolio_audio.mp3" type="audio/mp3"/>
<source src="Audio/portfolio_audio.wav" type="audio/wav"/>
<source src="Audio/portfolio_audio.ogg" type="audio/ogg"/>
</audio>
```

The five lines of HTML5 code play the portfolio_audio sound files as follows:

Line 1: Audio controls will be displayed with a Play button and a Pause button. The autoplay attribute sets the audio to start playing as soon as the file is available. Because "autoplay" is the default value for the autoplay attribute, you can omit it and still have the browser play the audio file automatically. The loop attribute specifies that the audio starts playing again immediately after it finishes.

Line 2: The source element specifies the name, location, and type of the MP3 file to play. The src attribute identifies the path and name of the audio file.

Line 3: The source element specifies the name, location, and type of the WAV file to play. The src attribute identifies the path and name of the audio file.

Line 4: The source element specifies the name, location, and type of the OGG file to play. The src attribute identifies the path and name of the audio file.

Line 5: This statement identifies the closing tag of the HTML5 audio element.

To Add an Audio File Using HTML5 Code

Insert the HTML5 audio element between the opening <body> and closing </body> tags in the HTML code for the Portfolio page. The following steps add HTML5 code to the Web page to include an audio file with controls on the page.

- Click the placeholder for the audio file plug-in on the Portfolio page and then press the DELETE key to delete it (Figure 6–14).

placeholder for audio plug-in is deleted

Figure 6–14

© Phase4 Photography / Shutterstock

2

- Click the Code button on the Standard toolbar to display the HTML code for the Portfolio page (Figure 6–15).

Q&A

The insertion point is in a different place in my code than it is in Figure 6–15. What should I do?

Move the insertion point so it appears where shown in Figure 6–15.

Code button

insertion point

Figure 6–15

● Press the ENTER key twice and then click the blank line to begin a new line of HTML5 code.

● Type `<audio controls autoplay="autoplay" loop>` to display the audio controls and to play the song continuously when the browser loads the page in an HTML5-supported browser (Figure 6–16).

Figure 6–16

● Press the ENTER key to begin a new line.

● Type `<source src= "Audio/portfolio_audio. mp3" type="audio/mp3" />` to play the audio file in a browser that supports .mp3 files (Figure 6–17).

Figure 6–17

5

- Press the ENTER key to begin a new line.

- Type `<source src= "Audio/portfolio_audio. wav" type="audio/wav" />` to play the audio file in a browser that supports .wav files (Figure 6–18).

code for .wav file

Figure 6–18

6

- Press the ENTER key to begin a new line.

- Type `<source src= "Audio/portfolio_audio. ogg" type="audio/ogg" />` to play the audio file in a browser that supports .ogg files (Figure 6–19).

code for .ogg file

Figure 6–19

7

- Press the ENTER key to begin a new line.

- Type `</audio>` to close the HTML5 audio tag (Figure 6–20).

Q&A

As I began to type `</audio>` to close the audio HTML5 code tag, why did Dreamweaver complete the tag for me?

When you establish an opening tag and begin to insert a closing tag, Dreamweaver automatically provides the text of the closing tag.

Figure 6–20

8

- Click the Save button on the Standard toolbar to save your changes.

To Display an HTML5 Audio Control in Different Browsers

When you include the HTML5 audio element in a Web page, each browser displays the audio playback control including a Play/Pause button, the time, a Mute button, and volume controls. In most situations, it is a best practice to display audio controls so users can mute the sound. The audio controls look different in various browsers. The following steps display the audio control in the Portfolio page in various browsers.

1

- Click the 'Preview/ Debug in browser' button on the Document toolbar and then click Preview in IExplore in the browser list to display the Portfolio page.

- If necessary, click the 'Allow blocked content' button to view the audio controls in the Internet Explorer browser (Figure 6–21).

Figure 6–21

2

- Click the Internet Explorer Close button to close the browser.

- Click the 'Preview/ Debug in browser' button on the Document toolbar, and then click Preview in Firefox in the browser list to display the Portfolio page and view the audio controls in the Firefox browser (Figure 6–22).

Q&A

When I click the 'Preview/Debug in browser' button, Firefox is not included in my list of browsers. What should I do?

© Phase4 Photography / Shutterstock; courtesy of Mozilla

Figure 6–22

If Firefox is installed on your computer, click Edit Browser List on the 'Preview/Debug in browser' list, click the plus button, enter the requested information in the Add Browser dialog box, click the OK button to close the dialog box, and then click the OK button to add Firefox to the list of browsers. If you do not have the Firefox browser installed on your computer, however, you cannot test the page using Firefox.

3

- Click the Firefox Close button to close the browser.

- Click the 'Preview/ Debug in browser' button on the Document toolbar, and then click Preview in chrome in the browser list to display the Portfolio page and view the audio controls in the Chrome browser (Figure 6–23).

Q&A

When I click the 'Preview/Debug in browser' button, Chrome is not included in my list of browsers. What should I do?

© Phase4 Photography / Shutterstock; courtesy of Google

Figure 6–23

If Chrome is installed on your computer, follow the instructions provided in Step 2, substituting Chrome for Firefox. If you do not have the Chrome browser installed on your computer, however, you cannot test the page using Chrome.

Q&A

Should I install multiple browsers on my computer for testing purposes?

Yes. Each browser behaves differently, so you should test your projects in multiple browsers.

 Experiment

- Allow the song to play all the way to the end. The song begins again because of the loop statement. Remove the loop statement from the HTML5 code. Save the code and refresh the page. The song only plays one time. Reinsert the loop statement and then save the document.

4

- Click the Chrome Close button to close the browser.

To Remove an HTML5 Audio Control and Loop

Audio on a Web page that plays repeatedly or too often can annoy visitors and people nearby them. With this in mind, the Gallery owners requested that you hide the audio controls on the Portfolio page and set the music to play only once. The following steps remove the audio control and the loop from the Portfolio page.

- If necessary, click the Code button on the Standard toolbar to return to Code view.

- Scroll down to find the audio tag, and then delete the word, controls, from the audio tag to remove the audio controls.

- Delete the word, loop, from the audio tag to remove the audio loop (Figure 6–24).

2

- Click the Close button on the portfolio.html tab to close the Portfolio page.

Figure 6–24

Break Point: If you wish to take a break, this is a good place to do so. To resume at a later time, start Dreamweaver and continue following the steps from this location forward.

Adding Video

By adding an appropriate amount of video to a Web page, you can entice your Web site visitors to learn more about your product and enrich their experience. Video clips should be only long enough to convey your meaning, and short enough so the video content loads quickly and creates a positive reaction from your customers. Each multimedia object should showcase your creativity and make your site stand apart from the average Web site.

Determine how to embed multimedia files.
As with audio files, you can embed video files by using a plug-in or using HTML5 code. The advantage of using a plug-in is that Dreamweaver CS6 provides tools for inserting plug-in objects without requiring you to enter HTML code. However, browsers are moving away from supporting plug-ins. So if you include plug-in objects, eventually your Web page will not be able to play the multimedia in the new browsers.

Instead of requiring plug-ins, browsers support HTML5 for multimedia objects. Embedding audio and video files by using HTML5 code means users can play the files in current and future browsers. However, embedding multimedia files with this method requires you to enter HTML5 code.

Understanding Video Formats

Many types of video formats such as MPEG-4 (.mp4), Windows Media (.wmv), Flash (.swf and .flv), RealVideo (.rm and .ram), and QuickTime (.mov) display full-motion video, which you can use to promote the message of your Web site. The MP4 format is the new and upcoming format for Web-based video. It is supported by YouTube, Flash players, and HTML5. Table 6–4 describes the various video formats.

BTW

Use Design Notes with Media Objects
If you want to store extra information with a media object, such as the name or location of the source file, you can add Design Notes to a media object. Right-click the media object in the document window, click Design Notes for Page on the context menu, and then enter the note.

Table 6–4 Video File Formats

File Name Extension	Description
.avi (Audio Video Interleave, or AVI)	AVI is supported by all computers running Windows.
.mov (QuickTime, developed by Apple)	QuickTime is a common format on the Internet for both Windows and Macintosh computers. The QuickTime Player is required to play QuickTime movies on a Windows computer.
.mpg or .mpeg (Moving Pictures Expert Group, or MPEG)	Files in the MPEG format run on Windows and Macintosh computers.
.mp4 (MPEG-4)	MPEG-4 (with H.264 video compression) is the new format for the Web. Online video publishers are moving to MP4 as the Internet sharing format for both Flash players and HTML5.
.rm or .ram (RealVideo, developed by RealMedia)	The RealVideo format allows the streaming of video, which reduces downloading time.
.swf (Flash SWF)	Files in the SWF format require the Adobe Flash Player.
.wmv, .wvx (Windows Media Format, or WMF)	The WMF format allows the streaming of video, uses the Windows Media Player, and plays on both Windows and Macintosh computers.

Embedding a Video File Using a Plug-In

To add rich media to a Web page, you can insert video files by using a plug-in or by entering HTML5 code. The most popular video plug-in is for the Flash player, which supports Flash videos such as animated text, business presentations, and visual effects and MP4 video files. The MP4 file type is the preferred modern video type that transmits over a narrower bandwidth compared to other video file types. The best format for smartphones and slate devices is MP4.

To Embed a Video Using a Plug-In

The Session page should open with an MP4 video named session_video.mp4, which features a guide to a Gallery photography session. The video highlights samples of the Gallery's photography. The following steps embed a video that plays using a browser plug-in.

1

- In the Files panel, double-click session.html to open the Session page.

- If necessary, click the Design button on the Document toolbar to display the page in Design view.

- Select the text, Insert page content here., and then press the DELETE key to delete the text (Figure 6–25).

Figure 6–25

2

- Click the Media button arrow on the Insert bar to display the Media menu (Figure 6–26).

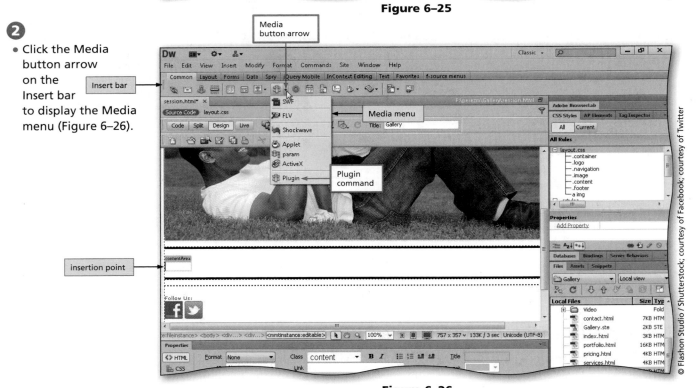

Figure 6–26

Dreamweaver Chapter 6

3

- Click Plugin to display the Select File dialog box.

- Double-click the Video folder to display the video files.

- Click the Up One Level button to navigate to the Gallery folder.

- Click session_video.mp4 to select the video file for the Session page (Figure 6–27).

Figure 6–27

4

- Click the OK button to insert a 32 × 32 pixel placeholder for the video (Figure 6–28).

Figure 6–28

- Double-click the W text box in the Property inspector and then type 480 to set the width of the video placeholder.

- Double-click the H text box in the Property inspector and then type 375 to set the height of the video placeholder.

- Press the ENTER key to resize the video placeholder (Figure 6–29).

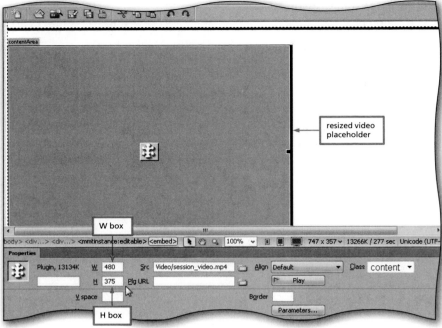

Figure 6–29

Other Ways

1. Insert menu, point to Media, click Plugin

To Set the Parameters of a Video File

The title of the session_video is Gallery Photography Session Guide. It should not start playing on the Session page until the visitor clicks the Play button in the video controls. The default setting for video plug-ins is to play the video automatically when the page opens. To allow the user to control the playback, you set the autoplay parameter to false. The following steps set the parameter of the video plug-in object.

- If necessary, select the video placeholder on the Session page.

- Click the Parameters button in the Property inspector to open the Parameters dialog box (Figure 6–30).

Figure 6–30

2

- Type autoplay to enter the name of the first parameter.

- Press the TAB key twice to move the insertion point to the Value column.

- Type false in the Value column to specify that the video must be started by the site visitor (Figure 6–31).

Figure 6–31

3

- Click the OK button to apply the parameter to the video file.

- With the placeholder selected, click Format on the Application bar to display the Format menu.

- Point to Align on the Format menu to display the Align submenu (Figure 6–32).

Figure 6–32

- Click Center on the Align submenu to center the video placeholder (Figure 6–33).

Figure 6–33

- Click the Save button on the Standard toolbar to save your changes.

- Click the 'Preview/ Debug in browser' button on the Document toolbar, and then click Preview in IExplore in the browser list to display the Session page in Internet Explorer.

- If necessary, click the 'Allow blocked content' button to give permission for playing the video file.

- Scroll down and click the Play button in the video controls to play the video (Figure 6–34).

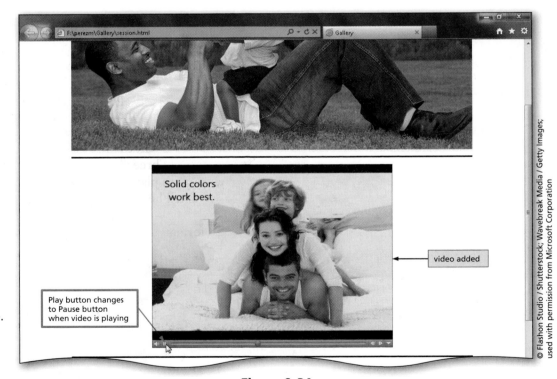

© Flashon Studio / Shutterstock; Wavebreak Media / Getty Images; used with permission from Microsoft Corporation

Figure 6–34

- Click the Internet Explorer Close button to close the browser.

Adding a Video File with HTML5 Code

In the same fashion as the audio file, modern browsers may not support the use of video plug-ins, but instead rely on the HTML5 video element. Table 6–5 lists the HTML5 video formats supported by the major browsers.

Table 6–5 HTML5 Video Formats	
Browser	**Supported Video Format**
Apple Safari 5	MP4
Google Chrome 6	MP4, WebM, Ogg
Microsoft Internet Explorer 9	MP4
Mozilla Firefox 4	WebM, Ogg
Opera 10.6	WebM, Ogg

Play video on the Web page.
You can add video to your Web page by having the browser download the video file to the user or by streaming the video content so that it plays while the file is downloading. Older browsers require their Web site visitors to download a plug-in to view common streaming formats such as Windows Media, RealMedia, and QuickTime. You then can use parameters to control the video object and how it is played on the Web page. Newer browsers support an HTML tag named <video> to play most video file types.

Plan Ahead

Coding HTML5 Video

As with the HTML5 audio element, you can embed a video on a Web page using the HTML5 video element, which is supported by Internet Explorer 9 and 10, Firefox, Opera, Chrome, and Safari. In the video element, you can include the *controls* attribute to display a control bar that viewers use to control the playback of the video file. Following the video element, use the HTML5 source element to list more than one format for the video file so it plays in multiple browsers. Three video formats are compatible with the video element: .mp4, .webm, and .ogg. To play one video file, include three source elements — one for each video format. The first source element typically specifies the file in the MP4 format.

The following code supports the three video file formats used in various browsers.

BTW

Video Size
If the file size of a video is too large, it can take a long time to download and play when it is displayed in a Web page. You should therefore limit the size of your videos without sacrificing their quality. By optimizing the video's file size, the video can play quickly and smoothly.

```
<video width="480" height="360" controls autoplay="autoplay">
<source src="Video/session_video.mp4" type="video/mp4"/>
<source src="Video/session_video.webm" type="video/webm"/>
<source src="Video/session_video.ogg" type="video/ogg"/>
</video>
```

The five lines of HTML5 code play the session_video video files as follows:
Line 1: The video appears in a video player with a width of 480 pixels and a height of 360 pixels. Video controls will be displayed with a Play button and a Pause button. The autoplay attribute sets the video to start playing as soon as the file is available. As with audio files, "autoplay" is the default value for this attribute, so you can omit the value to still have the video play when the page is opened.

Displaying a Video in Live View
If QuickTime is installed on your computer, you can preview an embedded video in Live view.

Line 2: The source element specifies the name, location, and type of the MP4 file to play. The src attribute identifies the path and name of the audio file.

Line 3: The source element specifies the name, location, and type of the WebM file to play. The src attribute identifies the path and name of the audio file.

Line 4: The source element specifies the name, location, and type of the OGG file to play. The src attribute identifies the path and name of the audio file.

Line 5: This statement identifies the closing tag of the HTML5 video element.

To Add a Video File Using HTML5 Code

The Session page can use HTML5 code to embed a video file that any modern browser can play. The following steps add HTML5 code to the Web page to play a video file in a player with playback controls.

1

• Select the video file placeholder in the Session page and then press the DELETE key to delete the plug-in (Figure 6–35).

placeholder for video plug-in is deleted

Figure 6–35

© Flashon Studio / Shutterstock

2

• Click the Code button on the Standard toolbar to display the HTML code for the Session page (Figure 6–36).

Code button

insertion point

Figure 6–36

❸

- Press the ENTER key twice and then click the blank line to begin a new line of code.

- Type `<video width="480" height="360" controls autoplay="autoplay">` to display the video controls and to play the video automatically when the browser loads the page in an HTML5-supported browser (Figure 6–37).

Q&A

Why do I need to specify width and height values for the video?

As the video loads in a browser, the width and height values determine how much space to reserve for the video in the player.

Figure 6–37

❹

- Press the ENTER key to begin a new line.

- Type `<source src="Video/session_video.mp4" type="video/mp4" />` to play the video file in a browser that supports .mp4 files (Figure 6–38).

Figure 6–38

5

- Press the ENTER key to begin a new line.

- Type `<source src="Video/session_video.webm" type="video/webm" />` to play the video file in a browser that supports .webm files (Figure 6–39).

Figure 6–39

6

- Press the ENTER key to begin a new line.

- Type `<source src="Video/session_video.ogg" type="video/ogg" />` to play the video file in a browser that supports .ogg files.

- Press the ENTER key to begin a new line.

- Type `</video>` to close the video HTML5 code tag (Figure 6–40).

Figure 6–40

7

- Click the Save button on the Standard toolbar to save your changes.

- Click the 'Preview/ Debug in browser' button on the Document toolbar, and then click Preview in IExplore in the browser list to display the Session page in the Internet Explorer browser.

- If necessary, click the 'Allow blocked content' button to display the video controls and play the video (Figure 6–41).

 Why did the video play automatically?

In the HTML5 code, the video was set to autoplay.

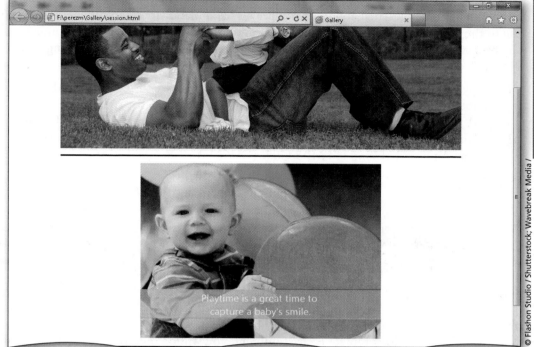

Figure 6–41

8

- Click the Internet Explorer Close button to close the browser.

- Click the Design button on the Document toolbar to display the page in Design view.

To Quit Dreamweaver

The following steps quit Dreamweaver and return control to the operating system.

1 Click the Close button on the right side of the Application bar to close the Dreamweaver window.

2 If Dreamweaver displays a dialog box asking you to save changes, click the No button.

Chapter Summary

In this chapter, you learned about Dreamweaver's audio and video multimedia objects. You added an audio file to the Portfolio page using both plug-ins and HTML5 code. You also customized the audio parameters of the background music. Next, you added a video to the Session page by first using a plug-in and then entering HTML5 code. The following tasks are all the new Dreamweaver skills you learned in this chapter:

1. Copy the Audio and Video folders (DW 337)
2. Embed a Background Sound Using a Plug-in (DW 338)
3. Set the Parameters of a Sound File (DW 341)
4. Add an Audio File Using HTML5 Code (DW 345)
5. Display an HTML5 Audio Control in Different Browsers (DW 348)
6. Embed a Video Using a Plug-in (DW 352)
7. Set the Parameters of a Video File (DW 354)
8. Add a Video File Using HTML5 Code (DW 358)

Apply Your Knowledge

Reinforce the skills and apply the concepts you learned in this chapter.

Adding a Video as a Plug-In

Note: To complete this assignment, you will be required to use the Data Files for Students. Visit www.cengage.com/ct/studentdownload for detailed instructions or contact your instructor for information about accessing the required files.

Instructions: In this activity, you insert a video as a plug-in and use the Property inspector to modify the width and height of the video. The completed Web page is displayed in Figure 6–42.

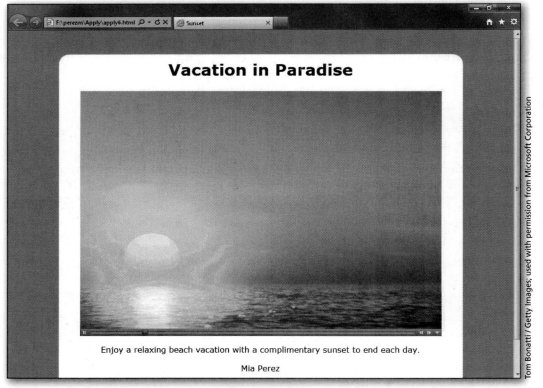

Figure 6–42

Perform the following tasks:

1. Copy the apply6.html file and the Video folder provided with your Data Files from the Chapter 06\Apply folder into the *your last name and first initial*\Apply folder.

2. Start Dreamweaver. Use the Sites button on the Files panel toolbar to select the Apply site. Open apply6.html.

3. Insert a blank line below the page heading, Vacation in Paradise, and then insert a plug-in on the blank line.

4. Navigate to the Video folder and select the sunset video file. Use the Property inspector to set the width to 720 and the height to 500.

5. Replace the text, Your name here, with your first and last names.

6. Save your changes and then view your document in your browser. If necessary, allow blocked content. Compare your document to Figure 6–42. Make any necessary changes, and then save your changes.

7. Submit the document in the format specified by your instructor.

Extend Your Knowledge

Extend the skills you learned in this chapter and experiment with new skills. You may need to use Help to complete the assignment.

Researching Audio and Video Converter Software

Instructions: In this activity, you research various audio and video converter software and write a summary of available converters.

Perform the following tasks:

1. Using your browser and favorite search engine, conduct some research to find software for at least two audio converters and two video converters.

2. Use a word processing program such as Microsoft Word to list each converter software you found. Include the name of the software, the cost of the software, the types of file format conversions that the software will perform, and the URL for each converter.

3. Save the document with the file name Extend6_*lastname_firstname*, using your first and last names as indicated. Submit the document in the format specified by your instructor.

Make It Right

Analyze a Web page and suggest how to improve its design.

Adding Video Using the HTML5 Video Tag

Note: To complete this assignment, you will be required to use the Data Files for Students. Visit www.cengage.com/ct/studentdownload for detailed instructions or contact your instructor for information about accessing the required files.

Instructions: In this activity, you insert the HTML5 video tag and three source file formats to accommodate various browsers. You also set the video to play automatically and make the controls visible on the Web page. The completed Web page is displayed in Figure 6–43.

Continued >

STUDENT ASSIGNMENTS

Make It Right *continued*

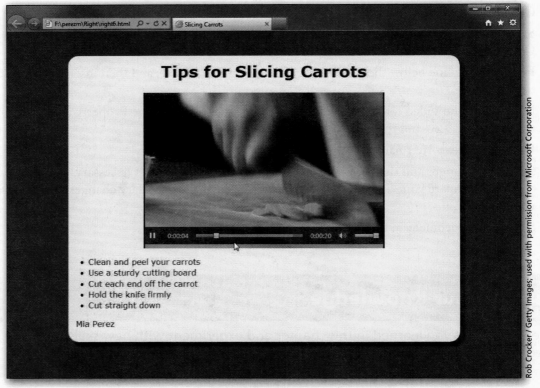

Rob Crocker / Getty Images; used with permission from Microsoft Corporation

Figure 6–43

Perform the following tasks:

1. Copy the right6.html file and the Video folder provided with your Data Files from the Chapter 06\Right folder into the *your last name and first initial*\Right folder.

2. Start Dreamweaver. Use the Sites button on the Files panel toolbar to select the Right site. Open right6.html.

3. Place the insertion point at the end of the Web page heading, Tips for Slicing Carrots, and then press the ENTER key to insert a new line.

4. Change to Code view.

5. Delete the text, , and then press the ENTER key twice.

6. In the blank line, insert the video tag. Use 480 for the width and 320 for the height. Include the controls and autoplay attributes within the tag to show the controls and to automatically play the video on the Web page.

7. Include three source tags — one for each type of video file format (.mp4, .webm, and .ogg) — to play the right6 video file stored in the Video folder. Identify each type of video format used within the source tag.

8. Add the closing video tag after the last source tag. Change to Design view.

9. Replace the text, Your name here, with your first and last names.

10. Save your changes and then view your document in your browser. Compare your document to Figure 6–43. Make any necessary changes, and then save your changes.

11. Submit the document in the format specified by your instructor.

In the Lab

Design and/or create a document using the guidelines, concepts, and skills presented in this chapter. Labs are listed in order of increasing difficulty.

Lab 1: Adding a Video as a Plug-In

Note: To complete this assignment, you will be required to use the Data Files for Students. Visit www.cengage.com/ct/studentdownload for detailed instructions or contact your instructor for information about accessing the required files.

Problem: You are creating an internal Web site for your company that features information about how to live a healthy lifestyle. Employees at your company will use this Web site as a resource for nutrition, exercise, and other health-related tips. In Chapter 2, you created the Exercise Web page. Now you need to add a video to the page. You need to insert a video as a plug-in and then define its width and height. The completed Exercise page is shown in Figure 6–44.

Figure 6–44

Perform the following tasks:

1. Copy the Video folder provided with your Data Files from the Chapter 06\Lifestyle folder into the *your last name and first initial*\Lifestyle folder.
2. Start Dreamweaver. Use the Sites button on the Files panel toolbar to select the Healthy Lifestyle site. Open exercise.html.
3. Delete the text within the editable region, Insert content here. Insert a plug-in.
4. Navigate to the Video folder and select the lifestyle video file. Use the Property inspector to set the width to 480 and the height to 340. Center the video in the editable region.
5. Save your changes and then view your document in your browser. Compare your document to Figure 6–44. Make any necessary changes, and then save your changes.
6. Submit the document in the format specified by your instructor.

In the Lab

Lab 2: Adding Video Using the HTML5 Video Tag

Note: To complete this assignment, you will be required to use the Data Files for Students. Visit www.cengage.com/ct/studentdownload for detailed instructions or contact your instructor for information about accessing the required files.

Problem: You are creating a Web site for Designs by Dolores, a Web site design company. The site provides information about the company and its services. In Chapter 2, you created the Web Hosting page. Now you need to add a video to this page.

In this activity, you insert the HTML5 video tag and specify three source file formats to accommodate various browsers. You also make the video play automatically and make the controls visible on the Web page. The completed Web page is displayed in Figure 6–45.

Perform the following tasks:

1. Copy the Video folder provided with your Data Files from the Chapter 06\Designs folder into the *your last name and first initial*\Designs folder.

2. Start Dreamweaver. Use the Sites button on the Files panel toolbar to select the Designs by Dolores site. Open hosting.html.

3. Delete the text within the editable region, Insert content here. Use the Format menu to center-align the contents of the editable region.

4. Change to Code view and press the ENTER key twice.

5. In the blank line, insert the video tag. Use 480 for the width and 320 for the height. Include the controls and autoplay attributes within the tag to show the controls and to play the video automatically on the Web page.

6. Include three source tags — one for each type of video file format (.mp4, .webm, and .ogg) — for the designs video file in the Video folder. Identify each type of video format used within the source tag.

7. Add the closing video tag after the last source tag. Change to Design view.

8. Save your changes and then view your document in your browser. Compare your document to Figure 6–45. Make any necessary changes, and then save your changes.

9. Submit the document in the format specified by your instructor.

Figure 6–45

In the Lab

Lab 3: Adding Video Using the HTML5 Video Tag

Note: To complete this assignment, you will be required to use the Data Files for Students. Visit www.cengage.com/ct/studentdownload for detailed instructions or contact your instructor for information about accessing the required files.

Problem: You are creating a Web site for Justin's Lawn Care Service, a lawn care company. The site provides information about the company and its services. In Chapter 3, you added content to the Contact page. Now you need to add a video to this page.

In this activity, you insert the HTML5 video tag and specify three source file formats to accommodate various browsers. You also make the video play automatically and make the controls visible on the Web page. The completed Web page is displayed in Figure 6–46.

Figure 6–46

Perform the following tasks:

1. Copy the Video folder provided with your Data Files from the Chapter 06\Lawn folder into the *your last name and first initial*\Lawn folder.

2. Start Dreamweaver. Use the Sites button on the Files panel to select the Justin's Lawn Care Service site. Open contact.html.

3. Place the insertion point at the end of the sentence in the editable region and then press the ENTER key. Center-align the new line.

4. Change to Code view, delete the text, , and then press the ENTER key twice.

5. In the blank line, insert the video tag. Use 480 for the width and 320 for the height. Include the controls and autoplay attributes within the tag.

6. Include three source tags — one for each type of video file format (.mp4, .webm, and .ogg) — for the lawn video file in the Video folder. Identify each type of video format used within the source tag.

7. Add the closing video tag after the last source tag. Change to Design view.

8. Save your changes and then view your document in your browser. Compare your document to Figure 6–46. Make any necessary changes, and then save your changes.

9. Submit the document in the format specified by your instructor.

Cases and Places

Apply your creative thinking and problem solving skills to design and implement a solution.

Note: To complete these assignments, you will be required to use the Data Files for Students. Visit www.cengage.com/ct/studentdownload for detailed instructions or contact your instructor for information about accessing the required files.

1: Adding Music as a Plug-In to the Moving Venture Tips Web Site

Personal

You have created all of the pages for Moving Venture Tips and now need to add content and music to the Tips page. Save the Audio folder provided with your Data Files into the *your last name and first initial*\Move folder. Create a page heading and then use an unordered list to make a list of moving tips on the Tips page. Insert an audio plug-in below the list and select the file in the Audio folder provided with your Data Files. Make the plug-in invisible on the page. Check the spelling using the Commands menu, and correct all misspelled words. Submit the document in the format specified by your instructor.

2: Adding Video Using HTML5 to Student Campus Resources

Academic

You have created all of the pages for Student Campus Resources and now can enhance the Home page with a video. You will embed the video file named campus using the HTML5 video tag. Save the Audio folder provided with your Data Files into the *your last name and first initial*\Campus folder. Use 480 for the width and 320 for the height. Show the controls on the page and set the video to autoplay. In the source tags, specify the three file formats of the video files in the Video folder provided with your Data Files: .mp4, .webm, and .ogg. Submit the document in the format specified by your instructor.

3: Adding Audio Using HTML5 to French Villa Roast Café

Professional

You have created all of the pages for French Villa Roast Café and now can enhance the home page with audio. You will embed the audio file named cafe_music using the HTML5 audio tag. Save the Audio folder provided with your Data Files into the *your last name and first initial*\Cafe folder. Do not show the controls. Set the audio to autoplay and loop. In the <source> tags, specify the .mp3 and .ogg files in the Audio folder provided with your Data Files. Submit the document in the format specified by your instructor.

Appendix A

Adobe Dreamweaver CS6 Help

Getting Help with Dreamweaver CS6

This appendix shows you how to use Dreamweaver Help. The Help system is a complete reference manual at your fingertips. You can access and use the Help system through the Help menu in Dreamweaver CS6, which connects you to up-to-date Help information online at the Adobe Web site. The Help system contains comprehensive information about all Dreamweaver features, including the following:

- A list of links to Dreamweaver help topics.
- A link to new features offered in Dreamweaver CS6.
- A link to Adobe TV, which features online tutorials.
- Search tools, which are used to locate specific topics.

The Dreamweaver Help Menu

One way to access Dreamweaver's Help features is through the Help menu and function keys. Dreamweaver's Help menu provides an easy system to access the available Help options (see Figure A–1 on the next page). Most of these commands open a Help window that displays the appropriate up-to-date Help information from the Adobe Web site. Table A–1 on the next page summarizes the commands available through the Help menu.

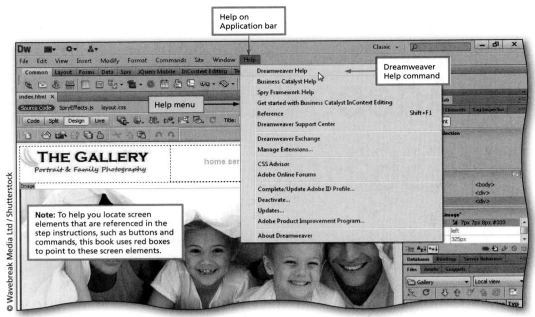

Figure A–1

Table A–1 Summary of Commands on the Help Menu

Command on Help menu	Description
Dreamweaver Help	Starts your default Web browser and displays the Dreamweaver CS6 online help system at the Adobe Web site.
Business Catalyst	Provides help for Adobe Business Catalyst, a unified hosting platform that enables Web designers to build Web sites that meet client requirements.
Spry Framework Help	Displays a complete Help document for the Spry framework for Ajax, a JavaScript library that provides the Web site developer with an option to incorporate XML data and other kinds of effects.
Get started with Business Catalyst InContext Editing	Provides information on how to make Web pages editable through any common browser so that content editors can revise Web page text while designers focus on design.
Reference	Opens the Reference panel group, which is displayed below the Document window. The Reference panel group contains the complete text from several reference manuals, including references on HTML, Cascading Style Sheets, JavaScript, and other Web-related features.
Dreamweaver Support Center	Provides access to the online Adobe Dreamweaver support center.
Dreamweaver Exchange	Links to the Adobe Exchange Web site, where you can download for free and/or purchase a variety of Dreamweaver add-on features.
Manage Extensions	Displays the Adobe Extension Manager window where you can install, enable, and disable extensions. An extension is an add-on piece of software or a plug-in that enhances Dreamweaver's capabilities. Extensions provide the Dreamweaver developer with the capability to customize how Dreamweaver looks and works.
CSS Advisor	Connects to the online Adobe CSS Advisor Web site, which provides solutions to CSS and browser compatibility issues, and encourages you to share tips, hints, and best practices for working with CSS.

Table A–1 Summary of Commands on the Help Menu (*continued*)

Command on Help menu	Description
Adobe Online Forums	Accesses the Adobe Online Forums Web page. The forums provide a place for developers of all experience levels to share ideas and techniques.
Complete/Update Adobe ID Profile	Create or update your Adobe Account information.
Deactivate	Deactivates the installation of Dreamweaver CS6. If you have a single-user retail license, you can activate two computers. If you want to install Dreamweaver CS6 on a third computer, you need to deactivate it first on another computer.
Updates	Lets you check for updates to Adobe software online and then install the updates as necessary.
Adobe Product Improvement Program	Displays a dialog box that explains the Adobe Product Improvement Program and allows you to participate in the program.
About Dreamweaver	Opens a window that provides copyright information and the product license number.

Exploring the Dreamweaver CS6 Help System

The Dreamweaver Help command accesses Dreamweaver's primary Help system at the Adobe Web site and provides comprehensive information about all Dreamweaver features. You can click a topic for more information or use a search tool to look for a particular topic. The Dreamweaver CS6 Help Web site is shown in Figure A–2.

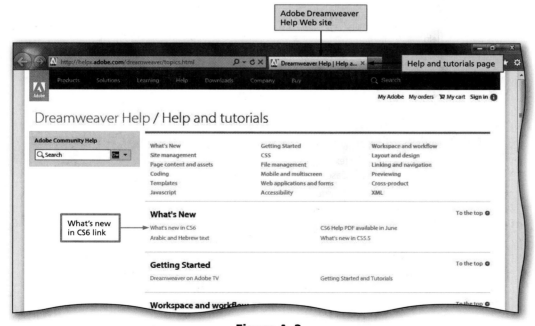

Figure A–2

Using the Help and Tutorials List

The **Help and tutorials list** is similar to a table of contents in a book and is useful for displaying Help when you know the general category of the topic in question, but not the specifics. You use the Help and tutorials list to navigate to the main topic, and then to the subtopic. When the information on the subtopic is displayed, you can read the information, click a link contained within the subtopic, or click the Previous or Next button to open the previous or next Help page in sequence. If a Comments link appears on the page, click it to view comments other users or experts have made about this topic.

To Find Help Using the Help and Tutorials List

To find help using the contents panel, you click a link to display a list of specific subtopics. You then can click a link to open a page related to that subtopic. The following steps use the Help and tutorials list to look up information about CSS3 transitions from the What's New topic on the Dreamweaver Help Web site.

● Click the link, What's new in CS6, below the What's New topic to view the list of new features in Adobe Dreamweaver CS6 (Figure A–3).

Figure A–3

● Click the topic, CSS3 transitions, to view the list of topics for CSS3 transitions (Figure A–4).

Q&A

How do I return to the main topic list?

Use your browser's Back button.

Figure A–4

Using the Search Feature

The quickest way to navigate the Dreamweaver help system is through the Adobe Community Help Search box in the left pane of the Dreamweaver Help Web window. Here you can type words, such as *CSS3 transitions* or *jquery mobile;* or you can type phrases, such as *how to insert Spry collapsible panel* or *Dreamweaver behaviors*. Adobe Community Help responds by displaying search results with a list of topics you can click.

The following are tips regarding the words or phrases you can enter to initiate a search:

1. Check the spelling of the word or phrase.

2. Keep your search specific, with fewer than seven words, to return the most accurate results.

3. If you search using a specific phrase, such as *option button*, put quotation marks around the phrase — the search returns only those topics containing all words in the phrase.

4. If a search term does not yield the desired results, try using a synonym, such as Web instead of Internet.

To Use the Adobe Community Help Search Feature

The following steps open Adobe Community Help and use the Search box to obtain useful information by entering the keywords, jquery mobile.

- If necessary, click Help on the Application bar and then click Dreamweaver Help to display the Dreamweaver Help Web site, open to the Help and tutorials page (Figure A–5).

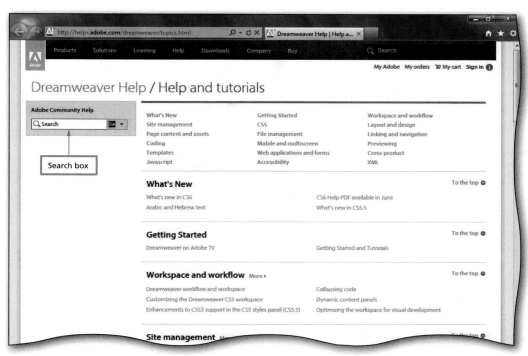

Figure A–5

2

- Click the Search box, type `jquery mobile`, and then press the ENTER key to display the search results (Figure A–6).

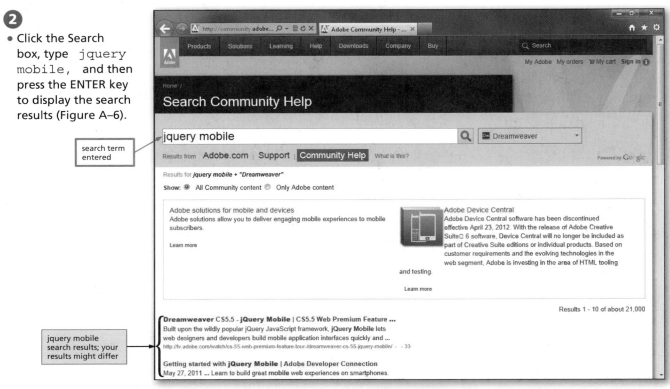

Figure A–6

Context-Sensitive Help

Using **context-sensitive help**, you can open a relevant Help topic in panels, inspectors, and most dialog boxes. To view these Help features, you click a Help button in a dialog box, choose Help on the Options pop-up menu in a panel group, or click the question mark icon in a panel or an inspector.

To Display Context-Sensitive Help on Text Using the Options Menu

Many of the panels and inspectors within Dreamweaver contain an Options Menu button in their upper-right corner. Clicking this button displays context-sensitive help. The following steps use the Options Menu button to view context-sensitive help through the Property inspector. In this example, the default Property inspector for text is displayed.

1

- Open a new document in Dreamweaver to prepare for using context-sensitive help.

- Display the Property inspector, if necessary, to gain access to the Options Menu button (Figure A–7).

Figure A–7

2

• Click the Options Menu button to display an online Help page on setting text properties in the Property inspector (Figure A–8).

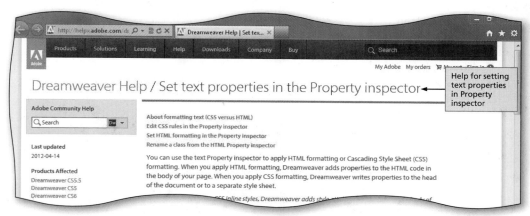

Figure A–8

Using the Reference Panel

The Reference panel is another valuable Dreamweaver resource. This panel provides you with a quick reference tool for HTML tags, JavaScript objects, Cascading Style Sheets, and other Dreamweaver features.

To Use the Reference Panel

The following steps access the Reference panel, review the various options, and select and display information on the <h1> tag.

1

• Click Help on the Application bar, and then click Reference to open the Reference panel.

• If necessary, click the Book button, and then click O'REILLY HTML Reference to display information about HTML tags (Figure A–9).

Figure A–9

● Click the Tag button to display the Tag menu (Figure A–10).

Figure A–10

● Click H1 to display information on the <h1> HTML tag (Figure A–11).

Help information about <h1> HTML tag

Figure A–11

● Click the Book button and then review the list of available reference books (Figure A–12).

● Click the Options Menu button on the Reference panel and then click Close Tab Group to close the panel.

Figure A–12

Apply Your Knowledge

Reinforce the skills and apply the concepts you learned in this appendix.

Viewing the Dreamweaver Help Resources

Instructions: Start Dreamweaver. Perform the following tasks using the Dreamweaver Help command.

1. Click Help on the Application bar and then click Dreamweaver Help.
2. Click the Site management link, then click the Connect to a remote server link.
3. Read the Connect to a remote server topic, and then use a word processing program to write a short overview of what you learned.
4. Submit the document in the format specified by your instructor.

Using the Search Box

Instructions: Start Dreamweaver. Perform the following tasks using the Search box in the Dreamweaver CS6 online Help system.

1. Press the F1 key to display the Using Dreamweaver CS6 Help page.
2. Click the Search box, type **adding sound**, and then press the ENTER key.
3. Click an appropriate link in the search results to open a Help page, click a link on the Help page about embedding a sound file, and then read the Help topic.
4. Use a word processing program to write a short overview of what you learned.
5. Submit the document in the format specified by your instructor.

Using Adobe Community Help

Instructions: Start Dreamweaver. Perform the following tasks using the Search box in the Dreamweaver CS6 online Help system.

1. Press the F1 key to display the Using Dreamweaver CS6 Help page.
2. Click the Search box, type **HTML5**, and then press the ENTER key.
3. Click an appropriate link in the search results to open a Help page and read the Help topic.
4. Review the 'Designing for web publishing' article.
5. Use your word processing program to prepare a report on what you learned.
6. Submit the document in the format specified by your instructor.

Appendix B
Changing Screen Resolution

This appendix explains how to change the screen resolution in Windows 7 to the resolution used in this book.

Changing Screen Resolution

Screen resolution indicates the number of pixels (dots) that the computer uses to display the letters, numbers, graphics, and background you see on the screen. When you increase the screen resolution, Windows displays more information on the screen, but the information decreases in size. The reverse also is true: As you decrease the screen resolution, Windows displays less information on the screen, but the information increases in size.

The screen resolution usually is stated as the product of two numbers, such as 1024×768 (pronounced "ten twenty-four by seven sixty-eight"). A 1024×768 screen resolution results in a display of 1,024 distinct pixels on each of 768 lines, or about 786,432 pixels. The figures in this book were created using a screen resolution of 1024×768.

This is the screen resolution most commonly used today, although some Web designers set their computers at a much higher screen resolution, such as 2048×1536.

To Change the Screen Resolution

The following steps change the screen resolution to 1024 × 768 to match the figures in this book.

1

- If necessary, minimize all programs so that the Windows 7 desktop appears.

- Right-click the Windows 7 desktop to display the Windows 7 desktop shortcut menu (Figure B–1).

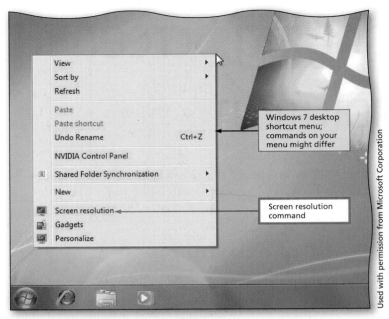

Figure B–1

2

- Click Screen resolution on the shortcut menu to open the Screen Resolution window (Figure B–2).

Figure B–2

3

● Click the Resolution button to display a list of resolution settings for your monitor.

● If necessary, drag the Resolution slider so that the screen resolution is set to 1024 × 768 (Figure B–3).

Figure B–3

4

● Click the OK button to set the screen resolution to 1024 × 768.

● Click the Keep changes button in the Display Settings dialog box to accept the new screen resolution (Figure B–4).

Figure B–4

Appendix C
For Mac Users

For the Mac User of this Book

For most tasks, running Adobe Dreamweaver CS6 with the Windows 7 operating system is not different from using it with the Mac OS X Lion 10.7 operating system. For some tasks, however, you might see some differences in the appearance or location of options, or you may need to complete the tasks using different steps. This appendix demonstrates how to start Adobe Dreamweaver CS6, create an HTML file, save a file, close a file, and quit Adobe Dreamweaver CS6 using the Mac operating system.

Keyboard Differences

One difference between a Mac and a PC is in the use of modifier keys. **Modifier keys** are special keys used to modify the normal action of a key when the two are pressed in combination. Examples of modifier keys include the SHIFT, CTRL, and ALT keys on a PC, and the SHIFT, COMMAND, and OPTION keys on a Mac (Figure C–1).

(a) PC Keyboard

(b) Mac Keyboard

Figure C–1

Table C–1 compares modifier keys on a Windows PC and a Mac. For instance, if the chapter instruction is to press CTRL+S to perform a task, Mac users would press COMMAND+S. For Mac modifier keys, many menu shortcut notations use the symbols instead of the key names. In addition, Mac users with a one-button mouse can press the CTRL key and then click (or CTRL+click) to display the shortcut or context menu.

Table C–1 PC and Mac Modifier Keys		
PC	Mac	Mac Symbol
CTRL key	CMD key	⌘
ALT key	OPT key	⌥
SHIFT key	SHIFT key	⇧
Right-click	CTRL-click	

To Start Adobe Dreamweaver CS6

The following steps, which assume Mac OS X Lion 10.7 is running, start Adobe Dreamweaver CS6 based on a typical installation. You may need to ask your instructor how to start Adobe Dreamweaver CS6 for your computer.

1

- Click the Spotlight button on the Mac desktop to display the Spotlight box.

- Type Adobe Dreamweaver CS6 as the search text in the Spotlight text box and watch the search results appear (Figure C–2).

Q&A

Where does Adobe Dreamweaver CS6 appear in the search results?

If Adobe Dreamweaver CS6 is installed on the computer, it should be the Top Hit in the Spotlight search results.

Figure C–2

2

- Click Adobe Dreamweaver CS6 to open the application.

- If the window is not maximized, click the green Zoom button on the title bar to maximize the window (Figure C–3).

Q&A

Does the PC version of Dreamweaver have a title bar?

On a PC, Dreamweaver CS6 has a title bar and a menu bar (called the Application bar). In all three applications, the clip control functions, minimize, maximize, and close, are inherited from the operating system and placed where the system user would expect to find them.

Figure C–3

Other Ways

1. Click Finder icon in Dock, navigate to Applications, double-click Adobe Dreamweaver CS6 folder, double-click

   Adobe Dreamweaver CS6 application icon

2. Click Dreamweaver icon on dock

To Create a New HTML File

The following steps, which assume Adobe Dreamweaver CS6 is open, create a new HTML file in Adobe Dreamweaver CS6.

1

- Click File on the menu bar to display the File menu (Figure C–4).

Figure C–4

2

- Click New on the File menu to display the New Document dialog box (Figure C–5).

Q&A

What does it mean when a menu command includes multiple symbols in the shortcut key notation?

Multiple symbols mean that you must hold down more than one key. For example, a notation of ⌥⌘O means to press and hold the OPTION and COMMAND keys while you press the O key. In this book, the instructions are formatted as OPT+COMMAND+O.

Figure C–5

3

- If necessary, click Blank Page in the left pane, click HTML in the Page Type pane, click <none> in the Layout pane, click the DocType button, and then click HTML 5 to select the settings.

- Click the Create button to create a page.

Other Ways

1. Press COMMAND+N

Save a File in Dreamweaver

The following steps, which assume a file is open, save an Adobe Dreamweaver CS6 file for the first time on the Mac operating system.

1

- Click File on the menu bar and then click Save As to display the Save As dialog box.

- Click the Save As text box and then type a name for the file, such as `index.html` (Figure C–6).

Q&A

Should I select a location for the file?

Dreamweaver usually saves the file in the root folder of a site. If necessary, click the Where button in the Save As dialog box to navigate to the correct location.

Figure C–6

2

- Click the Save button to save the file.

Other Ways
1. Press SHIFT+CTRL+S, type name, click Save button

Print a File in Dreamweaver

The following steps print an Adobe Dreamweaver CS6 file on the Mac operating system.

1

- Click File on the menu bar and then click Print Code to display the Print dialog box (Figure C–7).

2

- If necessary, click the Printer button and then click a printer name to select a printer.

- Click the Print button to print the document.

Figure C–7

Other Ways
1. Press COMMAND+P, click Printer button, click printer name, click Print button

Close a File in Dreamweaver

The following step closes an Adobe Dreamweaver CS6 file on the Mac operating system.

- Click File on the menu bar and then click Close.

Other Ways
1. Press COMMAND+W

Quit Dreamweaver

The following steps quit Adobe Dreamweaver CS6 on the Mac operating system.

- Click Dreamweaver on the menu bar to display the Dreamweaver menu (Figure C–8).

- Click Quit Dreamweaver to quit Dreamweaver.

Figure C–8

Other Ways
1. Press COMMAND+Q
2. Click Dreamweaver icon on dock, click Quit

Appendix D
Project Planning Guidelines

Using Project Planning Guidelines

The process of communicating specific information to others is a learned, rational skill. Computers and software, especially Adobe Dreamweaver CS6, can help you develop ideas and present detailed information to a particular audience.

Using Adobe Dreamweaver CS6, you can create and publish Web sites. Computer hardware and Web site design software, such as Adobe Dreamweaver CS6, reduces much of the laborious work of drafting and revising projects. Some design professionals use sketch pads or storyboards, others compose directly on the computer, and others have developed unique strategies that work for their own particular thinking and design styles.

No matter what method you use to plan a project, follow specific guidelines to arrive at a final product that presents one or more Web pages clearly and effectively (Figure D–1). Use some aspects of these guidelines every time you undertake a project and others as needed in specific instances. For example, in determining content for a project, you may decide a new Web page with a different layout would communicate the idea more effectively than an existing Web page. If so, you would create this new Web page from scratch.

PROJECT PLANNING GUIDELINES

1. DETERMINE THE PROJECT'S PURPOSE
Why are you undertaking the project?

2. ANALYZE YOUR AUDIENCE
Who are the people who will use your work?

3. GATHER POSSIBLE CONTENT
What graphics exist, and in what forms?

4. DETERMINE WHAT CONTENT TO PRESENT TO YOUR AUDIENCE
What image will communicate the project's purpose to your audience in the most effective manner?

Figure D–1

Determine the Project's Purpose

Begin by clearly defining why you are undertaking this assignment. For example, you may want to create a personal Web page or modify an existing one. Or you may want to create a Web site for a business or other organization. Once you clearly understand the purpose of your task, begin to draft ideas of how best to communicate this information.

Analyze Your Audience

Learn about the people who will use, analyze, or view your work. Where are they employed? What are their educational backgrounds? What are their expectations? What questions do they have? How will they interact with your product? What kind of computer system and Internet connection will they have? Web design experts suggest drawing a mental picture of these people or finding photographs of people who fit this profile so that you can develop a project with the audience in mind.

By knowing your audience members, you can tailor a project to meet their interests and needs. You will not present them with information they already possess, and you will not omit the information they need to know.

Example: Your assignment is to raise the profile of your college's nursing program in the community. Your project should address questions such as the following: How much does the audience know about your college and the nursing curriculum? What are the admission requirements? How many of the applicants admitted complete the program? What percent of participants pass the state nursing boards?

Gather Possible Content

Rarely are you in a position to develop all the material for a project. Typically, you would begin by gathering existing information, images, and photos, or writing and designing new text and graphics based on information that may reside in spreadsheets or databases. Web design work for clients often must align with and adhere to existing marketing campaigns or other business materials. Web sites, pamphlets, magazine and newspaper articles, and books could provide insights into how others have approached your topic. Personal interviews often provide perspectives not available by any other means. Consider video and audio clips as potential sources for material that might complement or support the factual data you uncover. Make sure you have all legal rights to any photographs and other media you plan to use.

Determine What Content to Present to Your Audience

Experienced Web designers recommend identifying three or four major ideas you want an audience member to remember after viewing your Web project. It also is helpful to envision your project's endpoint, the key fact or universal theme that you want to emphasize. All project elements should lead to this ending point.

As you make content decisions, you also need to think about other factors. Presentation of the project content is an important consideration. For example, will the content of your Web pages look good when printed on paper? How will the content look when viewed on a screen for a mobile device? Determine relevant time factors, such as the length of time to develop the project, how long editors will spend reviewing your project, or the amount of time allocated for presenting your Web site designs to the customer. Your project will need to accommodate all of these constraints.

Decide whether a graphic, a photograph, or an artistic element can express or emphasize a particular concept. The right hemisphere of the brain processes images by attaching an emotion to them; so in the long run, audience members are more apt to recall themes from graphics rather than those from the text.

Finally, review your project to make sure the theme still easily is identifiable and has been emphasized successfully. Is the purpose of each page clear and presented without distraction? Does the project satisfy the requirements?

Summary

When creating a Web site project, it is beneficial to follow some basic guidelines from the outset. By taking some time at the beginning of the process to determine the project's purpose, analyze the audience, gather possible content, and determine what content to present to the audience, you can produce a project that is informative, relevant, and effective.

Index

A

Abode Roundtrip technology,
  DW 19
absolute links
  adding, DW 172–173
  described, **DW 169**
accessibility
  adding alt text to provide, DW 150
  guidelines for Web sites,
    DW 12–13
accessing
  Dreamweaver Help, DW 65
  Internet, DW 6–7
  mobile sites, DW 8
  preferences, DW 41–42
accounts, creating Adobe,
  DW 300–302
Accredited Registrar Directory,
  DW 14
Acrobat Reader, DW 335
Action text box, Property
  inspector, DW 234
adding
  See also inserting
  Adobe widgets to Web pages,
    DW 309–314
  alt tags, DW 163, DW 165
  alternative text, DW 184
  audio files with HTML5 code,
    DW 343–348
  CSS rules, DW 178–180
  CSS styles, DW 92–93
  div tags, DW 93–96
  editable regions, DW 146–148
  form objects, DW 237
  image placeholders, DW 184–185
  initial values to Text Fields,
    DW 247
  labels to tables, DW 236–237
  links to Facebook, Twitter,
    DW 172–173
  menus to forms, DW 243–246
  multimedia with plug-ins or
    HTML5, DW 334–335
  navigation div tags, DW 104–106
  panel headings, DW 296–297
  Radio Groups, DW 248–250
  Spry Collapsible Panel widgets to
    Web pages, DW 292–296
  Spry to Web pages, DW 274
  Spry validation to Radio Group,
    DW 287–289
  Spry validation to text fields,
    DW 276–286

Submit, Reset buttons to forms,
  DW 250–252
Text Fields to forms, DW 238–242
text to tables, DW 209–210
video, DW 351–356
video files with HTML5 code,
  DW 357–361
Web pages, DW 58
widgets from Adobe Exchange,
  DW 303–305
Adobe BrowserLab
  comparing Web pages in multiple
    browsers using, DW 64
  testing Web pages with, DW 16
Adobe Community Help, APP 5–6
Adobe Creative Suite 6, **DW 26**
Adobe Dreamweaver CS6
  See also Dreamweaver
  described, **DW 19**, DW 20–21
Adobe Exchange, **DW 297**,
  DW 303–305
Adobe Fireworks, DW 143,
  DW 180
Adobe Flash Player plug-ins,
  DW 42
Adobe Integrated Runtime (AIR)
  checking your computer for and
    installing, DW 298–300
  described, **DW 297**
Adobe Photoshop, DW 143,
  DW 149
Adobe Widget Browser, **DW 297**
  reviewing, adding widgets,
    DW 303–305
  signing in to, DW 303
  using, DW 297–306
AirCard, **DW 8**
AJAX (Asynchronous JavaScript
  and XML), **DW 272**
aligning
  table cells, DW 227–228
  tables, DW 222–223
alignment, setting for .logo style,
  DW 102
All mode, **DW 144**
"Allow blocked content" button,
  DW 290
alt tags
  adding, DW 163
  described, **DW 150**
alternative text
  adding, DW 163, DW 165,
    DW 184
  described, **DW 150**

Americans with Disabilities Act
  (ADA), DW 13
anchor tags, **DW 178**
App Developer workspace, DW 31
Apple Safari, DW 4
Application bar, DW 29
  Commands menu (fig.), DW 63
  described, **DW 31**
ASP (Active Server Pages), **DW 18**
asterisk (*), unsaved file changes,
  DW 33, DW 51
audience, target, DW 9, APP 22
audio
  See also sound
  adding files using HTML5,
    DW 343–348
  HTML5 formats (table), DW 344
  planning use of, DW 334
  plug-in parameters (table), DW 340

B

background colors, DW 83
  changing, DW 108, DW 109
  removing, DW 145
  setting table cell, DW 229–230
  Web page, DW 11
background sounds, embedding
  using plug-ins, DW 338–340
backslash (\) in path structures,
  DW 44
behaviors, **DW 232**
bitmap images, **DW 149**
bitmaps, **DW 149**
bit-resolution, **DW 149**
Biz.ly, DW 15
blogs
  described, **DW 2**
  illustrated (fig.), DW 3
blue underlined text, DW 171
bold in tables, DW 221–222
borders
  defining CSS rules for, DW 110
  displaying CSS rule options,
    DW 179
  table, DW 208
Bravenet, DW 15
brightness, adjusting image's,
  DW 158
browsers, **DW 4**
  Adobe Widget Browser. *See*
    Adobe Widget Browser
  displaying HTML5 audio control
    in different, DW 348–350

HTML5 standards, DW 334–335
mobile, DW 8
previewing Web pages in,
    DW 63–65
testing forms in, DW 290–291
viewing sites in, DW 185
viewing widgets in, DW 320–321
business (Web sites)
described, **DW 2**
illustrated (fig.), DW 3
buttons on Insert bar, DW 32

C

captions, table, DW 206, DW 208,
    DW 215–216
Cascading Style Sheets, **DW 78**
Cascading Style Sheets (CSS)
    styles, **DW 20–21**
cells, **DW 204**
alignment options, DW 227–229
merging, splitting, DW 219
properties, DW 211–212
setting background colors,
    DW 229–230
Cengage Learning Web site,
    DW 11, DW 14
charts, Web page navigation,
    DW 7
Check Spelling command, DW 63
Chrome, DW 349, DW 357
class div tags, DW 94
classes, **DW 81**
Classic workspace, DW 29
illustrated (fig.), DW 31
resetting, DW 39–40
closing
files (Macintosh), APP 20
and opening panels, DW 37–39
templates, DW 114
Web page, DW 49
code, displaying Web page, DW 35
Code Navigator icon, DW 171
Code view, **DW 35**
codecs, **DW 336**
Coder workspace, DW 31
coding HTML5 video, DW 357–358
collapsing panel groups, DW 38
colons (:), properties and values,
    DW 82
colors
background. *See* background
    colors
hexadecimal codes for, DW 230
image placeholders, DW 182

selecting, DW 105
for visited links, DW 176
as Web site design tool, **DW 10–11**
columns, **DW 204**
adjusting width, DW 225–227
deleting, DW 219
properties, DW 211–212
commands
See also specific command
accessing with Insert bar, DW 32
on Help menu, APP 2–3
multiple symbols in shortcut key
    notation, APP 18
Spry widgets (table), DW 274
Commands menu, Application bar
    (fig.), DW 63
Common Gateway Interface (CGI)
    scripts, DW 232
compound selectors
adding new CSS rules using,
    DW 178–180
described, **DW 178**
compound styles, creating,
    DW 178–180
Contact form, DW 202–203
contact pages, creating,
    DW 166–168
.container class, defining CSS rules
    for, DW 97–99
.content class, defining CSS rules
    for, DW 109–111
context-sensitive help, **APP 6–7**
controls
adding HTML5 audio, DW 344
form, DW 238
Copy Dependent Files dialog box,
    DW 278
copying
files, DW 310
folders, DW 337–338
copying images into folders,
    DW 150–151
copyright, **DW 149**
creating
Adobe accounts, DW 300–302
blank HTML document, DW 30
compound styles, DW 178–180
contact pages, DW 166–168
cross-platform sites, DW 10
CSS rules, DW 97
Dreamweaver Web templates,
    DW 84
editable region of template,
    DW 113–115
folders, DW 310

forms, DW 231
HTML templates, DW 88–91
links, DW 56–57, DW 169
new HTML files (Macintosh),
    APP 17–18
two-column fixed layout pages,
    DW 51
unordered lists, DW 59–60
Web pages from templates,
    DW 115–117, DW 159–168
Web sites, DW 43–65,
    DW 86–88
widget preset for LightBox
    Gallery, DW 306–322
Crop tool, DW 148
cross-platform sites, **DW 10**
CSS, **DW 78**
.css, DW 96
CSS files
creating folders for, DW 87–88
described, **DW 43**
CSS Rule Definition dialog box
categories in (table), DW 97
displaying, DW 96
CSS rule definitions, **DW 80**
defining for .logo class,
    DW 100–103
selecting, DW 97–99
CSS rules
adding, DW 178–180
creating, DW 97
defining for .image class,
    DW 107–108
CSS style sheets
anatomy of, benefits of, DW 80–81
creating, DW 97
modifying, DW 178
CSS styles
adding, DW 92–93
formatting links using, DW 175
CSS3, overview of, DW 43
CSS3 styles, DW 21
curly braces ({ }) and declaration
    blocks, DW 82
Current mode, **DW 144**

D

Data Files for Students,
    DW 150–151, DW 310
data plans
described, **DW 8**
illustrated (fig.), DW 7
date text field, adding Spry
    validation to, DW 284–286

declaration blocks, DW 82
declarations, **DW 81**
defining image placeholders,
    DW 181–182
definition lists, **DW 59**
deleting
    See also removing
    links, DW 53–54
    table rows, columns, DW 219
Design button, DW 30
Design view, **DW 36**
designing
    Web pages, DW 43
    Web sites, DW 2
DHTML (Dynamic HTML),
    DW 18
directories, **DW 44**
disability types and Web page
    design strategies (table), DW 13
displaying
    context-sensitive help, APP 6–7
    document views, DW 35–37
    Standard toolbar, DW 40–41
    Web page code, DW 35
div tags, **DW 93**
    adding, DW 93–96
    adding content, DW 109–111
    adding navigation, defining CSS
        rules, DW 104–106
    using, DW 143
DocType, **DW 42**
document tabs, **DW 33**
Document toolbar, **DW 33**
Document Type Definition
    (DTD), **DW 42**
Document window, **DW 33**
documents
    creating blank HTML, DW 30
    displaying views, DW 35–37
    headings, DW 54
    inserting line breaks, DW 155
    updating those attached to
        template, DW 147, DW 173
Domain Name System (DNS),
    DW 14
domain names, **DW 14**
downloading Adobe AIR
    application, DW 299–300
dragging to create hyperlinks,
    DW 56–57
Dreamweaver
    Help, obtaining, DW 65, DW 92
    quitting, DW 65, DW 118,
        DW 186
    quitting (Macintosh), APP 20

quitting and restarting, DW 45
starting, DW 28–30, DW 85
starting (Macintosh), APP 16–17
touring Dreamweaver window,
    DW 30
Dreamweaver CS6 described,
    DW 26
Dreamweaver workspace,
    DW 30–31
drop-down menus, DW 243
Dual Screen option, DW 31
.dwt, **DW 84**

E

e-commerce
    described, **DW 4**
    illustrated (fig.), DW 3
Edit menu, DW 31–32
editable regions, **DW 84**, DW 91
    adding, DW 146–148
    creating, DW 113–115
editing
    CSS rules, DW 144–146
    graphics, DW 148
    navigation link text, DW 53–54
    Spry widgets, DW 306
e-mail links
    adding, DW 174–175
    described, **DW 169**
e-mail text field, adding Spry
    validation to, DW 281–282
embedding, **DW 338**
    multimedia files, DW 351
    sound files using plug-ins,
        DW 338–340
    video files using plug-in,
        DW 351–354
entertainment (Web sites)
    described, **DW 4**
    illustrated (fig.), DW 3
expanding panels, DW 38
external style sheets, **DW 82**

F

Facebook, **DW 153–154**
    adding links to, DW 172
    links, DW 6, DW 13–14
    marketing sites with,
        DW 153–158
file extensions htm, html, DW 115
file formats
    common sound (table), DW 336
    video, DW 351

files
    copying, DW 310
    creating new HTML (Macintosh),
        APP 17–18
    opening, DW 29
    printing (Macintosh), APP 20
    saving (Macintosh), APP 19
Files panel, DW 34
    icons on, DW 53
    Local Files, DW 45
Firefox, DW 349, DW 357
fixed layouts, **DW 50**
Flash Player, DW 335, DW 351
float property, **DW 100**
focal points, **DW 10**
folder icons, DW 53
folders
    copying, DW 337–338
    copying images into, DW 150–151
    creating for your Web site,
        DW 48, DW 87–88
    creating Lightbox, DW 310
    Dreamweaver, DW 44
    resource, DW 87
    Template, DW 84
fonts
    selecting for Web pages, DW 12
    serif and sans-serif, DW 101
.footer class, defining CSS rules
    for, DW 110–111
form objects, adding, DW 237
form Property inspector, using,
    DW 234–235
formats
    for image files, DW 149–150
    for video files (table), DW 351
formatting, **DW 54**
    digital photos as JPEG files,
        DW 148
    forms, DW 231
    links, DW 175–177
    table text, DW 214–216
    text using heading styles, **DW 54**
    using CSS styles, DW 92
forms, **DW 231**
    adding menus, DW 243–246
    adding Submit, Reset buttons to,
        DW 250–252
    adding Text Fields to, DW 238–242
    creating, form processing, DW 231
    designing using table, DW 235–236
    elements (table), DW 235
    inserting into Web pages,
        DW 232–234
    testing in browsers, DW 290–291

Forms tab, insert bar, DW 238
FTP (File Transfer Protocol),
   DW 16

G

Gallery site, DW 78–79, DW 306,
   DW 308
GIF, **DW 149**
Gmail, DW 174
Google Chrome (fig.), DW 4
graphics
   See also images
   editing, DW 148
Graphics Interchange Format,
   DW 149

H

hash symbol (#) and ID selectors,
   DW 81
<head> section, DW 83
headings, **DW 54**
   adding panel, DW 296–297
   Web page, DW 49
Help
   context-sensitive, APP 6–7
   exploring, APP 3–6
   menu, APP 1–3
   obtaining Dreamweaver, DW 65,
      DW 92
   Reference panel, using, APP 7–8
   searching, APP 5–6
Help and tutorials list, **APP 4**
hiding
   panels, DW 37–38
   toolbars, DW 40
Hint property, DW 284
home pages, **DW 6**, **DW 51**
   for Gallery Web site (fig.),
      DW 80
   inserting images on, DW 157–158
   naming, saving, DW 51–53
   saving, DW 57
Hotmail, DW 174
.htm, .html, DW 115–117
HTML templates, creating,
   DW 88–91
HTML5, **DW 18**, DW 27,
   DW 42, DW 334–336
   adding audio files using,
      DW 343–348
   adding video files with,
      DW 357–361
   audio formats (table), DW 344

vs. plug-ins, DW 351
   removing audio control, DW 350
HTTP. *See* Hypertext Transfer
   Protocol (HTTP)
https:// vs. http://, DW 172
hyperlinks
   See also links
   described, **DW 6**
Hypertext Markup Language
   (HTML), **DW 17**
   and creating Web pages with
      Dreamweaver, DW 19–20
   displaying Web page code, DW 35
   structure of tables, DW 216–217
Hypertext Transfer Protocol
   (HTTP)
   described, **DW 5**
   and encryption, DW 172

I

icons in Files panel, DW 53
.image class, defining CSS rules
   for, DW 107–108
Image Placeholder dialog box,
   DW 184–185
image placeholders, **DW 180**
   adding, DW 180, DW 184–185
   defining, DW 181–182
   replacing, DW 183
   setting color, DW 182
Image Tag Accessibility Attributes
   dialog box, DW 153, DW 156,
   DW 158, DW 161
image tags, DW 178
images
   acquiring, formatting, DW 148
   adding to widgets, DW 314–320
   adjusting brightness, DW 158
   copying into folders, DW 150–151
   designing Web site, DW 12
   file formats, DW 149–150
   and image placeholders, DW 180,
      DW 183
   inserting on home pages,
      DW 157–158
   linking to, DW 168
   placing in folders, DW 84,
      DW 87–88
   preparing, DW 142
   rollover, DW 175
   thumbnail, DW 309
importing Web pages with Adobe
   Roundtrip technology, DW 19
index pages, **DW 6**

index.htm, index.html, DW 51
informational/educational
   (Web sites)
   described, **DW 2**
   illustrated (fig.), DW 3
Init val, **DW 247**
inline styles, **DW 83**
Input Tag Accessibility Attributes
   dialog box, DW 238–242,
   DW 244, DW 252
Insert bar, **DW 32**
Insert Div Tag dialog box, DW 94
Insert panel, **DW 32**
inserting
   See also adding
   forms into Web pages,
      DW 232–234
   images on home pages,
      DW 157–158
   logo images in templates,
      DW 152–153
   tables on Web pages,
      DW 207–209, DW 217–219
   tables to design forms,
      DW 235–236
internal style sheets, **DW 83**
Internet Corporation for Assigned
   Names and Numbers (ICANN),
   DW 14
Internet Explorer, DW 348–350
   closing, DW 185
   illustrated (fig.), DW 4
   important features (table), DW 5
   Internet Explorer 9, DW 28
Internet service providers (ISPs)
   described, **DW 6**
   selecting for Web sites,
      DW 14–15
IP addresses (Internet Protocol
   addresses), **DW 14**
ISPs. *See* Internet service providers
   (ISPs)
Item Labels, DW 245

J

JavaScript
   behaviors, DW 232
   and jQuery, DW 18
Joint Photographic Experts Group,
   DW 149
JPEG, **DW 149**
JPEG files, formatting photos as,
   DW 148
jQuery, **DW 18–19**

L

labels, **DW 236**
layouts
  CSS, DW 21
  fixed, liquid, DW 50
  sketching using wireframes,
    DW 92–93
  table, DW 205–206
  template, DW 49
LightBox Gallery, DW 270
LightBox Gallery widget, DW 297,
    DW 306–322
line breaks, inserting, DW 155
link tags, **DW 83**
links, **DW 56**
  adding to templates, DW 168–175
  adding to Web pages, DW 61
  and blue underlined text, DW 171
  changing, deleting, DW 53–54
  creating, DW 56–57
  creating unordered, DW 59–60
  formatting, DW 175–177
liquid layouts, **DW 50**
lists, **DW 243**
  types of, DW 59
  Web page, DW 49
Live view, viewing sites in, DW 118
load testing, DW 17
Local Files, **DW 45**
local root folders, **DW 44**
local site folders, **DW 44**
local sites, defining, DW 43–44
locked regions, DW 113, DW 146
.logo class, defining CSS rule
    definitions for, DW 100–103
logos, DW 100
logos, inserting images in
    templates, DW 152–153
logs, server, **DW 15**

M

Macintosh
  keyboard differences, APP 15–16
  quitting Dreamweaver, DW 66
  saving Web pages, DW 52,
    DW 57
maintaining Web sites, DW 16–17
margin, **DW 97**
marketing sites with Facebook,
    Twitter, DW 153–158
markup languages, Document
    Type Definition (DTD), DW 42
master folders, **DW 44**
maximizing windows, DW 30

menus
  adding to forms, DW 243–246
  choosing, DW 31–32
  Dreamweaver Help, APP 1–3
  Item Labels, DW 245
  using, DW 32
merging
  described, **DW 219**
  table cells, DW 220
Microsoft Notepad, DW 19
Mobile Applications view, DW 31
modems, AirCard, DW 8
modes, All and Current, DW 144
modifier keys, **APP 15**
monitors, and Dual Screen option,
    DW 31
moving
  panels, DW 39
  toolbars, DW 40–41
Mozilla Firefox (fig.), DW 4
MP3 files, DW 336
MP4 format, DW 351–354
multimedia
  adding with plug-ins or HTML5,
    DW 334–335
  embedding files, DW 351
multiplatform display, DW 9–10

N

naming
  forms, DW 234
  home pages, DW 51
navigating Web sites, DW 7
navigation, identifying for sites,
    DW 168
.navigation class, defining CSS rule
    definitions for, DW 104
Network Solutions, DW 14–15
New CSS Rule dialog box, DW 95,
    DW 100–101, DW 107–108
New Documents dialog box,
    DW 88–91, DW 159–160
New Editable Region dialog box,
    DW 147
news (Web sites)
  described, **DW 2**
  illustrated (fig.), DW 3
noneditable regions, **DW 84**,
    DW 113

O

.ogg files, DW 347
opening
  and closing panels, DW 37–39

files, DW 29
  Gallery Template, DW 143
  templates, DW 143, DW 169
Opera browser, DW 4, DW 357
Options menu, displaying context-
    sensitive help on text, APP 6–7
ordered lists, **DW 59**
organizing site structures,
    DW 84–85
Outlook, DW 174

P

padding, **DW 109**
Page Properties button, Property
    inspector, DW 175
panel dock, **DW 34**
panel groups
  described, **DW 34**
  opening, closing, moving, DW 37
panels, **DW 34**
  adding headings, DW 296–297
  opening, closing, DW 37–39
  switching from Insert bar to,
    DW 32
paragraphs, Web page, DW 49
paths, **DW 44**
personal (Web sites)
  described, **DW 2**
  illustrated (fig.), DW 3
phone number text field, adding
    Spry validation to, DW 283–284
PHP (Hypertext Preprocessor),
    DW 18
picture elements, **DW 149**
pixels (px)
  described, **DW 97**, **DW 149**
  vs. points (pt), DW 101
placeholders, image. *See* image
    placeholders
planning
  layout, formatting of Web sites,
    DW 93
  multimedia additions, DW 334,
    DW 335
  projects, DW 204, APP 21–23
  Spry widgets use, DW 272,
    DW 273
  Web sites, DW 2, DW 8–10
plug-ins, **DW 334**
  embedding sound files using,
    DW 338–340
  embedding video files using,
    DW 351–354
  video, DW 351

PNG, **DW 150**
pointer with "not" symbol,
  DW 117
pop-up menus, DW 243
Portable Network Graphics,
  DW 150
portals
  described, **DW 2**
  illustrated (fig.), DW 3
preferences
  accessing, DW 41–42
  described, **DW 41**
preset, **DW 306**
Preview states of widgets, DW 275
previewing Web pages in browsers,
  DW 63–65, DW 230
printing files (Macintosh), APP 19
Professional Photographers of
  America (PPA) Web site,
  DW 169
progressive JPEG, **DW 149**
project management, DW 16
projects
  custom template and style sheet,
    DW 78–79
  formatted tables and forms,
    DW 202–203
  general guidelines, DW 28,
    DW 79, DW 142, DW 204
  interactive Web pages, DW
    270–271
  planning guidelines, DW 26,
    APP 21–23
  promotional images,
    DW 140–141
  small business incubator Web site
    plan, DW 26–27
  Web pages with multimedia,
    DW 332–333
properties, **DW 81**
  changing with Property inspector,
    DW 34
  setting for images, DW 183
  values, DW 82
Property inspector, **DW 34**
  applying headings styles,
    DW 54–56
  form, DW 234–235
  formatting tables, DW 210–211,
    DW 216
  merging table cells, DW 220
prototype, **DW 143**
pt (points), DW 101
publishing Web sites, DW 16
px (pixels), DW 101

Q
QuickTime Player, DW 335
quitting
  Dreamweaver, DW 45, DW 65,
    DW 118, DW 186
  Dreamweaver (Macintosh), APP 20

R
radio buttons
  adding in Radio Groups, DW 248
  adding Submit, Reset buttons to
    forms, DW 250–252
Radio Group, **DW 248**
  adding, DW 248–250
  adding Spry validation to,
    DW 287–289
readability and using tables, DW 205
Reference panel, using, APP 7–8
Rehabilitation Act, Section 508,
  DW 12
REI, DW 9
relative links
  adding, DW 170–171
  described, **DW 169**
removing
  See also deleting
  HTML5 audio control, loop,
    DW 350
  image borders, DW 179–180
renaming home pages, DW 51
replacing image placeholders,
  DW 183
Reset buttons, adding to forms,
  DW 250–252
resizing
  forms, DW 231
  tables, DW 213
resource folders, **DW 87**
restarting Dreamweaver, DW 45
rollover images, DW 175
rollover links, **DW 175**
  formatting, DW 175–177
  testing, DW 177–178
root, **DW 44**
rows, **DW 204**
  deleting, DW 219
  properties, DW 211–212

S
Save As dialog box, DW 52–53,
  DW 160
Save As Template dialog box,
  DW 91–92

Save Style Sheet File As dialog box,
  DW 95–96
Save vs. Save All buttons, DW 62
saving
  CSS style sheets, DW 95–96
  documents, DW 160
  files (Macintosh), APP 19
  files to USB flash drives, DW 47
  files with htm extension, DW 115
  home pages, DW 57
  HTML pages as templates,
    DW 90–91
  templates, DW 102, DW 114,
    DW 147
screen readers, DW 150
screen resolution
  changing, DW 28, APP 12–13
  described, **DW 10**, **APP 11**
scripts described, DW 232
search engines illustrated (fig.),
  DW 3
searching Help system, APP 5–6
Secure Sockets Layer (SSL),
  DW 15
Select Image Source dialog box,
  DW 152, DW 156, DW 158,
  DW 163, DW 184
selecting
  colors, DW 105
  CSS rule definitions, DW 97–99
  table elements, DW 213–216
  text, DW 54–55
selectors, **DW 81**
server logs, **DW 15**
servers
  locating ISP for hosting
    Web sites, DW 14–15
  Web, **DW 5**
server-side scripts, DW 232
Sharpen button, DW 148
ship's wheel icon, DW 171
showing
  See also displaying, viewing
  panels, DW 37–38
single-line text field properties,
  DW 246
Site Setup dialog box, DW 45,
  DW 46–49
sites
  defining local, DW 43–44
  described, DW 43–44
Small Business Incubator Web site,
  DW 26
social networking, role of,
  DW 13–14

social networking sites
  described, **DW 153**
  marketing with Facebook,
    Twitter, DW 153–158
social networks
  described, **DW 2**
  illustrated (fig.), DW 3
sound
  See also audio
  adding to Web pages,
    DW 335–336
  common file formats (table),
    DW 336
  embedding background, using
    plug-ins, DW 338–340
  embedding files using plug-ins,
    DW 338–340
  setting file parameters,
    DW 340–343
space between text and border,
  DW 109
spell-checking Web pages, DW 63
Split view, **DW 36**
Spry category, Insert bar, DW 273,
  DW 275–276
Spry Collapsible Panel widget,
  DW 274
  adding to Web pages, DW 292–296
  described, DW 292
Spry framework for AJAX, **DW 272**
Spry validation, **DW 270**
  adding to Radio Group,
    DW 287–289
  adding to text fields, DW 276–286
Spry Validation Radio Group
  widget, DW 274
Spry Validation Text Field widget,
  DW 274
Spry widgets, **DW 272**
  commands (table), DW 274
  editing, formatting, DW 306
  options, DW 273–274
SpryAssets folder, DW 279
SpryValidationTextField.js,
  DW 278
Standard toolbar, displaying and
  hiding, DW 40–41
starting
  Dreamweaver, DW 28–30,
    DW 85
  Dreamweaver (Macintosh),
    APP 16–17
  lists with different number or
    letter, DW 60
  restarting Dreamweaver, DW 45

status bar
  described, **DW 33**
  displayed options, DW 34
<style>, DW 83
style sheets
  See also CSS style sheets
  described, DW 80
  types of, DW 82–83
styles
  See also specific styles
  adding CSS, DW 92–93
  anatomy of, DW 81
  creating compound, DW 178–180
  described, DW 80
  headings, **DW 54**
  inline, **DW 83**
subfolders, **DW 44**
Submit buttons, adding to forms,
  DW 250–252
summaries of table data, DW 206
switching from Insert bar to panel,
  DW 32

T

table data, **DW 217**
Table dialog box, DW 205–206
table row, **DW 217**
tables
  adding labels, DW 236–237
  adding summary for accessibility,
    DW 206
  adjusting width, DW 223–227
  aligning, DW 222–223
  captions, DW 206, DW 208,
    DW 215–216
  cell, row, column properties,
    DW 211–212
  described, DW 202, DW 204–205
  designing layouts, DW 205–206
  formatting, DW 210–211
  HTML structure of, DW 216–217
  inserting, to design forms,
    DW 235–236
  inserting on Web page,
    DW 207–209, DW 217–219
  merging, splitting cells,
    DW 219–227
  properties (table), DW 211
  selecting elements, formatting,
    DW 213–216
tags
  See also specific tags
  inline style code within, DW 83
target audience, DW 9, APP 22

templates, **DW 43**
  adding div tags, DW 93–96
  adding relative links,
    DW 170–171
  closing, DW 114
  creating editable region of,
    DW 113–115
  creating HTML, DW 84,
    DW 88–91
  creating Web pages from,
    DW 115–117
  inserting logo images in,
    DW 152–153
  inserting social networking icons
    in, DW 155–157
  modifying, DW 143–148
  opening, DW 143, DW 169
  saving, DW 102, DW 114
  saving HTML pages as,
    DW 90–91
  selecting predefined, DW 49–51
Templates folder, DW 88–89
testing
  forms in browsers, DW 290–291
  links, DW 168
  load, DW 17
  rollover links, DW 177–178
  Web pages, DW 16
text
  adding to tables, DW 209–210
  aligning within table cells,
    DW 227–229
  blue underlined, DW 171
  designing Web site, DW 11–12
  editing navigation link,
    DW 53–54
  formatting using heading styles,
    DW 54–56
  linking to, DW 168
  organizing, formatting guidelines,
    DW 49
text editors, **DW 19**
Text Fields, **DW 238**
  adding initial values, DW 247
  adding Spry validation to,
    DW 276–286
  adding to forms, DW 238–242
  properties, DW 246
thumbnail images, **DW 309**
title bar (Macintosh), APP 17
titles, changing Web page,
  DW 62
toolbars, displaying and hiding,
  DW 40–41
tutorials list, APP 4

Twitter, **DW 154**
  adding links to, DW 173
  links, DW 6, DW 13–14
  marketing sites with, DW 153–158
typography, **DW 11**

U

undocking and moving toolbars,
  DW 40–41
Uniform Resource Locators
  (URLs), **DW 5**
United States Department of
  Agriculture nutrition site, DW 10
unordered lists, **DW 59**
Update Pages dialog box, DW 157
Update Template dialog box,
  DW 147, DW 157, DW 173
USB flash drives, when to create
  sites on, DW 44
US/Canada format, DW 284
user accounts, creating Acrobat,
  DW 300–302

V

validation, Spry. *See* Spry validation
values, **DW 82**
video
  adding, DW 351
  adding files with HTML5 code,
    DW 357–361
  coding HTML5, DW 357–358
  embedding files using plug-ins,
    DW 351–354
  formats (table), DW 351
  planning use of, DW 334
  playing on Web pages, DW 357
  setting file parameters,
    DW 354–356
viewing
  sites in browsers, DW 185
  sites in Live view, DW 118
  widgets in browsers, DW 320–321
views, displaying document,
  DW 35–37
visited links, DW 176

W

WAV files, DW 336

Web 2.0
  described, **DW 2**
  illustrated (fig.), DW 3
Web forms
  See also forms
  described, DW 202
Web page authoring programs,
  DW 19
Web Page command, DW 19
Web page titles
  changing, deleting, DW 62
  described, **DW 62**
Web pages
  adding, DW 58
  adding Adobe widgets to,
    DW 309–314
  adding graphics, DW 140
  adding links, DW 61
  adding sound to, DW 335–336
  adding Spry Collapsible Panel
    widgets, DW 292–296
  adding Spry to, DW 274
  adding tables, DW 207–209,
    DW 217–219
  creating for Web sites,
    DW 159–168
  creating from templates,
    DW 115–117
  described, DW 6
  editable and noneditable regions,
    DW 113
  enhancing with audio, video,
    DW 332
  inserting forms into,
    DW 232–234
  playing video on, DW 357
  previewing in browsers, DW 63–65
  spell-checking, DW 63
  testing, DW 16
Web programming languages,
  DW 17–19
Web servers, **DW 5**
Web site hosting
  domain name, obtaining, DW 14
  publishing Web site, DW 16
  server space, obtaining,
    DW 14–15
Web sites, **DW 6**
  accessibility guidelines, DW 12–13
  creating new, DW 43–65,
    DW 86–88

  creating Web pages for,
    DW 159–168
  navigating, DW 7
  organizing structure, DW 84–85
  planning, DW 2, DW 8–10
  publishing, DW 16
  types of, DW 2–3
  viewing in browsers, DW 185
  viewing in Live view, DW 118
Web templates. *See* templates
Weblogs. *See* blogs
Webmaster, **DW 16**
webs. com, DW 15
What You See Is What You Get
  (WYSIWYG), **DW 19**
white space on Web pages, **DW 10**
widget behavior, **DW 272**
widget structure, **DW 272**
widget styling, **DW 272**
widgets
  adding images to, DW 314–320
  adding to Web pages,
    DW 309–314
  Spry. *See* Spry widgets
  viewing in browsers, DW 320–321
Wi-Fi (Wireless Fidelity), DW 8
windows
  Document, DW 33
  maximizing, DW 30
  touring Dreamweaver, DW 30
wireframes, **DW 92**, **DW 143**
workspaces
  Classic, DW 29, DW 39–40
  Dreamweaver, **DW 30–31**
  switching, DW 31
World Wide Web Consortium
  (W3C), **DW 13**, **DW 80**
World Wide Web (WWW),
  DW 4
WYSIWYG text editors, DW 19

X

XHTML (Extensible Hypertext
  Markup Language), **DW 17–18**
XML (Extensible Markup
  Language), **DW 18**

Y

YouTube links, DW 13–14

Quick Reference Summary

Adobe Dreamweaver CS6 Quick Reference Summary

Task	Page Number	Mouse	Menu	Context Menu	Keyboard Shortcut
Absolute link, create	DW 172	Link text box on Property inspector			
Add button to form	DW 250	Button button on Forms tab of Insert bar	Insert | Form | Button		
Add div tag	DW 94	Insert Div Tag button on Insert bar			
Add menu to form	DW 244	Select (List/Menu) button on Forms tab of Insert bar	Insert | Form | Select (List/Menu)		
Add Radio Group to form	DW 248	Radio Group button on Forms tab of Insert bar	Insert | Form | Radio Group		
Add Spry Collapsible Panel to page	DW 292	Spry Collapsible Panel button on Spry tab of Insert bar	Insert | Spry | Spry Collapsible Panel		
Add Spry validation to date text field	DW 284	Spry Validation Text Field button on Spry tab of Insert bar, click Type button in Property inspector, select Date	Insert | Spry | Spry Validation Text Field, Type button in Property inspector, select Date		
Add Spry validation to Radio Group	DW 287	Spry Validation Radio Group button on Spry tab of Insert bar	Insert | Spry | Spry Validation Text Field		
Add text field to form	DW 239	Text Field button on Forms tab of Insert bar	Insert | Form | Text Field		
Adobe Widget Browser, display	DW 303	Extend Dreamweaver button on title bar, click Widget Browser			
Align table	DW 224	Align button in Property inspector			
Align table text	DW 214		Format | Align | alignment command	Align | alignment command	
Alignment, horizontal, set for table cell	DW 228	Horz button in Property inspector			
Alignment, vertical, set for table cell	DW 228	Vert button in Property inspector			
Audio, add to page as plug-in	DW 338	Media button arrow on Insert bar, click Plugin	Insert menu | Media | Plugin		
Background color, set for table	DW 228	Bg button in Property inspector			
Background sound, add to page as plug-in	DW 338	Media button arrow on Insert bar, click Plugin	Insert menu | Media | Plugin		
Bold, apply to text	DW 68	Bold button on Property inspector	Format | Style | Bold	Style	CTRL+B

Adobe Dreamweaver CS6 Quick Reference Summary *(continued)*

Task	Page Number	Mouse	Menu	Context Menu	Keyboard Shortcut
Brightness and contrast, adjust for image	DW 158	Brightness and Contrast tool on Property inspector	Modify	Image	Brightness/Contrast		
Browser, select for preview	DW 64	Preview/Debug in browser on Document toolbar	File	Preview in Browser	Preview in Browser	F12
Bulleted list, create	DW 59	Unordered List button on Property inspector	Format	List	Unordered List	List	Unordered List	
Button, add to form	DW 250	Button button on Forms tab of Insert bar	Insert	Form	Button		
Center text	DW 68		Format	Align	Center	Align	Center	CTRL+ALT+SHIFT+C
Check spelling	DW 63		Commands	Check Spelling		SHIFT+F7
Classic workspace, switch to	DW 29	Workspace switcher button, Classic	Window	Workspace Layout	Classic		
Code view, display	DW 35	Code button on Document toolbar	View	Code		
Collapse Property inspector	DW 37	Double-click Properties tab	Window	Properties	Minimize	CTRL+F3
Color, background, set for table	DW 228	Bg button in Property inspector			
Column, table, change width	DW 226	W box in Property inspector *or* Select column, drag right border			
Contrast, adjust for image	DW 158	Brightness and Contrast tool on Property inspector	Modify	Image	Brightness/Contrast		
Create editable region	DW 146		Insert	Template Objects	Editable Region		
Create link	DW 56	Point to File button on Property inspector *or* Link text box on Property inspector	Insert	Hyperlink	Make Link	
Create page	DW 51	HTML or More folder on Welcome screen, Blank Page	File	New	New File	CTRL+N
Create page from template	DW 116	More folder on Welcome screen, Page from Template			
Create site	DW 46	Dreamweaver Site on Welcome screen	Site	New Site		
Create template	DW 88	More folder on Welcome screen, Blank Template	File	New		
Create unordered list	DW 59	Unordered List button on Property inspector	Format	List	Unordered List	List	Unordered List	
CSS rule, create	DW 95	New CSS Rule button on CSS Styles panel			
CSS rule, edit	DW 145	Edit Rule button on CSS Styles panel *or* CSS button on Property inspector *or* Double-click selector on CSS Styles panel	Window	CSS Styles		
CSS rule, set for new div	DW 95	Insert Div Tag button on Insert bar, enter name, click New CSS Rule button, click Rule Definition button			
Design view, display	DW 36	Design button on Document toolbar	View	Design		
Display Adobe Widget Browser	DW 303	Extend Dreamweaver button on title bar, click Widget Browser			

Adobe Dreamweaver CS6 Quick Reference Summary (continued)

Task	Page Number	Mouse	Menu	Context Menu	Keyboard Shortcut
Display site in Live view	DW 118	Live button on Document toolbar			ALT+F11
Display Spry category on Insert bar	DW 275	Spry tab on Insert bar			
Div tag, add	DW 94	Insert Div Tag button on Insert bar			
Document, create	DW 51	HTML or More folder on Welcome screen	File | New		CTRL+N
Document, save	DW 51	Save button on Standard toolbar	File | Save or File | Save As	Save or Save As	CTRL+S CTRL+SHIFT+S
Dreamweaver, quit	DW 65	Close button	File | Exit		CTRL+Q
Dreamweaver, start	DW 29	Dreamweaver icon on desktop	Start | All Programs | Adobe Dreamweaver CS6		
Edit CSS rule	DW 145	Edit Rule button on CSS Styles panel or CSS button on Property inspector or Double-click selector on CSS Styles panel	Window | CSS Styles		
Edit text	DW 53	Drag to select text, type text or Type text			
Editable region, create	DW 146		Insert | Template Objects | Editable Region		
E-mail link, create	DW 174		Insert | Email Link		
E-mail text field, add Spry validation to	DW 281	Spry Validation Text Field button on Spry tab of Insert bar, click Type button in Property inspector, select E-mail	Insert | Spry | Spry Validation Text Field, Type button in Property inspector, select E-mail		
Expand Property inspector	DW 37	Properties tab	Window | Properties	Expand Panel	CTRL+F3
Folder, create for site files	DW 48			New Folder	CTRL+ALT+SHIFT+N
Form, insert	DW 233	Form button on Insert bar	Insert | Form | Form		
Format link as rollover text	DW 176	Page Properties button on Property inspector, Links (CSS) category			
Format, apply to paragraph	DW 56	Format button on Property inspector	Format | Paragraph Format	Paragraph Format	
Help	DW 65		Help | Dreamweaver Help		F1
Image brightness or contrast, adjust	DW 158	Brightness and Contrast tool on Property inspector	Modify | Image | Brightness/Contrast		
Image placeholder, insert	DW 182	Image button on Insert bar, Image Placeholder	Insert | Image Objects | Image Placeholder		
Image placeholder, replace with image	DW 183	Double-click placeholder or Browse for File button on Property inspector			
Image, align	DW 193		Format | Align	Align	
Image, insert into page	DW 157	Drag image from Assets panel or Files panel	Insert | Image		CTRL+ALT+I

Adobe Dreamweaver CS6 Quick Reference Summary *(continued)*

Task	Page Number	Mouse	Menu	Context Menu	Keyboard Shortcut
Image, specify Alt text image	DW 158	Alt text box on Property inspector *or* drag image to page, enter Alt text (Image Tab Accessibility Attributes dialog box)			
Indent text	DW 68	Blockquote button on Property inspector	Format | Indent	List	CTRL+ALT+]
Insert bar, display	DW 30		Window | Insert		CTRL+F2
Insert div tag	DW 94	Insert Div Tag button on Insert bar			
Insert form	DW 233	Form button on Insert bar	Insert | Form | Form		
Insert image	DW 157	Drag image from Assets panel or Files panel	Insert | Image	Insert	
Insert image placeholder	DW 182	Image button arrow on Insert bar, Image Placeholder	Insert | Image Objects | Image Placeholder		
Insert table	DW 207	Table button on Insert bar	Insert | Table		
Italic, apply to text	DW 68	Italic button on Property inspector	Format | Style	Style	CTRL+I
Layout, select template	DW 50	More folder on Welcome screen, click layout	File | New		CTRL+N
Line break, insert	DW 72		Insert | HTML | Special Characters | Line Break	Insert HTML | br	SHIFT+ENTER
Link, create absolute	DW 172	Link text box on Property inspector			
Link, create e-mail	DW 174		Insert | Email Link		
Link, create relative	DW 170	Point to File button on Property inspector *or* Link text box on Property inspector *or* Browse for File button next to Link text box on Property inspector	Insert | Hyperlink	Make Link	
Link, format as rollover text	DW 176	Page Properties button on Property inspector, Links (CSS) category			
List, create unordered	DW 59	Unordered List button on Property inspector	Format | List | Unordered List	List | Unordered List	
Live view, display	DW 118	Live button on Document toolbar			ALT+F11
Menu, add to form	DW 244	Select (List/Menu) button on Forms tab of Insert bar	Insert | Form | Select (List/Menu)		
Merge cells in table	DW 220	'Merges selected cells using spans' button in Property inspector	Modify | Table | Merge Cells	Merge Cells	
Open site	DW 159	Site button on Files panel, *site*			
Open template	DW 143	Open on Welcome screen	File | Open		CTRL+O
Page title, enter	DW 54	Title text box on Document toolbar			
Page, create	DW 51	More folder on Welcome screen	File | New	New File	CTRL+N
Page, create from template	DW 116	More folder on Welcome screen, Page from Template			
Page, preview in browser	DW 64	Preview/Debug in browser on Document toolbar	File | Preview in Browser	Preview in Browser	F12
Page, save	DW 51	Save button on Standard toolbar	File | Save *or* File | Save As	Save *or* Save As	CTRL+S CTRL+SHIFT+S
Page, save as template	DW 97		File | Save As Template		

Adobe Dreamweaver CS6 Quick Reference Summary (continued)

Task	Page Number	Mouse	Menu	Context Menu	Keyboard Shortcut
Panel, collapse or expand	DW 37	Click Collapse to Icons button or Expand Panels button		Minimize or Expand Panel	
Panel, move	DW 37	Drag panel by its tab			
Panel, open or close	DW 37	Click panel options button, click Close or click Close Tab Group	Window | Hide Panels	Close Tab Group	F4
Paragraph, center	DW 68		Format | Align | Center	Align | Center	CTRL+ALT+SHIFT+C
Parameters, set for sound file	DW 341	Parameters button in Property inspector			
Parameters, set for video file	DW 354	Parameters button in Property inspector			
Phone number text field, add Spry validation to	DW 283	Spry Validation Text Field button on Spry tab of Insert bar, click Type button in Property inspector, select Phone Number	Insert | Spry | Spry Validation Text Field, Type button in Property inspector, select Phone Number		
Placeholder, insert image	DW 182	Image button arrow on Insert bar, Image Placeholder	Insert | Image Objects | Image Placeholder		
Plug-in sound file, add to page	DW 338	Media button arrow on Insert bar, click Plugin	Insert menu | Media | Plugin		
Preferences, set	DW 41		Edit | Preferences		
Preview Web page	DW 64	Preview/Debug in browser on Document toolbar	File | Preview in Browser	Preview in Browser	F12
Property inspector, collapse or expand	DW 37	Double-click Properties tab	Window | Properties	Minimize/ Expand Panel	CTRL+F3
Quit Dreamweaver	DW 65	Close button	File | Exit		CTRL+Q
Radio Group, add to form	DW 248	Radio Group button on Forms tab of Insert bar	Insert | Form | Radio Group		
Region, create editable	DW 146		Insert | Template Objects | Editable Region		
Relative link, create	DW 170	Point to File button on Property inspector *or* Link text box on Property inspector *or* Browse for File button next to Link text box on Property inspector	Insert | Hyperlink	Make Link	SHIFT+drag to file
Reset button, add to form	DW 250	Button button on Forms tab of Insert bar	Insert | Form | Button		
Rule definition, create	DW 95, DW 170	New CSS Rule button on CSS Styles panel			
Rule definition, edit	DW 145	Edit Rule button on CSS Styles panel *or* CSS button on Property inspector *or* Double-click selector on CSS Styles panel	Window | CSS Styles		
Save document	DW 51	Save button on Standard toolbar	File | Save *or* File | Save As	Save *or* Save As	CTRL+S CTRL+SHIFT+S
Save page as template	DW 97		File | Save As Template		
Select List/Menu, add to form	DW 244	Select (List/Menu) button on Forms tab of Insert bar	Insert | Form | Select (List/Menu)		

Adobe Dreamweaver CS6 Quick Reference Summary *(continued)*

Task	Page Number	Mouse	Menu	Context Menu	Keyboard Shortcut
Select template layout	DW 50	More folder on Welcome screen, click layout	File | New		
Site, create site	DW 46	Dreamweaver Site on Welcome screen	Site | New Site		
Site, open	DW 159	Site button on Files panel, *site*			
Sound file, set parameters for	DW 341	Parameters button in Property inspector			
Sound, add to page as plug-in	DW 338	Media button arrow on Insert bar, click Plugin	Insert menu | Media | Plugin		
Spelling, check	DW 63		Commands | Check Spelling		SHIFT+F7
Spry category, display on Insert bar	DW 275	Spry tab on Insert bar			
Spry Collapsible Panel, add to page	DW 292	Spry Collapsible Panel button on Spry tab of Insert bar	Insert | Spry | Spry Collapsible Panel		
Spry validation, add to date text field	DW 284	Spry Validation Text Field button on Spry tab of Insert bar, click Type button in Property inspector, select Date	Insert | Spry | Spry Validation Text Field, Type button in Property inspector, select Date		
Spry validation, add to e-mail text field	DW 281	Spry Validation Text Field button on Spry tab of Insert bar, click Type button in Property inspector, select E-mail	Insert | Spry | Spry Validation Text Field, Type button in Property inspector, select E-mail		
Spry validation, add to phone number text field	DW 283	Spry Validation Text Field button on Spry tab of Insert bar, click Type button in Property inspector, select Phone Number	Insert | Spry | Spry Validation Text Field, Type button in Property inspector, select Phone Number		
Spry validation, add to Radio Group	DW 287	Spry Validation Radio Group button on Spry tab of Insert bar	Insert | Spry | Spry Validation Text Field		
Spry validation, add to text field	DW 276	Spry Validation Text Field button on Spry tab of Insert bar	Insert | Spry | Spry Validation Text Field		
Standard toolbar, display	DW 40		View | Toolbars | Standard	Standard	
Style rule, set for new div	DW 95	Insert Div Tag button on Insert bar, enter name, click New CSS Rule button, click Rule Definition button			
Submit button, add to form	DW 250	Button button on Forms tab of Insert bar	Insert | Form | Button		
Table cell, set horizontal alignment	DW 228	Horz button in Property inspector			
Table cell, set vertical alignment	DW 229	Vert button in Property inspector			
Table column, change width	DW 226	W box in Property inspector *or* Select column, drag right border			
Table text, align	DW 214		Format | Align | alignment command	Align | alignment command	
Table, align	DW 224	Align button in Property inspector			
Table, change width	DW 224	W box in Property inspector			

Adobe Dreamweaver CS6 Quick Reference Summary *(continued)*

Task	Page Number	Mouse	Menu	Context Menu	Keyboard Shortcut
Table, insert	DW 207	Table button on Insert bar	Insert | Table		
Table, merge cells in	DW 220	'Merges selected cells using spans' button in Property inspector	Modify | Table | Merge Cells	Merge Cells	
Template layout, select	DW 50	More folder on Welcome screen, click layout	File | New		
Template, create	DW 88	More folder on Welcome screen, Blank Template	File | New		
Template, create from page	DW 116	More folder on Welcome screen, Page from Template			
Template, open	DW 143	Open on Welcome screen			
Text field, add Spry validation to	DW 276	Spry Validation Text Field button on Spry tab of Insert bar	Insert | Spry | Spry Validation Text Field		
Text field, add to form	DW 239	Text Field button on Forms tab of Insert bar	Insert | Form | Text Field		
Text, center	DW 68		Format | Align | Center	Align | Center	CTRL+ALT+SHIFT+C
Text, edit	DW 53	Drag to select text, type text *or* Type text			
Title, enter for page	DW 54	Title text box on Document toolbar			
Unordered list, create	DW 59	Unordered List button on Property inspector	Format | List | Unordered List	List | Unordered List	
Video, add to page as plug-in	DW 352	Media button arrow on Insert bar, click Plugin	Insert menu | Media | Plugin		
Web page, preview in browser	DW 64	Preview/Debug in browser on Document toolbar	File | Preview in Browser	Preview in Browser	F12 CTRL+F12
Widget, add to page	DW 311		Insert | Widget		
Width, change for table	DW 224	W box in Property inspector			
Width, change for table column	DW 226	W box in Property inspector *or* Select column, drag right border			
Window, maximize	DW 30	Maximize button			
Workspace, reset to default settings	DW 39	Workspace Switcher button, Reset *workspace*	Window | Workspace Layout | Reset *workspace*		
Workspace, switch	DW 31	Workspace Switcher button	Window | Workspace Layout | *workspace*		